THE JUDAICA IMPRINT
FOR THOUGHTFUL PEOPLE

הגדה של פסח
משעבוד לגאולה

# TO FREEDOM

## The Passover Haggadah

### with a commentary illuminating the liberation of the spirit

# FROM BONDAGE

*by*

Rabbi Abraham J. Twerski, M.D.

*with* Rabbi Hirsh Michel Chinn, MSW

*and* Rabbi Benzion Twerski, Ph.D.

First edition – First impression / February 1995
Second impression / February 1996
Third impression / January 1998
Fourth impression / February 1999
Fifth impression / December 2001
Sixth impression / January 2004
Seventh impression / February 2007
Eighth impression / February 2010



Published by **SHAAR PRESS**
Distributed by MESORAH PUBLICATIONS, LTD.
4401 Second Avenue / Brooklyn, N.Y 11232 / (718) 921-9000

Distributed in Israel by SIFRIATI / A. GITLER
6 Hayarkon Street / Bnei Brak 51127

Distributed in Europe by LEHMANNS
Unit E, Viking Business Park, Rolling Mill Road / Jarrow, Tyne and Wear, NE32 3DP/ England

Distributed in Australia and New Zealand by GOLDS WORLD OF JUDAICA
3-13 William Street / Balaclava, Melbourne 3183 / Victoria Australia

Distributed in South Africa by KOLLEL BOOKSHOP
Ivy Common / 105 William Road / Norwood 2192, Johannesburg, South Africa

ISBN 10: 0-89906-396-9 ISBN 13: 978-0-89906-396-6 Hard Cover

Printed in the United States of America by Noble Book Press
Custom bound by Sefercraft, Inc. / 4401 Second Avenue / Brooklyn N.Y. 11232

# FROM BONDAGE TO FREEDOM

# ◆§ *Introduction*

*The Meaning of the Exodus*

*Preparation for Passover*

*Nissan and Tishrei:*
*Passover and Rosh Hashanah*

*The Haggadah: A Lesson in Humility*

# ⥈ Introduction

There is a quaint Yiddish song about a *chazzan* (cantor) who chanted a prayer service as an audition for the position in a congregation. The worshipers, who were very pleased with his rendition, expressed their evaluation of his performance in terms most familiar to each. Thus, the tailor said that the *chazzan's* melody was as pleasant as a row of neat, evenly spaced stitches. The blacksmith said that it was as pleasant as when one delivers a firm blow with the hammer on the anvil, and the cobbler said it was like piercing a piece of leather with a sharp awl.

When analyzing something, we undoubtedly all apply standards which are most familiar to us from the tasks of our everyday life, and I am no exception to this rule. After twenty-five years of treating some 40,000 alcoholics and other chemically addicted people, it should come as no surprise that my thinking is influenced by the various experiences, insights, and feelings that I have encountered in my work.

However, in my case, I may have more justification for using the examples of my practice than do the various craftsmen. The melody of the *chazzan* has little in common with the needle, the hammer and anvil, or the awl. There is, however, great similarity between the problems of chemical addiction and various other inadequate lifestyles. Essentially, addiction results when one attempts to escape from what one perceives to be a difficult reality, rather than try to confront it and cope with it. This maladjustment can occur just as well even in the complete absence of use of any chemical. Thus, if we were to take the life history of an alcoholic and substitute any self-destructive, escapist behavior for the word "alcohol," we would find that many inappropriate lifestyles are virtually identical to that of the alcoholic. By the same token, techniques which are helpful in overcoming alcoholism can also be effective in correcting any other inadequate lifestyle. I will therefore ask the reader to bear with me in my frequent references to the problems of alcohol and other substance abuse.

I am indebted for the inspiration for the theme of this Haggadah to a young man who underwent treatment for a very severe drug problem. At his first *Seder* at home, his father began reciting the Haggadah, "We were slaves unto Pharaoh." The young man interrupted, "Father," he said, "when were you ever a slave? I can relate to having been a slave. I was a slave to drugs, and there has never been so demanding and inconsiderate a taskmaster, so absolute an enslavement, as addiction to chemicals.

"I had no choice whether to use them or not. I did things in my addiction that I swore I would never do, because a slave must do as he is told. I not only used drugs when I liked them, but I even used some drugs whose effect I hated. If there ever was a slave in the world, it was me. I know what it means to be a slave, and I know what it means to be free."

This young man's description of being enslaved by drugs is an example of the slavery of addiction. However, drugs are not the only taskmasters to which many people may be subject. There are people who never use drugs, but are nevertheless slaves to money, or to power, or to acclaim, or to food indulgence, and yes, to cigarettes. An intelligent person who wishes very much to live and, in spite of his awareness that cigarettes can take his life, smokes them nevertheless, is a slave to cigarettes. In brief, anyone who loses control over any kind of behavior is a slave.

We should be proud to be free people, and the concept of slavery should be repulsive to us. Like our forefathers in Egypt, we should cry out to God to deliver us from enslavement to any self-destructive behavior.

The Haggadah is a message of hope. If we pray sincerely and truly wish to be free, God will answer our prayers.

❦ ❦ ❦

It is not an original discovery of mine that other inappropriate lifestyles have similarities to alcoholism. The prophet Isaiah, in rebuking people for their deviation from Torah observance, states, "They drift albeit without wine, they wander about aimlessly without ale" (*Isaiah* 29:9). Isaiah thus compares the abandonment of Torah living to the errors of inebriation, the two differing only in the use or non-use of intoxicants. In various places throughout the Scriptures we find references to inebriation as the prototype of improper behavior; e.g., *Isaiah* 19:14, 24:20, 28:1, 51:21; *Jeremiah* 23:9; *Joel* 1:5; *Obadiah* 1:16; *Zechariah* 9:15; *Psalms* 107:27; *Proverbs* 20:1; *Job* 12:25. These abundant Scriptural comparisons of improper behavior to that resulting from imbibing more than justify my drawing upon my work experiences to illustrate and clarify other unhealthy lifestyles.

Chemical addiction is characterized by a lack of spirituality, and recovering from these conditions requires the development of spirituality. Applying the hypothesis that many other inadequate life adjustments are in numerous ways similar to addiction may help us realize that in these, as well as in chemical addiction, there is a dearth of spirituality, and that living a more spiritual life can correct many of these other problems of life much as it brings about recovery from addiction. The blatancy of the features of addiction provides us with a valuable analogy which enables us to more easily identify the defects in other inadequate life adjustments, which might be less apparent and might otherwise go unnoticed.

This commentary is not a compendium on addiction, but rather an elaboration on the issues of spirituality, and how a lack of spirituality may result in a faulty lifestyle and what steps one may take to achieve spirituality. It is my belief that the Haggadah, like many other great works of Jewish theology, delivers this important message.

## ◆§ *The Meaning of the Exodus*

**"Remember this day on which you departed from Egypt from the house of bondage, for with a strong hand God removed you from there"** (*Exodus* 13:3).

This is perfectly understandable. The day that a nation was liberated certainly deserves to be commemorated and perpetuated for generations. The United States celebrates its independence day on the Fourth of July, with parades, firecrackers, patriotic speeches, and picnics.

But wait. "Matzos shall be eaten throughout the seven-day period (eight in the diaspora); and no *chametz* may be seen in your possession nor may leaven be seen in all your borders" (*ibid.* 13:7).

Isn't this a bit much for an independence day celebration? Given all the laws and practices that have been derived from the rigid restrictions against *chametz,* culminating in weeks of preparation and cleaning one's home to the point of virtual surgical sterility, isn't this an overkill for a commemorative event?

There is yet more. Not only is Passover designated in commemoration of the Exodus from Egypt, but so is Shavuos (Pentecost), Sukkos (Tabernacles), Rosh Hashanah (New Year), and Yom Kippur (Day of Atonement). And each week we refer to Shabbos as commemorating the Exodus, as it is written, "Safeguard the day of Shabbos to sanctify it . . . and you shall remember that you were a slave in the land of Egypt, and God has taken you out from there with a strong hand and an outstretched arm" (*Deuteronomy* 5:12-15).

Each week? Nay, every day! "And they (the *tefillin* [phylacteries]) shall be for you as a sign on your arm and a reminder between your eyes . . . for with a strong hand God removed you from Egypt" (*Exodus* 13:9). So also the *talis* (four-cornered fringed garment), "and they shall be unto you for fringes . . . I am the Lord Your God Who has removed you from the land of Egypt" (*Numbers* 15:39-41).

This seems to be getting a bit out of hand for an independence day rite. But we are not yet finished. The *mitzvah* of redemption of the first-born is meant to commemorate the Exodus (*Exodus* 13:15); as is giving a bonus to an indentured servant when his term of servitude is completed (*Deuteronomy* 15:14-15); the judging of a false prophet or a seducer to idolatry (*ibid.* 13:6-11); the maintenance of honest and accurate weights and measures (Leviticus 19:35-36); the prohibition against eating unclean animals (*ibid.* 11:44-47); and many other *mitzvos.* Even the most ardent nationalist would not prescribe such broad, varied, and taxing practices, both active and restrictive, merely to celebrate the historic event of a nation's coming into being. Clearly the Exodus from Egypt must represent something other than national independence.

That the Exodus from Egypt is inextricably bound to the revelation at Sinai is evident in the message transmitted to Moses at the burning bush: "When you bring forth the people from Egypt, you shall serve God on this mountain" (*Exodus* 3:12); and the opening words of the Ten Commandments given at Sinai were: "I am the Lord your God Who has taken you out of the land of Egypt from the house of bondage" (*ibid.* 20:2).

The liberation from Egypt was thus not merely a nationalistic incident, but the creation of a nation with a universal mission. "You have seen that which I did unto Egypt . . . and I brought you unto Me . . . and you shall be unto Me a kingdom of priests and a sacred people" (*ibid.* 19:4-6). The entire nation was to be priestly, and each individual a holy person. This was far more than just the formation of another political entity.

The full-scale saga of Egypt, the bondage as well as the liberation, must therefore be understood as components of an ultimate purpose: the formation of a *spiritual* people. Every incident in the saga can serve as a prototype for the development of spirituality, and the teachings that can be derived from each event have their application in our strivings toward spirituality thousands of years later. From the torture of enslavement — the "purifying furnace" (*Deuteronomy* 4:20) — to the miraculous dividing of the waters of the Red Sea, everything we do and everything that is done to us is a guide towards spirituality.

The mission of the Jew today is no different than that of his ancestors who left Egypt: to become priestly and sacred, or in other words, *spiritual.* Inasmuch as the forces that deter one from spirituality are powerful, ubiquitous, and constant, so must our efforts to vanquish these forces be constantly renewed and reinforced. It is for this reason that we continually refer back to the Exodus, as the source and wellspring of our armamentarium in the struggle to achieve spirituality.

The more thoroughly we understand the Exodus, the greater will be our resources to achieve spirituality. This is the function of the Haggadah, which is much more than a historical account. Let us therefore study the Haggadah with the realization that it contains teachings of the Exodus that are applicable not only on Passover, but also every day of the year, and indeed, many times each day: the ways in which we can attain the true freedom of spirituality.

## ◆§ *Preparation for Passover*

Cleaning the house in preparation for Passover is a formidable task, and as such may bear resemblance to cleansing ourselves of our defects so that we may become more pure spiritually. Both require a great deal of effort on our part, but neither can succeed without Divine assistance.

There is a story of a very devout individual who began his Passover housecleaning many weeks before the holiday, during which time he did not permit any *chametz* to enter the house. He meticulously cleaned and examined every nook and cranny in the house, removing each book in his substantial library to be shaken out lest a crumb of *chametz* had fallen in if anyone had read a book while eating. There was simply no possibility that anything was overlooked.

On Passover night, the man sat down to the *Seder* with his family, content that he had achieved perfection in regard to making his home absolutely *chametz*-free. He continued these most stringent precautions throughout the entire festival.

On one of the intermediate days of Passover, when the man went to fetch water from the well, he was shocked to discover, floating in the well, a loaf of bread! He realized that he had used water during Passover that had been contaminated by *chametz,* and was overcome with grief that he had inadvertently violated the laws of Passover.

The man consulted a *tzaddik* and related his tale of woe. He was particularly concerned that he had committed so grievous a sin, although he had exerted himself to the utmost to be sure that there was no *chametz* in his environs. Why had God permitted this to happen to him?

The *tzaddik* told him that the answer to his question was simple. God had not protected him because he had not prayed for His help. "The laws of Passover are so strict and demanding," the *tzaddik* said, "that it is impossible for unaided human efforts to achieve perfection in compliance. While we must do whatever is within our means, we must remember to ask God to complete whatever it is that is beyond our capabilities.

"You were extremely diligent in your efforts," the *tzaddik* said, "but you neglected to pray for Divine assistance. What happened should prove to you that a human being can only *try* to do his utmost, but must never forget to pray for Divine assistance."

Whether in ridding our homes of *chametz* or divesting ourselves of our character defects, we must indeed make a maximum effort, but always remember that without the help of God, even our utmost efforts cannot succeed.

❦ ❦ ❦

Another chassidic tale indicates how God does provide for someone who has done everything within his means, but places his trust in God.

There was a chassid who operated a small brewery. Inasmuch as beer is *chametz,* it was his practice to sell the brewery to a non-Jew before Passover and then buy it back after the festival, in order not to have possession of any *chametz* on Passover. He generally spent the Passover holidays visiting his wife's family away from his hometown.

One year, a fellow citizen who was hostile toward Jews and who was familiar with Jewish practices plotted against this chassid. He spread the word that under no circumstances should anyone transact to buy the Jew's brewery for the Passover holiday. On the morning before Passover, the chassid was shocked to discover that none of his usual contacts wished to make this transaction, and he was then left with a huge inventory of beer which he could not dispose of before Passover.

The chassid had no other option than to rid himself of ownership of the beer by abandoning the brewery and declaring it *hefker,* that is, he relinquished his ownership thereof. In compliance with Jewish law, he left the doors to the brewery wide open, and took off with his family for Passover, knowing that he had parted with a small fortune, since the citizens of the community would certainly help themselves to his entire stock while he was away for the week.

When he returned after Passover, he was confronted by members of the community, who said, "If you were sincere in abandoning ownership of your brewery, why did you place ferocious dogs to guard the entrances?" The chassid was bewildered, not knowing of what they were speaking, but everyone in the village corroborated the story that vicious-looking dogs were guarding all the entrances.

The chassid consulted his rebbe, asking whether he is permitted to take possession of the inventory, since it was *chametz* that had remained over the Passover. The rebbe replied, "This *chametz* was not yours over Passover, since you had sincerely and wholeheartedly abandoned it and given up ownership. If God saw fit to reward you with a miracle, that does not affect your having declared it *hefker.* You are certainly permitted to regain possession."

When a person does that which he is supposed to, with utmost sincerity and turning over to God that which is beyond his own wherewithal, God does respond.

❦ ❦ ❦

The "Netziv" of Volozhin once said, "Passover is brimming with mitzvos: the disposal of *chametz,* eating the matzah, drinking the four cups of wine at the *Seder,* eating the bitter herbs. One can become euphoric with the *simchah* of doing so many mitzvos.

"On the other hand one may say, 'Perhaps I did not clean the house well enough, and a few crumbs of *chametz* may have escaped my attention. Perhaps the matzah was not baked with adequate caution, and God forbid became *chametz.* Perhaps the making of the wine was not supervised properly. Perhaps the vegetables for the bitter herbs were not inspected carefully enough for insect infestation.' Instead of having the joy of doing mitzvos, one then has the worry of having sinned.

"But there is a requirement to rejoice on Passover, which means that once we have done what we are required to do, we can trust God to do the rest. We should rejoice with the mitzvos."

❦ ❦ ❦

Prior to the *Seder,* Rabbi Levi Yitzchak of Berditchev called on a person who was known to deal in contraband. "Can you get me some Turkish wool?" he asked. (At that time of hostilities between Russia and Turkey, possession of Turkish goods was punishable by death.)

"For a price I will get you anything," the man said.

"How many meters can you get me?" the Rabbi asked.

"As many as you wish," the man answered.

Rabbi Levi Yitzchak thanked him and then knocked on the door of a Jewish home. "Pardon me," he said. "Do you have any bread in your house? I need it desperately for a medicinal preparation."

The dweller looked astonished. "Bread? Certainly you jest, Rabbi. There hasn't been a crumb of bread in this house since yesterday."

Rabbi Levi Yitzchak turned his eyes to heaven. "Dear God," he said. "The Czar with his mighty police force cannot stop people from possessing contraband, even under threat of execution. But You have no police and no guns, yet Your commandment not to possess *chametz* is faithfully heeded. Are Your chosen people not wonderful?"

❦ ❦ ❦

In my book, *Generation to Generation,* I recounted some of my favorite Passover memories. As a child, I looked forward to Passover, because for me it was all fun. It undoubtedly was hard work for my mother, but carrying the dishes up and down to and from the cellar and hanging around the kitchen to absorb the fragrances of the Passover delicacies was a delight. We were far from wealthy, but I could never imagine that the table of a king could be more royally bedecked than our *Seder* table, with the few silver items. For nostalgic reasons, I have on my *Seder* table a small plate which was on my parents' *Seder* table when I was a young child. It is merely an inexpensive earthenware plate, not delicate porcelain, but as a child of five, there was nothing more beautiful in the world than the blue and pink floral design on this set of dinnerware. Now, some sixty years later, even though this plate would be relatively worthless in comparison to fine bone china, it still retains regal beauty for me.

The memories of the *Seder* night will never fade. Many gifts which parents and grandparents give to their offspring may be damaged or lost. However, memories of Passover never disappear. If you really wish to give something everlasting to your children and grandchildren, give them appropriate memories.

## ◆§ *Nissan and Tishrei: Passover and Rosh Hashanah*

In Exodus (12:2), God says to Moses, "This month shall be unto you the first month of the year." This has given rise to somewhat of a discrepancy. In the secular calendar, for example, the new year begins with January, which is also the first month of the year. The Jewish calendar is a bit different. The new year begins with Rosh Hashanah, but the first month of the year is not Tishrei, the month of Rosh Hashanah, but rather Nissan, the month of the Exodus.

There is a reason for this two-fold beginning. When a child is born, it is indeed a happy occasion. Yet, is it not a tragic reality that a person may live his life in such a manner that people may regret that he was born? Birth of a child is celebrated because of hope: hope that the child will lead a life that will be constructive and productive both for himself and for others.

The Talmud states that there was an extended philosophical dispute among the rabbis. Is man better off having been created, or would it have been better that man had not been created? When one looks at the sufferings of mankind, and particularly at the depravity of some humans and the capacity of man to be degenerate, cruel, and corrupt, one may be inclined to agree with those angels who, according to the Midrash, pleaded with God not to create the human being.

Rosh Hashanah commemorates creation of the world and creation of man. But the mere existence of man is not yet adequate cause for celebration. What reason is there to believe that man will harness his abundant capacities for what is good and noble? Lower forms of life may have great strength, but even the strength of a lion is limited in its scope. Not so the strength of man, whose intellect can be distorted to create weapons of mass destruction that can wipe out an entire population in a matter of just a few seconds.

Man underwent a second creation in Nissan, a spiritual creation. A rather small nation which had been enslaved, and which had experienced the cruelty and distress of the loss of liberty and human dignity, was now freed. This nation, with its appreciation of liberty and respect for human life, was given the Torah as a guide to proper living. The Exodus thus ushered in a chapter which was to give meaning to human life. Man could now embark on a spiritual life, instead of being only a *Homo sapiens,* an animal with intellect. To emphasize this, the Torah provided for *two* beginnings of the calendar, the first on Rosh Hashanah, the beginning of man as a physical being, and the second in Nissan, the beginning of man as a spiritual being.

It is quite characteristic that the secular world, which has only one new year, celebrates it with frivolity and often intoxication. From the secular aspect, all there is to life is pleasure seeking, and that is how New Year's Day is celebrated. The Jewish attitude is quite different. Rosh Hashanah is a very solemn day. Mankind has just come into being, but what will come of it, no one yet knows. The month of Nissan, in which Passover occurs, marks the appreciation of liberty, and the first steps towards receiving the Torah. That is the beginning of man's spiritual life, and this is then an appropriate time for celebration.

Well, why not then have Rosh Hashanah occur in the month of Nissan? Because that would be denying the significance of the physical world. The entire universe is the work of God, and it must be appreciated as such. Judaism does not teach escaping from the physical world into a life of ascetism, but, as with pronouncing a *berachah* on everything one consumes, emphasizes transforming the physical world into a sanctuary, where everything created can be dedicated to the glory of God. This is the teaching of the dual beginning of Tishrei and Nissan, of Rosh Hashanah and Passover.

## ◆§ *The Haggadah: A Lesson in Humility*

Every astute reader of the Haggadah will be struck with a glaring omission: The central figure of the Exodus is absent from the account. Except for a single incidental and seemingly accidental mention, the great liberator, Moses, who is associated with every facet of the Exodus, does not appear in the Haggadah. Is this not strange?

The answer is rather simple. The first mitzvah of relating the story of the Exodus appears in *Exodus* 10:2, where God says to Moses, "In order that you may tell your children . . . the miracles that I did." The immediate application of this mitzvah could not have been meant for the Israelites that were in Egypt and who participated in the Exodus, because their children had personally witnessed each stage — the enslavement, the ten plagues, and dividing of the Red Sea — and there was no point in reiterating these events to them. The only Israelites who did not experience these miraculous events firsthand were the children of Moses, who were in Midian with Jethro. Therefore, the first actual narration of the Exodus was when Moses told his children all that had transpired. Moses' narrative to his children thus constituted the first Haggadah.

Now Moses was the most humble of all men on earth (*Numbers* 12:3). Moses therefore minimized his own role, and did not say, "I did this" or "I did that." Since he composed the first Haggadah, he deleted any reference to himself from the narrative. Subsequently when the narrative was elaborated and expanded, it followed the very first model, with the role of Moses omitted.

In addition to everything else we learn from the Haggadah, it also contains the invaluable teaching of humility.

# ☙ Spirituality and the Festivals

## ◆§ Spirituality and the Festivals

Whereas Passover can be seen as the holiday of spiritual liberation, all the other festivals of the Jewish calendar also reflect the same theme. In the prayers for the various festivals, we refer to Rosh Hashanah, Yom Kippur, Succos, and Shavuos as "commemorating the Exodus from Egypt." While Chanukah and Purim do not relate to the Exodus, they are each celebrations of liberation on their own. Chanukah commemorates liberation from the tyranny of the Syrian Greeks, and Purim marks the liberation from the decree of annihilation by Haman.

It is therefore appropriate that in addition to Passover, we should analyze the other festivals for the particular messages of spiritual liberation that they convey.

### ROSH HASHANAH

The beginning of the Jewish year is a period of utmost solemnity. The memories of frivolities, amusements or other pleasant occasions are cast aside in favor of profound meditation and acceptance of Hashem as the Sovereign of the Universe. We rededicate ourselves to Him as our Master, and renew our commitment to follow His will. The liturgies of the lengthy services are replete with messages of faith. Rosh Hashanah is only part of a series, a program of *teshuvah* (repentance) that begins with the first day of Elul and culminates with Yom Kippur. Let us explore the precise role of this forty-day period.

*Teshuvah* implies the existence of sin and is the process whereby one can rid oneself of its lasting impressions. The month of Elul is set aside for this process as a preparation for Rosh Hashanah and Yom Kippur, the days of judgment, and it is only logical that a person should be spiritually prepared when appearing before the heavenly tribunal. What is not clear is why so much time must be devoted to this. Why would one day or two days not be enough? Why a full month? Why cannot the days of Rosh Hashanah and Yom Kippur be combined into one?

We may safely assume that no human being can achieve perfection, and the forty-day period of *teshuvah* is a mandatory venture in order to examine one's imperfections and to implement change. At one extreme there are people who have been grossly deviant, and at the other extreme is the *tzaddik,* the truly righteous person who has few blemishes. Interestingly, there is no mention anywhere that the time assigned for *teshuvah* is any less for the *tzaddik* than for anyone else.

The answer to some of the above questions lies in an understanding of *teshuvah,* which is more than a reckoning of the transgressions of the past year and an expression of remorse. A simple confession and a ritual of forgiveness would have sufficed for that. *Teshuvah* requires a change of character, and it is necessary to allow adequate time for changes in behavior to become part of an individual's personality.

Even a period of forty days does not suffice to accomplish a change in character, and indeed, our ethical works state that one should constantly be engaged in *teshuvah.* The fact, however, that more than one-tenth of the year was designated as a period of *teshuvah* serves as a symbol to remind us that *teshuvah* is more than an expression of regret, and even more than a resolve not to repeat improper acts.

In his epochal work, *Shaarei Teshuvah* (Gates of Repentance), Rabbeinu Yonah states that there are two approaches to *teshuvah.* Someone who sinned only occasionally needs to examine what it was that led him to commit the sin. This is not the approach, however, for someone who is more habitually sinful. This person must first concern himself with making a change in his behavior. Analysis of what might have caused his deviance must be left for later, after the behavioral changes have been firmly ingrained.

The validity of the concept of *teshuvah* as changing one's character rather than as remorse or even resolutions is substantiated by the *halachah* that requires a person who believes he is in his last days of life to recite the *vidui,* confession of sins. Here we have a single event that appears to be adequate to achieve forgiveness. This is in bold contrast to the lengthy period of *teshuvah* of Elul through Yom Kippur.

The major distinction between these two forms of *teshuvah* lies in the ultimate purpose. The dying person needs to cleanse himself of sin prior to appearing before the heavenly tribunal. However, for him a change in behavior and character is not an issue. *Teshuvah* can therefore be accomplished with a single ritual performed in sincerity. The *teshuvah* of Elul through Yom Kippur, however, is designed for a person who is praying to be inscribed for an additional year of life. This is a *teshuvah* with an eye to the future, and it therefore requires making the necessary modifications in one's character so that one's behavior in the future will be right and proper.

There is an interesting episode in the Talmud that further confirms this distinction. Elazar Ben Doradia was a person who led a totally depraved and dissolute life. One day, while in a house of ill repute, someone told him that he was hopelessly doomed, beyond the point of *teshuvah.* For some reason this comment pierced to his very soul, and he sat among the mountains appealing to all the forces of nature to intercede for him to attain Divine forgiveness. When he realized that there could be no such intercession, he wept incessantly until his soul departed from him. The Talmud states that at that moment, a heavenly echo was heard announcing that "Rabbi" Elazar Ben Doradia has achieved entrance to Paradise.

The Talmud relates that when Rabbi Yehudah HaNasi (the Prince) heard of this episode, he too wept, commenting that a person can earn entrance into Paradise in only a brief moment of *teshuvah.* Many Talmudic commentaries question why Rabbi Yehudah wept, since the possibility of redeeming oneself with sincere *teshuvah* should elicit joy rather than sorrow.

Perhaps Rabbi Yehudah's tears were for a *teshuvah* that reflected only on the past. Had Elazar Ben Doradia been allowed to survive, he could have so modified his character that he would have been capable of performing many mitzvos. While his *teshuvah* was sincere, it was not a *teshuvah* with a future, and that is a tragic occurrence.

In contrast to the confession of the dying person, the *teshuvah* of the Rosh Hashanah season is one of a new beginning, with a perspective for the future. Such *teshuvah* requires a great deal of time and effort, initiating the changes in character that will make one a better and more spiritual person.

❧ ❧ ❧

In the Rosh Hashanah prayers we say, "Remember us for life, for Your sake. . ." What do we mean: for Your sake?

A merchant who is unable to pay his bills may appeal to his supplier saying, "At this time I do not have the money to pay you. However, if you will advance me some additional merchandise on credit, I may be able to earn enough to pay the debt." In other words, he argues that it is to the supplier's advantage to extend his credit.

Similarly, on Rosh Hashanah, we say to God, "Perhaps we are not deserving of an extension. However, the only way we can do *teshuvah* and redeem ourselves is if You grant us life in which to do so. It is thus to Your advantage to grant us a year of health and prosperity so that we may be able to grow in spirituality."

*Our sages tell us that every person is judged on Rosh Hashanah, and his fortune for the coming year is decreed. One of the Baal Shem Tov's disciples asked that this appears to contradict a Talmudic statement that a person is judged each day.*

*The Baal Shem Tov looked out the window and saw the water carrier with his two buckets of water hanging from his shoulders. He beckoned to him saying, "How are things with you, Chikel?"*

*"How can they be?" Chikel responded angrily. "At my age I have to shlep buckets of water uphill all day. And for what? To earn a piece of dark bread and onion to satisfy my hunger!"*

*Several days later the Baal Shem Tov again beckoned to Chikel. "Nu, Chikel, how are things with you?"*

*Chikel smiled broadly. "Thank God, Rebbe, I am well. If at my age I can shlep water uphill and digest dark bread with onion, I shouldn't complain."*

*The Baal Shem turned to his disciples. "You see, it was decreed on Rosh Hashanah that Chikel will earn his living as a water carrier, but how he reacts to this can vary from day to day. God decrees on Rosh Hashanah, but each person judges himself each day."*

Like Chikel, we share with God in our judgment. Whether we are happy or unhappy depends a great deal on us.

*Rabbi Levi Yitzchak of Berditchev told his congregation that he was in need of someone to blow the shofar on Rosh Hashanah. One candidate after another applied, and when he asked them what was their kavanah, on what they concentrated when they blew the shofar, each one responded with various profound, esoteric, Kabbalistic concepts. Rabbi Levi Yitzchak was obviously not satisfied.*

*At the side stood a man who appeared hesitant to apply. "Do you know how to blow the shofar?" Rabbi Levi Yitzchak asked. "Yes," the man replied. "And what would you think about at the time?" Rabbi Levi Yitzchak asked.*

*The man began crying. "Rebbe," he said, "I am not learned in Kabbalah, and I do not know any esoteric meanings. I am destitute, and I do not have any money for a dowry for my daughter, and I fear she will be unable to marry. I therefore think, 'Father in Heaven, I am doing Your will and blowing the shofar as You commanded. Please do my will and give me the means to marry off my daughter.' "*

*Rabbi Levi Yitzchak beamed with delight. "You are my man! That is the most sincere kavanah I have heard all day."*

It pays to keep things simple.

**YOM KIPPUR**

We know Yom Kippur to be a most solemn day. Not only do we abstain from satisfying various physical appetites, but we also spend the entire day in prayer and pleas for Divine forgiveness. The abstentions of Yom Kippur are similar to those of Tishah B'Av, but whereas the latter is a day of mourning commemorating the destruction of the Temple, Yom Kippur is a *Yom Tov,* a festival. Historically, there were celebrations on Yom Kippur, such as that cited by the Talmud in which young men and women were introduced through *shidduchim* (matrimonial matches). The successful completion of the service for Divine forgiveness by the *Kohen Gadol* (High Priest) was celebrated on Yom Kippur. Indeed, Rabbeinu Yonah states that the festive meal on the day prior to Yom Kippur is in anticipation of the forthcoming forgiveness.

*Simchah* (joy) is not at all incompatible with the solemnity of the day. The Torah concept of *simchah* is not the merrymaking and gaiety which is so often thought to be synonymous with joy, but rather a feeling of jubilation in one's good fortune to be able to fulfill the Divine will and be a servant unto God.

*The Baal Shem Tov once asked a cantor, who sang the Al-Cheit (confession of sins) with a lively melody, why he did not chant this prayer with the traditional solemn strain. The cantor replied, "If I were cleaning the palace for the king and beautifying his throne room, would that not be a cause for joy? When I confess my sins, I remove all the trash from myself and make myself into a suitable dwelling place for the Divine spirit. Is this not a cause for joy?"*

Spiritual joy is in fulfillment of the Divine will. The practice of *shidduchim* on Yom Kippur described by the Talmud was in keeping with the concept of the mitzvah of raising families and transmitting to them the legacy of Sinai. The forgiveness of Yom Kippur was seen as an opportunity to rid oneself of the burdens of past mistakes, which then enables a person to progress in one's character development free of the depressing guilt which impedes optimum growth.

The abstentions of Tishah B'Av are maintained with an attitude of grief for the spiritual greatness we have lost. The abstinence of Yom Kippur symbolizes our liberation from the physical drives that may hinder our spiritual growth. The solemnity of the prayer for forgiveness emphasizes our awareness of the gravity of sinful behavior resulting from our character defects, and thus paves the way for true *teshuvah* and spiritual development. Whereas on Tishah B'Av we bewail the spiritual greatness we have lost, on Yom Kippur we are jubilant for the spiritual greatness that we can achieve.

❧ ❧ ❧

*Someone asked Rabbi Bunim of P'shichah why the Al-Cheit confession enumerates the sins in alphabetical order.*

*Rabbi Bunim responded, "If they were not listed according to the aleph-beis, how would one know when to stop?"*

❧ ❧ ❧

*One Yom Kippur eve, Rabbi Levi Yitzchak of Berditchev looked over his congregation, as all were standing with great reverence and solemnity, wearing the talis and the white kittel. He then approached the open ark and said, "Dear God, You commanded that on a day before Yom Kippur eve we are all to have feasts, and that it is as much a mitzvah to eat on the ninth day of Tishrei as it is to fast on the tenth day.*

*"Now suppose that non-Jews were told to have feasts. Why, most of them would be drunk or have so engorged themselves with food that they would not be able to attend prayers. But look at Your children. They have eaten and drank as You commanded, yet each one is here in shul, resembling the very heavenly host in their sanctity. Now I ask You, dear Heavenly Father, do they not warrant Your complete forgiveness?"*

A spiritual person can feast, and enjoy food and drink without it detracting from his spirituality.

In listing the various sins in the *Al-Cheit* confession, we ask forgiveness "for the sins we have done because of the *yetzer hara* (the Evil Inclination)." But aren't *all* sins done because of the *yetzer hara*?

One of the chassidic masters wittily said, "Rarely does a person think he is committing a sin with the *yetzer hara.* Most often he rationalizes that what is doing is good and proper, and perhaps a mitzvah, and that he is actually carrying out the dictates of the *yetzer tov*!"

How careful we must be not to deceive ourselves.

In the Yom Kippur confession we say, "We are before You like a vessel full of shame."

The chassidic master of Belz commented, "A vessel full of shame can be emptied and filled with healthy pride."

Yom Kippur deals with guilt over mistakes one has made. We can atone for mistakes and can make amends and rid ourselves of guilt. If we allow ourselves to feel destructive shame, to feel badly about ourselves because we are somehow inherently bad, then we are without means to dispose of this feeling.

This is why the Rabbi of Belz pointed out that "a vessel full of shame" says nothing about the nature of the vessel itself. It may be very beautiful. It may be valuable, perhaps made of gold or silver. If it does contain shame, the latter should be emptied and the shame replaced with self-esteem.

## SUKKOS

Rosh Hashanah and Yom Kippur are the start of a new period, one in which the person who has done sincere *teshuvah* wishes to make the necessary changes in order to become more spiritual.

We may learn much from people who have had to abandon a self-destructive lifestyle and, in order to make the necessary changes to develop a healthy lifestyle, have adopted certain effective techniques. People who recover from addiction to alcohol or drugs are instructed to avoid "people, places, and things" — i.e., associations which had previously been conducive to chemical use — and to establish new associations in order to prevent return to previous practices.

Having made a decision during the days of *teshuvah* to make various modifications in our lives in order to become more spiritual, we must now implement this decision. Sukkos helps us begin this process by providing us with changes in "people, places, and things."

For one whole week we change our customary dwelling place, leaving our "permanent" home, and living in the *sukkah.* Historically, the *sukkah* commemorates the protective clouds of glory which encircled the Israelites through their journey in the desert following the Exodus, and in this way we are reminded of God's providence, and that we can be secure if we place our lives in His trust. Living in the *sukkah,* a temporary hut, for seven days should also make us aware that what we generally consider to be our "permanent" home is nothing but a temporary dwelling, and that after our sojourn on earth we return to our truly permanent homes. This perspective on life should enable us to place our priority on those things that will provide for us in our permanent dwelling, rather than be preoccupied with the fleeting pleasures that characterize this ephemeral world.

On Sukkos we change "people," as we invite into the *sukkah* the seven shepherds of Israel — Abraham, Isaac, Jacob, Moses, Aaron, Joseph, and David — whose lives as paragons of spirituality can serve as models for us to emulate. According to Kabbalah, each of the seven shepherds represents one of the seven Divine traits which we are to incorporate into our lives: compassion, strength, beauty, triumph, glory, foundation, and sovereignty. Our associations with these "people" during Sukkos can serve as a springboard toward spirituality.

Finally, we change "things." Each day of Sukkos we take the four species, which are the items that are the centerpiece of the festival. The Midrash states that whereas God provides for growth of all vegetation via the natural physical cycles of weather, these four species — the citron, the palm, the myrtle, and the willow — are under direct Divine care. We thus identify with these four species, since Israel too is beyond the realm of physical law, and is under the immediate supervision of God. Anyone who has any doubt about this will find it difficult to explain the survival of the Jewish people throughout history. Mighty, populous empires that were secure within their borders have perished from the face of the earth, while this handful of people, driven from land to land, always among hostile neighbors, and repeatedly decimated by pogroms, inquisitions, and holocaust, has stubbornly survived.

The "people, places, and things" provided by Sukkos enable us to make a quantum leap into the spirituality for which we have prepared ourselves during the days of *teshuvah*. Sukkos is therefore the "festival of rejoicing," but brings us closer to fulfillment of our ultimate purpose in life: becoming spiritual people.

❦ ❦ ❦

*Rabbi Levi Yitzchak of Berditchev used to make an extra effort to invite homeless, street people into his sukkah. The obvious reason was that these were often "undesirables" who might not be invited elsewhere.*

*However, Rabbi Levi Yitzchak gave this explanation. "We are told that in the World to Come, God will make a huge sukkah and invite all the tzaddikim. I would love to be there, but what right will I have to expect an invitation? I will therefore argue, 'I deserve to enter, because even though I do not have any merits, my practice was to have all the "undesirables" in my sukkah, and measure for measure, I should be permitted into the sukkah even though I too may be undesirable.' "*

❦ ❦ ❦

*One year there was a dearth of esrogim (citrons), and the Gaon of Vilna was very distressed that he would not be able to fulfill the precious mitzvah of the four species. He asked his disciples to find out whether an esrog was available anywhere and to pay whatever price was asked.*

*One disciple encountered a wealthy man who had procured an esrog and was on his way home. The Gaon's student, having been told to pay any price, told him, "If you remain in Vilna so that the Gaon can also use your esrog, I assure you that the reward for his mitzvah will be ascribed to you." Hearing this, the man agreed to remain in Vilna for Sukkos.*

*When the Gaon heard about the conditions of the transaction, he was overjoyed. "Ideally one should perform mitzvos without consideration of reward," he said, "yet one cannot totally eliminate the knowledge that reward will be forthcoming, and this may blemish the performance of the mitzvah. But now that I know I will not receive the reward for the mitzvah, I can do it without any personal interest whatever."*

The epitome of spirituality is doing what is right without any consideration of personal gain. The Gaon of Vilna was spirituality at its finest.

**SHAVUOS**

Perhaps the prominent feature of spirituality is the dedication of oneself to a purpose in life other than self-gratification, whether the latter takes the form of physical drives or ego aspirations.

According to the Midrash, the giving of the Torah to the Israelites on Shavuos was met with opposition by the heavenly angels, who claimed that mortals were not deserving of the Torah. While Moses successfully refuted the angels' claim, the question is why did the angels think that they had a greater right to the Torah.

While we do not know much about how angels operate, it is revealed to us in our daily services that "They each give to one another, with love, permission to sanctify their Creator with a pleasant spirit." In other words, there is no competitiveness among the angels who will merit to sing the hymns to God. Each one lovingly yields the privilege to another.

Unfortunately, human beings are not free of competitiveness, even when the Divine service is involved. In some situations there is fierce competition over who will perform a certain ritual, and non-spiritual vanity finds its way into religious services. We need only note, for example, the rancor which may develop when someone feels slighted because he was not selected for one of the earlier *hakafos* (processions) on Simchas Torah. If one truly rejoices with the Torah, what difference is it whether one had the second or the sixth *hakafah*?

A king once removed a general from his command following his loss of an important battle, and it was rumored that the general had committed treason by intentionally losing the battle. When the war was finally won and a victory celebration was held, the first general participated heartily in honoring the triumph of his successor. The king concluded that there could not have been a breach of loyalty, else he would not have rejoiced in his successor's triumph.

Spirituality is put to the test when there is a question whether a mitzvah will be done, or whether one insists that *only he* must do it. Whereas striving to do mitzvos may occasionally permit zeal, the latter can be distorted into an ego trip. The Talmud relates that during the Second Temple period, when there had been a deterioration of spirituality, two *Kohanim* (priests) competed for the privilege to perform a particular service. The spat led to strife, and one priest stabbed the other. When zeal from mitzvos results in any degree of harm to another person, it is misguided and reprehensible.

The angels knew the foibles of mortals. "Give them the Torah," they claimed, "and they will use it to further themselves. Leave the Torah with us, where there is no bickering as to who is privileged to perform the Divine service."

Moses' triumph over the angels was due to a phenomenon which occurred only once in the history of our people. The Talmud states that at Sinai "all Jews were united, like one person with one heart." At that particular moment all Israelites shed their self-seeking behavior, and their dedication to God was absolute and sincere. It was this unity that earned the Israelites the gift of the Torah.

Alas! Rashi states that this unity was of brief duration, and that petty bickering began soon thereafter, never again to leave us.

The spiritual message of Shavuos is not merely the historic event of receiving the Torah, but rather how it was that we merited it. Shavuos should stimulate us to set aside our self-seeking behavior and to dedicate ourselves fully to the service of God, for only with this as our goal can we overcome the divisiveness that has plagued us throughout history.

Let us remember that we are separate only in our physical bodies. The *neshamah,* the spirit which inhabits us, is of Divine origin, and all *neshamos* are a single entity. To the degree that we relegate our physical selves to a subordinate position and make the spirit the essence of our lives, to that degree we can all be one. Spirituality and unity are one and the same.

❦ ❦ ❦

The Midrash states that when Moses came to receive the Torah, the heavenly angels protested, claiming that the Torah should remain with them in the heavens and not be given to earthly creatures.

> *The Maggid of Dubno explained this Midrash with a parable. A rabbi who was very unpopular in his community accepted a position in another city. When the committee from the city came to escort the rabbi to his new pulpit, the townsfolk assembled and began shouting, "No! You cannot take our rabbi from us. We will not allow it!"*
>
> *The rabbi was bewildered. He turned to the community leaders and asked, "Why are you making this protest? You never did care for me."*
>
> *The community leaders took the rabbi aside. "You see," they said, "if we seem pleased with your departure, the people who have come to take you to their city will suspect that you are not liked, and they may renege on the contract. We therefore want them to believe you are very well liked, so that they will indeed accept you as their rabbi."*
>
> *"Similarly," said the Maggid of Dubno, "the angels protested that they wished the Torah to remain in heaven, simply to increase Moses' desire to bring it down to earth."*

Shavuos is essentially the culmination of the Exodus, inasmuch as the Torah, which is the ultimate goal of the Jewish nation, was given on Shavuos.

The spiritual values of the Torah are of the highest order: "to be a nation of priests and a sacred people" (*Exodus* 19:6). How is it possible, even with a leader as great as Moses, to take a population that had been enslaved, oppressed, and crushed for so many decades under the influence of Egyptian paganism and transform them in so short a period of time to the heights of spirituality?

The method was given by God to Moses in the mitzvah of *sefirah,* the counting of the *Omer.* Beginning with the second day of Passover, Jews are to count forty-nine days, and celebrate Shavuos on the fiftieth day. Each day we say, "This is the first day, this is the second day," etc.

Giving an oppressed and enslaved people so lofty a goal would appear to be preposterous. But to tell them that they have to do just a little bit of character improvement each day brings the challenge down to bite size. In our *siddurim,* the specific character traits which are to be rectified each day are enumerated. This is the method that Moses used with the Israelites.

It is a most successful technique. When we assume tasks that are within our capacities to perform, we can succeed. The success of this method is attested to by the declaration of the Israelites at Sinai, "We shall do and we shall listen," with the acceptance of absolute subjugation to God and turning over one's life and one's will to the will of God. This is a technique which we should use all year around, not only during *sefirah.* We may set high goals for ourselves, and we should work at them one day at a time.

## CHANUKAH

Although the history of Chanukah commemorates a later event in Jewish history and is not of Biblical origin, its spiritual message is particularly important. Chanukah marks the rededication of the Temple after the stunning military triumph of the Maccabeans, and we celebrate Chanukah not by commemorating the military conquest, but rather by lighting the Chanukah candles, to remind us of the miracle of the oil, whereby one day's supply lit brightly for eight days. The priority given to the miracle of the oil over the miraculous triumph of a mere handful of inadequately supplied warriors against the overwhelmingly superior forces of the Syrian army indicates where the emphasis of Judaism lies. As Scripture says, "Not by might and not by force, but by spirit, said God" (*Zechariah* 4:6). The military triumph is mentioned in our prayers only to express our gratitude to God for this miracle, but the message of Chanukah that was intended for posterity was that of the oil.

We might ask: Why is it that the miracle of Chanukah is perpetuated in an annual celebration, while such marvelous occurrences such as Joshua's stopping the sun and moon in their orbits (*Joshua* 10:13) are not commemorated? The answer is that we commemorate only those miracles which convey a message that is of practical value today. Miracles that are of historical significance only, regardless how great, are not celebrated.

The message of the miracle of the oil has many implications. Firstly, it conveys the concept of the *menorah,* a service which we emulate on Shabbos and Yom Tov by lighting candles. If one lights a candle for oneself, one makes the room brighter for everyone else. If one lights a candle for another person, one benefits from the light as well. Lighting the candles reminds us that no one is an island. We are all in this world together, and no one can stand alone.

Secondly, the episode of the *menorah* characterizes the resolve of the Maccabeans, a principle which should guide us throughout our lives. When the Temple was liberated, all the vials of oil had been rendered unfit for the *menorah* because they had been defiled by use in pagan rights. A single vial was found that was untouched, but it could last for only one day, whereas it would be eight days before a fresh supply of oil could be procured.

No doubt that there were some who were resigned to using defiled oil, arguing that it was futile to insist on using the single vial of uncontaminated oil, since the other oils would have to be used eventually. Better judgment prevailed, however, and it was decided to do the best one can today, and to leave tomorrow's worries for tomorrow. The Maccabeans championed the concept of "One day at a time," and it was this message that the Sages of the Sanhedrin wish to perpetuate.

We often create difficulties for ourselves when we try to deal with tomorrow's problems today. There are many times when we must do things to prepare for the future, but this is appropriate only when our doing something today is constructive. Too often we worry about problems about which we can do nothing, and we anticipate the worst when it is just as likely that the best will occur. For such situations the message of Chanukah serves as a true beacon of light. "Do your very utmost with what you have, and pray for Divine help for whatever is beyond your ability to control."

Chanukah is a very spiritual holiday, and appropriately enough, we celebrate it by beginning with one light on the first day, and adding to it each day. This is the way spirituality should develop. We may begin with just a small nucleus of brightness, but we must add to it each day of our lives.

## PURIM

Second only to Passover, Purim is observed in commemoration of our salvation from the decree of the annihilation by Haman. Purim is observed by the public reading of the Book of Esther, by giving charity to the poor, and by exchanging gifts of food with friends. There is one aspect of the Purim celebration, however, that makes us raise our eyebrows. We are to have a feast, and according to the interpretation of the Talmud provided by the early commentaries, one should "imbibe until one does not know between 'cursed is Haman and blessed is Mordechai.' "

Inasmuch as excessive drinking is soundly condemned by all halachic authorities, how can we explain this apparent aberration, to drink until reaching a stage of confusion?

Various explanations have been given for this exceptional rule, but none of them are really satisfactory, and the question remains essentially unanswered. However, what should concern us is not the theoretical explanation of this Talmudic passage, but its application as it affects us today, in our own observance of Purim.

Many later halachic authorities make no exception in the condemnation of intoxication for Purim. Rabbi Chezkia de Silva, a respected halachic authority, wrote some 200 years ago, "In our generation, where excessive drinking may result in improper behavior, one should not drink inordinately." Many recent halachic authorities have concurred.

It goes without saying that any person who has an alcohol problem is absolutely forbidden to consume liquor in any quantity at any time, including

Purim. People who are truly safe drinkers may drink just a bit more wine on Purim than they do on Shabbos.

This opinion of the later halachic authorities does not contradict the Talmudic rule. One must analyze the words of the Talmud carefully. The Talmud certainly does not use the term that refers to intoxication, nor does it even use the word "to drink." Rather, the Talmud chose an unusual term, *l'avsiumi,* which literally means "to be perfumed" or "to absorb a fragrance." The connotation appears to be that one should absorb the idea of Purim until one does "not *know* between 'cursed is Haman and blessed is Mordechai.' "

Purim is indeed a day of joyous celebration, but it is a sacred day, not to be profaned by intoxication and improper levity.

What then may be the meaning of "not know between 'cursed is Haman and blessed is Mordechai'?" Again it is important to carefully analyze the words of the Talmud. The passage does not read "not *distinguish*" between the two, because that might have indeed conveyed the idea of a state of confusion. Rather, the choice of words is "not *know*" and this is a significant choice of words.

Mordechai and Haman are two extremes, the personification of good and evil. Good is blessed and evil is accursed.

In many values there are extremes at either pole, and a broad intermediate zone. Indeed, for many values Rambam recommends avoiding the extremes and adopting what he refers to as "the golden path," which is some point between the two extremes. This is not true of good and evil, for which there can be no compromise. Good must always be sought in its purest form, and evil must always be avoided.

The Talmud states that Haman's threatened decrees were the results of the Jews having deviated from the Torah, and having compromised on Torah values. Under the guidance of Mordechai they corrected their errant ways and accepted the Torah just as their ancestors had done generations earlier at Sinai.

There is a zone that is "between" Haman and Mordechai, an intermediate area between good and evil, which represents a compromise. The message one should absorb, *"l'avsiumi,"* from Purim is that there is no compromise, no acceptance of a grey area when the values of good and evil are under consideration. Our salvation on Purim was the result of absolute rejection of evil and totally embracing good. This is identical to our salvation from Egypt, where, as we have seen, the Israelites totally rejected paganism and idolatry, and accepted upon themselves servitude to Hashem. This is the message of Purim as well as that of Passover.

## ◆ *The Order of the Seder*

## ◆ *The Four Cups*

# ☙ The Order of the Seder

***Kaddesh, Urechatz, Karpas, Yachatz, Maggid, Rachtzah, Motzi, Matzah, Maror, Korech, Shulchan Orech, Tzafun, Barech, Hallel, Nirtzah.***

The above mnemonic consists of fifteen terms, which correspond to the fifteen parts of the *Seder.* In the Haggadah the *Seder* is arranged in a manner that symbolizes not only the national trek from slavery to freedom, but also one's personal journey of self-discovery and growth.

### ☙ *Kaddesh* (Chanting the *kiddush*)

There are people who approach the royal *Seder* table with no advance spiritual preparation. They may think, "I don't really belong here. If anyone knew the real me, I certainly wouldn't be invited." Therefore, we begin the *Seder* with the *kiddush,* in which we state "*Mikadesh Yisrael,*" *God* sanctifies each Jew. There is an element of intrinsic sanctity in every individual. Even though we may not feel worthy and deserving at this point, we have to take God's word for it. Each person is holy, sanctified, and unique.

### ☙ *Urechatz* (Washing the hands, without reciting the blessing)

We have just been told that whether we believe it or not, we are indeed holy. We therefore respond with a washing of the hands, a token act of cleansing. We may not yet believe that we are capable of being purified and becoming spiritual, and our lack of belief in our self-worth is indicated by our abstention from reciting a *berachah* (blessing) for this washing. But that is quite all right. One may act "as if" as long as one is not deceiving oneself. We know that this act of purification is not yet the real thing, but we hope it will eventually lead us to genuine purification.

### ☙ *Karpas* (Dipping the vegetable in salt water)

Many reasons have been given for this ritual, but one of them conveys a particularly important message. We take a vegetable that had, up until now, existed in the ground. If it were capable of thought, it would have a self-perception of being lowly and would feel discomfort. On Passover night this vegetable is given a place of distinction and honor in the ritual of the *Seder.* Thus, Passover elevates even the earth-fettered tuber.

Rabbi Yosef Chaim Sonnenfeld was asked why he immersed himself in the *mikveh* so often. He replied, "If *mikveh* can effect a conversion and make a lowly soul more spiritually elevated, imagine what it can do to a soul that has already reached some level of loftiness!"

If Passover can uplift a simple vegetable, allowing it to raise its head and participate at the royal *Seder,* imagine what hope it offers to the person whose feelings of inferiority have resulted in a profound sense of shame. *Karpas* thus beckons to those who have feelings of unworthiness, inviting them to take their places around the table of God, even before one has achieved authentic purification.

Like the dipping of the *karpas* in salt water, we too have the opportunity to cleanse ourselves. True, sometimes this cleansing process may feel like salt water on an open wound. Let us remember that this initial discomfort is removing a superficial defect. The beauty and value that now presents itself at the *Seder* has always been there, having only been concealed by a thin layer of grime.

### ☙ ***Yachatz*** (Breaking the matzah)

As we will see, matzah has a dual symbolism. On the one hand it is the bread of affliction, and on the other hand it is the bread of liberation. Matzah can portray both the subservience and lowliness of enslavement, and yet also the hope of a brighter future. This second aspect of matzah emanates from the fact that the Israelites left Egypt with the dough unbaked, following Moses into the barren desert solely on the basis of their belief in God.

We break the matzah and conceal the larger portion beneath the pillow upon which we lean. Perhaps this symbolizes that even when our source of salvation is concealed from us, we nevertheless know it is there, and we may lean on it. We achieve a measure of serenity from the knowledge that the bread of salvation is there, and, even if not visible at present, will be manifest in the future.

We have thus progressed in the order of the *Seder* from a lack of belief in our potential to achieve *kedushah* (sanctity), to acting "as if," and then to a modicum of comfort and serenity with trust that God will help us achieve spiritual grandeur.

### ☙ ***Maggid*** (Reciting the Haggadah)

The narrative of the Haggadah tells what things were like, what happened, and how things are now. This narrative must be recited aloud, so that it is shared with others. As we relate the imperfections of our collective past, and follow the theme through to the glory of the ultimate redemption, those whose self-images have been shame-ridden may experience this liberating experience. The theme initiated at the *kiddush,* "I am worthwhile and spiritual," is now reinforced.

### ☙ ***Rachtzah*** (Washing the hands and reciting the blessing)

With this second washing, upon which we invoke the name of God, we indicate that we have progressed from a state of "as if" to an experience of genuine purification.

### ☙ ***Motzi-Matzah*** (Eating the matzah)

The first blessing that is recited over the matzah is the traditional blessing for bread, acknowledging that it is God Who brings forth bread from the earth. The "natural" phenomenon of seeds sprouting into grain is the handiwork of God. We elevate this bread to a level of a mitzvah, and ingest it so that it may become part of our very person. Every physical object can similarly be transformed into a mitzvah when it contributes to the service of God.

### ☙ ***Maror-Korech*** (Eating the bitter herbs by themselves and with the matzah)

Many people may experience moments of bitterness in life, but these can be mitigated when taken together with the matzah. The bitterness is pungent only when taken by itself, but in presence of the trust and hope in a better future symbolized by the matzah, the distress of the bitterness is decreased.

### ☙ ***Shulchan Orech*** (Partaking of the meal)

Having come to the awareness that even the distresses of life can be mitigated, we are now capable of enjoying the good things of life. The anxiety and fear that prevent a person from enjoying the good things of life have now been largely removed by the preceding steps in the *Seder.* Life can now not only be tolerated, but even enjoyed.

### ☙ *Tzafun* (Eating the hidden matzah)

Having negotiated the earlier steps, the previous trust now blossoms into visible deliverance. The bread of deliverance which had, up to this point, been concealed, is now uncovered. That which was hidden by the mysterious ways of God now becomes overtly manifest. Faith and trust will mature into freedom and spirituality.

### ☙ *Barech* (Reciting the Prayer of Thanks after the meal)

The process of growth from enslavement to freedom, from feelings of inadequacy to self-esteem, was not an easy one. At many points along the way we may have resented the distress of the "growing pains." However, we now appreciate the growth process, and realize that we must express our gratitude to God for providing us with the strength and sustenance to achieve this level of spirituality.

### ☙ *Hallel* (Reciting the praises of God)

Whereas the first two chapters of *Hallel* were recited prior to the meal, we now conclude *Hallel* with those chapters that relate to the ultimate redemption of Israel. Our recognition of the Divine benevolence and our awareness that even the moments of distress were constructive periods of growth enable us to face the future, and give thanks to God for all that we will yet experience, even if we must yet face adversities. According to the Talmud, the ultimate redemption may be preceded by the "agonies of redemption," but our experience of spiritual growth which the *Seder* order symbolizes allows us to accept even these agonies with serenity.

### ☙ *Nirtzah* (Whoever has completed the order of the *Seder* finds favor in the eyes of God)

The great theologian and ethicist, Rabbi Moshe Chaim Luzzatto, states that the entire existence of man is one vast set of challenges. The Divine wisdom has decreed that it must be so, for reasons known only to God. By accepting this and following the ascent to spirituality, we fulfill the Divine will, and find favor in the eyes of God.

## ☙ The Four Cups

The Midrash states that one reason we have four cups of wine (or grape juice) at the *Seder* is to correspond to the four expressions of liberation that are found in *Exodus* (6:6-7), whereby God tells Moses that he will deliver the Israelites from their Egyptian captivity and take them as His nation. The four expressions used are: (1) I will take them out of Egypt, (2) I will save them, (3) I will deliver them, and (4) I will take them to be My nation.

The liberation of the Israelites was not a unique event in the history of mankind. Many nations have come into being by separating themselves from the domination of a ruler and declaring their independence. Even today we witness new countries arising as the nationalistic spirit of a group leads them to form their own government.

But there is something very special about the Exodus which distinguishes it from other liberations. Nationalistic aspirations are invariably the desire of a people to free themselves from someone's domination and to be their own masters. The formation of a breakaway nation is founded on the supposition that "No one is going to tell us what to do. We wish to be independent and rule ourselves." Rarely, if ever, has a group of people declared its independence in order to put itself under the absolute rule of another power.

As dear and as desirable as liberty is, it is thus essentially a negative phenomenon in the sense that it is the throwing off of a yoke. The Exodus was strikingly different. In his first dialogue with Moses, God says, "When you take the people out of Egypt, you will serve God on this mountain" (*Exodus* 3:12). The deliverance from Egypt was not going to represent independence in the usual sense of the word. The Israelites were not being taken out to become a nation that would be its own master. Rather, they would emerge as a nation that would come under the absolute rule of God, with every facet of life dictated by Torah law, what they must do and what they may not do. God explicitly states, "The children of Israel are servants unto Me" (*Leviticus* 25:55). The Exodus was not meant to be a negative phenomenon, the *rejection of a yoke,* but a positive one, the *acceptance* of a yoke.

One might ask, what kind of independence is this? It appears to be merely a trade-off, a substitution of one subjugation for another.

True; but let us note what the Talmud says. The Torah states that the Ten Commandments were inscribed on the Tablets, the word חָרוּת meaning "inscribed." This same word can be read phonetically as חֵרוּת, which means "liberated," and the verse thus reads that liberation is inherent in the commandments of the Torah.

How are we to understand this? Let me give you an example from my daily work, treating people with addiction. Never in your life have you seen any enslavement as total and as absolute as that of the addict to his chemical substance. The addict has no choice whatsoever. He is not free to do as he may wish. When the urge for the chemical overtakes him, he will do whatever is necessary to get it, no holds barred. The chemical dictates and the addict obeys.

But chemicals are not the only human addiction. People may be addicted to power, to greed, to lust, to acclaim from others. These people, too, may be helpless in regard to whatever drive dominates them and dictates their behavior. They may think they are acting as free people, but nothing could be farther from the truth. They are slaves to lust, to money, to power, to acclaim, and there is no respite from these taskmasters. In their sleep as well as in their waking hours, they are subject to this dictatorship.

The Torah gives a person the capacity to use his human intellect to regulate his behavior, rather than being under the domination of one's physical drives. Accepting the rule of God, which elevates people above passions, is thus the true freedom.

The first three of the four expressions of liberation refer solely to the deliverance from the Egyptian captivity, but this is grossly incomplete. Many nations have come into being with no ultimate goal other than not being dominated by a ruler. Throwing off the yoke is only part of liberation, and if this is not followed by something which allows man to be master over himself, then nothing has really been accomplished.

The fourth expression, "I will take them to be My nation," which indicates the servitude to God and acceptance of Torah as the way of life, thus completes the Exodus, and gives meaning to the first three expressions.

We pride ourselves on being free. Let us reflect a bit on whether we are truly free, or only delude ourselves about our freedom. Such reflection will help us realize the truth of the Talmudic statement, that true freedom is inscribed on the Tablets, consisting of the Divine commandments.

# ◆ *Preparing for Passover*

*The Search for Chametz*

*Burning the Chametz*

*Eruv Tavshilin*

*Kindling Lights*

*Preparing for the Seder*

# בדיקת חמץ

On the night of 14 Nissan, the night before the Pesach *Seder,* the search for *chametz* (leaven) is made. It should be done with a candle as soon as possible after nightfall. [When the first *Seder* is on Saturday night, the search is conducted on Thursday night (13 Nissan).]
Before the search is begun, the following blessing is recited.
If several people assist in the search, only one recites the blessing for all.

**בָּרוּךְ** אַתָּה יהוה, אֱלֹהֵינוּ מֶלֶךְ הָעוֹלָם, אֲשֶׁר קִדְּשָׁנוּ בְּמִצְוֹתָיו, וְצִוָּנוּ עַל בִּעוּר חָמֵץ.

After the search, the *chametz* is wrapped and put aside in a safe place to be burned in the morning. Then the following declaration is made:

**כָּל חֲמִירָא** וַחֲמִיעָא דְּאִכָּא בִרְשׁוּתִי, דְּלָא חֲמִתֵּהּ וּדְלָא בִעַרְתֵּהּ וּדְלָא יְדַעְנָא לֵהּ, לִבָּטֵל וְלֶהֱוֵי הֶפְקֵר כְּעַפְרָא דְאַרְעָא.

# ביעור חמץ

In the morning, after the *chametz* has been burned, the following declaration is made.

**כָּל חֲמִירָא** וַחֲמִיעָא דְּאִכָּא בִרְשׁוּתִי, דַּחֲזִתֵּהּ וּדְלָא חֲזִתֵּהּ, דַּחֲמִתֵּהּ וּדְלָא חֲמִתֵּהּ, דְּבִעַרְתֵּהּ וּדְלָא בִעַרְתֵּהּ, לִבָּטֵל וְלֶהֱוֵי הֶפְקֵר כְּעַפְרָא דְאַרְעָא.

# ערוב תבשילין

When Pesach falls on Thursday and Friday, an *eruv tavshilin* is made on Wednesday.
The *eruv*-foods are held while the following blessing and declaration are recited.

**בָּרוּךְ** אַתָּה יהוה, אֱלֹהֵינוּ מֶלֶךְ הָעוֹלָם, אֲשֶׁר קִדְּשָׁנוּ בְּמִצְוֹתָיו, וְצִוָּנוּ עַל מִצְוַת עֵרוּב.

**בַּהֲדֵין** עֵרוּבָא יְהֵא שָׁרֵא לָנָא לַאֲפוּיֵי וּלְבַשּׁוּלֵי וּלְאַטְמוּנֵי וּלְאַדְלוּקֵי שְׁרָגָא וּלְתַקָּנָא וּלְמֶעְבַּד כָּל צָרְכָּנָא, מִיּוֹמָא טָבָא לְשַׁבְּתָא [לָנָא וּלְכָל יִשְׂרָאֵל הַדָּרִים בָּעִיר הַזֹּאת].

## THE SEARCH FOR CHAMETZ

On the night of 14 Nissan, the night before the Pesach *Seder,* the search for *chametz* (leaven) is made. It should be done with a candle as soon as possible after nightfall. [When the first *Seder* is on Saturday night, the search is conducted on Thursday night (13 Nissan).]
Before the search is begun, the following blessing is recited.
If several people assist in the search, only one recites the blessing for all.

**בָּרוּךְ** Blessed are You, HASHEM, our God, King of the Universe, Who has sanctified us with His commandments and has commanded us concerning the removal of *chametz.*

After the search, the *chametz* is wrapped and put aside in a safe place to be burned in the morning. Then the following declaration is made:

**כָּל חֲמִירָא** Any *chametz* or leaven that is in my possession, which I have not seen, have not removed and do not know about, should be annulled and become ownerless, like dust of the earth.

## BURNING THE CHAMETZ

In the morning, after the *chametz* has been burned, the following declaration is made.

**כָּל חֲמִירָא** Any *chametz* or leaven that is in my possession, whether I have recognized it or not, whether I have seen it or not, whether I have removed it or not, should be annulled and become ownerless, like dust of the earth.

## ERUV TAVSHILIN

When Pesach falls on Thursday and Friday, an *eruv tavshilin* is made on Wednesday.
The *eruv*-foods are held while the following blessing and declaration are recited.

**בָּרוּךְ** Blessed are You, HASHEM, our God, King of the Universe, Who has sanctified us with His commandments and has commanded us concerning the *mitzvah* of *eruv.*

**בַּהֲדֵין** Through this *eruv* may we be permitted to bake, cook, insulate, kindle flame, prepare, and do anything necessary on the Festival for the sake of the Shabbos [for ourselves and for all Jews who live in this city].

# הדלקת הנרות

On each Yom Tov night of Pesach two blessings are recited. When Pesach coincides with the Sabbath, light the candles, then cover the eyes and recite the blessings. Uncover the eyes and gaze briefly at the candles. When Pesach falls on a weekday, some follow the above procedure, while others recite the blessings before lighting the candles. When Pesach coincides with the Sabbath, the words in brackets are added.

[It is forbidden to create a new flame — for example, by striking a match — on Yom Tov. Therefore, on the second night the candles must be lit from a flame that has been burning from before Yom Tov.]

**בָּרוּךְ** אַתָּה יהוה אֱלֹהֵינוּ מֶלֶךְ הָעוֹלָם, אֲשֶׁר קִדְּשָׁנוּ בְּמִצְוֹתָיו, וְצִוָּנוּ לְהַדְלִיק נֵר שֶׁל [שַׁבָּת וְשֶׁל] יוֹם טוֹב.

**בָּרוּךְ** אַתָּה יהוה אֱלֹהֵינוּ מֶלֶךְ הָעוֹלָם, שֶׁהֶחֱיָנוּ וְקִיְּמָנוּ וְהִגִּיעָנוּ לַזְּמַן הַזֶּה.

It is customary to recite the following prayer after the kindling. The words in brackets are included as they apply.

**יְהִי רָצוֹן** לְפָנֶיךָ, יהוה אֱלֹהַי וֵאלֹהֵי אֲבוֹתַי, שֶׁתְּחוֹנֵן אוֹתִי [וְאֶת אִישִׁי, וְאֶת בָּנַי, וְאֶת בְּנוֹתַי, וְאֶת אָבִי, וְאֶת אִמִּי] וְאֶת כָּל קְרוֹבַי; וְתִתֶּן לָנוּ וּלְכָל יִשְׂרָאֵל חַיִּים טוֹבִים וַאֲרוּכִים; וְתִזְכְּרֵנוּ בְּזִכְרוֹן טוֹבָה וּבְרָכָה; וְתִפְקְדֵנוּ בִּפְקֻדַּת יְשׁוּעָה וְרַחֲמִים; וּתְבָרְכֵנוּ בְּרָכוֹת גְּדוֹלוֹת; וְתַשְׁלִים בָּתֵּינוּ; וְתַשְׁכֵּן שְׁכִינָתְךָ בֵּינֵינוּ. וְזַכֵּנִי לְגַדֵּל בָּנִים וּבְנֵי בָנִים חֲכָמִים וּנְבוֹנִים, אוֹהֲבֵי יהוה, יִרְאֵי אֱלֹהִים, אַנְשֵׁי אֱמֶת, זֶרַע קֹדֶשׁ, בַּיהוה דְּבֵקִים, וּמְאִירִים אֶת הָעוֹלָם בַּתּוֹרָה וּבְמַעֲשִׂים טוֹבִים, וּבְכָל מְלֶאכֶת עֲבוֹדַת הַבּוֹרֵא. אָנָּא שְׁמַע אֶת תְּחִנָּתִי בָּעֵת הַזֹּאת, בִּזְכוּת שָׂרָה וְרִבְקָה וְרָחֵל וְלֵאָה אִמּוֹתֵינוּ, וְהָאֵר נֵרֵנוּ שֶׁלֹּא יִכְבֶּה לְעוֹלָם וָעֶד, וְהָאֵר פָּנֶיךָ וְנִוָּשֵׁעָה. אָמֵן.

# KINDLING LIGHTS

On each Yom Tov night of Pesach two blessings are recited. When Pesach coincides with the Sabbath, light the candles, then cover the eyes and recite the blessings. Uncover the eyes and gaze briefly at the candles. When Pesach falls on a weekday, some follow the above procedure, while others recite the blessings before lighting the candles. When Pesach coincides with the Sabbath, the words in brackets are added.

[It is forbidden to create a new flame – for example, by striking a match – on Yom Tov. Therefore, on the second night the candles must be lit from a flame that has been burning from before Yom Tov.]

**בָּרוּךְ** Blessed are You, HASHEM, our God, King of the Universe, Who has sanctified us with His commandments, and has commanded us to kindle the light of [the Sabbath and of] the Festival.

**בָּרוּךְ** Blessed are You, HASHEM, our God, King of the Universe, Who has kept us alive, sustained us, and brought us to this season.

It is customary to recite the following prayer after the kindling. The words in brackets are included as they apply.

**יְהִי רָצוֹן** May it be Your will, HASHEM, my God and God of my forefathers, that You show favor to me [my husband, my sons, my daughters, my father, my mother] and all my relatives; and that You grant us and all Israel a good and long life; that You remember us with a beneficent memory and blessing; that You consider us with a consideration of salvation and compassion; that You bless us with great blessings; that You make our households complete; that You cause Your Presence to dwell among us. Privilege me to raise children and grandchildren who are wise and understanding, who love HASHEM and fear God, people of truth, holy offspring, attached to HASHEM, who illuminate the world with Torah and good deeds and with every labor in the service of the Creator. Please, hear my supplication at this time, in the merit of Sarah, Rebecca, Rachel, and Leah, our mothers, and cause our light to illuminate that it be not extinguished forever, and let Your countenance shine so that we are saved. Amen.

## ◆ Preparing for the Seder

The *Seder* preparations should be made in time for the *Seder* to begin as soon as the synagogue services are finished. It should not begin before nightfall, however. Matzah, bitter herbs and several other items of symbolic significance are placed on the *Seder* plate in the arrangement shown below.

ג' מצות
3 MATZOS

**Matzah** — Three whole matzos are placed one atop the other, separated by a cloth or napkin. Matzah must be eaten three times during the *Seder,* by itself, with *maror,* and as the *afikoman.* Each time, the minimum portion of matzah for each person should have a volume equivalent to half an egg. Where many people are present, enough matzos should be available to enable each participant to receive a proper portion.

**Maror** and **Chazeres** — Bitter herbs are eaten twice during the *Seder,* once by themselves and a second time with matzah. Each time a minimum portion, equal to the volume of half an egg, should be eaten. The Talmud lists several vegetables that qualify as *maror,* two of which are put on the *Seder* plate in the places marked *chazeres* and *maror.* Most people use romaine lettuce (whole leaves or stalks) for *chazeres,* and horseradish (whole or grated) for *maror,* although either may be used for the mitzvah of eating *maror* later in the *Seder.*

**Charoses** — The bitter herbs are dipped into *charoses* (a mixture of grated apples, nuts, other fruit, cinnamon and other spices, mixed with red wine). The *charoses* has the appearance of mortar to symbolize the lot of the Hebrew slaves, whose lives were embittered by hard labor with brick and mortar.

**Z'roa** [Roasted bone] and **Beitzah** [Roasted egg] — On the eve of Passover in the Holy Temple in Jerusalem, two sacrifices were offered and their meat roasted and eaten at the *Seder* feast. To commemorate these two sacrifices, we place a roasted bone (with some meat on it) and a roasted hard-boiled egg on the *Seder* plate.

The egg, a symbol of mourning, is used in place of a second piece of meat as a reminder of our mourning at the destruction of the Temple — may it be rebuilt speedily in our day.

**Karpas** — A vegetable (celery, parsley, boiled potato) other than bitter herbs completes the *Seder* plate. It will be dipped in salt water and eaten. (The salt water is not put on the *Seder* plate, but it, too, should be prepared beforehand, and placed near the *Seder* plate.)

৺ *The Haggadah*

# קדש

*Kiddush* should be recited and the *Seder* begun as soon after synagogue services as possible — however, not before nightfall. Each participant's cup should be poured by someone else to symbolize the majesty of the evening, as though each participant had a servant.

On Friday night begin here:

(quietly— וַיְהִי עֶרֶב וַיְהִי בֹקֶר)

**יוֹם הַשִּׁשִּׁי:** וַיְכֻלּוּ הַשָּׁמַיִם וְהָאָרֶץ וְכָל צְבָאָם. וַיְכַל אֱלֹהִים בַּיּוֹם הַשְּׁבִיעִי מְלַאכְתּוֹ אֲשֶׁר עָשָׂה, וַיִּשְׁבֹּת בַּיּוֹם הַשְּׁבִיעִי מִכָּל מְלַאכְתּוֹ אֲשֶׁר עָשָׂה. וַיְבָרֶךְ אֱלֹהִים אֶת יוֹם הַשְּׁבִיעִי וַיְקַדֵּשׁ אֹתוֹ, כִּי בוֹ שָׁבַת מִכָּל מְלַאכְתּוֹ אֲשֶׁר בָּרָא אֱלֹהִים לַעֲשׂוֹת.[1]

KIDDUSH CONTINUES ON NEXT PAGE

1. *Genesis* 1:31-2:3.

### קַדֵּשׁ / וּרְחַץ — *Kaddesh / Urechatz*

In addition to dictating the order of the *Seder,* these words indicate an order that is unique to the Exodus.

The word "*kaddesh*" means to sanctify, and can be taken as an imperative, "Sanctify yourself." *Urechatz* can also mean, "Cleanse yourself."

Usually, cleansing oneself must precede sanctification, as we read in *Psalms,* "Abstain from evil, and do that which is good" (34:15). There is no point in trying to cleanse someone who is wallowing in mud until he emerges from the mud, and there is no purpose in adorning oneself in fine clothes until the dirt has been washed away. Similarly, one cannot expect to achieve *kedushah* (sanctity) unless one has first abandoned sinful behavior.

According to the Talmudic sages, the Exodus was an exception to this rule. The Jews under Egyptian bondage had lost their spirituality as well as their freedom. Under Egyptian influence, they had degenerated into the idolatry of their environment. Indeed, the sacrifice of the paschal lamb, which was an Egyptian totem, was intended to express their rejection of the paganism in which they had become immersed. Yet, even before emerging from the depths of spiritual decadence, they merited an unprecedented Divine revelation. The vision of Divinity witnessed at the Splitting of the Sea by the lowliest Jew of the Exodus surpassed the marvelous revelations of the prophet Ezekiel (*Mechilta*).

# KADDESH

*Kiddush* should be recited and the *Seder* begun as soon after synagogue services as possible – however, not before nightfall. Each participant's cup should be poured by someone else to symbolize the majesty of the evening, as though each participant had a servant.

On Friday night begin here:

(quietly – And there was evening and there was morning)

**יוֹם הַשִּׁשִּׁי:** The sixth day. Thus the heavens and the earth were finished, and all their array. On the seventh day God completed His work which He had done, and He abstained on the seventh day from all His work which He had done. God blessed the seventh day and hallowed it, because on it He abstained from all His work which God created to make.[1]

KIDDUSH CONTINUES ON NEXT PAGE

---

*The Exodus thus had the unique feature of enabling a person to be elevated to the ultimate heights of spirituality even prior to divesting himself of objectionable behavior!*

This unique *chesed* (favor) which accompanied the historical Exodus remains available to us at any time. It is ours for the asking, if only we invoke it.

There are some people who become disillusioned with their lifestyle, and might consider adopting a more spiritual mode of living, but are reluctant to do so because they consider spirituality to be beyond their reach. "There is no point in my trying to make a change now," they may say. "I am too far gone, too set in my habits. My trying to observe any part of the Torah in my present state would be hypocritical."

This is not true. Observance of any of the many mitzvos which have been designated as representing or being associated with the Exodus carries with it the unique favor of bestowing sanctity even prior to shedding one's depravity.

We read and hear about the lives of our eminent *tzaddikim* (pious individuals), and although we admire their greatness, we may nevertheless not seek to emulate them, thinking, "How could I ever aspire to achieve such devotion and saintliness?" We give up because we think it to be an act of futility. Such greatness is clearly beyond our reach.

Again, not true. A person can redeem himself with one moment of sincere

On all nights other than Friday, begin here;
on Friday night include all passages in parentheses.

סַבְרִי מָרָנָן וְרַבָּנָן וְרַבּוֹתַי:

**בָּרוּךְ** אַתָּה יהוה אֱלֹהֵינוּ מֶלֶךְ הָעוֹלָם, בּוֹרֵא פְּרִי הַגָּפֶן:

**בָּרוּךְ** אַתָּה יהוה אֱלֹהֵינוּ מֶלֶךְ הָעוֹלָם, אֲשֶׁר בָּחַר בָּנוּ מִכָּל עָם, וְרוֹמְמָנוּ מִכָּל לָשׁוֹן, וְקִדְּשָׁנוּ בְּמִצְוֹתָיו. וַתִּתֶּן לָנוּ יהוה אֱלֹהֵינוּ בְּאַהֲבָה (שַׁבָּתוֹת לִמְנוּחָה וּ)מוֹעֲדִים לְשִׂמְחָה, חַגִּים וּזְמַנִּים לְשָׂשׂוֹן, אֶת יוֹם (הַשַּׁבָּת הַזֶּה וְאֶת יוֹם) חַג הַמַּצּוֹת הַזֶּה, זְמַן חֵרוּתֵנוּ (בְּאַהֲבָה) מִקְרָא קֹדֶשׁ, זֵכֶר לִיצִיאַת מִצְרָיִם, כִּי בָנוּ בָחַרְתָּ וְאוֹתָנוּ קִדַּשְׁתָּ מִכָּל הָעַמִּים, (וְשַׁבָּת) וּמוֹעֲדֵי קָדְשֶׁךָ (בְּאַהֲבָה וּבְרָצוֹן) בְּשִׂמְחָה וּבְשָׂשׂוֹן הִנְחַלְתָּנוּ. בָּרוּךְ אַתָּה יהוה, מְקַדֵּשׁ (הַשַּׁבָּת וְ)יִשְׂרָאֵל וְהַזְּמַנִּים.

KIDDUSH CONTINUES ON NEXT PAGE

---

devotion. The Talmud tells of a reprobate whose entire life was dissolute, and because of a single sincere effort at *teshuvah* (repentance) was proclaimed by a heavenly voice to have merited *Gan Eden* (Paradise).

The Exodus was distinct because of an act of faith by our ancestors. Two million people left a land of abundance, following the prophet of an invisible God into a desolate and barren desert, where there was neither food nor water for such a multitude, clinging only to the belief that God would provide for them. It is this supreme act of trust which is constantly before God, as the prophet says, "I remember to your merit the kindness of your youth . . . when you followed Me into the desert, into a barren wilderness" (*Jeremiah* 2:2).

What we repeatedly refer to when commemorating the Egyptian saga is *yetzias mitzrayim,* the act of *leaving* Egypt, because it is this absolute, unwavering trust in God that is the foundation of spirituality.

*Kaddesh urechatz*! What a precious Divine gift!

On all nights other than Friday, begin here;
on Friday night include all passages in parentheses.

By your leave, my masters and teachers:

בָּרוּךְ Blessed are You, HASHEM, our God, King of the Universe, Who creates the fruit of the vine.

בָּרוּךְ Blessed are You, HASHEM, our God, King of the Universe, Who has chosen us from all nations, exalted us above all tongues, and sanctified us with His commandments. And You, HASHEM, our God, have lovingly given us (Sabbaths for rest), appointed times for gladness, feasts and seasons for joy, (this Sabbath and) this Feast of Matzos, the season of our freedom (in love,) a holy convocation in memoriam of the Exodus from Egypt. For You have chosen and sanctified us above all peoples, (and the Sabbath) and Your holy festivals (in love and favor), in gladness and joy have You granted us as a heritage. Blessed are You, HASHEM, Who sanctifies (the Sabbath,) Israel, and the festive seasons.

KIDDUSH CONTINUES ON NEXT PAGE

---

### ◆§ חַג הַמַּצּוֹת הַזֶּה — *this Feast of Matzos*

Whereas we refer to the festival as Passover, the Torah refers to it only as "the festival of the matzos." Why?

Rabbi Levi Yitzchak of Berditchev explained. The matzah represents the total devotion of the Israelites to God, as it is said in *Exodus* (12:39), that the Israelites were in such haste to leave Egypt that they baked their dough before it had a chance to rise, and they took no other provisions with them. So great was their trust in God at this moment that they followed Moses into the barren desert, not thinking how they would get food or water. This trust and devotion is remembered as a virtue, as the prophet says (*Jeremiah* 2:2), "I remember you following Me into the desolate desert."

The word "Passover," on the other hand, indicates the miraculous salvation, whereby God smote the firstborn of Egypt, but "passed over" the homes of the Israelites (*Exodus* 12:13). It is thus a term of gratitude and praise of G-d.

The Jews and God thus reciprocate in praising one another. The Torah refers to the festival as that of the *matzos,* extolling the loyalty of the Jews, whereas the Jews refer to this as *Passover,* in praise of the Divine miracle.

By the way these terms are used, we learn to always be appreciative of the merits of others.

On Saturday night, add the following two paragraphs:

**בָּרוּךְ** אַתָּה יהוה אֱלֹהֵינוּ מֶלֶךְ הָעוֹלָם, בּוֹרֵא מְאוֹרֵי הָאֵשׁ.

**בָּרוּךְ** אַתָּה יהוה אֱלֹהֵינוּ מֶלֶךְ הָעוֹלָם, הַמַּבְדִּיל בֵּין קֹדֶשׁ לְחוֹל, בֵּין אוֹר לְחֹשֶׁךְ, בֵּין יִשְׂרָאֵל לָעַמִּים, בֵּין יוֹם הַשְּׁבִיעִי לְשֵׁשֶׁת יְמֵי הַמַּעֲשֶׂה. בֵּין קְדֻשַּׁת שַׁבָּת לִקְדֻשַּׁת יוֹם טוֹב הִבְדַּלְתָּ, וְאֶת יוֹם הַשְּׁבִיעִי מִשֵּׁשֶׁת יְמֵי הַמַּעֲשֶׂה קִדַּשְׁתָּ, הִבְדַּלְתָּ וְקִדַּשְׁתָּ אֶת עַמְּךָ יִשְׂרָאֵל בִּקְדֻשָּׁתֶךָ. בָּרוּךְ אַתָּה יהוה, הַמַּבְדִּיל בֵּין קֹדֶשׁ לְקֹדֶשׁ.

On all nights conclude here:

**בָּרוּךְ** אַתָּה יהוה אֱלֹהֵינוּ מֶלֶךְ הָעוֹלָם, שֶׁהֶחֱיָנוּ וְקִיְּמָנוּ וְהִגִּיעָנוּ לַזְּמַן הַזֶּה.

The wine should be drunk without delay while reclining on the left side. It is preferable to drink the entire cup, but at the very least, most of the cup should be drained.

# ורחץ

The head of the household — according to many opinions, all participants in the *Seder* — wash their hands as if to eat bread [pouring water from a cup, twice on the right hand and twice on the left], but without reciting a blessing.

# כרפס

All participants take a vegetable other than *maror* and dip it into salt water. A piece smaller in volume than half an egg should be used. The following blessing is recited [with the intention that it also applies to the *maror* which will be eaten during the meal] before the vegetable is eaten.

**בָּרוּךְ** אַתָּה יהוה אֱלֹהֵינוּ מֶלֶךְ הָעוֹלָם, בּוֹרֵא פְּרִי הָאֲדָמָה.

On Saturday night, add the following two paragraphs:

בָּרוּךְ Blessed are You, HASHEM, our God, King of the Universe, Who creates the illumination of the fire.

בָּרוּךְ Blessed are You, HASHEM, our God, King of the Universe, Who distinguishes between sacred and secular, between light and darkness, between Israel and the nations, between the seventh day and the six days of activity. You have distinguished between the holiness of the Sabbath and the holiness of a Festival, and have sanctified the seventh day above the six days of activity. You distinguished and sanctified Your nation, Israel, with Your holiness. Blessed are You, HASHEM, who distinguishes between holiness and holiness.

On all nights conclude here:

בָּרוּךְ Blessed are You, HASHEM, our God, King of the Universe, Who has kept us alive, sustained us, and brought us to this season.

The wine should be drunk without delay while reclining on the left side. It is preferable to drink the entire cup, but at the very least, most of the cup should be drained.

---

## URECHATZ

---

The head of the household — according to many opinions, all participants in the *Seder* — wash their hands as if to eat bread [pouring water from a cup, twice on the right hand and twice on the left], but without reciting a blessing.

---

## KARPAS

---

All participants take a vegetable other than *maror* and dip it into salt water. A piece smaller in volume than half an egg should be used. The following blessing is recited [with the intention that it also applies to the *maror* which will be eaten during the meal] before the vegetable is eaten.

בָּרוּךְ Blessed are You, HASHEM, our God, King of the Universe, Who creates the fruits of the earth.

# יחץ

The head of the household breaks the middle matzah in two. He puts the smaller part back between the two whole matzos, and wraps up the larger part for later use as the *afikoman*. Some briefly place the *afikoman* portion on their shoulders, in accordance with the Biblical verse recounting that Israel left Egypt carrying their matzos on their shoulders, and say, בִּבְהִלוּ יָצָאנוּ מִמִּצְרָיִם, *"In haste we went out of Egypt."*

# מגיד

The broken matzah is lifted for all to see and the participants begin the recitation of the Haggadah with the following brief explanation of the proceedings.

**הָא לַחְמָא עַנְיָא דִּי אֲכָלוּ אַבְהָתָנָא בְּאַרְעָא דְמִצְרָיִם. כָּל דִּכְפִין יֵיתֵי**

### ◆§ יַחַץ — *Yachatz*

The instructions at *Yachatz* are to break the matzah in two, and put the greater piece aside for the *afikoman*.

> *At the Seder table of Rabbi Menachem of Lubavitch, the Tzemach Tzedek, one of the guests was carefully measuring the two pieces to see which was the larger one. Noticing this the Rabbi remarked, "When greatness has to be measured in millimeters, it is not greatness at all. In such instances the lesser may actually be the greater."*

Sometimes the world is impoverished in leadership. Presidents, prime ministers, and kings do not demonstrate any outstanding qualities. Their superiority, if it exists, is measured in millimeters. In such instances, the common man is apt to be greater, because he meets the criteria for a common man, whereas the leader is not meeting the criteria of leadership.

### ◆§ הָא לַחְמָא עַנְיָא דִּי אֲכָלוּ אַבְהָתָנָא בְּאַרְעָא דְמִצְרָיִם — *This is the poor bread that our fathers ate in the land of Egypt.*

The Torah refers to the years of enslavement in Egypt as Israel's "furnace of purification" (*Deuteronomy* 4:20), and although we may not fully understand how we were purified and why purification was needed, it is clear that this experience should help us identify with those who are suffering and to come to their aid. In several places the Torah requires us to be sensitive to

# YACHATZ

The head of the household breaks the middle matzah in two. He puts the smaller part back between the two whole matzos, and wraps up the larger part for later use as the *afikoman*. Some briefly place the *afikoman* portion on their shoulders, in accordance with the Biblical verse recounting that Israel left Egypt carrying their matzos on their shoulders, and say, בְּבְהִלוּ יָצָאנוּ מִמִּצְרָיִם, *"In haste we went out of Egypt."*

# MAGGID

The broken matzah is lifted for all to see and the participants begin the recitation of the Haggadah with the following brief explanation of the proceedings.

**הָא לַחְמָא עַנְיָא** This is the poor bread that our fathers ate in the land of Egypt. Whoever is hungry,

---

the needs of the stranger. "And you shall love him (the stranger in your midst) like yourself, for you were strangers in the land of Egypt" (*Leviticus* 19:34).

Eating the "bread of affliction" should remind us of those who do not yet enjoy the blessing of freedom. We should bear in mind that as long as even one person is enslaved, all mankind is not yet free.

**הָא לַחְמָא עַנְיָא דִּי אֲכָלוּ אַבְהָתָנָא בְּאַרְעָא דְמִצְרָיִם — *This is the poor bread that our fathers ate in the land of Egypt.***

The ultimate in the obligation and appreciation for any considerations one has received is taught in the Torah commandment, "Do not abhor an Egyptian, for you were a sojourner in his land" (*Deuteronomy* 23:8). Rashi anticipates the question, "Because we sojourned? They enslaved us and threw our infants into the Nile!" True. Yet there is no denying that we lived in their land, ate of its produce, and received shelter from the elements. The harm they did to us must not obscure the appreciation that is due to them for the benefits they bestowed. The Torah's emphasis on the primacy of gratitude is so great that even in this relationship of servitude, the suffering sustained at the hands of the Egyptians should not abrogate this obligation. As we shall see, gratitude is fundamental to spirituality.

Inasmuch as this introductory paragraph is written in Aramaic rather than Hebrew, it must have been composed during the Babylonian exile. Passover, the festival of liberation and independence, was being celebrated under conditions of disenfranchisement and oppression. This paragraph thus served as a reassurance. The Babylonian Jews were saying, "We may again be eating the bread of affliction in exile, but just as we had once been oppressed and were redeemed, so we can again look forward to redemption."

*In a village there was a rather simple Jew who enjoyed his daily drink. On the day before Passover, knowing that he could not have whiskey for eight whole days, he decided to imbibe all he could and he drank himself into a stupor. When night fell, his wife tried to wake him to conduct the Seder, but all in vain. Finally, shortly before dawn she was able to arouse him.*

*"Wake up, Chaim," she said. "It is still time to make the Seder."*

*Grudgingly, he sat up. He looked at the matzos and the wine on the table, washed his hands, made the berachah hamotzi, gulped down four goblets of wine, and said,*

*"What do I know about making a Seder?" All I know is that our ancestors were slaves to a wicked Egyptian king, and God took us out of Egypt. And just as He saved us then He will always save us from cruel oppressors." And with that he went back to sleep.*

*The following day the chassidic master sent for the wife. "Tell me about your husband's Seder," he said. Much embarrassed, the woman related what had happened.*

*"What a shame that he has fallen to drink," the Rebbe said. "The sincerity of his belief in Divine salvation was warmly received in Heaven. His genuine feelings captured the message of the Seder."*

In everyone's life there are peaks and valleys. At times of distress we should remember that we have emerged from similar episodes in the past, and that we will survive this ordeal as well. There is never any reason for despair. Passover carries the message for the individual as well as for the nation.

### ◆§ כָּל דִּכְפִין יֵיתֵי וְיֵכוֹל — *Whoever is hungry, let him come and eat.*

Let all who are hungry come and eat. All, without discrimination.

*The chassidic master, Rabbi Zusia of Hanipoli, had a chassid who was very successful in his business and used to help in his support. One time the chassid came and was told that Rabbi Zusia was away visiting his*

let him come and eat! Whoever is needy, let him come and celebrate Pesach! This year we are here; next year

---

*Rabbi, the Maggid of Mezeritch. The chassid reasoned, If my Rabbi has a Rabbi, then the latter must be greater yet, and he then began sending his support to the Maggid. As he did so, his business eventually began to fail, and he asked Rabbi Zusia why this was happening to him.*

*"Very simple," Rabbi Zusia said. "God relates to us accordingly as we act. When you were less choosy and you gave to Zusia, not looking for greater tzaddikim, then God gave to you without investigating whether you were really deserving. But when you began to pick and choose and give only to great tzaddikim, then God began to investigate whether you were deserving of prosperity."*

On a night when we pray for the ultimate Redemption, even though we may not be meritorious enough to deserve it, we say, "Let all who are hungry come," without exception. If we do not discriminate, then we can expect that God will not be too discriminating with us.

*On the day before Passover a man asked the Rabbi of Brisk whether it is permissible to use four cups of milk instead of wine at the Seder, since he was unable to afford wine.*

*The Rabbi gave the man several rubles, instructing him to buy wine and all other Seder needs.*

*The Rabbi's wife, who had observed this, asked, "Why did you give him so much money? He doesn't need that much to buy wine."*

*The Rabbi explained, "How could he have considered using milk at the Seder, since the Seder meal is traditionally fleischig (with meat)? Obviously, he could not afford to buy meat either, so that is why I gave him enough money for all his needs."*

### ◆§ כָּל דִּצְרִיךְ יֵיתֵי וְיִפְסַח — *Whoever is needy, let him come and celebrate Pesach.*

Inasmuch as the Haggadah can be seen as a text on spirituality, this invitation is for those who seek spirituality to come and join in.

Judaism does not proselytize. We have no missionaries who knock on doors seeking converts. Quite the contrary, anyone who applies for conversion to Judaism is thoroughly discouraged from making such a move. Only after one has mastered the many demands of Judaism, and perseveres

הַבָּאָה בְּאַרְעָא דְיִשְׂרָאֵל. הָשַׁתָּא עַבְדֵי, לְשָׁנָה הַבָּאָה בְּנֵי חוֹרִין.

The *Seder* plate is removed and the second of the Four Cups of wine is poured. The youngest present asks the "Four Questions" regarding the unusual proceedings of the evening.

מַה נִּשְׁתַּנָּה הַלַּיְלָה הַזֶּה מִכָּל הַלֵּילוֹת?

---

in the desire to embrace Judaism in spite of all its requirements, only then is conversion permitted.

In other words, our public relations are based on attraction, not promotion. This drawing power must come from our living a spiritual life that provides a serenity such that it will cause others to gravitate to our lifestyle. "And you shall observe and fulfill (the teachings of the Torah), for it is your wisdom and understanding before the eyes of other nations, who shall hear all these decrees and will say, 'Surely, this great nation is a wise and understanding people' " (*Deuteronomy* 4:6).

While we do not recruit, our doors are open. The allure must result from our demonstrating how we emerge from our enslavement of today to our freedom of tomorrow.

### כָּל דִּצְרִיךְ — *Whoever is needy*

It has been wisely said that much of the evil that has befallen the world is a result of people's concern about their own *physical* well-being, while showing concern only for other people's *spiritual* well-being.

Yes, we will share our spiritual wealth with those who are deprived in this area, but let us also remember that there are those whose neediness lies in food, clothing, and shelter.

### כָּל דִּכְפִין יֵיתֵי וְיֵכוֹל . . . לְשָׁנָה הַבָּאָה בְּאַרְעָא דְיִשְׂרָאֵל — *Whoever is hungry, let him come and eat . . . next year may we be in the Land of Israel.*

"Let all who are hungry come and eat. . . Today we are here, but in the year to come we will be in the Land of Israel."

The prophet says that the ultimate redemption and our return to Zion will come about by virtue of the mitzvah of *tzedakah* (*Isaiah* 1:27). Inasmuch as all of the mitzvos of the Torah are incomplete if they are not performed with the proper *kavanah* (concentration), who can say that one has properly fulfilled any mitzvah, with its many esoteric meanings?

may we be in the Land of Israel! This year, we are slaves; next year may we be free men!

The *Seder* plate is removed and the second of the Four Cups of wine is poured. The youngest present asks the "Four Questions" regarding the unusual proceedings of the evening.

**מַה נִּשְׁתַּנָּה** Why is this night different from all other nights?

---

The one exception is the mitzvah of *tzedakah.* The purpose of this mitzvah is to relieve the suffering of the needy. How and why this is achieved is irrelevant. Rashi (*Deuteronomy* 24:19) states that if someone loses a coin and a poor person finds it, the former has the merit of the mitzvah of *tzedakah,* even though he was totally unaware of having helped the poor person. This is why the ultimate redemption will be by virtue of *tzedakah.* It is *always* a complete mitzvah.

We can now understand the reason the Haggadah juxtaposes the two statements above. "Let all who are hungry come and join at our table" — by virtue of caring for those in need, we will merit the ultimate redemption, and in the year to come be in our homeland.

### מַה נִּשְׁתַּנָּה — *Mah Nishtanah*

The Passover *Seder* is dedicated to children. The Talmud records a practice of giving the children confections to keep them awake for the *Seder.* It is also recommended not to delay the beginning of the *Seder,* so that children will be awake, and furthermore, the *Seder* begins with the youngest child asking the "Four Questions."

In the story of the Exodus, Pharoah conceded that he would allow the Israelites to leave to worship in the desert, but insisted only the adults go and the children be left behind (*Exodus* 10:9-11), to which Moses responded, "We will go with our young and our old," and the fact that he placed the young before the old indicates the importance which he gave to youth.

Our coming into being as a nation contains the elements of our survival as a nation, which is that priority must be given to the youth. Budgets that give low priority to education, whether it is a household budget or the community budget, are making a grave mistake.

The word "*Seder*" means order. The order of things is that acquainting children with Judaism must be at the very top of the list.

## שֶׁבְּכָל הַלֵּילוֹת אָנוּ אוֹכְלִין חָמֵץ וּמַצָּה, הַלַּיְלָה הַזֶּה – כֻּלּוֹ מַצָּה.

The spiritual life is an intelligent life, one of knowledge and wisdom, not of ignorance.

Prior to the invention of the printing press, books were laboriously hand-written, and were generally owned either by the aristocracy or by the clergy. The laity was largely ignorant of religious writings, as Scriptures were not readily accessible to them. Indeed, when the printing press made Scriptures available to all, the church was most displeased. It is little wonder that the Reformation which succeeded in challenging existing dogma followed the popularization of Scriptures by means of the printing press. Dogma thrives on ignorance.

Judaism, to the contrary, has always emphasized education, and primarily knowledge of the Torah. The first concern of a community was always the *cheder* (school), which had primacy even over the synagogue. There tots would be taught Hebrew and given access to the Torah in the original. Inquiry was never discouraged. Even the fundamental principles of faith which are essential to Jewishness did not escape philosophical inquiry.

It is most appropriate, therefore, that at the very outset of a treatise on spirituality, we begin with asking, Why?

The "Four Questions" emphasize yet another aspect of spirituality: the ability to live with conflict. The emphasis of modern psychology on the resolution of contention has resulted in people eschewing all conflict. Living with ongoing stress has become unthinkable, and many individuals who find themselves entangled in struggles that are not readily resolvable may attempt to escape therefrom by rather desperate methods, not the least of which is seeking the oblivion or euphoria of alcohol, mind-altering substances, or diversionary activities.

The loss of tolerance for conflict has had a profound impact on interpersonal relationships as well as on the intrapersonal psyche. The unprecedented divorce rate is, to a great measure, due to the inability to withstand conflict, and to seek immediate relief from all frustrating situations.

The "Four Questions" point out that the *Seder,* the feast of spirituality, is characterized by the co-existence of conflicting ideas. We eat the dry matzah, the bread of the slave, and the bitter herbs to commemorate our enslavement, yet we recline on couches and dip appetizers into dressings according to the custom of the free and wealthy nobility. How can we reconcile these opposites?

**1.** On all other nights we may eat *chametz* and matzah, but on this night — only matzah.

---

The answer is that we do not need to reconcile all conflicts. The concept of freedom as espoused in Torah is quite distinct from the secular concept. According to the latter, the ultimate aim of freedom is the absence of all discord, a state rarely encountered in reality. Torah freedom includes the capacity to live *with* stress, and to be able to achieve serenity in the face of conflict.

### ◆§ הַלַּיְלָה הַזֶּה כֻּלּוֹ מַצָּה — *this night — only matzah*

The prohibition against *chametz* on Passover is much more stringent than that of any other forbidden food. For example, if a tiny bit of *treifah* food is accidentally mixed with a large quantity of food that is kosher, so that the proportion of kosher to non-kosher is greater than 60:1, the mixture may be eaten. With *chametz,* this is not so. If a tiny crumb of *chametz* were to fall into a huge vat of matzah dough, and the proportion of matzah to *chametz* were a million to one, the entire dough would be condemned. What is different about *chametz* on Passover that renders it more detrimental than other forbidden foods?

The difference between *chametz* and matzah is a simple one. Matzah dough that is allowed to remain unbaked will spontaneously ferment and become *chametz.* It remains matzah only if from the very first contact of the flour with the water it is kneaded, rolled, and promptly baked. *Halachah* requires continuous contact; working with the mixture of flour and water up to the very moment of its baking. No change occurs in the matzah except that which is brought about by the hands of the kneader. This is not so with *chametz,* which ferments and rises when it is left to itself. *Chametz* undergoes spontaneous changes.

Matzah and *chametz* thus symbolize two distinct philosophical perspectives. Matzah represents constant Divine providence. Nothing happens unless God makes it happen. Nothing occurs "by itself." The minutest event in the universe does not escape God's attention. *Chametz* represents spontaneous change. A "big bang" occurs, and things then progress without anyone directing the changes.

The dramatic narrative of the Exodus indicates that God was directing the scenario, overriding the rules of nature. Judaism teaches that not only is the hand of God present in such obvious miracles, but in everything that occurs in the universe. The growth of every blade of grass is determined under Divine providence. Nothing takes place without God willing it to happen.

To impress upon us the extension of the Divine providence evident in the

**שֶׁבְּכָל הַלֵּילוֹת** אָנוּ אוֹכְלִין שְׁאָר יְרָקוֹת,
הַלַּיְלָה הַזֶּה – מָרוֹר.
**שֶׁבְּכָל הַלֵּילוֹת** אֵין אָנוּ מַטְבִּילִין אֲפִילוּ פַּעַם אֶחָת,
הַלַּיְלָה הַזֶּה – שְׁתֵּי פְעָמִים.
**שֶׁבְּכָל הַלֵּילוֹת** אָנוּ אוֹכְלִין בֵּין יוֹשְׁבִין וּבֵין מְסֻבִּין,
הַלַּיְלָה הַזֶּה – כֻּלָּנוּ מְסֻבִּין.

The Seder plate is returned. The matzos are kept uncovered as the Haggadah is recited in unison. The Haggadah should be translated if necessary, and the story of the Exodus should be amplified upon.

**עֲבָדִים** הָיִינוּ לְפַרְעֹה בְּמִצְרָיִם, וַיּוֹצִיאֵנוּ יהוה אֱלֹהֵינוּ מִשָּׁם בְּיָד חֲזָקָה וּבִזְרוֹעַ נְטוּיָה. וְאִלּוּ לֹא הוֹצִיא הַקָּדוֹשׁ בָּרוּךְ הוּא אֶת אֲבוֹתֵינוּ מִמִּצְרַיִם, הֲרֵי אָנוּ

---

Exodus to all events of the world, we eat the matzah, which, in contrast to *chametz,* represents an entity which undergoes no spontaneous change. To emphasize that not even the most infinitesimal event escapes God's attention, the *halachah* is that the minutest crumb of *chametz* is prohibited. We must believe that there is nothing so insignificant as to be beyond Divine providence.

Perhaps this is why the kabbalistic writings refer to matzah as the "bread of faith." Matzah teaches us that, except for those moral free decisions which are relegated to man, everything in the world occurs because God designs it so.

❧ ❧ ❧

After asking the "Four Questions," a child heard his father recite, "We were slaves unto Pharaoh." The child asked, "How is that an answer to my four questions?"

The father responded, "Look, when we were slaves to Pharaoh, did we ask why he wanted us to do something? He gave orders and we obeyed. No questions asked. Now we do things at the *Seder* because God said that this is what we are supposed to do. No questions asked. Understand?"

### ◆§ עֲבָדִים הָיִינוּ לְפַרְעֹה בְּמִצְרָיִם — *We were slaves to Pharaoh in Egypt*

Why is it so certain that without Divine intervention we could not have freed ourselves at some later point in time? Is history not replete with ac-

2. On all other nights we eat many vegetables, but on this night — *maror.*
3. On all other nights we do not dip even once, but on this night — twice.
4. On all other nights we eat either sitting or reclining, but on this night — we all recline.

The Seder plate is returned. The matzos are kept uncovered as the Haggadah is recited in unison. The Haggadah should be translated if necessary, and the story of the Exodus should be amplified upon.

**עֲבָדִים** We were slaves to Pharaoh in Egypt, but HASHEM our God took us out from there with a mighty hand and an outstretched arm. Had not the Holy One, Blessed is He, taken our fathers out from Egypt, then we,

---

counts of captive nations that achieved liberty without miraculous intervention by God?

Rabbi Isaac Meir of Gur provided the answer. In commissioning Moses to liberate the Israelites from Egypt, God said, "I will extract them from beneath the burden (*sivlus*) of Egypt" (*Exodus* 6:6). Rabbi Isaac Meir points out that the word "*sivlus*" also means "tolerance," and the sentence then reads, "I will extract them from their *tolerance* of Egypt."

During the many years of enslavement, the Israelites had become so accustomed to their status that they considered it to be the normal state of affairs. Not only had they resigned themselves to being slaves, but also had come to believe that this was their natural state, much like the proverbial worm who infests the horseradish and undoubtedly considers this, the bitterest of all vegetables, to be the best place in the world.

A slave may reason, "What is wrong with being a slave? A slave's stomach is always full, and he carries no responsibilities. The master is the one who has the burden of providing for the slaves. Of what use is liberty with its accompanying obligations?"

Moses' first task was to convince the Israelites that liberty was indeed desirable. As the Torah relates, they were not all that enthused with the idea, and when their initial quest for a modicum of freedom of worship resulted in greater oppression, they rejected the project and heaped calumny upon Moses for having increased their misery (*Exodus* 5:21).

The Haggadah thus correctly states that without Divine intervention we would not have extricated ourselves from Egypt, because we had no aspiration for liberty.

וּבָנֵינוּ וּבְנֵי בָנֵינוּ מְשֻׁעְבָּדִים הָיִינוּ לְפַרְעֹה בְּמִצְרָיִם. וַאֲפִילוּ כֻּלָּנוּ חֲכָמִים, כֻּלָּנוּ נְבוֹנִים, כֻּלָּנוּ זְקֵנִים, כֻּלָּנוּ יוֹדְעִים אֶת הַתּוֹרָה, מִצְוָה עָלֵינוּ לְסַפֵּר בִּיצִיאַת מִצְרָיִם. וְכָל הַמַּרְבֶּה לְסַפֵּר בִּיצִיאַת מִצְרַיִם, הֲרֵי זֶה מְשֻׁבָּח.

---

This facet of the story of the Exodus is of great importance to us even thousands of years later. Many people have adjusted to a lifestyle in which they feel comfortable, and have never given a thought that perhaps an alternate lifestyle might be preferable. Some people are enslaved to their own passions, to the standards of living set by their neighbors, to prevailing cultural values, or to addictions to food, alcohol, or other chemicals. Some people may live an entire lifetime in this state of servitude, failing to exercise their right to independent thinking or to extricate themselves from harmful habits that are ruinous to both body and soul.

The story of the Exodus should serve as an arousal to every individual. It should alert one to think, "Is it possible that I may be in a rut, but similar to my enslaved ancestors, fail to recognize it?" This should stimulate one to a rigorous self-examination, and to a determination that if there is indeed a more worthy lifestyle, one should be ready and willing to bear the temporary discomfort in making the necessary changes in one's life to achieve the true liberty that dignifies a human being.

Spirituality does not come easily. Cows in the pasture undoubtedly have greater contentment than an intelligent being who struggles to achieve mastery over oneself and grow in character. But are we willing to relegate ourselves to a state of bovine contentment when we are capable of achieving Divine spirituality?

### ◆§ וַאֲפִילוּ כֻּלָּנוּ חֲכָמִים — *Even if we were all men of wisdom*

In the introduction to his epochal *Path of the Just,* Luzzatto says that he will not provide any new information in his book. Everything that he will present is well known to everyone, but precisely because people are familiar with these ethical principles, they tend to take them for granted, give them little thought, and fail to enact them in their daily lives. He therefore suggests that his book be reviewed frequently, and be used as a reminder, to alert people to actually do what they already know to be proper.

our children, and our children's children would have remained enslaved to Pharaoh in Egypt. Even if we were all men of wisdom, understanding, experience, and knowledge of the Torah, it would still be an obligation upon us to tell about the Exodus from Egypt. The more one tells about the Exodus, the more he is praiseworthy.

---

This is why the Haggadah states that regardless of how wise and learned one may be, it is incumbent upon one to relate the story of the Exodus. In fact, it is precisely those who are most learned and most familiar with the story of the Exodus who are most vulnerable to take it for granted, as Luzzatto says.

The more frequently one thinks about the Exodus, the more likely one is to put its teachings into practice.

### ◆§ וְכָל הַמַּרְבֶּה לְסַפֵּר בִּיצִיאַת מִצְרַיִם הֲרֵי זֶה מְשֻׁבָּח — *The more one tells about the Exodus, the more he is praiseworthy.*

If we had maintained the status of independence that we acquired at the Exodus, we could easily understand why it should be celebrated. But why is the narration of the story of the Exodus important in times when we are in exile and suppressed by hostile rulers, when there is no remnant of our independence?

This may be explained by a parable of a poor person who won a great deal of money in a sweepstakes. Realizing that he never had the opportunity of an education, he used his funds to hire tutors, and he became quite a learned person. Each year he would celebrate the anniversary of the day of his winnings.

As time went by, he lost all his money, and was again impoverished. Yet, he continued the practice of celebrating the day of his enrichment. When asked why he continued to do so after he had lost all his wealth, he replied, "Yes, the money is gone, but the education and the knowledge that I acquired thereby is still with me."

Even if we have lost the political independence we achieved at the Exodus, we have retained the spirituality which resulted from repudiating the pagan lifestyle of Egypt and accepting the Torah soon after our deliverance. Our celebrating Passover even in exile indicates that we value the spiritual gains above the material. One who abounds in the narration of the story of the Exodus is thus indeed praiseworthy, because this shows that he gives the highest priority to spirituality.

מַעֲשֶׂה בְּרַבִּי אֱלִיעֶזֶר וְרַבִּי יְהוֹשֻׁעַ וְרַבִּי אֶלְעָזָר בֶּן עֲזַרְיָה וְרַבִּי עֲקִיבָא וְרַבִּי טַרְפוֹן שֶׁהָיוּ מְסֻבִּין בִּבְנֵי בְרַק, וְהָיוּ מְסַפְּרִים בִּיצִיאַת מִצְרַיִם כָּל אוֹתוֹ הַלַּיְלָה. עַד שֶׁבָּאוּ תַלְמִידֵיהֶם וְאָמְרוּ לָהֶם, רַבּוֹתֵינוּ הִגִּיעַ זְמַן קְרִיאַת שְׁמַע שֶׁל שַׁחֲרִית.

---

**וְכָל הַמַּרְבֶּה לְסַפֵּר בִּיצִיאַת מִצְרַיִם הֲרֵי זֶה מְשֻׁבָּח — *The more one tells about the Exodus, the more he is praiseworthy.***

The human being is a composite, consisting of a Divine spirit which inhabits an essentially animal body. The latter has powerful strivings, not the least of which is to remain calm and undisturbed, maintaining the status quo. Change of any kind is likely to be uncomfortable, and in seeking to avoid the discomfort of change, the human being may find abundant reasons why change is unnecessary. This is the well-known phenomenon of *rationalization,* which enables us to delude ourselves into believing that things are fine just as they are.

To counter these powerful forces, even periodic self-examination is not sufficient. If we are not on *constant* alert, rationalizations are likely to once again dominate. Thus, regardless of how wise and learned one may be, the Haggadah urges and stimulates us to perform self-examination with the same frequency that our rationalizations are likely to occur. The more one recalls this vital teaching, the more one is likely to emerge from one's rut and strive for spirituality.

Struggling with the *yetzer hara* (evil inclination) is like playing a tennis match. Each stroke must be returned, and the opponent is obviously going to try to hit the ball out of one's reach. One must exert much effort to return the stroke, because failure to do so results in losing the game.

How aptly does the Haggadah say, "The more one relates the story of the Exodus, the more praiseworthy one becomes."

Why is it so meritorious to elaborate on the story of the Exodus?

A *maggid* (preacher) once delivered a long-winded sermon in the Chofetz Chaim's synagogue. Although the sermon was rather insipid, the Chofetz Chaim complemented the *maggid* lavishly, whereupon the latter humbly said, "I did not really think my talk was that good."

The Chofetz Chaim said, "My dear friend, the entire time that you delivered your address, no one in the audience had an opportunity to speak *lashon hara* (gossip). Your lengthy sermon thus prevented a grievous sin."

At the *Seder,* where there is often a gathering of family members who have

**מַעֲשֶׂה** It happened that Rabbi Eliezer, Rabbi Yehoshua, Rabbi Elazar ben Azaryah, Rabbi Akiva, and Rabbi Tarfon were reclining (at the *Seder*) in Bnei Brak. They discussed the Exodus all that night until their students came and said to them: "Our teachers, it is the time [daybreak] for the reading of the morning *Shema.*"

---

not seen each other for months, it is quite likely that the conversation would turn to talk about relatives and friends, and unfortunately, much *lashon hara* might be communicated. Therefore, the more one relates about the Exodus at the *Seder,* the more praiseworthy one is, because it prevents the exchange of *lashon hara*!

### ❧ וְהָיוּ מְסַפְּרִים בִּיצִיאַת מִצְרַיִם כָּל אוֹתוֹ הַלַּיְלָה — *They discussed the Exodus all that night*

Why are we told about the gathering of scholars who discussed the Exodus all night until dawn?

Perhaps this is to tell us that fatigue is as much a psychological phenomenon as it is a physiological condition.

We know all too well what "*Erev Pesach*" is like in the Jewish home. Until the onset of the *Yom Tov,* one is busy with last-minute preparations, and by the time one sits down to the *Seder,* one is fairly exhausted. Add to this four cups of wine and a heavy meal, and physiology brings on drowsiness. Some of us do not even make it through the end of the Haggadah. Those that do are soon deep in slumber.

To remain awake all night after "*Erev Pesach*" and the *Seder,* by virtue of discussing the miracles of the Exodus, indicates how something which is psychologically stimulating can override physiology.

Next time we delay doing something important because "we're too tired," let us think of this portion of the Haggadah.

### ❧ עַד שֶׁבָּאוּ תַלְמִידֵיהֶם וְאָמְרוּ לָהֶם, רַבּוֹתֵינוּ הִגִּיעַ זְמַן קְרִיאַת שְׁמַע שֶׁל שַׁחֲרִית — *until their students came and said to them, "Our teachers, it is the time [daybreak] for the reading of the morning Shema."*

When scholars of the caliber of these Talmudic giants are engaged in a discussion of the wonders of the Exodus, how do students have the audacity to interrupt them, especially to imply that they are derelict in delaying the reciting of the *Shema*?

**אָמַר** רַבִּי אֶלְעָזָר בֶּן עֲזַרְיָה, הֲרֵי אֲנִי כְּבֶן שִׁבְעִים שָׁנָה, וְלֹא זָכִיתִי שֶׁתֵּאָמֵר יְצִיאַת מִצְרַיִם בַּלֵּילוֹת, עַד שֶׁדְּרָשָׁהּ בֶּן זוֹמָא, שֶׁנֶּאֱמַר, לְמַעַן תִּזְכֹּר אֶת יוֹם צֵאתְךָ מֵאֶרֶץ מִצְרַיִם כֹּל יְמֵי חַיֶּיךָ.[1] יְמֵי חַיֶּיךָ הַיָּמִים, כֹּל יְמֵי חַיֶּיךָ הַלֵּילוֹת. וַחֲכָמִים אוֹמְרִים, יְמֵי חַיֶּיךָ הָעוֹלָם הַזֶּה, כֹּל יְמֵי חַיֶּיךָ לְהָבִיא לִימוֹת הַמָּשִׁיחַ.

(1) *Deuteronomy* 16:3.

---

The Talmud states that the reading of the evening *Shema* should consist of an expression of trust in God, and the reading of the morning *Shema* should be an affirmation of faith in the unity of God and the acceptance of subjugation to His will (*Berachos* 12a). These are mutually reinforcing, because the greater an individual's faith in God, the deeper is his trust, and the more he trusts in God, the more firm becomes his conviction of His Oneness and subservience to His will.

The students, seeing the intensity of their masters' trust in God which they had achieved as a result of their elaboration of His many miracles of the Exodus, wished to share in the greater affirmation of faith as they themselves prepared to recite the morning *Shema*. The comment of the disciples was thus: "*We* are about to recite the morning *Shema*. Please help us do so in the light of the greater spiritual insights you have achieved in your discussion of the Exodus." This was a request to be taught, and not an admonition of their teachers.

Asking to be taught is never considered *chutzpah*. "One who is shy is not likely to learn," say the Sages (*Ethics of the Fathers* 2:5).

A shy person who is in desperate need of water will overcome his shyness and ask for water. One who realizes that spirituality is vital to life will not hesitate to seek spiritual guidance from anyone who can provide it.

### ☙ יְמֵי חַיֶּיךָ הַיָּמִים, כֹּל יְמֵי חַיֶּיךָ הַלֵּילוֹת — *The phrase "the days of your life" would have indicated only the days; the addition of the word 'all' includes the nights as well.*

Torah concepts of work and rest differ markedly from secular concepts. This is most evident in how the weekly day of rest is observed. In the secular

**אָמַר** Rabbi Elazar ben Azaryah said: I am like a seventy-year-old man, but I could not succeed in having the Exodus from Egypt mentioned every night, until Ben Zoma expounded it: "In order that you may remember the day you left Egypt all the days of your life."[1] The phrase "the days of your life" would have indicated only the days; the addition of the word "all" includes the nights as well. But the Sages declare that "the days of your life" would mean only the present world; the addition of "all" includes the era of *Mashiach.*

---

world, the purpose of a day of rest is to renew one's energies for the work week that is to follow. Rest is subordinate to work, and the day of rest is thus the means, while the workweek becomes the goal. According to Torah, however, one works six days in order to be able to observe the Shabbos, which is the goal and ultimate purpose of creation.

If the liberation from Egypt were only an achievement of political independence and the throwing off of the burden of physical enslavement, then it is only daytime that should be emphasized, because that is when the forced labor took place. Nights were rest periods during which there was respite from work. Slaves are essentially "free" at night.

If, however, we conceptualize enslavement as oppression of the spirit as well as of the body, then the nights are as worthy of commemoration as the days, because they were nothing but preparatory periods for yet more work. When work is a means to a higher goal, then work is work and rest is rest. However, if work is the *ultimate* goal, then work is work, but rest that is in the interest of work is nothing loftier than work.

It has been said that a person who does not meditate each day on one's place and purpose in the world is not much of a person. Someone who returns home after a day of hard work, kicks off his shoes, and sinks into a comfortable recliner has certainly earned a period of relaxation, but after appropriate respite has been achieved, one should direct one's attention to Torah study, prayer, and meditation, which then gives the workday a true value. If one spends the rest of the evening glued to the television screen, and rises from the lounge chair only to retire to one's bed, the entire day remains rather similar to that of the ox who pulls the plow by day and sleeps away the night. The fact that man has a TV to watch, whereas oxen do not, is hardly a distinctive feature dignifying the human being as someone "created in the image of God."

**בָּרוּךְ** הַמָּקוֹם, בָּרוּךְ הוּא. בָּרוּךְ שֶׁנָּתַן תּוֹרָה לְעַמּוֹ יִשְׂרָאֵל, בָּרוּךְ הוּא. כְּנֶגֶד אַרְבָּעָה בָנִים דִּבְּרָה תוֹרָה: אֶחָד **חָכָם**, וְאֶחָד **רָשָׁע**, וְאֶחָד **תָּם**, וְאֶחָד **שֶׁאֵינוֹ יוֹדֵעַ לִשְׁאוֹל.**

**חָכָם** מָה הוּא אוֹמֵר? מָה הָעֵדֹת וְהַחֻקִּים

---

It is not how we spend our days that attests to our spirituality, but rather how we spend our nights.

❧ ❧ ❧

The Talmud relates that Rabbi Elazar Ben Azariah was only eighteen when he was elevated to his post as head of the academy. Miraculously, his beard turned white to provide him with the dignified appearance of maturity.

The *Zohar* states that God, the Torah, and Israel are one and the same. Since God and the Torah are infinite and timeless, every Jew should have the capacity to rise above time.

> *My great-grandfather, the first Rabbi of Bobov, was conversing with some of his chassidim, when someone mentioned that this was a special day and should be celebrated with some refreshments. The Rabbi then arose, saying, "Good. I will send my young boy to bring some."*
>
> *After a bit, the Rabbi returned, and it was evident that he himself had run the errand. To the embarrassed chassidim he said, "I did not lie to you. As I grew older, I took my youth along with me, and I still have the 'young boy' within me."*

One can be seventy at eighteen, and one can also be eighteen at seventy.

**◆ בָּרוּךְ הַמָּקוֹם, בָּרוּךְ הוּא. בָּרוּךְ שֶׁנָּתַן תּוֹרָה לְעַמּוֹ יִשְׂרָאֵל, בָּרוּךְ הוּא — *Blessed is the Omnipresent; Blessed is He. Blessed is the One Who has given the Torah to His people Israel; Blessed is He.***

The Haggadah introduces the dialogue with the four sons with the phrase, "Blessed is the One Who has given the Torah to His people Israel."

The *brachah* we recite when reading the Torah closes with, "Blessed is God Who gives the Torah": *gives* rather than *has given.* The giving of the Torah was not a historical event of the past, but is an ongoing process which continues to the present and beyond.

**בָּרוּךְ** Blessed is the Omnipresent; Blessed is He. Blessed is the One Who has given the Torah to His people Israel; Blessed is He. Concerning four sons does the Torah speak: a **wise** one, a **wicked** one, a **simple** one, and one **who is unable to ask.**

**חָכָם** **The wise son** — what does he say? "What are the the testimonies, decrees, and ordinances which

---

Let us reflect a moment. What other book written thousands of years ago continues to be studied and analyzed with its teachings applied to everyday life? The philosophical works of Aristotle and Plato may be studied by students of philosophy, but are essentially of little more than academic interest. The great scientific discoveries of the Renaissance may be appreciated as breakthroughs, but their content has long been obsolete. Theories of physics that were held to be true just several decades ago have now been discarded. Torah, on the other hand, has continued to be relevant to this very day, its teachings finding application in everyday life. Torah has not been and never will be obsolete. Every generation since Sinai has found its needs addressed in Torah. Why? Because the Author of the Torah knew the needs of every generation until the end of time, and provided for all eventualities. This is why we say, "He *gives* the Torah," rather than, "He *gave* the Torah."

Throughout centuries of Jewish history, children have been asking questions about Torah, and parents have been able to respond. Parents can respond in the age of jet planes and microwaves as well as when people traveled by mule and cooked over wood fires. The Torah is and will be relevant unto eternity.

Spirituality is similarly timeless. Material quests and lifestyles may undergo change. Truth, selflessness, compassion, patience, diligence, and all other components of spirituality are today what they were thousands of years ago. There can be continuity throughout generations, provided that we bequeath and transmit spiritual values to our children.

### ◆§ חָכָם מָה הוּא אוֹמֵר? — *The wise son — what does he say?*

As was pointed out earlier, Judaism encourages inquiry. However, this must be inquiry with a sincere intent to learn and to gain knowledge, and not provocative, derisive scoffing.

The question posed by the wise person is essentially that which we raised in our chapter on the meaning of the Exodus. Why are so many and varied

וְהַמִּשְׁפָּטִים אֲשֶׁר צִוָּה יהוה אֱלֹהֵינוּ אֶתְכֶם?[1] וְאַף אַתָּה אֱמָר לוֹ כְּהִלְכוֹת הַפֶּסַח, אֵין מַפְטִירִין אַחַר הַפֶּסַח אֲפִיקוֹמָן.

**רָשָׁע** מָה הוּא אוֹמֵר? מָה הָעֲבֹדָה הַזֹּאת לָכֶם?[2] לָכֶם וְלֹא לוֹ, וּלְפִי שֶׁהוֹצִיא אֶת עַצְמוֹ מִן הַכְּלָל, כָּפַר בְּעִקָּר – וְאַף אַתָּה הַקְהֵה אֶת שִׁנָּיו וֶאֱמָר לוֹ, בַּעֲבוּר זֶה עָשָׂה יהוה לִי בְּצֵאתִי מִמִּצְרָיִם.[3] לִי וְלֹא לוֹ, אִלּוּ הָיָה שָׁם לֹא הָיָה נִגְאָל.

(1) *Deuteronomy* 6:20. (2) *Exodus* 12:26. (3) 13:14.

mitzvos related to the Exodus? What is so significant about this historic incident that warrants its pervading every facet of daily life?

The response to the wise person is that which we have presented in this treatise. "You may not eat after partaking of the Paschal sacrifice." Why? Because the latter is the symbol of spiritual liberation. The offering of the paschal lamb represents our rejection of paganism with all its inherent materialism and self-indulgence. Therefore, the taste of spiritual liberty must be permitted to linger, and we are to savor it as long as it can last. There are many pleasantries that titillate our temptation, and we must be aware that pleasant-tasting condiments might obscure the taste of our precious spiritual freedom, and hence must be avoided. Physical pleasures may be so seductive that we are always at risk of sacrificing our spirituality in their favor. We therefore need to be constantly reminded of the teachings of the Exodus. This is a thoughtful response to a reasonable question.

### ◆§ רָשָׁע מָה הוּא אוֹמֵר? — *The wicked son — what does he say?*

The depraved person, however, does not ask in order to know. His mind is closed because he has already made his decisions. He prefers earthly pleasures to spiritual strivings, and his attitude is, "Who needs all this ritual anyway? If you do wish to celebrate Passover as an independence day, do so with a parade, picnic, and firecrackers, and then go about the business of

HASHEM, our God, has commanded you?"[1] Therefore explain to him the laws of the Pesach offering: that one may not eat dessert after the final taste of the Pesach offering.

**רָשָׁע The wicked son** — what does he say? "Of what purpose is this work to you?"[2] He says, "To you," thereby excluding himself. By excluding himself from the community of believers, he denies the basic principle of Judaism. Therefore, blunt his teeth and tell him: "It is because of this that HASHEM did so for me when I went out of Egypt."[3] "For me," but not for him — had he been there, he would not have been redeemed.

---

living and forget about it until next year!" This can hardly be considered a question, but is rather a statement of defiance.

There is little value in trying to reason with a person like this, because he does not want to listen. So to this person we say, "There were the likes of you in Egypt, who refused to follow Moses into the desert. There were also those who did leave with Moses but relapsed into paganism with the worship of the Golden Calf, and there were those who complained about the manna, saying, 'We wish we were back in Egypt, when we had fish, onions, garlic, and melons' (*Numbers* 11:5). There were those who said, 'Let us appoint a new leader and return to Egypt' (ibid. 14:4). Had you been there, you might have grudgingly exited from Egypt along with everyone else, but you would have willingly traded the hard-won, precious liberty for physical indulgences. You are far more interested in feeding your stomach rather than nurturing your mind. Yes, you might have left Egypt, but you would not have been *redeemed*. You would have maintained a slave mentality well into the liberation."

We should fashion ourselves after the wise person, who constantly seeks to gain knowledge, so that we may always progress in our quest of spiritual growth.

### ◆§ וְאַף אַתָּה הַקְהֵה אֶת שִׁנָּיו — *Therefore, blunt his teeth.*

The response to the depraved son appears to be very harsh. Is this the way parents should discipline an unruly child?

Unfortunately, there are times when such extreme measures may be necessary. For example, in working with young people who have become involved with drugs and who turn a deaf ear to all reasoning, parents must be

**תָּם** מָה הוּא אוֹמֵר? מַה זֹּאת? וְאָמַרְתָּ אֵלָיו, בְּחֹזֶק יָד הוֹצִיאָנוּ יהוה מִמִּצְרַיִם מִבֵּית עֲבָדִים.[1]

---

taught to institute "tough love." If necessary, they must say, "Our home is drug free. If you continue to use drugs, you must find yourself somewhere else to live." It is most difficult for parents to evict their own child, but the destructive and even lethal consequence of drug use may require a radical approach.

Parents should not be supportive of any lifestyle that is destructive. Not all defiance is destructive and, while certainly unpleasant, may not require application of such extreme measures. However, when a child engages in behavior that the parents know to be self-destructive, the parents may have no option but to implement "tough love," which is exactly what the very words mean. "Tough" because it is harsh on the child, "love" because it is applied out of concern for the child's welfare.

The Haggadah tells us that with a son who lives a degenerate lifestyle, rejecting all spirituality, there is a need for "tough love."

> *The Rabbi of Ropschitz asked, "Why is it that every year new editions of the Haggadah appear?" He answered, "It is because last year's 'wicked person' has become this year's 'wise person'."*

How prophetic the Rabbi's words were. The lists of best sellers invariably contain books by criminals whose trials and convictions made national news.

Last year's criminals are this year's wise men.

### ☙ *The rasha of Passover vs. the rasha of Sukkos*

On Sukkos we observe the mitzvah of the four species. The Midrash states that the *esrog* (citron), which has both taste and fragrance, symbolizes the person with both Torah knowledge and good deeds. The myrtle, which is fragrant but tasteless, represents a person with good deeds but who is unlearned. The palm branch, of a tree whose fruit is tasty but without fragrance, represents a person with Torah knowledge but with no meritorious deeds, and the willow branch, which is both tasteless and without fragrance, personifies the *rasha*, one who is ignorant of Torah and barren of good deeds.

**תָּם The simple son** — what does he say? "What is this?" Tell him: "With a strong hand did HASHEM take us out of Egypt, from the house of bondage."[1]

(1) *Exodus* 13:8.

---

Yet the willow branch (the *rasha*) is part of the mitzvah on Sukkos, whereas the *rasha* of Passover is rejected. Why?

The answer is that the *rasha* of Sukkos is bound with the other species, and unites himself with his brethren. Even if he disagrees with them, this is his redeeming feature. The *rasha* of Passover — who observes the family celebrating the beautiful *Seder* ritual and defiantly rejects them with his derisive, "What good is all this anyway?" — has no redeeming features whatever, and is therefore excluded from the mitzvah.

A person may not yet be spiritual, but if he associates with spiritual people, there is hope that he will embrace spirituality.

### תָּם מָה הוּא אוֹמֵר? — *The simple son — what does he say?*

In contrast to the wise person — who understands the value of spiritual freedom and therefore his only question is "In what way is the Exodus related to so many varied mitzvos?" — The simple person is overwhelmed by all the ritual of Passover. He does not reject it like the depraved person, but in his bewilderment sincerely asks, "What is all this for?" and he deserves an answer.

The answer provided, that God delivered us from the Egyptian bondage with a mighty hand, refers not only to the coercion of Pharaoh, but to the fact that even many of the Israelites had to be coerced to leave Egypt. As we noted earlier, Moses had to convince the slaves that liberty was preferable to enslavement, and not all Israelites accepted his message. We therefore explain to the simple person that even today there are many people who may adapt themselves to contentment, and whose primary goal in life is to be comfortable. These people may reject the message of being liberated from the tyranny of one's physical drives, and that striving for spirituality, even though it may interfere with one's tranquility, is the primary goal that makes man worthy of being created in the Divine image. The simple person, because he is sufficiently aware to ask, may accept an answer and be willing to investigate the spiritual life.

# וְשֶׁאֵינוֹ יוֹדֵעַ לִשְׁאוֹל, אַתְּ פְּתַח לוֹ. שֶׁנֶּאֱמַר, וְהִגַּדְתָּ לְבִנְךָ בַּיּוֹם הַהוּא לֵאמֹר, בַּעֲבוּר זֶה עָשָׂה יהוה לִי בְּצֵאתִי מִמִּצְרָיִם.[1]

(2) *Exodus* 13:8.

---

### ◆§ וְשֶׁאֵינוֹ יוֹדֵעַ לִשְׁאוֹל, אַתְּ פְּתַח לוֹ — *As for the son who is unable to ask, you must initiate the subject for him*

The person who does not know enough to ask unfortunately represents a considerable segment of the population. These people do not analyze, do not reject, and do not even question, because there is nothing that even stimulates their curiosity. They hardly reflect on goals in life. Their lives consist of work, rest, relaxation, and entertainment. At the end of the workday they partake of a meal, then while away their precious time in trivial pursuits, and they may remain there until it is time to retire for the night. They look forward to the weekend and to vacations as times for play or otherwise indulge themselves. No thought of a higher purpose in life, of something beyond self-gratification, ever occurs to them, and if one tried to convey such a message, it would fall on deaf ears, not because they are defiant, but because the whole concept is something alien to them. If they can pay their bills, keep their family fed and clothed, and have as much fun as their circumstances permit, that is just fine. As far as they are concerned that is all that there is to life, and if anyone tries to argue otherwise, he is dismissed as a zealous evangelist.

The prototype of this group is the alcoholic in the early stages of addiction, who has not yet experienced any of the devastation incident to alcoholism, which may not occur until he reaches a more advanced stage. This person soothes himself with drink whenever he so desires, which is quite frequently, but still works every day, socializes, relates fairly well to his family, and has not been apprehended for drunk driving. Although his functioning may have become dependent on alcohol and he is indeed addicted to it, any such suggestion would be totally rebuffed. There is no way of convincing him that he is living dangerously because he experiences no distress whatever from his drinking, and anyone who suggests otherwise is nothing but a crackpot temperance zealot.

It is futile to try to reason with this person. Unfortunately, all one can do is wait for nature to take its inevitable and inexorable course. Given enough time, he will come to a crucial point; then and only then will the

**וְשֶׁאֵינוֹ יוֹדֵעַ לִשְׁאוֹל** As for **the son who is unable to ask,** you must initiate the subject for him, as it is stated: You shall tell your son on that day: "It is because of this that HASHEM did so for me when I went out of Egypt."[1]

---

person perhaps be amenable to the suggestion that his lifestyle is self-destructive.

This, the Haggadah tells us, is what we must do with the person who does not know enough to ask; i.e., who is satisfied with the status quo, with a life consisting of nothing more than work, rest, and fun, and who will reject any suggestion that all is not right with him. With this person you must wait until a crisis occurs, until some event in life shakes him out of his complacency and makes him willing to consider that there may be something more to life. Delivering the message of spiritual liberation any earlier is premature and futile, and you must wait "until the matzah and maror are present before him"; i.e., until he can palpably sense the bitterness of being a slave to one's physical desires and can perceive that there may be value in spirituality, in being liberated from the tyranny of one's bodily strivings.

Is it not tragic that so many people plod along in a lifestyle far inferior to that which should dignify the crown of God's creation? Indeed it is. The psalmist bewails the folly of people who do not conceive of anything beyond earthly goods and pleasure. "They are much like animals, whom they resemble" (*Psalms* 49:21). The message of Passover is designed to elevate us beyond this lowly state.

### וְשֶׁאֵינוֹ יוֹדֵעַ לִשְׁאוֹל, אַתְּ פְּתַח לוֹ — *As for the son who is unable to ask, you must initiate the subject for him*

In chassidic lore there is a quote from Rabbi Hirsh of Rimanov. "Take my word for it. The one who does not know what to ask comes away with the best." Just what could he have meant with this?

At one week-end dedicated to the search for spirituality for people recovering from various addictions, there was a session called "Ask the Rabbi." One woman, Bernice, who had little exposure to Judaism, spoke up.

"This morning I was frustrated, more than I have ever been in my entire life. I passed by the room where you were having services, and I saw all of you praying. I wanted to join you, but I don't know how to pray. It's not that I can not read the Hebrew, because I could read the English. It's just that my family was not religious, and we never went to Temple. I don't know the first thing about prayer. I stood outside the room, wanting to go in, but not knowing what I would do if I was inside."

I said to Bernice, "Let me understand this. You were frustrated because you saw us praying, but you did not know how to pray.

"That's how things appeared in your prospective. But let us look at how God perceived this.

"When God sees us entering the shul, He may very well say, "Oh, Oh, look who's coming. Some more people with their selfish requests: 'God give me this' or 'God give me that.' All they can think about is their own needs.

"Then God saw you standing outside the room, broken hearted, wanting desperately to pray but not knowing how. God then said, "Look at My child, Bernice. She is in such agony because she wants to reach Me, but does not know how.

"Now tell me, Bernice," I said, "whose prayer was more sincere? My prayers for all that I desire, or your silent prayer for wishing to be able to come closer to God?"

❦ ❦ ❦

Chassidic lore is replete with stories of people who wanted to pray but knew nothing about prayer.

> *One of my favorite stories is that of Rabbi Levi Yitzchak of Berditchev, who held up services on Rosh Hashanah. He later explained.*
>
> *"There is a young lad in town who is a shepherd. He was orphaned at a young age, and never had the opportunity to go to cheder (Hebrew school) and learn how to read Hebrew. This morning, when he saw everyone streaming towards the synagogues, and upon inquiring was told that today was the solemn day of Rosh Hashanah, he felt very bad that he could not join others in prayer.*
>
> *"The young lad went out into the field and turned his eyes upward towards heaven. 'Dear God,' he said. "I have never learned to pray like others have. All I know is the aleph-beis. I will recite the letters for You, and You put them together to make the proper words." The lad began reciting aleph, beis, gimmel, daled, etc.*
>
> *"The lad is now reciting the aleph-beis, and God is busy putting the letters together to form the proper words. We must delay our*

*prayers until the lad is finished with his, at which time God can be attentive to us."*

*The Baal Shem Tov often quoted the phrase, "God prefers the sincerity of the heart." Everyone should, of course, become as fluent in prayer as possible. However, the essence of prayer is in the emotional investment one places in it.*

I believe this is what the Rabbi of Rimanov meant. The one who does not know what to ask for and is heart-broken because he would like to pray but does not know how, his prayer may be the most precious of all.

### ◆§ תָּם. . . וְשֶׁאֵינוֹ יוֹדֵעַ לִשְׁאוֹל — *The simple son. . . The son who is unable to ask*

*The Baal Shem Tov went out of his way to befriend and favor simple folk. At one seudah shlishis (the third Sabbath meal), the Baal Shem Tov expounded to his disciples on the secrets of Torah, while the simple folk sat in an adjacent room reciting Tehillim (Psalms). Some of the disciples reflected how fortunate they were to be able to grasp the profound teachings of the master, unlike the general public whose erudition was limited to reciting Tehillim.*

*The Baal Shem Tov asked his disciples to join hands and close their eyes. They suddenly felt themselves transported into a celestial, spiritual sphere, where they heard the heart-rending pleas, "Merciful Father, my soul longs for the courtyard of God, where my heart can sing to God." Another voice cried out, "As a deer calls longingly for a stream of water, so my soul calls longingly for You, O God. My soul thirsts for God." The disciples were enchanted by these sincere pleas for closeness to God, and as their tears flowed freely they thought, "If only we were able to achieve such profound devotion and longing for God, just once in a lifetime."*

*The Baal Shem Tov then instructed them to open their eyes, and he said, "The prayers that you heard were those of the ordinary people who are in the next room reciting Tehillim. While they may lack your scholarship, their hearts are sincere in wishing to come closer to God."*

The simple son asks sincerely, "What is this?" and the one who may not know enough to ask is nevertheless willing to listen and to be taught. These children are dear to God, and they should be dear to us as well.

**יָכוֹל** מֵרֹאשׁ חֹדֶשׁ, תַּלְמוּד לוֹמַר בַּיּוֹם הַהוּא. אִי בַּיּוֹם הַהוּא, יָכוֹל מִבְּעוֹד יוֹם, תַּלְמוּד לוֹמַר בַּעֲבוּר זֶה. בַּעֲבוּר זֶה לֹא אָמַרְתִּי אֶלָּא בְּשָׁעָה שֶׁיֵּשׁ מַצָּה וּמָרוֹר מֻנָּחִים לְפָנֶיךָ.

**מִתְּחִלָּה,** עוֹבְדֵי עֲבוֹדָה זָרָה הָיוּ אֲבוֹתֵינוּ, וְעַכְשָׁו קֵרְבָנוּ הַמָּקוֹם לַעֲבוֹדָתוֹ. שֶׁנֶּאֱמַר, וַיֹּאמֶר יְהוֹשֻׁעַ אֶל כָּל הָעָם, כֹּה אָמַר יהוה אֱלֹהֵי יִשְׂרָאֵל, בְּעֵבֶר הַנָּהָר יָשְׁבוּ אֲבוֹתֵיכֶם מֵעוֹלָם, תֶּרַח

---

**אֶלָּא בְּשָׁעָה שֶׁיֵּשׁ מַצָּה וּמָרוֹר מֻנָּחִים לְפָנֶיךָ — *Only when matzah and maror lie before you — at the Seder***

Some may say, "Granted, the message of the Exodus is most important. But why must we have all the intricate Passover restrictions and the complicated rituals? Is it not sufficient to just set some time aside to meditate about the meaning of the Exodus?"

Modern psychology has provided an answer to this question. In earlier times it was thought that the approach to solving a behavioral or emotional problem was to analyze it carefully so that one could obtain "insight" into the origin of the problem, how the problem developed, and what particular meaning the symptom had for the individual. This insight was supposed to resolve the underlying problem and eliminate the symptom.

The only trouble with this very logical theory is that it frequently does not work. Patients are likely to say, "Doctor, I understand everything thoroughly, but I don't feel any different."

Modern psychology has therefore taken a different approach: Change behavior first, and insight will eventually follow.

Merely meditating on the meaning of the Exodus may indeed result in attaining intellectual insight, but this may not contribute much to spiritual growth. One must eat the dry matzah, the bread of affliction which was the mainstay of our ancestors' diet because it was the cheapest thing available to fill the slave's stomach and to satiate his hunger. One must eat the bitter herbs and "taste" bitterness, to identify with the bitterness of their oppression. These symbolic acts may sufficiently reinforce the message of the Exodus so that it has an impact on how we feel and consequently on how

**יָכוֹל** One might think [that the obligation to discuss the Exodus commences] from the first day of the month [of Nissan], but the Torah says: "[You shall tell your son] on that day." By "on that day" one might think [that the obligation to discuss the Exodus commences] while it is still day; therefore the Torah adds: "It is because of this [that HASHEM did so for me when I went out of Egypt]." The pronoun "this" [implies something tangible, thus, "You shall tell your son"] applies only when matzah and *maror* lie before you — at the *Seder.*

**מִתְּחִלָּה,** Originally our ancestors were idol worshipers, but now the Omnipresent has brought us near to His service, as it is written: Yehoshua said to all the people, "So says HASHEM, God of Israel: Your fathers always lived beyond the Euphrates River, Terach

---

we behave, rather than being a mental experience which may be intellectually enlightening, but emotionally unproductive.

Spirituality is more readily achieved by spiritual behavior than by spiritual thought.

### ◆§ *Action before Contemplation*

Let us remember that we came into being as a nation at Sinai, where the rallying cry was *na'aseh v'nishma,* "We will do and we will listen." We understood at that crucial moment of our initiation as a people that waiting for contemplation to lead to action may result in insufferable delays. We accepted the Divine commandments on the premise that we would put them into action and only subsequently allow ourselves to contemplate them.

### ◆§ מִתְּחִלָּה, עוֹבְדֵי עֲבוֹדָה זָרָה הָיוּ אֲבוֹתֵינוּ — *Originally our ancestors were idol worshipers . . .*

According to one opinion in the Talmud, the Haggadah should begin with this paragraph, which refers to a period several centuries prior to the Egyptian saga, rather than with, "We were slaves unto Pharaoh in Egypt." What is the rationale underlying this opinion?

The essence of idolatry is not that one prays to a figurine of wood, metal, or clay. It is simply unthinkable that sensible human beings could

אֲבִי אַבְרָהָם וַאֲבִי נָחוֹר, וַיַּעַבְדוּ אֱלֹהִים אֲחֵרִים.
וָאֶקַּח אֶת אֲבִיכֶם אֶת אַבְרָהָם מֵעֵבֶר הַנָּהָר, וָאוֹלֵךְ
אוֹתוֹ בְּכָל אֶרֶץ כְּנָעַן, וָאַרְבֶּה אֶת זַרְעוֹ, וָאֶתֶּן לוֹ אֶת
יִצְחָק. וָאֶתֵּן לְיִצְחָק אֶת יַעֲקֹב וְאֶת עֵשָׂו, וָאֶתֵּן
לְעֵשָׂו אֶת הַר שֵׂעִיר לָרֶשֶׁת אוֹתוֹ, וְיַעֲקֹב וּבָנָיו יָרְדוּ
מִצְרָיִם.[1]

---

be so foolish as to believe that these inanimate objects which were the creation of their own hands were indeed deities that possess supernatural powers.

The principle underlying idolatry is stated very simply in the Talmud, in regard to the recurrence of this practice among the ancient Israelites. "The Israelites knew that these images were of no substance, but they used them in order to achieve positive sanction for otherwise forbidden relationships" (*Sanhedrin* 63b).

Various temptations to which humans are subject are forbidden by edict of the Torah, while others are proscribed by one's conscience. A person who wishes to indulge his desires, yet appease his conscience and be free of guilt for being in violation of any moral principles, may reach a rather simple solution: Establish an authority that will set moral standards that will satisfy one's whim and will pronounce edicts that will permit one to behave in whatever way one wishes. In order for this authority to have the right to dictate moral and ethical standards, it must be imbued with those properties that qualify it for this function, and what better qualification can there be than for it to be a god?

The distinction between Torah belief in God versus the belief in idols is thus very elementary. According to Torah, God created man and dictates how man should behave. In idolatry, man creates his own gods and dictates to them to tell him what he wishes to hear.

The idolater is thus a person who is under domination of his physical desires, and who, in order to placate his conscience, obtains a *hechsher* (authorized positive sanction) from the gods he creates for himself. This is essential to him because he is either unable or unwilling to resist his physical drives. In other words, the idolater is a person who is dominated by his impulses and is a slave to his own passions.

The two opinions in the Talmud as to how to begin the Haggadah, the text of spiritual freedom, are thus really quite similar, differing only in emphasis.

the father of Avraham and Nachor, and they served other gods. Then I took your father Avraham from beyond the river and led him through all the land of Canaan. I multiplied his offspring and gave him Yitzchak. To Yitzchak I gave Yaakov and Esav; to Esav I gave Mount Seir to inherit it, but Yaakov and his children went down to Egypt."[1]

(1) *Joshua* 24:2-4.

---

The first opinion is that beginning the Haggadah with "We were slaves unto Pharaoh in Egypt" is most appropriate because it refers to the total enslavement, both physical and spiritual, to which the Israelites were subject, and from which God extricated them. The second opinion contends that this approach might be misinterpreted and lead one to think that we are celebrating primarily our liberation from captivity. We might thereby lose sight of the primacy of the *spiritual* liberation of the Exodus. It is therefore preferable to begin with an account of our humble origins, our being descendants of idolaters, people enslaved by the drives of the human body.

This helps us better understand the greatness of the patriarch Abraham, who was the first person to categorically reject idolatry and to come to an awareness of the true God. It was Abraham's spiritual character, his rising above the tyranny of passion, that enabled him to grasp the truth. It was because Abraham consciously chose to became subservient to the will of God that he was able to *master* himself rather than be a *slave* to his physical drives, and he was therefore able to see through the spurious nature of the prevailing pagan beliefs. At this point God revealed Himself to him, and commissioned him to spread the truth of spirituality.

We cannot expect to succeed in the search for truth as long as we are unwilling to accept the consequences that follow our finding the truth, which includes frustrating some of our animal drives.

Truth and spirituality are inseparable.

## ◆§ *Ancient vs. Modern*

*During the haskalah (enlightenment) movement, many Jews became free thinkers and considered themselves to be "progressive" when they discarded traditional practices. One of these maskilim met the Rabbi of Tchortkov, and chided him as to why chassidic*

**בָּרוּךְ** שׁוֹמֵר הַבְטָחָתוֹ לְיִשְׂרָאֵל, בָּרוּךְ הוּא. שֶׁהַקָּדוֹשׁ בָּרוּךְ הוּא חִשַּׁב אֶת הַקֵּץ, לַעֲשׂוֹת כְּמָה שֶׁאָמַר לְאַבְרָהָם אָבִינוּ בִּבְרִית בֵּין הַבְּתָרִים, שֶׁנֶּאֱמַר, וַיֹּאמֶר לְאַבְרָם, יָדֹעַ תֵּדַע כִּי גֵר יִהְיֶה זַרְעֲךָ

---

*Jews continue to adhere to outdated practices and refuse to embrace modernism.*

*The Rabbi replied, "You seem to have reversed the facts. The Haggadah states otherwise, that you are the ancients and we are the moderns. Originally, our early ancestors were idolaters, essentially freethinkers who gave into every desire and temptation by establishing for themselves gods that would tell them what they wished to hear. We are the moderns, who have accepted upon ourselves the rule of Divinely ordained morals and ethics. All you have done is to go back to the early behavior of pre-civilized mankind.*

*"You are the ancients. We are the moderns."*

### ◆§ בָּרוּךְ שׁוֹמֵר הַבְטָחָתוֹ לְיִשְׂרָאֵל, בָּרוּךְ הוּא — *Blessed is He Who keeps His pledge to Israel; Blessed is He!*

Jews acknowledge God as their King, and we are grateful that He is our Ruler.

We can best understand this when we observe how political leaders come to power, and how they behave after they have been elected. They seek to seduce the electorate with sweet words, with promises of utopia. There will be no new taxes, but rather full employment, with health care for all and elimination of crime. No sooner are they elected than they reverse themselves on everything.

God is a a True King; i.e., a King of truth. Yes, He promises, but He does not deceive, and He delivers on His promises. "You will indeed reap reward, but first there will be much suffering." Perhaps not what we would wish to hear, but it is the truth.

Leaders of nations could be spiritual if they would learn from this example. Spirituality is truth. Blessed is the One Who keeps His promise, and since we are to emulate the Divine attribute, the message of the Haggadah is that all those who keep these promises will be blessed.

**בָּרוּךְ** Blessed is He Who keeps His pledge to Israel; Blessed is He! For the Holy One, Blessed is He, calculated the end of bondage in order to do as He said to our father Avraham at the Covenant between the Parts, as it is stated: He said to Avram, "Know with certainty that your offspring will be aliens

---

### ◆§ יָדֹעַ תֵּדַע כִּי גֵר יִהְיֶה זַרְעֲךָ בְּאֶרֶץ לֹא לָהֶם — *Know with certainty that your offspring will be aliens in a land not their own*

Many reasons have been given for the Divine decree that the Israelites be enslaved. It appears that all are true, and that the decree was a consequence of multiple causes. Among the many is the patriarch Abraham's response to the Divine promise to give the land of Canaan to his descendants. "And he (Abraham) said, 'My Lord, Hashem/Elokim, whereby shall I know that I am to inherit it?' " (*Genesis* 15:8). Rashi explains that Abraham was not in any way questioning God's promise, but rather asking, "Why do I deserve this?" Yet the Torah commentaries take the patriarch to task for even this apparently innocent question.

This reprimand appears rather strange. The Talmud lauds Abraham's humility as one of his greatest virtues, and praises his words when he pleaded for mercy on behalf of the sinful people of Sodom. "I am only dust and ashes," Abraham said (ibid. 18:27), and this is cited as one of the most sincere expressions of humility of all time. Inasmuch as humility is so great a virtue, why then is Abraham taken to task when he expresses his belief that he is undeserving of God's beneficence? The answer to this question provides an important clarification about *anivus* (humility).

Indeed a person must be humble. One should always consider oneself as not having adequately fulfilled one's obligations, and should therefore always strive to improve oneself in every way possible and do even more than in the past. When one asks something of God, it should therefore always be expressed as a request for a favor, as a gift flowing from Divine benevolence rather than an assertion that God owes one something. Thus, when interceding for the Sodomites, Abraham was correct in effacing himself and asking for Divine mercy.

However, when God gives something to a person, one should accept the gift gracefully and with appreciation. This is not the time to assert that one is not deserving of the Divine gift. When a father gives his child a gift, the child

בְּאֶרֶץ לֹא לָהֶם, וַעֲבָדוּם וְעִנּוּ אֹתָם, אַרְבַּע מֵאוֹת שָׁנָה. וְגַם אֶת הַגּוֹי אֲשֶׁר יַעֲבֹדוּ דָּן אָנֹכִי, וְאַחֲרֵי כֵן יֵצְאוּ בִּרְכֻשׁ גָּדוֹל.[1]

(1) *Genesis* 15:13-14.

---

need not ask, "What did I do to deserve this?" The gift may be one of love for the child rather than a reward for performance.

Many people are unable to enjoy that which God has given them because they are haunted by a morbid fear that if they did enjoy it, it would be taken from them. A typical example is a young woman who suffered from severe anxiety, and every morning approached her infant's crib with painful dread, fearing that she will find her child a victim of crib death. What was the reason for her fear? "I don't believe I deserve to have such a beautiful child."

Although we cannot attribute "feelings" to God, we are permitted to draw analogies from human experience. How would a person feel if he gave a gift to a dear friend or loved one, and later discovered that his gift had never been used because the recipient was afraid it might be damaged? Would the giver not be far more pleased to know that his gift was used, enjoyed, and appreciated?

When God gives us gifts, we are to use them and enjoy them, and not live in dread of losing them. We should, of course, use them wisely, and not abuse them or put them to use in a way which would displease God. But it is wrong to live in constant dread, and not be able to appreciate God's kindnesses. As King David says in his description of the God-fearing person, "He will not fear bad tidings; his heart is steadfast, trusting in God" (*Psalms* 112:7).

Abraham's humility was praiseworthy when it was in its proper place. However, when it extended a bit too far so that he was unable to enjoy the Divine promise because he considered himself undeserving, he was reprimanded.

A spiritual person must be truly humble, yet be able to enjoy God's blessings, accepting them as gifts of love, and even if not "deserved," to be able to enjoy them nonetheless.

in a land not their own, they will serve them and they will oppress them four hundred years; but also upon the nation which they shall serve will I execute judgment, and afterwards they shall leave with great possessions."[1]

---

### ◆§ וַעֲבָדוּם וְעִנּוּ אֹתָם. . . וְאַחֲרֵי כֵן יֵצְאוּ בִּרְכֻשׁ גָּדוֹל — *They will serve them and they will oppress them . . . and afterwards they shall leave with great possessions*

We express our gratitude to God for fulfilling His promise to the patriarch Abraham. However, that promise certainly had its drawbacks, because while it did contain the Divine pledge of redemption and reward, it also contained a decree of enslavement and torture. How can we then be grateful for the entire promise when it had such negative implications?

> *During the lifetime of the great Maggid of Mezeritch, no new, harsh anti-Semitic decrees were issued in Czarist Russia. These were renewed after the Maggid's death, and the Maggid's disciples, who were certain that the period of reprieve was due to their great master's ability to intercede before God to prevent these harsh decrees, were perplexed. Why was he no longer interceding for his people now that he was in Heaven in even closer proximity to God?*
>
> *The Maggid appeared in a dream to one of his disciples and said, "When I was an inhabitant of Earth and I perceived a decree to be evil, I interceded to have it revoked. However, from my vantage place in Heaven, I now see that these harsh decrees have an ultimate good, and in the final analysis are to our people's advantage. I cannot intercede to revoke something which eventually is for our welfare."*

The period of enslavement in Egypt was indeed one of great suffering, but, as the Torah says, it was a "purifying crucible" which forged us into the only nation that has survived throughout history. This passage in the Haggadah is therefore an application of the Talmudic dictum, that one must be grateful to God for the bad that happens just as for the good, because everything that emanates from God is for our ultimate good, even if we do not appreciate it at the moment.

The matzos are covered and the cups lifted as the following paragraph is proclaimed joyously. Upon its conclusion, the cups are put down and the matzos are uncovered.

**וְהִיא** שֶׁעָמְדָה לַאֲבוֹתֵינוּ וְלָנוּ, שֶׁלֹּא אֶחָד בִּלְבָד עָמַד עָלֵינוּ לְכַלּוֹתֵנוּ. אֶלָּא שֶׁבְּכָל דּוֹר וָדוֹר עוֹמְדִים עָלֵינוּ לְכַלּוֹתֵנוּ, וְהַקָּדוֹשׁ בָּרוּךְ הוּא מַצִּילֵנוּ מִיָּדָם.

---

**וְהִיא שֶׁעָמְדָה לַאֲבוֹתֵנוּ וְלָנוּ — *It is this that has stood by our fathers and us.***

This verse may be relating an unfortunate pattern in Jewish history. We tend to be at our finest when we are oppressed. Moses predicted this when he said, "Israel grew fat and became defiant" (*Deuteronomy* 30:15). When we prosper, we become more vulnerable to assimilation.

The prophets exhorted people to *teshuvah,* but although their words can penetrate into the very core of one's being, they may sometimes not achieve their goal. The Talmud says that when King Achashverosh gave Haman his ring, thereby empowering him to issue whatever decrees he wished, this aroused Jews to *teshuvah* more than all the exhortation of the forty-eight prophets. Like wayward children, we may not listen to reason and may require harsh discipline.

This may be one meaning of this verse in the Haggadah. Unfortunately, what has stood for our ancestors and for us and has enabled us to remain strong to our faith is that in every generation we were faced with persecution and threats of destruction. As with the transfer of the ring to Haman, this may be what it takes to remind us that we are Jews.

It is time that we learn from history. If we take the words of the prophets to heart, there will be no need for any Hamans. We should be proud of our Jewishness and live it to its fullest. How happy we are when our children listen to us and behave properly because we tell them to do so, rather than cause us the distress of having to punish them. We can give God the joy of living the way He wishes us to without His having to discipline us harshly.

**אֶלָּא שֶׁבְּכָל דּוֹר וָדוֹר עוֹמְדִים עָלֵינוּ לְכַלּוֹתֵנוּ — *But in every generation they rise against us to annihilate us.***

The human *spirit* is comprised of a number of qualities that are unique to human beings, and because these are the factors that distinguish man from lower forms of life, they constitute the essence of his *humanity*. To the

The matzos are covered and the cups lifted as the following paragraph is proclaimed joyously. Upon its conclusion, the cups are put down and the matzos are uncovered.

**וְהִיא** It is this that has stood by our fathers and us. For not only one has risen against us to annihilate us, but in every generation they rise against us to annihilate us. But the Holy One, Blessed is He, rescues us from their hand.

---

degree that a person lacks any of these *spiritual* components, to that degree one is incomplete in one's humanity.

One of the features that is unique to man is the capacity to learn from history. It is unlikely that animals have a conscious awareness of what transpired in times past, nor are they capable of using this information to improve themselves or avoid repeating mistakes of the past. A thoroughbred race horse probably does not know what miscalculation his sire made that resulted in his losing a race, and hence is incapable of making a conscious effort to avoid the same error.

Humans, however, do have the capacity to learn from the past, and if they fail to do so, they will indeed demonstrate the truth of the adage, "Those who fail to learn from history are doomed to repeat it."

Failure to learn from the past has doomed both individuals and nations. History has abundantly demonstrated that every nation that has sought to expand by subduing and subjugating other peoples has risen to an apogee, only to eventually disintegrate into oblivion. Yet, this has not deterred nations from building empires and dominating over others, in the belief that they will be the exception to the rule of history.

The failure to learn from history is probably the single greatest cause of human misery. In working with addicted individuals, it is striking to see how the alcoholic, drug addict, or compulsive gambler repeats his destructive behavior in spite of incontrovertible evidence that such behavior has been utterly ruinous. Analysis of this repetitive behavior reveals that these people usually think, "This time will be different."

Much suffering could have been avoided if people would have learned from history and not considered themselves to be immune to the effects of behavior that has been proven to be destructive.

There are many lessons that Jews can learn from our painful history. We can learn that trying to deny our Jewishness will not spare us from oppression by those who despise us. We can learn that each time we have fled persecution and found a benign and tolerant environment, it was only a matter of time before we had to pick up the staff and begin our wandering again and seek less hostile domicile. We can learn how futile it is to think that "ethical" people will not harm us. We may note that religious leaders who pontificated in the name of their god felt it was their sacred duty to have Jews burned at the stake, and that it was the most enlightened, sophisticated and cultured nation in the world that committed the unspeakable atrocities of the Holocaust. We can learn that we have only each other and our God, and that if we abandon one another or God we are sealing our own doom.

If we realize that "in every generation there have been those who wished to destroy us, but that God has saved us from their hand," we can be secure in the knowledge that He will not forsake us now. We may never be able to fathom why God permitted the massacres of the Crusades, the Inquisition, the pogroms, and the Holocaust. Nonetheless, the fact that this people though few in number, uprooted from its homeland, driven from land to land, and repeatedly subjected to mass extermination *has* survived, while mighty civilizations who remained secure within their borders have perished, leaves no other conclusion than that God has a mission for Israel, and that Israel must and will survive, because God is the guardian of Israel.

Failure to learn these important lessons of history is a dereliction of spirituality.

It is customary when reciting this paragraph, to lift up the cup of wine (or grape juice).

In this paragraph we testify to the history of repeated persecutions that Jews have suffered throughout the ages. One might ask: What is the secret of Jewish survival? Having been driven from our homeland, and repeatedly subjected to pogroms, inquisitions, and holocausts, how is it that we have survived? Why did Jews simply not assimilate with their surroundings to escape these repetitive tortures? What is the secret of the strength of our survival?

Many Torah commentaries point out that the Torah attitude toward the Jew and his environment is to have the utmost consideration and respect for the people among whom we live, to pray for their peace and welfare, but to avoid intimate relationships which can erode our identity. In order to maintain our distinct identity, many Jewish practices constitute a barrier to assimilation. One of these is a rabbinic ordinance not to share wine with

**צֵא** Go and learn what Lavan the Aramean attempted to do to our father Yaakov! For Pharaoh decreed only against

---

other than fellow Jews. The reason? Drinking together may promote intimacy rather than just friendship, and may eliminate the inhibitions and restraints that can serve as a barrier to intermarriage. The "kosher wine" can thus be seen as a symbol of Jewish identity.

In referring to our stubborn perseverance throughout the ages, we lift up the cup of kosher wine as an answer to the implied question: How is it that we are still here?

### ☙ צֵא וּלְמַד מַה בִּקֵּשׁ לָבָן הָאֲרַמִּי לַעֲשׂוֹת לְיַעֲקֹב אָבִינוּ — *Go and learn what Lavan the Aramean attempted to do to our father Yaakov*

In this passage, the Haggadah seems to attribute the Egyptian saga as a consequence of Laban's hostility to Jacob. Why is this so?

As we read in Scriptures, Jacob loved Rachel, and Laban deceived Jacob by substituting Leah for Rachel. Jacob subsequently did marry Rachel, who was obviously his cherished wife.

Joseph, the child of the beloved Rachel, was Jacob's favorite, which resulted in his incurring the envy of his brothers, causing his being sold into slavery, and thence the complete Egyptian incident. Had Laban not tricked Jacob into marrying Leah, Joseph would have been the legitimate oldest child, entitled to the privileges of the first-born, and the entire Egyptian episode would have been avoided.

It was thus Laban's sly behavior that was the cause of the children of Jacob being enslaved in Egypt.

### ☙ צֵא וּלְמַד — *Go and learn.*

*Rabbi Shneur Zalman was once asked what he had learned at Mezeritch. He answered, "Tzei u'lemad, if you wish to learn, you must go out from yourself." As long as you are totally absorbed with yourself, you cannot succeed in learning. You may not have the requisite objectivity to accept all valid knowledge. If you can set your self-interest aside, and search only for truth, regardless of where it may lead, even if it should result in personal inconvenience, then you are open to accumulating knowledge.*

הַזְּכָרִים, וְלָבָן בִּקֵּשׁ לַעֲקוֹר אֶת הַכֹּל. שֶׁנֶּאֱמַר:
אֲרַמִּי אֹבֵד אָבִי, וַיֵּרֶד מִצְרַיְמָה וַיָּגָר שָׁם בִּמְתֵי
מְעָט, וַיְהִי שָׁם לְגוֹי, גָּדוֹל עָצוּם וָרָב.[1]
וַיֵּרֶד מִצְרַיְמָה — אָנוּס עַל פִּי הַדִּבּוּר.

(1) *Deuteronomy* 26:5.

---

### ◆§ וְלָבָן בִּקֵּשׁ לַעֲקוֹר אֶת הַכֹּל — *Lavan attempted to uproot everything*

In reading the Biblical account of the episode of Jacob and Laban, it is not immediately evident from the text that Laban wished to totally annihilate Jacob. To the contrary, when Laban pursued the fleeing Jacob, he reprimanded him saying, "The daughters are my daughters and the sons are my sons and the sheep are my sheep, and all that you see is mine. What harm did you think I would do to my own daughters or to their children?" (*Genesis* 31:43). It appears that Laban actually wished to maintain a closeness with Jacob, rather than to destroy him.

However, this is precisely the point of the story. In contrast to Pharaoh who wished to *physically* destroy all Jewish males, Laban did not desire the physical destruction of Jacob and his family. Rather, he wished to maintain their association so that he could influence them to accept his pagan practices. Whereas we are generally on the alert for those who may wish to physically harm us, we are far more vulnerable to the danger of spiritual harm.

We may not be aware that there are real dangers that lurk in the environment which surrounds us, and that we may be adversely influenced by the culture in which we live. This may be because we fail to understand the magnitude of the spiritual damage that we may suffer if we adopt the prevailing non-Torah values of our neighbors.

In my work with people who are recovering from addiction, I note that veterans in recovery caution newcomers to be aware of "people, places, and things," by which they mean that a recovering person should avoid associating with those "people, places, or things" that may be conducive to resumption of their addiction. The painful course in the school of experience has taught them that regardless of how sincere and determined a person may be not to relapse, exposure to influences that encourage addiction may overwhelm even the finest intentions.

the males, Lavan attempted to uproot everything, as it is said:

**An Aramean attempted to destroy my father. Then he descended to Egypt and sojourned there, with few people; and there he became a nation — great, mighty and numerous.**[1]

**Then he descended to Egypt** — compelled by Divine decree.

---

If we truly value our spirituality and understand that loss of spirituality can be lethal, we will be most cautious in associating with "people, places, and things" that may constitute a threat to our spirituality. For example, allowing ourselves to be preoccupied with the pursuit of material success and indulgence in physical pleasures, which appears to be the predominant drive in Western civilization, can place us at great risk. The spiritual destruction of Jacob was the evil intent of the cunning Laban.

### ◆§ וַיֵּרֶד מִצְרַיְמָה – אָנוּס עַל פִּי הַדִּבּוּר — *Then he descended to Egypt — compelled by Divine decree*

The literal translation of the text is, "compelled by the word." The most common interpretation of "the word" is that Jacob was ordered by God to go to Egypt (*Genesis* 46:3). However, one of the Torah commentaries offers another interpretation. The embryonic origin of the Egyptian saga began with Joseph's bearing tales of his brothers' improper behavior to Jacob (*Genesis* 37:2), which resulted in their hatred of him, their selling him into slavery, Joseph's rise to power in Egypt, and Jacob's eventual descent to Egypt with his entire family, which then culminated in the enslavement of the Israelites. Had Jacob refused to accept Joseph's gossip about his brothers, the entire tragic Egyptian epic might never have come to pass.

These are the bitter roots of *lashon hara,* the carrying of tales. The great sage of a recent generation, the Chofetz Chaim, dedicated his life toward eradication of *lashon hara,* and in his many writings on the subject repeatedly points out that listening to tales about another person is every bit as grievous a sin as carrying tales. Not only is listening to *lashon hara* a passive sin on its own, but by providing a listening ear to one who speaks *lashon hara,* one is an accomplice to the active sin.

The spiritual perfection of the Patriarchs was so great that even a microscopic defect was considered a blemish. Yet, the fact that the Torah and the Talmud call attention to their "faults" indicates that we must learn from these and improve upon our own shortcomings, even though the two may be light years apart.

A spiritual person should have no need either to speak *lashon hara* or to listen to it. One chassidic master said, "Every person has imperfections that could bear improvement. Why concern yourself with faults of others when you have your own to deal with?"

A popular aphorism is "Sticks and stones will break my bones but names will never harm me." This is wrong, very wrong. The Talmud compares the spoken word to a sharp arrow, and the spoken word can be even deadlier than the arrow since it can harm someone who is miles away, far beyond the reach of physical harm.

Jacob was compelled to go down to Egypt, setting into motion the ordeal of his descendants, all this the result of just a few spoken words.

### ◆§ וַיֵּרֶד מִצְרַיְמָה — *Then he descended to Egypt*

A careful analysis of the syntax in *Genesis* will reveal that the move from Canaan to Egypt is generally referred to as a "descent." However, once Jacob and his sons came to Egypt, the Torah no longer uses the word "descended" to Egypt, but rather "came" to Egypt. Why?

Egypt is described in the Midrash as being the depth of immorality and corruption. When the children of Jacob first came to Egypt, they experienced this as a spiritual *descent.*

We tend to rather rapidly acclimatize to an environment of immorality and corruption, so that it gradually loses its repugnant character, and it no longer repels us. The initial exposure to a decadent environment elicits a shock reaction, but afterwards, this effect wanes. This is what the Torah indicates with the change of verbs. After the Israelites came to Egypt, they no longer perceived it as being a descent. They became rather indifferent to the evils of the environment.

A spiritual person must at all times be aware that he is in an environment that is conducive to physical indulgences, and that he can easily fall prey to its lure. He must at all times be alert so that he does not compromise his spirituality. Frequent readings of literature that teaches spiritual growth is an excellent way to maintain one's spiritual standards. Luzzatto's *Path of the Just* is a primer of spirituality, and one should read several paragraphs daily, as the author discusses the development of character traits that elevate one to *ruach haKodesh,* identification with the Divine Spirit.

While we do not think of ourselves as superior to others, because that would be vanity, we should nevertheless recognize that when we associate with a non-spiritual secular world, we are in danger of accepting its values.

## ☙ Hold on Above

*In the village of Premislan, the mikveh was located at the top of a hill. Ascending the hill on a snowy winter day was hazardous, as one was prone to slip. The chassidic master, Rabbi Meir, would walk up the icy slope without any difficulty. When asked how he did this, he responded, "It is simple. When you hold on above, you do not slip below."*

Living in a hedonistic culture is like climbing an icy slope. If you wish to avoid falling, you must hold on tightly to what is above you.

## ☙ Let Silence Be My Judge

The spoken word carries great weight in both *halachah* and *mussar.*

*There is a charming story of one Reb Shmelke, who was a chassid of the Rabbi of Bluzhov. Shmelke was a rather simple man, certainly not a scholar. He had a strange practice; once he put on his talis for prayer, he would not speak until he had removed his talis after completion of the service. When he was asked for the source of this practice, he said "There is no source. It is my own idea. You see, I heard that when we stand in judgment before the Heavenly Tribunal, we have to relate everything we did during our sojourn on earth, and on the basis of our own testimony, we are judged. Obviously, one cannot lie before the Divine Tribunal, and telling the truth about everything we did will certainly result in being condemned to gehinnom (hell).*

*"I have thought of a way to escape punishment. Inasmuch as we are buried in a talis, I will simply indicate to the tribunal that I cannot speak because I am wearing a talis. Since this was my practice during my entire life, I doubt that they will force me to do otherwise. Since I will not be able to testify against myself, they will not be able to condemn me."*

*All the other chassidim smiled at Shmelke's naiveté. Years went by, and Shmelke died at a ripe old age. Several weeks after Shmelke's death, the Rabbi of Bluzhov went into a trance, and upon awakening, he smiled brightly and said, "Shmelke's strategy worked for him! He was promptly admitted to Gan Eden" (Paradise).*

**וַיָּגָר שָׁם** — מְלַמֵּד שֶׁלֹּא יָרַד יַעֲקֹב אָבִינוּ לְהִשְׁתַּקֵּעַ בְּמִצְרַיִם, אֶלָּא לָגוּר שָׁם. שֶׁנֶּאֱמַר, וַיֹּאמְרוּ אֶל פַּרְעֹה, לָגוּר בָּאָרֶץ בָּאנוּ, כִּי אֵין מִרְעֶה לַצֹּאן אֲשֶׁר לַעֲבָדֶיךָ, כִּי כָבֵד הָרָעָב בְּאֶרֶץ כְּנָעַן, וְעַתָּה יֵשְׁבוּ נָא עֲבָדֶיךָ בְּאֶרֶץ גֹּשֶׁן.[1]

**בִּמְתֵי מְעָט** — כְּמָה שֶׁנֶּאֱמַר, בְּשִׁבְעִים נֶפֶשׁ יָרְדוּ אֲבֹתֶיךָ מִצְרָיְמָה, וְעַתָּה שָׂמְךָ יהוה אֱלֹהֶיךָ כְּכוֹכְבֵי הַשָּׁמַיִם לָרֹב.[2]

(1) *Genesis* 47:4. (2) *Deuteronomy* 10:22.

---

### ☙ וַיָּגָר שָׁם — *He sojourned there*

The word וַיָּגָר that the Torah uses in referring to Jacob's dwelling in Egypt has its origin in the word גר which connotes temporary residence rather than permanent citizenship.

The Talmud states that although the Israelites lived in Egypt for two hundred and ten years, they maintained their identity by retaining their Hebrew language, by retaining the traditional Hebrew garb, and by giving their children Hebrew rather than Egyptian names. It was this preservation of their identity that allowed them to remain a distinct people, by virtue of which they were redeemed at the Exodus.

Throughout history, some Jews have sought to avoid discrimination and persecution by phasing out their Jewish identities and by frank assimilation. While one can hardly be condemned for seeking a way to avoid the suffering of anti-Semitism, we must remember that we were commissioned by God to be a spiritual people and to carry the message of Godliness and spirituality to the world. We cannot carry out our mission if we lose our identity by assimilation, and become part of the non-Jewish world.

A spiritual person does not shirk responsibilities, even at the cost of personal distress.

### ☙ *Never Lost Our Identity*

*An anti-Semitic Russian minister of education once challenged one of the leading rabbis. "You Jews do not observe the teachings of your own Torah. Your Torah states that you must follow the majority. You constitute only a small minority among a vast majority of non-Jews, yet you*

**He sojourned there** — this teaches that our father Yaakov did not descend to Egypt to settle, but only to sojourn temporarily, as it says: They (the sons of Yaakov) said to Pharaoh: "We have come to sojourn in this land because there is no pasture for the flocks of your servants, because the famine is severe in the land of Canaan. And now, please let your servants dwell in the land of Goshen."[1]

**With few people** — as it is written: With seventy persons, your forefathers descended to Egypt, and now HASHEM, your God, has made you as numerous as the stars of heaven.[2]

---

*are obstinate in being different. You are violating your own laws."*

*The scholar replied, "Your Excellency is not applying the Torah law accurately. We indeed do follow the majority, but only when we are in doubt about the nature of something, do we assume that the benefit of doubt lies with the majority. Or if there is an admixture of kosher with non-kosher food, so that the non-kosher food is not recognizable, we may then apply the majority rule. However, the latter does not apply in absence of doubt or when something is clearly recognizable.*

*"We Jews are never in doubt. We know who we are and have never lost our identity. Furthermore, we are easily recognizable. Hence the principle of following the majority does not apply."*

Jacob knew that his descendants would have a lengthy stay in Egypt. His message to them was that they must always consider themselves *geirim,* foreigners in an alien society. They must always remain distinct, and never allow themselves to be absorbed by the dominant culture.

### בִּמְתֵי מְעָט — *with few people*

Sometimes a nucleus of people join together for a worthy cause, and when they fail to interest a larger number of people in their project, they may become discouraged and give it up as unrealistic.

A while ago I visited a Jewish community which was trying to stimulate local interest in identification, treatment, and prevention of alcoholism and drug abuse among Jews, particularly among Jewish youth. The organizers of the program were disappointed that in spite of the publicity, only sixteen people attended the meeting, and they apologized for the poor showing.

I told them that there were no grounds for disappointment and no need for an apology. In 1936, Alcoholics Anonymous began with only two people who had an idea, and the fellowship had now grown to millions of people over the entire globe.

The Torah tells us that Jacob came to Egypt with only a handful of people, but with Divine blessing they multiplied and became very populous and, after two hundred and ten years, left Egypt a mighty nation of over 600,000 people.

Meager beginnings are not grounds for discouragement. If one has a worthy cause, one should continue to champion it. Even if it is not immediately successful, it will eventually bear fruit. In *Ethics of the Fathers* (2:21) we are told, "You may not have the responsibility to complete the task, but you are not at liberty to abstain from working at it." If we believe in an idea and are convinced that it is right, we should work for it and not despair because we are few in number. The Torah states, "God will bless you in all the things that you do" (*Deuteronomy* 14:29). We will indeed receive the Divine blessing, but we must initiate the action.

### בִּמְתֵי מְעָט — *with few people*

The term *bimsei me'at* may also refer to little in quality as well as in quantity. Even after the death of the sons of Jacob and under the cruel oppression of Egypt, the Israelites were able to produce spiritual giants, the likes of Moses, Aaron, and Miriam. They knew how to nurture the tiny seeds of greatness.

Spiritual growth cannot be stifled. In recent times, Jews living under the terror of Communism managed to learn Torah. One Russian Jew brought out with him a hand-written copy of the *Mishnah,* which his father had managed to laboriously write from memory and had used to teach his children in the shadow of the Kremlin.

It is as natural to grow spiritually as it is to grow physically, as long as one provides the proper nutrients of Torah and *mitzvos.*

### *Seeds of Greatness*

*It is told that Rabbi Heschel of Cracow was a child prodigy, and when a community interviewed candidates for a rabbinic position, young Heschele applied, putting the older scholars to shame with his brilliance. The community leaders told him that while he indeed surpassed all others in learning, he could not expect the community to engage an eleven-year-old child as their rabbi.*

**There he became a great nation** — this teaches that the Israelites were distinctive there.

---

*"Why not?" Heschele asked. "Every person has some defect. I am the only one who can guarantee to improve upon his defect every single day."*

We are all deficient in spirituality. We should also guarantee to improve on our defect with daily spiritual growth.

### ◆§ וַיֵּרֶד מִצְרַיְמָה וַיָּגָר שָׁם בִּמְתֵי מְעָט — *He descended to Egypt and sojourned there, with few people.*

The structure of this sentence appears a bit awkward. It should rather have read, "He descended to Egypt, few in number, and dwelt there."

The Rabbi of Gur quoted a passage from the Jerusalem Talmud which relates that a scholar was once shown a beautiful synagogue in one of the lands of the Diaspora. Instead of being pleased, he quoted the verse from *Hosea* (8:12), "Israel forgot his Maker and built beautiful edifices." The prophet appears to have foretold that grandiose buildings would be erected as synagogues, but this would not constitute a better relationship with God.

The Rabbi of Gur continued, "In the Diaspora we are not to build luxurious edifices, even as synagogues. The place for these is in our homeland. In the Diaspora we should live with modesty."

This is the reason for the structure of the above verse, according to the Rabbi of Gur. Jacob descended to Egypt, and he dwelt there, as if few in number, not ostentatiously, but with profound modesty.

Too often we delude ourselves that by erecting a handsome synagogue, we have enhanced our spirituality. Even of the Sanctuary which God commanded Moses to build, it is said, "Let them build Me a Sanctuary, and I will dwell within them," upon which the commentaries remark, "God does not mean that He will dwell within *it,* i.e., the Sanctuary, but rather within *them,* within each individual." Rather than assigning to God a building in which He may reside, we should render ourselves appropriate dwelling places for the Divine Spirit, so that He may dwell with us.

### ◆§ וַיְהִי שָׁם לְגוֹי גָּדוֹל — *There he became a great nation*

Just as *bimsei me'at* refers to our beginnings in Egypt with qualitative as well as quantitative paucity, so does the statement "There he became a great nation" refer to greatness in character as well as in number.

**עָצוּם** – כְּמָה שֶׁנֶּאֱמַר, וּבְנֵי יִשְׂרָאֵל פָּרוּ וַיִּשְׁרְצוּ וַיִּרְבּוּ וַיַּעַצְמוּ בִּמְאֹד מְאֹד, וַתִּמָּלֵא הָאָרֶץ אֹתָם.[1] **וָרָב** – כְּמָה שֶׁנֶּאֱמַר, רְבָבָה כְּצֶמַח הַשָּׂדֶה נְתַתִּיךְ, וַתִּרְבִּי וַתִּגְדְּלִי וַתָּבֹאִי בַּעֲדִי עֲדָיִים, שָׁדַיִם נָכֹנוּ

(1) *Exodus* 1:7.

Israel was indeed forged into a nation in Egypt, which the Torah refers to as the "iron crucible" (*Deuteronomy* 4:20). A crucible is a furnace where the intense heat melts the ore and separates the pure metal from impurities with which it is mixed. But why did the Israelites need to be put through a crucible? What impurities did they have which required cleansing?

The exile began with Jacob and his family going down to Egypt, where Joseph was the viceroy. Joseph was in Egypt because his envious brothers had sold him into slavery. The root of our Egyptian ordeal lies therefore in fraternal divisiveness and hatred. While Joseph may have provoked his brothers' anger and envy, people should not allow such emotions to lead them into behavior as cruel as selling a brother into slavery.

Under the whip of the Egyptian taskmasters, the Israelites joined together to support one another. Divisiveness generally occurs only amidst comfort and luxury. Suffering tends to eliminate differences among kin, as they realize that in a hostile world they have only each other to rely on. Oppression does away with the petty feelings that cause dissension. It was thus in the Egyptian exile, under cruel oppression, that the Israelites achieved greatness, the greatness of unity.

Many of our *tzaddikim* felt that exile is essential for character development, and voluntarily took upon themselves exile. Particularly noted for this are the great chassidic masters, the brothers Rabbi Elimelech of Lizensk and Rabbi Zusia of Hanipoli, who wandered for years from village to village in Poland. How else could they learn to identify with the hapless Jew thrown into debtor's prison, the disenfranchised orphan, or the plight of the penniless widow? These *tzaddikim* felt that sharing in the suffering enhanced their sensitivity and compassion.

Empathy and compassion are components of spirituality. The exile in Egypt may have begun with the pettiness of divisiveness, but it ended with the greatness of unity and brotherly love.

**Mighty** — as it says: And the Children of Israel were fruitful, increased greatly, multiplied, and became very, very mighty; and the land was filled with them.[1]

**Numerous** — as it says: I made you as numerous as the plants of the field; you grew and developed, aand became charming, beautiful of figure; and your

---

### ◆§ עָצוּם וָרָב — *Mighty and numerous*

This paragraph, which is dissected here into its component parts and substantiated by quotes from *Exodus,* can be found in *Deuteronomy* (26:5-8), and is recited as part of the ritual of *bikkurim.* When the first fruits (*bikkurim*) ripen, they are to be brought to the Sanctuary in Jerusalem as an offering, and after they are placed before the Altar, the owner gives thanks to God for so fertile a land.

We have already mentioned that gratitude is a most important component of spirituality. Here the Torah teaches us *how* to express gratitude. It is not enough to be grateful for a favor received. True appreciation requires a full awareness of how things came to be: how things were, what happened, and how they are now. Failure to thoroughly understand these phases renders one's gratitude incomplete.

The narrative recited at the *bikkurim* offering thus begins with the distress of the patriarch Jacob, who was persecuted by Laban, and then, following the agony of the disappearance of Joseph, went down to Egypt. It tells how our ancestors suffered the tortures of cruel enslavement, how they prayed, and how God redeemed them. It then closes with an expression of gratitude for the bountiful land one now enjoys.

### ◆§ *True Gratitude*

*The chassidic master Rabbi Baruch of Medziboz was reciting the traditional prayer before Friday night kiddush, when he paused at the phrase, "I thank You, God, for all the kindnesses You have done for me, and for those You are yet to do for me in the future." Rabbi Baruch reflected, "Why should I thank God now for future favors? Why do I not just wait and express my gratitude for them when they occur?"*

*Rabbi Baruch then said, "I know why. It may be that certain kindnesses may occur in a fashion that they will not appear to me to be favors. In fact, they may come in an unpleasant vehicle, and I will not know to thank God for these favors. That is why I must thank him in advance."*

וּשְׂעָרֵךְ צִמֵּחַ, וְאַתְּ עֵרֹם וְעֶרְיָה; וָאֶעֱבֹר עָלַיִךְ וָאֶרְאֵךְ מִתְבּוֹסֶסֶת בְּדָמָיִךְ, וָאֹמַר לָךְ, בְּדָמַיִךְ חֲיִי, וָאֹמַר לָךְ, בְּדָמַיִךְ חֲיִי.[1]

(1) *Ezekiel* 16:7,6.

---

*The rabbi then began to weep. How tragic, that my intelligence is so limited that God will be doing kindnesses for me, yet I will not be appreciative of them at the time.*

The Haggadah elaborates on the theme of gratitude by emphasizing that it is not enough to simply recount the past. Gratitude is not complete until an individual analyzes the past in its minutest details, both the intensity of the suffering he had experienced and the wonderful ways whereby God redeemed him.

The rite of *bikkurim* was carried out on Shavuos, the day on which the Torah was given at Sinai. It is of interest that in referring to the festival of Shavuos, the Torah does not designate it as the day on which we received the Torah, but rather as "the day of *bikkurim*" (*Numbers* 28:26). Perhaps the message in this is that the mitzvah of *bikkurim* expresses the essence of Torah: True gratitude is the key to spirituality.

### ◆§ וָרָב כְּמָה שֶׁנֶּאֱמַר — *Numerous — as it says: I made you as numerous as the plants of the field*

The metaphor wherein the Israelites in Egypt are compared to plants may contain an important message.

The Midrash states that on every blade of grass there is a higher power that dictates: "Grow!" Why is this necessary? Is growth not a natural phenomenon? Why must there be a force that commands it to grow?

This Midrash reveals a vital concept in spirituality. *Inertia* is a strong natural force to overcome, both physically and spiritually. If you wish to move a heavy box, the first push requires a greater energy expenditure, because the natural inclination is for an object to remain in its place. To get it to move, one must overcome this inertia.

This is true of any change, even more so in living things than in inanimate objects. We are creatures of habit, and to bring about any changes we must overcome the powerful resistance of inertia, which would have us maintain our status quo.

hair grown long; but you were naked and bare. And I passed over you and saw you downtrodden in your blood and I said to you: "Through your blood shall you live!" And I said to you: "Through your blood shall you live!"[1]

---

This is why each blade of grass must be prodded to grow. Without such prodding, inertia would maintain it at its lowly status. This was also true of the Israelites in Egypt, who needed to be prodded out of their inertia, out of their complacency and acceptance of slavery as a normal way of life. Hence the comparison of the Israelites to the grass of the field is very appropriate.

The first step in spiritual growth is to be dissatisfied with one's present level of spirituality. This dissatisfaction can help overcome the natural inertia, the tendency to do nothing, to make no changes.

*A disciple of the chassidic master of Karlin once complained to him that he was frustrated because he was unable to progress spiritually. "What can I do for you, my son?" the master said. "I have been unable to find the key to open your heart."*

*"A key?" the young man cried out in desperation. "Who needs a key? Open it with an ax!"*

*"Never mind," the master said. "It has just been opened."*

When we are desperate with dissatisfaction over our present spiritual status, we have taken a major step towards spiritual growth.

### ◆§ וְאַתְּ עֵרֹם וְעֶרְיָה — *but you were naked and bare*

The commentaries explain that this refers to the Israelites being barren of mitzvos prior to the Exodus. They were therefore given the mitzvah of the Paschal offering, in order to have some merit.

*The Tzaddik of Sanz was told about a wealthy landowner who was about to evict a tenant. The Tzaddik reprimanded the landowner for his cruelty.*

*"But this tenant does not deserve any mercy," the landowner said. "He is a flagrant sinner who deserves to be buried. It is a mitzvah to bury him!"*

*The Tzaddik responded, "Obviously, burying a sinner is not so great a mitzvah. The Midrash states that there were many sinful, assimilated*

**וַיָּרֵעוּ** אֹתָנוּ הַמִּצְרִים, וַיְעַנּוּנוּ, וַיִּתְּנוּ עָלֵינוּ עֲבֹדָה קָשָׁה.[1]

**וַיָּרֵעוּ אֹתָנוּ הַמִּצְרִים** – כְּמָה שֶׁנֶּאֱמַר, הָבָה נִתְחַכְּמָה לוֹ, פֶּן יִרְבֶּה, וְהָיָה כִּי תִקְרֶאנָה מִלְחָמָה, וְנוֹסַף גַּם הוּא עַל שֹׂנְאֵינוּ, וְנִלְחַם בָּנוּ, וְעָלָה מִן הָאָרֶץ.[2]

(1) *Deuteronomy* 26:6. (2) *Exodus* 1:10.

*Jews who refused to leave Egypt with Moses, and that they perished during the three days of darkness. Without a doubt, they must have been brought to burial by other Jews. If so, why were the Jews considered barren of mitzvos? They had so many mitzvos burying the sinful who had perished.*

*"The only conclusion," the Tzaddik continued, "is that it is not so great a mitzvah to bury a sinful person. Therefore, acting in this fashion is a waste of your precious time."*

### ❧ וַיָּרֵעוּ אֹתָנוּ הַמִּצְרִים — *The Egyptians did evil to us*

The phrase וַיָּרֵעוּ which is generally translated as "they (the Egyptians) did evil to us" can also be translated as a conjugation of the word רֵעַ (friend), and the phrase would then read "they befriended us." In other words, prior to the period of manifest enmity, the Egyptians behaved toward the Israelites in a superficially friendly manner, concealing their nefarious designs behind a facade of brotherhood.

The Midrash states that the enslavement of the Israelites began very insidiously. Initially, the nobility of Egypt and indeed the king himself worked on the construction projects, and under the banner of egalitarianism invited the Jews, as honored citizens, to participate. Slowly the Egyptians began withdrawing from the work force, acting only as supervisors and advisers, until the ultimate state of absolute enslavement of the Israelites was achieved. Indeed, the Talmud recommends that the herb used for *maror* be one that is sweet when it first begins growing and turns bitter only in its maturity, because that was precisely the process experienced by our ancestors.

The message conveyed by this interpretation of the Haggadah is that

**וַיָּרֵעוּ The Egyptians did evil to us and afflicted us; and imposed hard labor upon us.**[1]

**The Egyptians did evil to us** — as it says: Let us deal with them wisely lest they multiply and, if we happen to be at war, they may join our enemies and fight against us and then leave the country.[2]

---

we must always be on our guard, not only against politically hostile forces, but even more so in protecting our spiritual well-being. The forces that threaten our spirituality seldom reveal their destructive character at the very onset. Quite the contrary, they are likely to appear benign and even benevolent, and only after they have established a firm foothold in our lives does their true nature become apparent. By then it may be most difficult to overcome them.

The development of any of the addictive conditions is a classic example of this phenomenon. In the early phase of habituation, a person is likely to think that his substance provides him with much-needed relaxation, allows him to socialize with greater ease, helps him sleep, and even enhances his work performance. The progression is likely to be insidious, with each step of the process being virtually undetectable, and by the time the destructive effects of his habit are apparent, the individual is deep in the clutches of an obstinate and devastating addiction.

Indeed, in describing the wily tactics of the *yetzer hara,* the Talmud states that it rarely begins by urging frank violation of the Torah. It may even urge a person to do things that may seem highly idealistic, but its goal is to bring a person under its domination, and the innocence of the early seduction is merely one feature of a well-planned stratagem of deception. Once the individual has begun to obey its instructions, the *yetzer hara* becomes ever more bold, eventually demanding total rejection of one's Jewish identity.

We can generally take steps to protect both our physical and our spiritual well-being when the threat is from overtly hostile sources. We are far more vulnerable when the enemy's tactics appear rather benign. In order to keep ourselves on guard, we must perform periodic self-evaluations, preferably with a trusted mentor who can alert us to possible self-deception. Being a slave to any habit robs one of a measure of personal freedom, and the loss of freedom to choose one's behavior, whether it is due to frank addiction or to less evident habituations, is a serious incursion on spirituality.

**וַיְעַנּוּנוּ** — כְּמָה שֶׁנֶּאֱמַר, וַיָּשִֽׂימוּ עָלָיו שָׂרֵי מִסִּים, לְמַֽעַן עַנֹּתוֹ בְּסִבְלֹתָם, וַיִּֽבֶן עָרֵי מִסְכְּנוֹת לְפַרְעֹה, אֶת פִּתֹם וְאֶת רַעַמְסֵס.[1]

**וַיִּתְּנוּ עָלֵינוּ עֲבֹדָה קָשָׁה** — כְּמָה שֶׁנֶּאֱמַר, וַיַּעֲבִדוּ מִצְרַיִם אֶת בְּנֵי יִשְׂרָאֵל בְּפָֽרֶךְ.[2]

**וַנִּצְעַק אֶל יהוה אֱלֹהֵי אֲבֹתֵינוּ, וַיִּשְׁמַע יהוה אֶת קֹלֵנוּ, וַיַּרְא אֶת עָנְיֵנוּ, וְאֶת עֲמָלֵנוּ, וְאֶת לַחֲצֵנוּ.**[3]

---

### ◆ לְמַֽעַן עַנֹּתוֹ בְּסִבְלֹתָם — *in order to oppress them with their burdens*

The text points out that the prime purpose of forcing the Israelites to work was not to have the cities built, but simply to oppress and torture them. The Talmud explains that they were told to build in a marshy area, where the bricks would inevitably sink into the ground. After laboriously erecting a brick wall, the slaves would return only to find that all their labor was for naught, having been swallowed by the swamp.

> *It is told that a man was once sentenced to twenty-five years of hard labor, and was shackled to a huge wheel fixed in the wall, which he had to crank during all his waking hours. As he turned the heavy wheel, he would often try to imagine what he might be achieving through his backbreaking work. Perhaps he was turning a millstone that was grinding grain into flour, or perhaps he was bringing water up from a deep well to irrigate a field.*
>
> *When the long sentence came to an end and the shackles were removed, the first thing this man did, broken in both body and spirit, was to go to the other side of the wall to see just what he had been accomplishing for twenty-five years. How shocked he was to discover that there was nothing there! Just a wheel in the wall, not attached to anything. At this point he broke down in tears. "Twenty-five years of hard work, all for nothing." The awareness that all his work was of no avail was far worse than the hard labor itself. The Egyptians knew this, and this is how they tortured their slaves.*

**And afflicted us** — as it says: They set taskmasters over them in order to oppress them with their burdens; and they built Pisom and Raamses as treasure cities for Pharaoh.[1]

**They imposed hard labor upon us** — as it says: The Egyptians subjugated the Children of Israel with hard labor.[2]

**וַנִּצְעַק We cried out to HASHEM, the God of our fathers; and HASHEM heard our voice and saw our affliction, our burden and our oppression.[3]**

(1) *Exodus* 1:11. (2) 1:13 (3) *Deuteronomy* 26:7.)

---

What does this tell us? We too put forth a great deal of effort in our lives. One day we too will reflect, "What was it all for?" That day can be a pleasant experience or one of dreadful anguish. If we live spiritual lives and constantly refine our character, we will be able to look back happily upon a very positive achievement. But if all we can see then is hours and days spent in surviving and in trying to satisfy our ephemeral desires, we will painfully discover that our lives were essentially futile, a very painful discovery indeed.

"Who is a wise person? One who can foresee the future" (*Tamid* 32a). There will be a time in the future when we will look back upon our lives, and we have the ability to make that a very pleasant experience, if we emphasize our spiritual lives rather than our material needs.

### ◆§ וַיִּתְּנוּ עָלֵינוּ עֲבֹדָה קָשָׁה — *They imposed hard labor upon us*

At one *Seder,* the reader of the Haggadah was explaining that in each generation we are to envision ourselves as though we personally participated in the Exodus.

The lady of the house, who had worked into the wee hours of the nights preceding Passover — scrubbing down the kitchen and transferring all the utensils in and out of the basement — said, "Oh, I have no trouble identifying with at least part of that. It says here that the Israelites were put to doing hard work. Well, that is one aspect of the Exodus that is still very much with us today."

### ◆§ וַנִּצְעַק אֶל ה׳ — *We cried to HASHEM*

The length of the enslavement in Egypt and the way it was brought to an end by the many miracles with manifest Divine intervention provides us with an important teaching.

**וַנִּצְעַק אֶל יהוה אֱלֹהֵי אֲבֹתֵינוּ** — כְּמָה שֶׁנֶּאֱמַר, וַיְהִי בַיָּמִים הָרַבִּים הָהֵם, וַיָּמָת מֶלֶךְ מִצְרַיִם, וַיֵּאָנְחוּ בְנֵי יִשְׂרָאֵל מִן הָעֲבֹדָה, וַיִּזְעָקוּ, וַתַּעַל שַׁוְעָתָם אֶל הָאֱלֹהִים מִן הָעֲבֹדָה.[1]

**וַיִּשְׁמַע יהוה אֶת קֹלֵנוּ** — כְּמָה שֶׁנֶּאֱמַר, וַיִּשְׁמַע אֱלֹהִים אֶת נַאֲקָתָם, וַיִּזְכֹּר אֱלֹהִים אֶת בְּרִיתוֹ אֶת אַבְרָהָם, אֶת יִצְחָק, וְאֶת יַעֲקֹב.[2]

**וַיַּרְא אֶת עָנְיֵנוּ** — זוֹ פְּרִישׁוּת דֶּרֶךְ אֶרֶץ, כְּמָה שֶׁנֶּאֱמַר, וַיַּרְא אֱלֹהִים אֶת בְּנֵי יִשְׂרָאֵל, וַיֵּדַע אֱלֹהִים.[3]

---

The redemption from Egypt did not come about through a gradual build-up of forces and the establishment of organized opposition by the enslaved Israelites. Had that happened, we could understand rather easily why it happened when it did and not earlier, because it had to wait until all conditions necessary for a successful rebellion had been met. But since it transpired by Divine intervention, why did it not occur earlier? Before God there is no such thing as "getting ready."

We say that we cried out onto God to be merciful and relieve our distress and that He heard our prayers. Yes, but why all the years of suffering? Why did He not intervene earlier?

While this question does not always have an answer that satisfies our logic, I did gain some insight on this in a pediatrician's office.

A mother had brought her infant to the doctor for immunization. As soon as the child saw the white-clad doctor he began crying, remembering only too well what had befallen him at this man's hands just several months earlier.

The mother assisted the physician by forcefully restraining the child, who clawed and kicked her. If we could enter the child's mind, we would no doubt discover that he was violently angry at his mother who had suddenly betrayed him, and who, instead of protecting him from harm as she always did, was now collaborating with this brutal aggressor who was going to stab him with a sharp instrument.

The moment the physician withdrew the needle and the mother released

**We cried out to Hashem, the God of our fathers** — as it says: It happened in the course of those many days that the king of Egypt died; and the Children of Israel groaned because of the servitude and cried; their cry because of the servitude rose up to God.[1]

**Hashem heard our voice** — as it says: God heard their groaning, and God recalled His covenant with Avraham, with Yitzchak, and with Yaakov.[2]

**And saw our affliction** — that is the disruption of family life, as it says: God saw the Children of Israel and God took note.[3]

---

(1) *Exodus* 2:23 (2) 2:24. (3) 2:25.

---

her restraining hold, the infant embraced her and clung to her for dear life. But why? Was she not the very person who had just betrayed him and had subjected him to such intense pain?

Obviously, the infant's trust in the mother was so great that even though he thought she had allowed him to be hurt, he nevertheless turned to her for comfort, protection, and relief from the pain. This is precisely how we relate to God. Although we cannot understand why He subjects us to suffering any more than the infant can understand his mother's behavior, our trust in Him is so great that it is not shaken by our suffering. Even when we angrily protest, we are nevertheless aware that God is a loving and caring Father, and that is why we appeal to Him in our distress.

We believe that God listens, and that He hears our prayers. Why He does not respond immediately and allows our anguish to continue is known only to Him. It is a serious mistake to assume that if God does not answer our prayers immediately it is because He is not listening. God always listens. We believe that God is the ultimate manifestation of kindness and is not sadistic. He does not withhold anything from us for any reason other than because in His infinite wisdom, which is unfathomable to the human mind, He knows it is somehow to our advantage.

The many miracles of the Exodus which attest to Divine intervention should reinforce our faith. "Behold, the Guardian of Israel does not slumber nor sleep" (*Psalms* 121:4). God always listens and He responds in the manner which He perceives as best.

**וְאֶת עֲמָלֵנוּ** — אֵלּוּ הַבָּנִים, כְּמָה שֶׁנֶּאֱמַר, כָּל הַבֵּן הַיִּלּוֹד הַיְאֹרָה תַּשְׁלִיכֻהוּ, וְכָל הַבַּת תְּחַיּוּן.[1]

**וְאֶת לַחֲצֵנוּ** — זוֹ הַדְּחַק, כְּמָה שֶׁנֶּאֱמַר, וְגַם רָאִיתִי אֶת הַלַּחַץ אֲשֶׁר מִצְרַיִם לֹחֲצִים אֹתָם.[2]

**וַיּוֹצִאֵנוּ יהוה מִמִּצְרַיִם בְּיָד חֲזָקָה, וּבִזְרֹעַ נְטוּיָה, וּבְמֹרָא גָּדֹל, וּבְאֹתוֹת וּבְמֹפְתִים.**[3]

**וַיּוֹצִאֵנוּ יהוה מִמִּצְרַיִם** — לֹא עַל יְדֵי מַלְאָךְ, וְלֹא עַל יְדֵי שָׂרָף, וְלֹא עַל יְדֵי שָׁלִיחַ, אֶלָּא הַקָּדוֹשׁ בָּרוּךְ הוּא בִּכְבוֹדוֹ וּבְעַצְמוֹ. שֶׁנֶּאֱמַר, וְעָבַרְתִּי בְאֶרֶץ מִצְרַיִם בַּלַּיְלָה הַזֶּה, וְהִכֵּיתִי כָל בְּכוֹר בְּאֶרֶץ מִצְרַיִם מֵאָדָם וְעַד בְּהֵמָה, וּבְכָל אֱלֹהֵי מִצְרַיִם אֶעֱשֶׂה שְׁפָטִים, אֲנִי יהוה.[4]

וְעָבַרְתִּי בְאֶרֶץ מִצְרַיִם בַּלַּיְלָה הַזֶּה — אֲנִי וְלֹא מַלְאָךְ. וְהִכֵּיתִי כָל בְּכוֹר בְּאֶרֶץ מִצְרַיִם —

---

### ◆§ וְעָבַרְתִּי בְאֶרֶץ מִצְרַיִם . . . אֲנִי וְלֹא מַלְאָךְ — *I will pass through the land of Egypt . . . I and no angel*

What difference would it make whether the redemption from Egypt was effected via an angel rather than by God Himself?

The entire concept of God operating via angelic emissaries requires understanding. A human being, who is limited as to how many things one can do at one time, may need to deputize others to accomplish additional tasks, but since God is infinite in power, why does He resort to angels to carry out His wishes?

Torah authorities state that inasmuch as God is eternal, all Divine actions are inseparable from Him, hence everything God does is also eternal. Since many things God wishes to have done are limited in duration, He sends an agent to perform them in His stead. The significance of our being told that the redemption from Egypt came about not via an angel but by God Himself is so that we should understand this to have been an eternal redemption. We declare this in the evening service: "He delivered His people Israel from there (Egypt) to an eternal liberty."

**Our burden** — refers to the children, as it says: Every son that is born you shall cast into the river, but every daughter you shall let live.[1]

**Our oppression** — refers to the pressure expressed in the words: I have also seen how the Egyptians are oppressing them.[2]

**וַיּוֹצִאֵנוּ** **HASHEM brought us out of Egypt with a mighty hand and with an outstretched arm, with great awe, with signs and wonders.**[3]

**HASHEM brought us out of Egypt** — not through an angel, not through a seraph, not through a messenger, but the Holy One, Blessed is He, in His glory, Himself, as it says: I will pass through the land of Egypt on that night; I will slay all the firstborn in the land of Egypt from man to beast; and upon all the gods of Egypt will I execute judgments; I, HASHEM.[4]

"I will pass through the land of Egypt on that night" — I and no angel; "I will slay all the firstborn in the land of Egypt" —

(1) *Exodus* 1:22. (2) 3:9. (3) *Deuteronomy* 26:8. (4) *Exodus* 12:12.

---

But inasmuch as we have been repeatedly oppressed throughout our history, in what way is our liberty eternal? The answer is that although we may have been in physical bondage, our *spiritual* emancipation is eternal. By delivering us from the idolatrous influences of paganism and giving us the Torah, God has given us the capacity for spiritual freedom, something which can never be taken from us.

Even a brief review of the Jewish past convinces one of our spiritual freedom. Mighty, populous empires, soundly rooted in their homelands, have disappeared from the world scene, and their existence is known to us only through archaeological relics. The Jewish nation, driven from its homeland, and subjected to repeated persecutions, culminating in the Holocaust, has stubbornly persisted, defying all dynamics of history. We are indeed an eternal people, and it is our Torah and our spirituality that has ensured our miraculous survival. Even the most ardent skeptic, reviewing the past history of the Jewish people, must conclude that our existence is a testimony to Divine protection. No other explanation makes sense.

There is nothing as dear to a person as the breath of life. If we are threatened with deprivation of oxygen, we instinctively struggle to breathe in

אֲנִי וְלֹא שָׂרָף. וּבְכָל אֱלֹהֵי מִצְרַיִם אֶעֱשֶׂה שְׁפָטִים – אֲנִי וְלֹא הַשָּׁלִיחַ. אֲנִי יהוה – אֲנִי הוּא, וְלֹא אַחֵר.

---

order to survive, because our body "knows" that it will perish without oxygen. That is how we must regard our spirituality. It is our very life, and our only means of existence.

But temptation can override even the drive for life itself, as evidenced by the person who is addicted to a dangerous chemical, and who puts his very life at risk because of the irresistible craving for the chemical. Other temptations may be no less lethal, although they are a greater danger to our spiritual life than to our physical survival. If we appreciate spirituality as being the essence of life, we must resist the temptation to act in ways that would jeopardize our spirituality.

### ⁂ אֲנִי וְלֹא מַלְאָךְ — *I and no angel*

Another interpretation of "I and not an angel" is related to the concept of idolatry as explained by Maimonides.

Maimonides explains that the first deviation that ultimately resulted in paganism was based on a falacious belief that God is too exalted to be concerned about the petty deeds of humans. People therefore reasoned that after God created the world, He abandoned it in order to occupy himself with more important things, entrusting the operation of the world to His underlings, the angels. The logic was therefore to pray to the angels who were in immediate charge of the world, and it was but a small step from there to bestowing the heavenly bodies with special powers and then to pay homage to them.

The Jewish faith began with the Exodus, which was followed shortly thereafter by the formal delineation of Judaism in the giving of the Torah. The first revelation at the Exodus was therefore of God Himself, not through any emissary, in order to impress the Israelites that in contrast to the pagan ideas that prevailed in their environment, they were to understand that man can have a personal, imminent, and direct contact with God, without any intermediaries, and that God relates directly to mankind and does intervene in the affairs of man when He wishes.

This is an important concept in prayer, which should be a bonding between man and God.

In many congregations, there is a plaque at the reader's pulpit that reads "Know before Whom you are standing." This is meant to serve as a reminder

I and no seraph; "And upon all the gods of Egypt will I execute judgments" — I and no messenger; "I, HASHEM" — it is I and no other.

---

that a person should maintain a proper attitude of reverence in the imminent presence of God. But it should also be a reminder of the intimate relationship we have with God. We are standing before Him, relating directly to Him, and in contrast to the mistaken belief of the early idolaters, God is very much interested in everything we do.

The concept of prayer had been more or less of an abstraction for me, until one day when I prayed at the *Kotel* (Western Wall). A blind man approached the wall, and after bestowing a gentle kiss on the sacred stones, he ran his fingers over the stones, feeling centuries of Jewish history in the ridges and troughs of the massive boulders. He began a conversation with God, relating many personal things. He then paused a few moments, and said, "Oh, I'm sorry. That I already told You yesterday," and continued his conversation. I was electrified by the character of this man's prayer. It appeared to me much different than the rather routine rituals of prayer which we so often practice. This was an intimate, one-to-one conversation between him and God.

To know that God listens, that He cares about us, that He desires our association, and that we can reach Him by following His will is a fundament of spirituality.

## ☙ *When an Angel Suffices*

Why does the Haggadah place emphasis on the fact that the smiting of the firstborn was done by God Himself and not through an angel?

*A rabbi was once approached by some people in the community who requested that he dismiss the shochet (ritual slaughterer) from his position because of rumors of improper behavior.*

*The rabbi refused to do so. "In the account of the Akeidah (the test of Abraham's willingness to sacrifice Isaac), the patriarch Abraham was given the command to bring Isaac as an offering by God Himself. However, the actual sacrifice was prevented by the intervention of an angel, who stayed Abraham's hand. It is obvious," the rabbi continued, "that to prevent taking a life, the authority of an angel suffices. To take someone's life, only Almighty God has the right to do that.*

*"You wish me to discharge this person from his position and deprive his family of a livelihood on the basis of a rumor? That would be tantamount to taking their lives. This can only be done by God Himself."*

**בְּיָד חֲזָקָה** — זוֹ הַדֶּבֶר, כְּמָה שֶׁנֶּאֱמַר, הִנֵּה יַד יהוה הוֹיָה בְּמִקְנְךָ אֲשֶׁר בַּשָּׂדֶה, בַּסּוּסִים בַּחֲמֹרִים בַּגְּמַלִּים בַּבָּקָר וּבַצֹּאן, דֶּבֶר כָּבֵד מְאֹד.[1]

**וּבִזְרֹעַ נְטוּיָה** — זוֹ הַחֶרֶב, כְּמָה שֶׁנֶּאֱמַר, וְחַרְבּוֹ שְׁלוּפָה בְּיָדוֹ, נְטוּיָה עַל יְרוּשָׁלָיִם.[2]

**וּבְמֹרָא גָּדֹל** — זוֹ גִּלּוּי שְׁכִינָה, כְּמָה שֶׁנֶּאֱמַר, אוֹ הֲנִסָּה אֱלֹהִים לָבוֹא לָקַחַת לוֹ גוֹי מִקֶּרֶב גּוֹי, בְּמַסֹּת, בְּאֹתֹת, וּבְמוֹפְתִים, וּבְמִלְחָמָה, וּבְיָד חֲזָקָה, וּבִזְרוֹעַ נְטוּיָה, וּבְמוֹרָאִים גְּדֹלִים, כְּכֹל אֲשֶׁר עָשָׂה לָכֶם יהוה אֱלֹהֵיכֶם בְּמִצְרַיִם לְעֵינֶיךָ.[3]

**וּבְאֹתוֹת** — זֶה הַמַּטֶּה, כְּמָה שֶׁנֶּאֱמַר, וְאֶת הַמַּטֶּה הַזֶּה תִּקַּח בְּיָדֶךָ, אֲשֶׁר תַּעֲשֶׂה בּוֹ אֶת הָאֹתֹת.[4]

---

**בְּיָד חֲזָקָה – זוֹ הַדֶּבֶר . . . וּבִזְרֹעַ נְטוּיָה – זוֹ הַחֶרֶב** — ***With a mighty hand — refers to the pestilence . . . With an outstretched arm — refers to the sword***

The phrase the Haggadah employs to explain "the outstretched arm" refers to a sword that has been withdrawn from its sheath, ready to be utilized as a weapon. Ready to be used — but not used.

The Talmud states that when punishment is inflicted, God does so with mercy, inflicting losses on one's belongings, but sparing one's life. The psalmist states that it is the evil that will destroy the evildoer (*Psalms* 34:22), and the Talmudic statement thus means that God had designed it so that the wicked are not immediately destroyed by their wrongdoings, but rather are given lesser losses which should serve as a warning so that they will correct errant ways.

We can see this occurring in people who behave in a self-destructive manner. The negative consequences of their actions should stimulate them to correct their ways. Unfortunately, some people are obstinate and simply refuse to get the message.

Pharaoh is a prime example of obstinacy and recalcitrance. The hand of God was stretched out in a stern warning, which he ignored. The cattle plague which was visited upon him affected animals rather than people. He could

**With a mighty hand** — refers to the pestilence, as it is stated: Behold, the hand of HASHEM shall strike your cattle which are in the field, the horses, the donkeys, the camels, the herds, and the flocks — a very severe pestilence.[1]

**With an outstretched arm** — refers to the sword, as it says: His drawn sword in His hand, outstretched over Jerusalem.[2]

**With great awe** — alludes to the revelation of the Shechinah, as it says: Or has a deity attempted to take unto Himself a nation from the midst of another nation by trials, miraculous signs, and wonders, by war and with a mighty hand and outstretched arm and by awesome revelations, as all that HASHEM your God did for you in Egypt, before your eyes?[3]

**With signs** — refers to [the miracles performed with] the staff as it says: Take this staff in your hand, that you may perform the miraculous signs with it.[4]

(1) *Exodus* 9:3. (2) *I Chronicles* 21:16. (3) *Deuteronomy* 4:34. (4) *Exodus* 4:17.

---

have spared himself greater suffering by heeding the warnings and yielding to the Divine will.

Obstinacy is a rather common trait. Its futility can be seen on a winter day, when some motorists continue to spin their wheels, refusing to recognize that they are only digging themselves ever deeper into a rut. A wise person recognizes when his actions are destructive rather than constructive, correct his behavior, and is able to avoid greater difficulties.

### ◆§ וּבְאֹתוֹת – זֶה הַמַּטֶּה — *With signs — refers to [the miracles performed with] the staff*

The wondrous staff of Moses has quite a history. According to the Midrash, this staff was in the Garden of Eden, and was transmitted from generation to generation, until Moses found it in possession of his father-in-law, Jethro.

There were two aspects to this staff. When it was held in the hands of Moses, it was an instrument of deliverance, punishing evildoers and dividing the sea to rescue the emancipated slaves. When it was not in the hands of Moses, it was converted to a venomous serpent.

**וּבְמֹפְתִים** — זֶה הַדָּם, כְּמָה שֶׁנֶּאֱמַר, וְנָתַתִּי מוֹפְתִים בַּשָּׁמַיִם וּבָאָרֶץ

As each of the words דָּם, *blood,* אֵשׁ, *fire,* and עָשָׁן, *smoke,* is said, a bit of wine is removed from the cup, with the index finger, or, if one is squeamish, by pouring.

**דָּם וָאֵשׁ וְתִמְרוֹת עָשָׁן.**[1]

דָּבָר אַחֵר: בְּיָד חֲזָקָה – שְׁתַּיִם; וּבִזְרֹעַ נְטוּיָה – שְׁתַּיִם; וּבְמֹרָא גָּדֹל – שְׁתַּיִם; וּבְאֹתוֹת – שְׁתַּיִם; וּבְמֹפְתִים – שְׁתַּיִם. אֵלּוּ עֶשֶׂר מַכּוֹת שֶׁהֵבִיא הַקָּדוֹשׁ בָּרוּךְ הוּא עַל הַמִּצְרִים בְּמִצְרַיִם, וְאֵלּוּ הֵן:

---

Perhaps this staff may symbolize the enormously potent forces of science and knowledge. These can bring benefits to mankind, but can also cause untold misery. Their ultimate effects depend on whether they are in the hands of responsible, spiritual people, or whether they slip from their control.

Atomic science, for example, has enabled doctors to diagnose disease and provide treatment. While it has saved many lives, one atomic explosion can annihilate an entire population.

"This staff you shall take in your hands" (*Exodus* 4:17). In order for the wondrous staff to perform miraculous deeds of benefit to mankind, it must be firmly in the hands of people like Moses.

### ◆§ אֵלּוּ עֶשֶׂר מַכּוֹת — *These are the ten plagues*

In the account of Creation in *Genesis,* we find ten utterances wherewith God brought the universe into existence. "The function of the Ten Plagues," said Rabbi Isaac Meir of Gur, "was to convert the ten utterances of Creation into the Ten Commandments."

The thought behind this relationship of the series of "tens" is that one's concept of the genesis of the universe has a profound impact on one's behavior. Those who deny Creation and who believe that the world evolved out of primordial matter do not attribute any ultimate purpose to life. To them, the word "teleology" is an anathema. The world is nothing but an accident, the result of multiple forces that happened to interact in such a manner that over billions of years elements combined to form molecules, then more complex chemicals, amino acids, proteins, and ultimately all living things, including the unbelievably complex human brain. Since there was no purposeful Creation, one cannot speak of an absolute

**With wonders** — alludes to the blood, as it says: I will show wonders in the heavens and on the earth

As each of the words דָּם, *blood,* אֵשׁ, *fire,* and עָשָׁן, *smoke,* is said, a bit of wine is removed from the cup, with the index finger, or, if one is squeamish, by pouring.

**Blood, fire, and columns of smoke.**[1]

Another explanation of the preceding verse: [Each phrase represents two plagues,] hence: with a mighty hand — two; with an outstretched arm — two; with great awe — two; with signs — two; with wonders — two. These are the ten plagues which the Holy One, Blessed is He, brought upon the Egyptians in Egypt, namely:

(1) *Joel* 3:3.

---

moral law. Laws are enacted as social controls, and can be modified as society sees fit.

The Torah concept is that the world came into being at the behest of God, Who created it for a purpose known only to Him. In order for that purpose to be achieved, God gave us the Torah which contains His instructions for the function of the world. There is an absolute moral law as prescribed by the Torah, and man is not free to abrogate the Divine laws.

A person is free to accept either concept. Of course, the atheistic concept is a more convenient one, since man is then not bound by any authority higher than himself.

The Ten Plagues, which were a suspension of all physical laws of nature and hence incontrovertible evidence of Divine intervention in the operation of the universe, proved the existence of a Creator. In modern terms, one might say that God generally lets the world operate on "automatic," i.e., according to natural laws, but that at any moment He may turn off the automatic and operate the world on "manual." This operation on manual, which occurred with the miraculous Ten Plagues, thus attested that there is an intelligent Being at the controls.

The demonstration of the existence of God made it possible to speak of absolute moral and ethical values, i.e., the Ten Commandments. Thus, the series of "tens" is indeed as Rabbi Isaac Meir explained.

This demonstration of Creation being of Divine origin was necessary only once. Thereafter we have to follow the teachings of the Torah as it was received by our ancestors at Mount Sinai and transmitted to us by the Torah authorities.

As each of the plagues is mentioned, a bit of wine is removed from the cup as above. The same is done by each word of Rabbi Yehudah's mnemonic.

**דָּם. צְפַרְדֵּעַ. כִּנִּים. עָרוֹב. דֶּבֶר. שְׁחִין. בָּרָד. אַרְבֶּה. חֹשֶׁךְ. מַכַּת בְּכוֹרוֹת.**

---

### ◆§ אֵלּוּ עֶשֶׂר מַכּוֹת — *These are the ten plagues*

The saga of the ten plagues had always puzzled me. Again and again Moses warns Pharaoh of the consequences that will befall him if he refuses to release the Israelites. Each time Moses' prediction comes true, and each time Pharaoh pleads for relief, promising to comply with his request. No sooner is there a moment of respite, however, than Pharaoh becomes obstinate, recalcitrant, and defiant.

Had this happened only one or twice, Pharaoh's refusal to learn from experience might be more easily understood. However, when there is a consistent and repetitive pattern, how can anyone fail to get the message? Is it conceivable that Pharaoh was so utterly dense that he could not learn from such intensely painful experiences?

I never understood how this was possible until I began treating addictive disease, and then I became aware that this failure to learn from experience has nothing to do with intelligence. There are some things that highly intelligent people appear to be incapable of learning, even when it is blatantly manifest to everyone else.

The life history of the addictive person is virtually identical to the saga of the ten plagues. The person's habit results in some type of disastrous consequence, and he swears that he will never resume this behavior. Before too long however, he does resume his destructive behavior, totally oblivious to the experiences of the past, or cleverly deluding himself as to why this time things will be different. This pattern may recur much more than ten times, and it is no exaggeration to state that it may recur a hundred times. As with Pharaoh, there may be no yielding until some utterly disastrous event occurs, and even then there may be a relapse. This is what transpired with Pharaoh when he pursued the Israelites after having released them following the most devastating of the Ten Plagues.

While this pattern is blatant in the addict, we may not be aware that, in more subtle forms, it may often be present in non-addicts as well. We are sometimes obstinate in refusing to yield to the dictates of logic, even when a particular behavior has proven itself to be repeatedly destructive.

Like Pharaoh and like the addict, our egos may blind us to the truth. We

As each of the plagues is mentioned, a bit of wine is removed from the cup as above. The same is done by each word of Rabbi Yehudah's mnemonic.

**1. Blood 2. Frogs 3. Vermin 4. Wild Beasts
5. Pestilence 6. Boils 7. Hail 8. Locusts
9. Darkness 10. Plague of the Firstborn.**

---

would therefore be wise to periodically examine our convictions and behavior, and be willing to consider the possibility that regardless of how certain we are that we are right in what we are doing, we may nevertheless be mistaken. Self-examination may not be fully reliable, however, because our biases may make us oblivious to the truth. We would therefore do well to enlist the assistance of a competent person whose counsel we trust, to help us avert the disasters that may occur as a result of refusing to consider that we may be fallible.

### ◆§ *A Diminishment of Joy*

It is customary, when reciting the ten plagues, to pour a bit of wine from one's cup.

In Psalm 23, the psalmist expresses his gratitude for the abundance of favors received with the phrase, "my cup runneth over." If this expression connotes that one is content and satisfied with everything one has, then pouring from one's cup and diminishing its contents symbolizes a lack, that one has lost something.

True, the cruelty of the Egyptians warranted their being punished. Nevertheless we are not happy if others are punished on our account, even if they deserved it. We ascribe to the words of Solomon, "Do not rejoice when your enemy falls" (*Proverbs* 24:17).

It is of interest that in regard to the other festivals, the Torah prescribes *simchah.* It is only in regard to Passover that this word is omitted, because although we do celebrate our independence, we cannot have a full measure of joy with the knowledge that our triumph was accompanied by the distress of the Egyptians, even though they were our sworn enemies.

### ◆§ *Obstinacy Viewed Constructively*

Chassidic writings emphasize that all character traits can be applied constructively. While envy is a deplorable trait, being envious of someone who has achieved greater knowledge and greater spirituality can stimulate one to higher achievement. While hatred is an abomination, one should hate evil and injustice.

רַבִּי יְהוּדָה הָיָה נוֹתֵן בָּהֶם סִמָּנִים:

דְּצַ״ךְ • עֲדַ״שׁ • בְּאַחַ״ב.

The cups are refilled. The wine that was removed is not used.

**רַבִּי יוֹסֵי** הַגְּלִילִי אוֹמֵר: מִנַּיִן אַתָּה אוֹמֵר שֶׁלָּקוּ הַמִּצְרִים בְּמִצְרַיִם עֶשֶׂר מַכּוֹת וְעַל הַיָּם לָקוּ חֲמִשִּׁים מַכּוֹת? בְּמִצְרַיִם מָה הוּא אוֹמֵר,

---

This is true of obstinacy as well. If the Jewish nation was not stubborn, we would long since have perished. Only a stubborn people rises again and again after repeated devastating persecutions. On an individual level, one may be obstinate in refusing to yield on moral principles. How can one, then, distinguish good obstinacy from bad?

The acid test is *mesiras nefesh*: accepting martyrdom. Does one believe strongly enough in one's principle to be able to sacrifice one's life for it?

Pharaoh was obstinate, and he withstood severe punishments because of his refusal to yield to Moses, even to the point of placing his entire country in jeopardy (*Exodus* 10:7). However, this was so only as long as he was not personally at risk. But when the firstborn were smitten, and he feared for his life because he, too, was a firstborn (*Rashi, ibid.* 12:32), he then told Moses to take the Israelites and leave. Pharaoh was not ready to surrender his life for his principles.

Jewish history is replete with incidents of *mesiras nefesh,* because for the Jew life is not an end in itself. Life is given for a purpose, and it would lose its value if that purpose were gone.

> *It is related that Rabbi Yosef Yitzchak of Lubavitch, who persisted in disseminating Torah in defiance of Bolshevik orders to the contrary, was once challenged by an officer who suddenly pulled a gun on him. When the Rabbi remained unperturbed, the officer asked him if he was not afraid of being killed. The Rabbi replied, "When one has a multiplicity of gods and only one world, one is afraid of dying. When one has only one God but two worlds, one is not afraid to die."*

If all there is to life is living, then surrendering one's life is unthinkable. If there is something beyond living, a purpose for which one lives, then *mesiras nefesh* becomes a possibility.

It has been said, "If there is nothing worth dying for, then there is really nothing to live for." Living for the sake of living is a characteristic of brute

Rabbi Yehudah abbreviated them by their Hebrew initials:

**D'TZACH, ADASH, B'ACHAV.**

The cups are refilled. The wine that was removed is not used.

**רַבִּי יוֹסֵי** Rabbi Yose the Galilean said: How does one derive that the Egyptians were struck with ten plagues in Egypt, but with fifty plagues at the Sea? — Concerning the plagues in Egypt the Torah states:

---

beasts. Paganism, which is nothing but institutionalized hedonism, recognizes only the physical world in which one can gratify one's desires, and giving up one's life is therefore senseless. The person who has one God and knows that this world is preparatory for the World to Come can accept martyrdom.

Pharoah's stubbornness was in the service of his ego, and crumbled when the ego itself was at risk. Obstinacy of *kedushah* is that which has resulted in our martyrs yielding their lives with the declaration of *Shema Yisrael.*

**רַבִּי יְהוּדָה הָיָה נוֹתֵן בָּהֶם סִמָּנִים: דְּצַ"ךְ עֲדַ"שׁ בְּאַחַ"ב — *Rabbi Yehudah abbreviated them by their Hebrew initials:* D'TZACH ADASH B'ACHAV.**

Countless explanations have been offered for Rabbi Yehudah's mnemonic. An amusing anecdote is that of Rabbi Heschel of Cracow.

> *Rabbi Heschel was a child prodigy. One time he accompanied his father on a trip, and they stayed at an inn. The innkeeper was extremely stingy, and served them in very tiny cups.*
>
> *When the innkeeper poured their drink into these tiny cups, the young Heschel remarked, "Now I understand Rabbi Yehudah's mnemonic in the Haggadah.*
>
> *"It is customary when reciting the ten plagues, to pour off a bit of wine at the mention of each plague. But if one were to do that at the Seder at this inn, one would be left without any wine remaining in the cup. To provide for such an exigency, Rabbi Yehudah therefore provided three words comprised of the initials of the plagues, so that one would only have to pour off three times instead of ten."*
>
> *Then the young Heschel said in a rather loud voice, "The innkeeper certainly has a larger cup for himself, so he can afford to pour off as he recites each of the ten plagues. So, the ten plagues are for the innkeeper, and the mnemonic is for the guests."*
>
> *All the guests laughed heartily, and the innkeeper got the message.*

וַיֹּאמְרוּ הַחַרְטֻמִּם אֶל פַּרְעֹה, אֶצְבַּע אֱלֹהִים הִוא.[1]
וְעַל הַיָּם מָה הוּא אוֹמֵר, וַיַּרְא יִשְׂרָאֵל אֶת הַיָּד
הַגְּדֹלָה אֲשֶׁר עָשָׂה יהוה בְּמִצְרַיִם, וַיִּירְאוּ הָעָם אֶת
יהוה, וַיַּאֲמִינוּ בַּיהוה וּבְמֹשֶׁה עַבְדּוֹ.[2] כַּמָּה לָקוּ
בְאֶצְבַּע? עֶשֶׂר מַכּוֹת. אֱמוֹר מֵעַתָּה, בְּמִצְרַיִם לָקוּ
עֶשֶׂר מַכּוֹת, וְעַל הַיָּם לָקוּ חֲמִשִּׁים מַכּוֹת.

(1) *Exodus* 8:15. (2) 14:31.

---

**וַיַּאֲמִינוּ בַּה׳ וּבְמֹשֶׁה עַבְדּוֹ — *And they believed in Hashem and in His servant Moshe.***

*A woman came to the Tzaddik of Sanz with a tale of woe. The Tzaddik reassured her to have faith in God, and He would surely help her.*

*The woman refused to be consoled. "That is not what it says in the siddur," she said. "In the siddur it says that God helped the Israelites and they saw His great wonders, and then they had faith in God. First He must help, and the faith comes afterward."*

*The Tzaddik smiled. "You are right," he said. "God must adhere to what it says in the siddur," and he gave her his blessing for a prompt salvation.*

There is a colloquial expression that "Seeing is believing." A bit of analysis will reveal that this is technically incorrect. One does not "believe" what one knows to be a fact by virtue of a sense experience. Thus, I do not "believe" that what is in front of me is a table, because I see it and I know it is there. If I am told there is a table in the next room, one which I do not see, then I may "believe" it is there. Seeing is actually the antithesis of believing.

Inasmuch as the Torah is always technically correct, why does it say that when the waters of the Red Sea divided, the Israelites "believed" in God? The Midrash states that when they said, "This is my God" (*Exodus* 15:2), the revelation of the Divine Presence was so obvious that they pointed at it with their fingers. Also, the Midrash states that the lowliest person had a greater revelation of the Divine Throne than did the prophet Ezekiel. If so, then there was nothing to "believe," because at this time the existence of God was a known fact.

As Jews are prone to do, we might answer this question with another question. There is a mitzvah of *emunah,* to believe in God. Was Moses unable to fulfill this mitzvah? Since Moses spoke to God directly, as the Torah says,

The magicians said to Pharaoh, "It is the finger of God."[1] However, of those at the Sea, the Torah relates: Israel saw the great "hand" which HASHEM laid upon the Egyptians, the people feared HASHEM and they believed in HASHEM and in His servant Moshe.[2] How many plagues did they receive with the finger? Ten! Then conclude that if they suffered ten plagues in Egypt [where they were struck with a finger], they must have been made to suffer fifty plagues at the Sea [where they were struck with a whole hand].

---

"face to face like a person speaks to a friend" (*Exodus* 33:11), then there was nothing for him to believe. Was Moses then deprived of the mitzvah of *emunah*?

The answer is that even though one knows that God exists, one cannot know the greatness of God. Even if God reveals Himself to a person, there is infinitely more about God that a person does not know. In fact, since God is in every way infinite, man cannot possibly grasp the greatness of God. Hence, as much as one factually knows, there is so much more that one does not know, and this is what one must believe. Moses fulfilled the mitzvah of *emunah* by believing in the infinity of God, the greatness of God, which far surpassed whatever was revealed to him. This is why the Torah refers to the Israelites' "belief" in God even when there was a vivid revelation. They believed about God that which they did not see.

As with belief in God so it is with spirituality. The *neshamah,* the human spirit, is the Divine soul, and as such it is infinite in capacity. One becomes spiritual by maximizing the components of one's soul, and since the soul is infinite, the development of spirituality should never come to an end. Physical growth comes to an end in early adult life, but spiritual growth should continue forever.

A person should never be satisfied with having reached a particular level of spirituality. Spiritual growth may be compared to pushing a wagon uphill. If one stops the upward movement, the wagon may roll back down, and within moments all the laborious effort expended in pushing it upward can be undone. So it is with spiritual growth. If one brings it to a halt, it may soon be lost. There have been tragic incidents in Jewish history [notably the case of Elisha ben Avuyah in the Talmud (*Chaggigah* 15a)] where such deteriorations have occurred.

Spirituality is thus a climb towards infinity, a goal which can never be reached, but towards which every spiritual person must nevertheless strive.

**רַבִּי אֱלִיעֶזֶר** אוֹמֵר: מִנַּיִן שֶׁכָּל מַכָּה וּמַכָּה שֶׁהֵבִיא הַקָּדוֹשׁ בָּרוּךְ הוּא עַל הַמִּצְרִים בְּמִצְרַיִם הָיְתָה שֶׁל אַרְבַּע מַכּוֹת? שֶׁנֶּאֱמַר, יְשַׁלַּח בָּם חֲרוֹן אַפּוֹ – עֶבְרָה, וָזַעַם, וְצָרָה, מִשְׁלַחַת מַלְאֲכֵי רָעִים.[1] עֶבְרָה, אַחַת. וָזַעַם, שְׁתַּיִם. וְצָרָה, שָׁלֹשׁ. מִשְׁלַחַת מַלְאֲכֵי רָעִים, אַרְבַּע. אֱמוֹר מֵעַתָּה, בְּמִצְרַיִם לָקוּ אַרְבָּעִים מַכּוֹת, וְעַל הַיָּם לָקוּ מָאתַיִם מַכּוֹת.

**רַבִּי עֲקִיבָא** אוֹמֵר: מִנַּיִן שֶׁכָּל מַכָּה וּמַכָּה שֶׁהֵבִיא הַקָּדוֹשׁ בָּרוּךְ הוּא עַל הַמִּצְרִים בְּמִצְרַיִם הָיְתָה שֶׁל חָמֵשׁ מַכּוֹת? שֶׁנֶּאֱמַר, יְשַׁלַּח בָּם חֲרוֹן אַפּוֹ, עֶבְרָה, וָזַעַם, וְצָרָה, מִשְׁלַחַת מַלְאֲכֵי רָעִים. חֲרוֹן אַפּוֹ, אַחַת. עֶבְרָה, שְׁתַּיִם. וָזַעַם, שָׁלֹשׁ. וְצָרָה, אַרְבַּע. מִשְׁלַחַת מַלְאֲכֵי רָעִים, חָמֵשׁ. אֱמוֹר מֵעַתָּה, בְּמִצְרַיִם לָקוּ חֲמִשִּׁים מַכּוֹת, וְעַל הַיָּם לָקוּ חֲמִשִּׁים וּמָאתַיִם מַכּוֹת.

---

◆ **מִנַּיִן שֶׁכָּל מַכָּה וּמַכָּה . . . אַרְבַּע מַכּוֹת** ◆ — ***How does one derive . . . four plagues***

What is the point of telling us the complexity of the plagues? Is the Scriptural version that there were ten severe plagues which ultimately brought Pharaoh to his knees not adequate? Furthermore, why do the Talmudic scholars differ as to the number of components of each plague?

Earlier we noted that the account of the plagues — with the repeated warnings to Pharaoh, his repeated submission under stress, and his repeated reneging on his promises — is very similar to the course of the addicted person, who is warned, who suffers, who promises, and who relapses. We also pointed out that even in the absence of addiction, a similar pattern of denial and recalcitrance may occur in a somewhat less dramatic fashion among many people.

**רַבִּי אֱלִיעֶזֶר** Rabbi Eliezer said: How does one derive that every plague that the Holy One, Blessed is He, inflicted upon the Egyptians in Egypt was equal to four plagues? — for it is written: He sent upon them His fierce anger: wrath, fury, and trouble, a band of emissaries of evil.[1] [Since each plague in Egypt consisted of] 1) wrath, 2) fury, 3) trouble, and 4) a band of emissaries of evil, therefore conclude that in Egypt they were struck by forty plagues and by the Sea two hundred!

**רַבִּי עֲקִיבָא** Rabbi Akiva said: How does one derive that each plague that the Holy One, Blessed is He, inflicted upon the Egyptians in Egypt was equal to five plagues? — For it is written: He sent upon them His fierce anger, wrath, fury, trouble, and a band of emissaries of evil. [Since each plague in Egypt consisted of] 1) fierce anger, 2) wrath, 3) fury, 4) trouble, and 5) a band of emissaries of evil, therefore conclude that in Egypt they were struck by fifty plagues and by the Sea two hundred and fifty!

(1) *Psalms* 78:49.

---

The saga of the plagues can be seen as a study of human nature. One might suppose that if each plague had been just a bit more severe, Pharaoh would have surrendered earlier. Rabbi Eliezer therefore tells us that each plague was indeed more severe than we generally assume, but Pharaoh remained recalcitrant nonetheless. In other words, obstinacy and self-righteousness might not be overcome even by severe distress. Rabbi Akiva goes one step further, asserting that the plagues were even more severe than Rabbi Eliezer believed them to be, and yet Pharaoh did not yield until the bitter end.

The point of all this is to emphasize how oblivious a person may be to his own self-destructive behavior and that refusal to admit he has been wrong, as well as denial and resistance to change, can persist even in the face of overwhelming suffering. All this emphasis on the resistance to change should help us realize that we are all susceptible to the foibles of human nature, and unless we understand this and become more willing to question the certainty of our opinions and be more amenable to change, we may bring about unimaginable harm to ourselves.

## כַּמָּה מַעֲלוֹת טוֹבוֹת לַמָּקוֹם עָלֵינוּ.

אִלּוּ הוֹצִיאָנוּ מִמִּצְרַיִם,
וְלֹא עָשָׂה בָהֶם שְׁפָטִים, דַּיֵּנוּ.
אִלּוּ עָשָׂה בָהֶם שְׁפָטִים,
וְלֹא עָשָׂה בֵאלֹהֵיהֶם, דַּיֵּנוּ.
אִלּוּ עָשָׂה בֵאלֹהֵיהֶם,
וְלֹא הָרַג אֶת בְּכוֹרֵיהֶם, דַּיֵּנוּ.
אִלּוּ הָרַג אֶת בְּכוֹרֵיהֶם,
וְלֹא נָתַן לָנוּ אֶת מָמוֹנָם, דַּיֵּנוּ.
אִלּוּ נָתַן לָנוּ אֶת מָמוֹנָם,
וְלֹא קָרַע לָנוּ אֶת הַיָּם, דַּיֵּנוּ.
אִלּוּ קָרַע לָנוּ אֶת הַיָּם,
וְלֹא הֶעֱבִירָנוּ בְתוֹכוֹ בֶּחָרָבָה, דַּיֵּנוּ.

---

**כַּמָּה מַעֲלוֹת טוֹבוֹת לַמָּקוֹם עָלֵינוּ — *The Omnipresent has bestowed so many favors upon us***

This is a rather strange hymn. At first glance, some of the verses do not stand to reason. For example, "Had He given us their wealth, but not split the Sea for us, it would have sufficed us." Of what possible value would wealth have been if the Sea would not have been divided for the Israelites? Inasmuch as they were trapped between the oncoming Egyptian army and the Sea, they were doomed to annihilation unless there would be an escape route through the Sea. Or, "Had he split the Sea for us, but not led us through it on dry land, it would have sufficed us." Of what use would the miraculous separation of the waters have been if the Israelites had not traversed the Sea? In what way would some of these acts without those which followed have been sufficient?

There is an important lesson to be derived from this hymn. We must learn to be grateful for every favor we receive, even if at the moment we cannot see its ultimate good. The refrain "It would have sufficed us" means that every incident in the many events of the Exodus was sufficient to elicit prompt gratitude from us, even though the eventual benefit

**The Omnipresent has bestowed so many favors upon us!**

Had He brought us out of Egypt,
  but not executed judgments against the Egyptians,
    it would have sufficed us.
Had He executed judgments against them,
  but not upon their gods, it would have sufficed us.
Had He executed judgments against their gods,
  but not slain their firstborn, it would have sufficed us.
Had He slain their firstborn,
  but not given us their wealth, it would have sufficed us.
Had He given us their wealth,
  but not split the Sea for us, it would have sufficed us.
Had He split the Sea for us,
  but not led us through it on dry land,
    it would have sufficed us.

---

might not have been immediately apparent.

The ability to feel and express gratitude is a vital component of spirituality. Many people have difficulty with gratitude, perhaps because they think that acknowledging gratitude obligates them to their benefactor, and generally people do not like to feel beholden to anyone. Some people may even consciously or unconsciously deny what was done for them in order to avoid feeling grateful. Even if there is no frank denial of the favor, there may be a tendency to postpone expressing gratitude until one sees whether the favor has indeed brought about the desired result.

Spirituality requires overcoming all resistances to gratitude. This hymn tells us that each favor the Israelites received warranted a prompt expression of gratitude to God, even for those incidents where the favor might have appeared to be futile.

One person said, "By thanking God for the day that has passed, I merit His blessing for the day that is to come." Acknowledging the Divine benevolence elicits further beneficence, so that we can earn the future by being grateful for the past. None of the acts that appeared to be futile were really so. For example, by being grateful for receiving the wealth of their captives, the Israelites merited the next step in their salvation, and so with all other occurrences listed.

As we advance in spirituality, we should advance in acknowledging the kindnesses we receive, and promptly express our gratitude for them.

אִלּוּ הֶעֱבִירָנוּ בְתוֹכוֹ בֶּחָרָבָה,
וְלֹא שִׁקַּע צָרֵינוּ בְּתוֹכוֹ, דַּיֵּנוּ.
אִלּוּ שִׁקַּע צָרֵינוּ בְּתוֹכוֹ,
וְלֹא סִפֵּק צָרְכֵּנוּ בַּמִּדְבָּר אַרְבָּעִים שָׁנָה, דַּיֵּנוּ.
אִלּוּ סִפֵּק צָרְכֵּנוּ בַּמִּדְבָּר אַרְבָּעִים שָׁנָה,
וְלֹא הֶאֱכִילָנוּ אֶת הַמָּן, דַּיֵּנוּ.
אִלּוּ הֶאֱכִילָנוּ אֶת הַמָּן,
וְלֹא נָתַן לָנוּ אֶת הַשַּׁבָּת, דַּיֵּנוּ.
אִלּוּ נָתַן לָנוּ אֶת הַשַּׁבָּת,
וְלֹא קֵרְבָנוּ לִפְנֵי הַר סִינַי, דַּיֵּנוּ.
אִלּוּ קֵרְבָנוּ לִפְנֵי הַר סִינַי,
וְלֹא נָתַן לָנוּ אֶת הַתּוֹרָה, דַּיֵּנוּ.

---

**אִלּוּ קֵרְבָנוּ לִפְנֵי הַר סִינַי, וְלֹא נָתַן לָנוּ אֶת הַתּוֹרָה, דַּיֵּנוּ** — ***Had He brought us before Mount Sinai, but not given us the Torah, it would have sufficed us.***

The obvious question is: What good would it have been to be at Sinai without receiving the Torah? The answer to this provides us with an important psychological principle: an understanding of the essential nature of man.

King Solomon says, "God made man straight" (*Ecclesiastes* 7:29). Straight and simple, but man sought to complicate things by deviating from the straight path.

The Talmud states that if the Torah had not been given, one could have learned proper behavior from the observation of animals in nature. One would have learned the sanctity of private property by observing ants; marital fidelity by observing pigeons; modesty by observing cats (*Eruvin* 100b). Various animals have traits which man could have adopted.

But who is to say that in absence of the Torah we would have emulated these admirable traits? Perhaps we would have learned promiscuity by observing dogs and rapaciousness from observing tigers. It must be that if we approached nature with an unbiased attitude, we would have known which traits to learn from whom, because man is fundamentally *yashar*. It is only

Had He led us through on dry land,
but not drowned our oppressors in it,
it would have sufficed us.
Had He drowned our oppressors in it, but not provided for our needs in the desert for forty years,
it would have sufficed us.
Had He provided for our needs in the desert for forty years,
but not fed us the Manna, it would have sufficed us.
Had He fed us the Manna,
but not given us the Shabbos, it would have sufficed us.
Had He given us the Shabbos,
but not brought us before Mount Sinai,
it would have sufficed us.
Had He brought us before Mount Sinai,
but not given us the Torah, it would have sufficed us.

---

because man gives into his physical drives that he rationalizes his behavior and thereby deviates from being *yashar.*

The Talmud states that the Patriarchs observed the entire Torah before it was given. How can this be? How could they have known what is proper and what is forbidden? The answer is that although Abraham was born into a family of idolaters, his clear thinking led him to the conclusion that idolatry is wrong, and he was able to grasp the truth of there being one God by sound reasoning. Abraham's search for the truth did not allow his intellect to be misled by his bodily urges. Abraham was spiritual.

The spiritual person is thus the pristine of *yashar,* the straight and simple being that God created. Like Abraham, someone who is willing to set aside one's personal temptations and search for absolute truth will find it, will become *yashar,* and by observance of nature will know which traits are admirable and which are condemnable. The *yashar* would learn the correct attitude towards private property from the ant and not from the tiger.

What happened at Sinai was that during the three days of preparation for receiving the Torah, under the tutelage of Moses, the Israelites achieved a status of spirituality similar to that of the Patriarchs, and like the Patriarchs, could have grasped the entire Torah even if it had not been given. Hence being at Sinai without actually receiving the Torah would have been a great accomplishment.

אִלּוּ נָתַן לָנוּ אֶת הַתּוֹרָה,
וְלֹא הִכְנִיסָנוּ לְאֶרֶץ יִשְׂרָאֵל, דַּיֵּנוּ.
אִלּוּ הִכְנִיסָנוּ לְאֶרֶץ יִשְׂרָאֵל,
וְלֹא בָנָה לָנוּ אֶת בֵּית הַבְּחִירָה, דַּיֵּנוּ.

**עַל** אַחַת כַּמָּה, וְכַמָּה טוֹבָה כְפוּלָה וּמְכֻפֶּלֶת לַמָּקוֹם עָלֵינוּ. שֶׁהוֹצִיאָנוּ מִמִּצְרַיִם, וְעָשָׂה בָהֶם שְׁפָטִים, וְעָשָׂה בֵאלֹהֵיהֶם, וְהָרַג אֶת בְּכוֹרֵיהֶם, וְנָתַן לָנוּ אֶת מָמוֹנָם, וְקָרַע לָנוּ אֶת הַיָּם, וְהֶעֱבִירָנוּ בְתוֹכוֹ בֶּחָרָבָה, וְשִׁקַּע צָרֵינוּ בְּתוֹכוֹ, וְסִפֵּק צָרְכֵּנוּ בַּמִּדְבָּר אַרְבָּעִים שָׁנָה, וְהֶאֱכִילָנוּ אֶת הַמָּן, וְנָתַן לָנוּ אֶת הַשַּׁבָּת, וְקֵרְבָנוּ לִפְנֵי הַר סִינַי, וְנָתַן לָנוּ אֶת הַתּוֹרָה, וְהִכְנִיסָנוּ לְאֶרֶץ יִשְׂרָאֵל, וּבָנָה לָנוּ אֶת בֵּית הַבְּחִירָה, לְכַפֵּר עַל כָּל עֲוֹנוֹתֵינוּ.

**רַבָּן גַּמְלִיאֵל** הָיָה אוֹמֵר: כָּל שֶׁלֹּא אָמַר שְׁלֹשָׁה דְבָרִים אֵלּוּ בַּפֶּסַח, לֹא יָצָא יְדֵי חוֹבָתוֹ, וְאֵלּוּ הֵן,

**פֶּסַח. מַצָּה. וּמָרוֹר.**

---

What this teaches us is that we have an innate concept of right and wrong, good and evil, because we were created *yashar.* If only we do not allow ourselves to be seduced by the wiles of the *yetzer hara,* we will be the spiritual beings that God meant us to be. The more we strive for spirituality, the greater will be the clarity of our perception of what is proper and what is improper. Perhaps that is the concept of *teshuvah,* which literally means return — to return to the nascent state of *yashar* in which we were created.

### ◆§ פֶּסַח מַצָּה וּמָרוֹר — *Pesach, Matzah and Maror*

Earlier we noted that merely meditating about a mitzvah is not sufficient, and that spirituality is affected more by behavior than by intellectual insights. However, the converse may also be true. Acts that are performed

Had He given us the Torah,
but not brought us into the Land of Israel,
it would have sufficed us.
Had He brought us into the Land of Israel,
but not built for us the *Beis HaMikdash,*
it would have sufficed us.

**עַל** Thus, how much more so, should we be grateful to the Omnipresent for all the numerous favors He showered upon us: He brought us out of Egypt; executed judgments against the Egyptians; and against their gods; slew their firstborn; gave us their wealth; split the Sea for us; led us through it on dry land; drowned our oppressors in it; provided for our needs in the desert for forty years; fed us the Manna; gave us the Shabbos; brought us before Mount Sinai; gave us the Torah; brought us to the Land of Israel; and built us the Temple, to atone for all our sins.

**רַבָּן גַּמְלִיאֵל** Rabban Gamliel used to say: Whoever has not explained the following three things on Passover has not fulfilled his duty; namely,

**PESACH** — the Pesach offering;
**MATZAH** — the unleavened bread;
**MAROR** — the bitter herbs.

---

without proper *kavanah* (thought and intent) are insipid and may even be useless.

In the Talmud there is a discussion on whether a mitzvah which is performed without *kavanah* has merit. While the conclusion in *halachah* is that the act itself is of value, there are some mitzvos where *kavanah* is absolutely essential, and lack of *kavanah* makes the mitzvah grossly incomplete. An example of this is the mitzvah of prayer, where recitation of words without thinking of their meaning is of little value. The *Shelah* comments on this very graphically: "Prayer without *kavanah* is like a body without a soul," and like a lifeless body, is functionless. Rabban Gamliel contends that the three Passover mitzvos are similar to prayer, and that *kavanah* is an absolute essential for all three. Unless one recognizes the significance of the Paschal offering as a repudiation of paganism, one has merely eaten a piece of broiled meat, and the same holds true for matzah and *maror.*

**פֶּסַח** שֶׁהָיוּ אֲבוֹתֵינוּ אוֹכְלִים בִּזְמַן שֶׁבֵּית הַמִּקְדָּשׁ הָיָה קַיָּם, עַל שׁוּם מָה? עַל שׁוּם שֶׁפָּסַח הַקָּדוֹשׁ בָּרוּךְ הוּא עַל בָּתֵּי אֲבוֹתֵינוּ בְּמִצְרַיִם. שֶׁנֶּאֱמַר, וַאֲמַרְתֶּם, זֶבַח פֶּסַח הוּא לַיהוה, אֲשֶׁר פָּסַח עַל בָּתֵּי בְנֵי יִשְׂרָאֵל בְּמִצְרַיִם בְּנָגְפּוֹ אֶת מִצְרַיִם, וְאֶת בָּתֵּינוּ הִצִּיל, וַיִּקֹּד הָעָם וַיִּשְׁתַּחֲווּ.[1]

---

Rabban Gamaliel does not refer to the significance of the matzah as the bread of *affliction,* as was mentioned at the beginning of the Haggadah, but rather as the bread of *deliverance,* since it represents the haste with which the Israelites fled from Egypt. *Maror,* on the other hand, clearly refers to the period of oppression. If so, the order in the Haggadah appears to be reversed, because chronologically there was first the *maror* of the oppression, and only later the matzah of the deliverance.

Earlier we noted that the Israelites in Egypt had not only resigned themselves to a life of slavery, but had so adapted to it that many opposed Moses' mission to achieve their freedom, and that Moses' first task was to convince them of the superiority of freedom over slavery. While Moses ultimately succeeded in doing so, we noted earlier that a residue of longing for the "good old days" of enslavement nevertheless persisted to some degree. It was only after the Israelites ultimately adapted to liberty that they were able to look back on the period of enslavement and see it for what it truly was: bitter, cruel oppression.

The realization of the bitterness of oppression thus did not occur until long *after* the deliverance; hence the symbolism of *maror* is performed *after* the symbolism of deliverance, the matzah, and herein lies an important teaching.

One recovered addict, who had resisted entering treatment for years, said, "The worst day of my sobriety is far better than the best day of my addiction." He did not make this statement until his third year of recovery. Not only had he been oblivious of the pathology of his addiction while it was active, he did not even appreciate its gravity until he was well into his recovery.

It is possible for us to have less-than-optimum lifestyles without being aware of it, and we may resist constructive changes even if we do become aware. But even when we are finally convinced of the necessity to effect modifications in our lifestyle and actually begin doing so, we may so resent the discomfort involved in making changes that we may revert to our previous habits. The acceptance that change was necessary may only have

**פֶּסַח** Pesach — Why did our fathers eat a Pesach offering during the period when the *Beis HaMikdash* stood? — Because the Holy One, Blessed is He, passed over the houses of our fathers in Egypt, as it is written: You shall say: "It is a Pesach offering for HASHEM, Who passed over the houses of the Children of Israel in Egypt when He struck the Egyptians and spared our houses; and the people bowed down and prostrated themselves."[1]

(1) *Exodus* 12:27.

---

been achieved on an intellectual level, and intellect may not be sufficient to withstand the temptation to revert to the old established, comfortable behavior. The emotional insight on the value of the changes may not occur for a while, and during this interval, much effort must be exerted to avoid relapse.

Reversing the chronological order and placing the *maror* after the matzah should remind us that we may need to wait a bit for an emotional appreciation to replace that which had only been an intellectual concept.

### ◆§ פֶּסַח — *A Pesach offering*

The Paschal offering consisted of sacrificing a lamb, which was the Egyptian totem (*Exodus* 8:22), and this ritual therefore represented the repudiation of paganism by the Israelites.

The Sages of the Talmud state that the Israelites had not only been physically enslaved in Egypt, but that they had also adopted much of the Egyptian ideology. The lamb, which was the Egyptian totem, was the zenith of the zodiac, and at the top of the hierarchy of their idol worship. This particular ideology was totally deterministic, with everything being subject to irrevocable laws of nature. There was no possible appeal to Divine guidance and Divine intervention. Man had no free will, and there was thus no place for spiritual aspirations. Such an ideology advocated: "Eat, drink, and be merry, for tomorrow we die."

Paganism or idolatry is not so much a religion of worshiping an idol as a philosophy of indulgence. The sole purpose of its being couched in religious terms is to provide sanction for a person to gratify all his desires without having to feel any guilt for doing so. Although paganism has assumedly been rejected for many centuries, the current trend to decriminalize various

The middle matzah is lifted and displayed while the following paragraph is recited.

**מַצָּה** זוּ שֶׁאָנוּ אוֹכְלִים, עַל שׁוּם מָה? עַל שׁוּם שֶׁלֹּא הִסְפִּיק בְּצֵקָם שֶׁל אֲבוֹתֵינוּ לְהַחֲמִיץ, עַד שֶׁנִּגְלָה עֲלֵיהֶם מֶלֶךְ מַלְכֵי הַמְּלָכִים הַקָּדוֹשׁ בָּרוּךְ הוּא וּגְאָלָם. שֶׁנֶּאֱמַר, וַיֹּאפוּ אֶת הַבָּצֵק אֲשֶׁר הוֹצִיאוּ מִמִּצְרַיִם עֻגֹת מַצּוֹת כִּי לֹא חָמֵץ, כִּי גֹרְשׁוּ מִמִּצְרַיִם, וְלֹא יָכְלוּ לְהִתְמַהְמֵהַּ, וְגַם צֵדָה לֹא עָשׂוּ לָהֶם.[1]

The *maror* is lifted and displayed while the following paragraph is recited.

**מָרוֹר** זֶה שֶׁאָנוּ אוֹכְלִים, עַל שׁוּם מָה? עַל שׁוּם שֶׁמֵּרְרוּ הַמִּצְרִים אֶת חַיֵּי אֲבוֹתֵינוּ בְּמִצְרַיִם.

(1) *Exodus* 12:39.

---

immoral behaviors is nothing but a sophisticated variation of paganism.

On the eve of Passover when the firstborn were smitten, the homes of the Israelites that were marked as having brought the Paschal offering were spared. The redemption from physical enslavement could be achieved with the defeat of the Egyptian army, but spiritual redemption required an indication that one was prepared to reject hedonism as a way of life, and opt for spiritual goals and values.

### ◆§ מַצָּה — *Matzah*

The Israelites had to leave Egypt in such great haste that they could not afford the few extra moments necessary to allow their dough to rise into bread. The reason for the haste, the Torah tells us, is "because they could not delay." The *Ari* explains that the Israelites had deteriorated to a very low level and lost their spirituality in the environment of immorality that prevailed in Egypt. Only a tiny spark of spirituality remained, and had they stayed in Egypt even one moment longer, that faint spark too would have been extinguished, and they would have then been beyond redemption. This haste in leaving resulted in the dough becoming matzah, which therefore represents the near totality of their loss of spirituality, and the great compassion by God to extract them before they would reach the stage of irreversibility.

*Chametz* has another connotation. *Chametz* is something which has extensive power to convert something to its own kind. I.e., if one were to take

The middle matzah is lifted and displayed while the following paragraph is recited.

**מַצָּה** Matzah — Why do we eat this unleavened bread? — Because the dough of our fathers did not have time to become leavened before the King of kings, the Holy One, Blessed is He, revealed Himself to them and redeemed them, as it is written: They baked the dough which they had brought out of Egypt into unleavened bread, for it had not fermented, because they were driven out of Egypt and could not delay, nor had they prepared any provisions for the way.[1]

The *maror* is lifted and displayed while the following paragraph is recited.

**מָרוֹר** Maror — Why do we eat these bitter herbs? — Because the Egyptians embittered the lives of our fathers in Egypt, as it says: They embittered their lives with hard labor,

---

a large batch of dough and introduce just a tiny morsel of sour dough, this small fragment can act enzymatically to cause the entire batch to ferment. This, too, is the nature of indulgence or immorality. It does not take an enormous force to cause spiritual deterioration. The infectious nature of physical indulgence is such that given the slightest opportunity to take hold, it can completely corrupt a previously spiritual person. Recovering alcoholics, for example, are well aware of this principle. Even after years of hard-won sobriety, allowing a single drop of alcohol to enter the system can very quickly undo everything that had been laboriously achieved. This is why *chametz* is forbidden even in the most infinitesimally small quantity.

The concepts of matzah and *chametz* thus stand side by side, representing principles vital to the maintenance of spirituality. *Chametz* teaches us that even a tiny fragment can have very far-reaching consequences, and matzah teaches us that it is possible for deterioration to be so complete that one may reach a state of irreversibility from which there is no redemption. Both concepts must be remembered by anyone who cherishes spirituality.

### ◆§ מָרוֹר — *Maror*

Although there is a widespread custom to use horseradish for *maror* because of its pungent taste, the *Shulchan Aruch* cites one opinion in the Talmud that a species of lettuce is preferable (particularly romaine lettuce, if it can be cleansed of all insects). The reason given by the Talmud is that this variety of lettuce begins as a very soft plant, but in time its core hardens. This symbolizes the insidious entrapment of the Israelites by the Egyptians. Initially they took a soft approach, hiring them as highly paid workers, and

שֶׁנֶּאֱמַר, וַיְמָרְרוּ אֶת חַיֵּיהֶם, בַּעֲבֹדָה קָשָׁה, בְּחֹמֶר וּבִלְבֵנִים, וּבְכָל עֲבֹדָה בַּשָּׂדֶה, אֵת כָּל עֲבֹדָתָם אֲשֶׁר עָבְדוּ בָהֶם בְּפָרֶךְ.[1]

**בְּכָל דּוֹר** וָדוֹר חַיָּב אָדָם לִרְאוֹת אֶת עַצְמוֹ כְּאִלּוּ הוּא יָצָא מִמִּצְרָיִם. שֶׁנֶּאֱמַר, וְהִגַּדְתָּ לְבִנְךָ בַּיּוֹם הַהוּא לֵאמֹר, בַּעֲבוּר זֶה עָשָׂה יהוה לִי, בְּצֵאתִי מִמִּצְרָיִם.[2] לֹא אֶת אֲבוֹתֵינוּ בִּלְבָד

---

then hardened their grasp on them as they gradually converted them into total slaves. The lesson to be learned therefrom, say the Commentaries, is that we must be on the alert for the cunning of the *yetzer hara,* which rarely conducts a frontal attack on one's spirituality. Rather, the individual is lured into an apparent innocent pastime, and the *yetzer hara* imperceptibly drives him into progressively greater indulgence, until he becomes totally devoid of morality and a slave to his biological drives.

For this reason, the matzah and *maror* are eaten with the Passover offering, and according to Hillel, combined together in *Korach.* All three relate to the maintenance of spirituality. *Maror,* by alerting one to the insidious cunning of the *yetzer hara,* matzah by symbolizing, as noted above, the depth of the deterioration into which a person may be drawn, and the Passover offering, the repudiation of idolatry, of any system which offers official approval for submitting to one's physical drives. Rabban Gamliel correctly points out that only when one has correctly grasped the meaning of these three symbols has one fulfilled one's spiritual obligations.

*A young man left his shtetl to immigrate to America but failed to write home. He was quite resourceful, and his mother learned from visitors that he had been successful and was living comfortably. They also told her his address. Inasmuch as she was illiterate, she went to the village scribe to have a letter written for her.*

*The mother dictated to the scribe: "Dear Son, I was glad to hear that you are well. Thank God I am well too. We have had a cold winter and I could not afford much firewood, but thank God I was able to keep the wind out by stuffing rags into the crevices. Now the winter is over, and when it rains the roof leaks, but thank God I have been able to patch it with tin sheets. Food is very expensive, but thank God it is possible to*

with mortar and bricks, and with all manner of labor in the field: whatever service they made them perform was with hard labor.[1]

**בְּכָל דּוֹר** In every generation it is one's duty to regard himself as though he personally had gone out of Egypt, as it is written: You shall tell your son on that day: "It was because of this that HASHEM did for **'me'** when I went out of Egypt."[2] It was not only our fathers

(1) *Exodus* 1:14. (2) 13:8.

---

*get day-old bread quite cheaply. Our cow stopped giving milk, but thank God I was able to find a customer who bought it for meat. I will manage somehow with God's help."*

*The scribe was horrified by the son's dereliction in helping his mother, and he wrote as follows: "Dear Son, I heard from visitors that you are well off, and I cannot understand why you have not helped me. During the harsh winter I had to stuff rags into the crevices to keep out the wind, but without fire the house was freezing. Now that the winter is over, the rain leaks in. All I can afford to eat is stale bread, and now that our cow stopped giving milk, I barely have enough food to survive."*

*When the scribe read aloud the letter he had written, the woman clapped her hands in grief. "Oy vay," she said. "I never knew how bad off I was."*

There is a proverb that a worm that infests a horseradish root must think, "This is the sweetest place in the world." We may be so accustomed to an inadequate living standard that we accept it as normal. We are more likely to become aware of material deprivation, but lack of spirituality may go unnoticed. It is only after the matzah of liberation that we may appreciate the *maror* of enslavement.

### ☙ בְּכָל דּוֹר וָדוֹר חַיָּב אָדָם לִרְאוֹת אֶת עַצְמוֹ כְּאִלּוּ הוּא יָצָא מִמִּצְרָיִם — *In every generation it is one's duty to regard himself as though he personally had gone out of Egypt*

In every generation one is obligated to see oneself as though he emerged from Egypt.

Although one recites the Haggadah and even elaborates on all the aspects of the story of the Exodus, one has not yet fulfilled one's obligation.

גָּאַל הַקָּדוֹשׁ בָּרוּךְ הוּא, אֶלָּא אַף אוֹתָנוּ גָּאַל עִמָּהֶם. שֶׁנֶּאֱמַר, וְאוֹתָנוּ הוֹצִיא מִשָּׁם, לְמַעַן הָבִיא אֹתָנוּ לָתֶת לָנוּ אֶת הָאָרֶץ אֲשֶׁר נִשְׁבַּע לַאֲבוֹתֵינוּ.[1]

---

It is mandatory that one experience the Exodus personally.

This is not as difficult as it sounds. Our imaginations are very creative, as evidenced by how vividly we can dream in our sleep, and how vividly we can daydream when we are awake. Our ingenious minds can create three-dimensional scenes in rich color, and we can see ourselves fully participating in these scenes. Being familiar with the story of the Exodus, one should meditate and create the various scenes in one's mind. One should see oneself in the straw pits, clearing the straw, mixing it with mud, and baking it into bricks in the tropical sun. One should hear the scolding of the Egyptian taskmasters, and feel the lashes of their whips on one's back. One should then visualize the various plagues and the panic of the Egyptians. Then one should see oneself as part of the throng leaving Egypt, following Moses into the barren desert. Finally, one should be standing at the edge of the Red Sea, and hear the thunder of Pharaoh's chariots approaching, feel the terror of being trapped, and then see the glory of God as the waters of the Red Sea divide.

Exercising one's imagination in this way is mandatory. The sweet taste of liberty cannot be appreciated as long as oppression is only an abstraction. The acceptance of the omnipotence of God is incomplete unless one has seen the many miracles with one's own eyes.

The *Seder* ritual facilitates this experience. We eat the matzah, the bread which the slaves were given to satiate their hunger. We taste the bitterness of the *maror*. We explain in great detail every step of the Exodus. Now one must close one's eyes and relive the Exodus oneself, for only then can we fully appreciate its greatness, and only then can we properly acknowledge our gratitude to God.

### ☙ *Maximizing One's Potential*

Ah! To be able to see oneself!

The primary theme that runs through many of my writings (*Let Us Make Man* [CIS Publications]; *When Do the Good Things Start?* [Pharos Books]; *Life's Too Short* [St. Martin's Press]) is the need for a person to have a valid self-perception. Many of people's psychological woes are due to a low self-esteem, which is in turn due to a distorted self-perception, with

whom the Holy One redeemed from slavery; we, too, were redeemed with them, as it is written: He brought **"us"** out from there so that He might take us to the land which He had promised to our fathers.[1]

(1) *Deuteronomy* 6:23.

---

unwarranted feelings of inadequacy, inferiority, and unworthiness. If only a person could see himself as he really is, many unhappy situations could be avoided. In every generation and at all times, a person is duty bound to see himself as he really is.

But what about the conclusion of the sentence, "as though he personally had gone out of Egypt"? What does that have to do with a self-image? The *Tiferes Yisrael* cites a Midrash that a king had heard about Moses' greatness, and he dispatched his artists to bring him back a likeness of Moses. When they returned, he submitted the portrait to his wise men who were physiognomists; i.e., they could deduce a person's character from the study of his facial features. The wise men reported that Moses was vain, greedy, lustful, arrogant, brutal, and in every way the polar opposite of what the king had heard. The king was perplexed, because he had utmost confidence in the accuracy of his artists and the competency of his wise men, and he decided to make the trip to the desert to see Moses for himself.

When the king met Moses, he saw that his artists' drawing had been perfect. He then shared with Moses how far off his physiognomists had been. Moses explained to the king that his experts were not wrong at all. "You see," he said, "all that they can gather from a study of facial features is what kind of character traits were inherent in a person from birth, and in this respect they were right. I was born with all the capacities to be decadent. However, I channeled all these tendencies towards spiritual goals, and converted them so that I am indeed greedy to achieve more spiritual wealth, and I do lust with a passion for an ever-closer relationship with God. These converted traits were not detectable to your wise men."

Many people might be alarmed to discover in themselves such negative character traits, and they may therefore either refuse to look at themselves or disown these components of their characters. In either case, they will not gain a knowledge of their true selves. Moses did neither. He became aware of them, was not frightened by them, and redirected them towards constructive goals.

We have already noted that the Exodus from *Mitzrayim,* from Egypt, is also to be understood as an escape from *metzarim,* from the limitations that

The matzos are covered and the cup is lifted and held until it is to be drunk. According to some customs, however, the cup is put down after the following paragraph, in which case the matzos should once more be uncovered. If this custom is followed, the matzos are to be covered and the cup raised again upon reaching the blessing אֲשֶׁר גְּאָלָנוּ, Who has redeemed us (p. 150).

**לְפִיכָךְ** אֲנַחְנוּ חַיָּבִים לְהוֹדוֹת, לְהַלֵּל, לְשַׁבֵּחַ, לְפָאֵר, לְרוֹמֵם, לְהַדֵּר, לְבָרֵךְ, לְעַלֵּה, וּלְקַלֵּס, לְמִי שֶׁעָשָׂה לַאֲבוֹתֵינוּ וְלָנוּ אֶת כָּל הַנִּסִּים הָאֵלּוּ, הוֹצִיאָנוּ מֵעַבְדוּת לְחֵרוּת, מִיָּגוֹן לְשִׂמְחָה, וּמֵאֵבֶל לְיוֹם טוֹב, וּמֵאֲפֵלָה לְאוֹר גָּדוֹל, וּמִשִּׁעְבּוּד לִגְאֻלָּה, וְנֹאמַר לְפָנָיו שִׁירָה חֲדָשָׁה, הַלְלוּיָהּ.

---

constrict a person and prevent him from maximizing his potential. A person may apply *Yetzias Mitzrayim* to himself, and by converting any negative traits towards positive goals, rise above his restraints, and like Moses, fully realize his potential for spirituality. Thus a person is duty bound to look at himself and apply the principles of the Exodus to liberate himself from the boundaries and limitations of his physical drives, to become fully spiritual.

### ◆§ וְנֹאמַר לְפָנָיו שִׁירָה חֲדָשָׁה — *Let us, therefore, recite a new song before Him*

Song has always occupied an important place in Judaism. The songs of the Levites were exquisite, and the training a Levite had to undergo before being permitted to perform in the Temple was most demanding. King David composed his beautiful songs to the tune of the harp. According to the Midrash, the harp was placed near his bed, and when the night breeze caused the strings to vibrate, King David awoke to sing his Divine songs in praise of God.

In recent history, the chassidic masters employed songs, both songs of devotion, whose profound tunes enhanced depth of meditation and soul searching, and songs of *simchah,* to arouse one to dance with the joy of being a servant of God, chosen to perform His *mitzvos.*

*There are many stories about the potency of song. It is told that a scholar once posed a most difficult problem in Talmud to Rabbi Schneur Zalman, who responded with singing a tune of dveikus, a serene melody of longing for God, one which can cleanse the mind of*

The matzos are covered and the cup is lifted and held until it is to be drunk. According to some customs, however, the cup is put down after the following paragraph, in which case the matzos should once more be uncovered. If this custom is followed, the matzos are to be covered and the cup raised again upon reaching the blessing אֲשֶׁר גְּאָלָנוּ, Who has redeemed us (p. 151).

**לְפִיכָךְ** Therefore it is our duty to thank, praise, pay tribute, glorify, exalt, honor, bless, extol, and acclaim Him Who performed all these miracles for our fathers and for us. He brought us forth from slavery to freedom, from grief to joy, from mourning to festivity, from darkness to great light, and from servitude to redemption. Let us, therefore, recite a new song before Him! Halleluyah!

---

*extraneous thoughts. By the time he finished the tune, the scholar had found the explanation for his difficult problem.*

### ☙ *A Temple Melody*

*A favorite story is that of the Tzaddik of Sanz, whose chassid, Abish Meir, was very gifted musically. One Friday, Abish Meir was attracted by a melody emanating from a tavern and could not tear himself away. He continued to hum the beautiful tune for hours.*

*That Friday night Abish Meir led the services, and when he sang the Lechah Dodi (My beloved, let us greet the Shabbos bride), he sang with the tune that had haunted him all day. Then, realizing that he may have profaned the services with a tavern melody, he quickly made his exit for fear that the Tzaddik would reprimand him.*

*Abish Meir had never missed being at the Tzaddik's table Friday night, but this time was afraid to attend. He decided he would wait until others had arrived, and he would then slip in unnoticed. But no sooner did he enter that he heard the Tzaddik call him. "Abish Meir! Why have you kept us waiting so long? Sing the Shabbos zemiros with the melody you sang for Lechah Dodi." During the singing, the Tzaddik was ecstatic.*

*The Tzaddik later explained. "When the Temple was destroyed and the Jews were driven into exile, what happened with all the beautiful music of the Levites? It, too, went into exile, and these Heavenly melodies have been taken captive by aliens. This music was originally ours, Abish Meir, and we have recaptured one of the Temple melodies."*

**הַלְלוּיָהּ** הַלְלוּ עַבְדֵי יהוה, הַלְלוּ אֶת שֵׁם יהוה. יְהִי שֵׁם יהוה מְבֹרָךְ, מֵעַתָּה וְעַד עוֹלָם. מִמִּזְרַח שֶׁמֶשׁ עַד מְבוֹאוֹ, מְהֻלָּל שֵׁם יהוה. רָם עַל כָּל גּוֹיִם יהוה, עַל הַשָּׁמַיִם כְּבוֹדוֹ. מִי כַּיהוה אֱלֹהֵינוּ, הַמַּגְבִּיהִי לָשָׁבֶת. הַמַּשְׁפִּילִי לִרְאוֹת, בַּשָּׁמַיִם וּבָאָרֶץ. מְקִימִי מֵעָפָר דָּל, מֵאַשְׁפֹּת יָרִים אֶבְיוֹן. לְהוֹשִׁיבִי עִם נְדִיבִים, עִם נְדִיבֵי עַמּוֹ. מוֹשִׁיבִי עֲקֶרֶת הַבַּיִת, אֵם הַבָּנִים שְׂמֵחָה, הַלְלוּיָהּ.[1]

---

### הַלְלוּיָהּ הַלְלוּ עַבְדֵי יהוה, הַלְלוּ אֶת שֵׁם יהוה — *Halleluyah! Praise, you servants of HASHEM, praise the Name of HASHEM*

The comment of the Midrash on this verse is, "Servants of God, and not servants of Pharaoh." In *Leviticus* 25:55, it says, "For the Children of Israel are servants unto Me . . . for I delivered them from the land of Egypt."

The desire for independence appears to be innate within humans rather than acquired. Even young tots who do not have an intellectual grasp of the value of freedom appear to manifest a desire to be independent. Like any other physiologic-psychologic urge, this drive for independence can be constructive or destructive.

A thorough understanding of the composition and function of the human psyche reveals the concept of absolute independence to be a fallacy. Brute animals are totally dominated by their bodily drives, and when hungry or thirsty, they must seek food and water. An animal cannot decide to fast and frustrate the bodily urge for food. Human beings, whose physical component is akin to that of animals, are similarly driven by powerful physical urges, but in contrast to animals, have the capacity to resist them, a capacity residing within the spiritual component. The force of the physical drives may be so overwhelming that without Divine assistance, people will ultimately be dominated by them. The Talmud states this clearly: "I have created the *yetzer hara* (the evil inclination), and I have created Torah as an antidote" (*Kiddushin* 30b). It is impossible, over the long term, to avoid domination by the *yetzer hara* without Divine assistance. The validity of this has been demonstrated by the phenomenon of the '60's and its aftermath. "Doing one's thing" became the alpha and omega of life, and the flower children celebrated the demise of God. The result? A

**הַלְלוּיָהּ** Halleluyah! Praise, you servants of HASHEM, praise the Name of HASHEM. Blessed be the Name of HASHEM from now and forever. From the rising of the sun to its setting, HASHEM's Name is praised. Raised above all nations is HASHEM, above the heavens is His glory. Who is like HASHEM, our God, Who is enthroned on high, yet deigns to look upon the heaven and earth? He raises the destitute from the dust, from the trash heaps He lifts the needy — to seat them with nobles, with nobles of His people. He transforms the barren wife into a glad mother of children. Halleluyah![1]

(1) *Psalms* 113.

---

culture of moral anarchy, with unrestrained violence and lust-induced diseases threatening the very survival of mankind. The Torah knew better. We are either subjects of God, or of Pharaoh, the personification of the *yetzer hara.*

But one may ask: Do we not relinquish freedom when we subject ourselves to God? Let us remember, the choice is not whether or not to relinquish freedom, but rather *to whom,* the body or the spirit. Subjugation to the body means being driven by irrational biological drives, whereas subjugation to God is an act of will and intellect, one which befits man. Yes, we have a concept of *ol malchus Shamayim,* the yoke of Heaven, but the full phrase is *kabbalas ol malchus Shamayim,* something which we willingly accept. Furthermore, this is an acceptance which man must make anew each day. The *eved Hashem,* the servant of God, is not an automaton, but a proud spiritual being, who exercises his freedom of choice every day, and willingly chooses to subject himself to the will of a Higher Power, a will whose goal is the betterment of man.

### ⁂ מְקִימִי מֵעָפָר דָּל — *He raises the destitute from the dust*

The very first paragraph of *Hallel* sets the tone for the entire *Hallel.* When we approach the idea of praising God, we are initially often afraid or at least very uncomfortable, either because God is so lofty or we think ourselves to be so lowly, or both. In order to communicate with God, we seem faced with the choice of either bringing God down to our level, which seems inappropriate, or for us to think of ourselves as great, which we may feel is dishonest.

**בְּצֵאת** יִשְׂרָאֵל מִמִּצְרָיִם, בֵּית יַעֲקֹב מֵעַם לֹעֵז. הָיְתָה יְהוּדָה לְקָדְשׁוֹ, יִשְׂרָאֵל מַמְשְׁלוֹתָיו. הַיָּם רָאָה וַיָּנֹס, הַיַּרְדֵּן יִסֹּב לְאָחוֹר. הֶהָרִים רָקְדוּ כְאֵילִים, גְּבָעוֹת כִּבְנֵי צֹאן. מַה לְּךָ הַיָּם כִּי תָנוּס, הַיַּרְדֵּן תִּסֹּב לְאָחוֹר. הֶהָרִים תִּרְקְדוּ כְאֵילִים, גְּבָעוֹת כִּבְנֵי צֹאן. מִלִּפְנֵי אָדוֹן חוּלִי אָרֶץ, מִלִּפְנֵי אֱלוֹהַ יַעֲקֹב. הַהֹפְכִי הַצּוּר אֲגַם מָיִם, חַלָּמִישׁ לְמַעְיְנוֹ מָיִם.[1]

(1) *Psalms* 114.

---

"He raises the destitute from dust." God makes the decision for us. He reaches out to the downtrodden, picks him up, and seats him at the royal table. It is not that the poor person is made wealthy, but he is lifted out of the dust.

We begin praising God by recognizing that He has given us opportunities to improve our lives. Recognizing this favor obligates us to make use of these opportunities.

### הַיָּם רָאָה וַיָּנֹס — *The Sea saw and fled*

In this paragraph we are told of the miraculous dividing of the waters of the Red Sea. There are many Midrashim surrounding this event, telling us, for example, that not only did the Sea split once into twelve separate paths, one for each tribe (different people need different paths for salvation!), but there was also a second splitting. Why?

When the Sea opened, the Israelites recognized God's might and benevolence. But there were two individuals, Dathan and Abiram, who were busy urging the Israelites not to trust Moses, not to trust God's promise, but rather to return to their Egyptian taskmasters. These two refused to step into the Sea, and the Children of Israel crossed to safety, leaving them behind. This could have been the end of these two, who were continuously a thorn for Moses and who consistently challenged God's sovereignty.

When Dathan and Abiram realized that they had backed the wrong side, they prayed to God and miraculously, the Midrash says, the Sea split again for them! God suspended the laws of nature, not just for an entire nation, not only for the righteous, but even for those people who were and would continue to be outcasts.

**בְּצֵאת** When Israel went forth from Egypt, Yaakov's household from a people of alien tongue, Yehudah became His sanctuary, Yisrael His dominion. The Sea saw and fled; the Jordan turned backward. The mountains skipped like rams, and the hills like young lambs. What ails you, O Sea, that you flee? O Jordan, that you turn backward? O mountains, that you skip like rams? O hills, like young lambs? Before the Master — tremble, O earth, before the presence of the God of Yaakov, Who turns the rock into a pond of water, the flint into a flowing fountain.[1]

---

Jews have often been mocked as people who bend down to pick up pennies. We learned this trait from none other than God alone! God "bends down" and saves the "small change," even those of seemingly little worth.

On Passover we celebrate redemption, not only as a nation, which we are, and not only as valuable contributors to society, which we can be. We also celebrate the redemption of the worn, meager penny, which may be me.

### ☙ *Victim of Circumstances*

In this psalm, reference is made to both the splitting of the Red Sea and to the revelation at Mount Sinai.

The Midrash states that at the miraculous dividing of the Red Sea, the angels asked God why He was favoring the Israelites over the Egyptians, since the former too had degenerated into pagan practices. God responded, "The Israelites did so under coercion, whereas the Egyptians did so of their own free will."

It is common practice today to attempt to exonerate a person of deviant behavior because he was a victim of circumstances, with an upbringing that did not provide him the opportunity to distinguish right from wrong. The fact is, however, that the rate of recidivism among people with antisocial behavior is high, and that even after being given the opportunity and the means to learn and to distinguish right from wrong, many revert to their antisocial acts.

The response to the angels mitigating the paganism of the Israelites would therefore have been of little substance, if it were not for the fact that the Israelites would enthusiastically accept the Torah and dedicate

According to all customs the cup is lifted and the matzos covered during the recitation of this blessing. (On Saturday night the phrase in parentheses substitutes for the preceding phrase.)

**בָּרוּךְ** אַתָּה יהוה אֱלֹהֵינוּ מֶלֶךְ הָעוֹלָם, אֲשֶׁר גְּאָלָנוּ וְגָאַל אֶת אֲבוֹתֵינוּ מִמִּצְרַיִם, וְהִגִּיעָנוּ הַלַּיְלָה הַזֶּה לֶאֱכָל בּוֹ מַצָּה וּמָרוֹר. כֵּן יהוה אֱלֹהֵינוּ וֵאלֹהֵי אֲבוֹתֵינוּ, יַגִּיעֵנוּ לְמוֹעֲדִים וְלִרְגָלִים אֲחֵרִים הַבָּאִים לִקְרָאתֵנוּ לְשָׁלוֹם, שְׂמֵחִים בְּבִנְיַן עִירֶךָ וְשָׂשִׂים בַּעֲבוֹדָתֶךָ, וְנֹאכַל שָׁם מִן הַזְּבָחִים וּמִן הַפְּסָחִים (מִן הַפְּסָחִים וּמִן הַזְּבָחִים) אֲשֶׁר יַגִּיעַ דָּמָם עַל קִיר מִזְבַּחֲךָ לְרָצוֹן. וְנוֹדֶה לְךָ שִׁיר חָדָשׁ עַל גְּאֻלָּתֵנוּ וְעַל פְּדוּת נַפְשֵׁנוּ. בָּרוּךְ אַתָּה יהוה, גָּאַל יִשְׂרָאֵל.

**בָּרוּךְ** אַתָּה יהוה אֱלֹהֵינוּ מֶלֶךְ הָעוֹלָם, בּוֹרֵא פְּרִי הַגָּפֶן.

The second cup is drunk while leaning on the left side — preferably the entire cup, but at least most of it.

---

# רחצה

---

The hands are washed for matzah and the following blessing is recited.
It is preferable to bring water and a basin to the head of the household at the *Seder* table.

**בָּרוּךְ** אַתָּה יהוה אֱלֹהֵינוּ מֶלֶךְ הָעוֹלָם, אֲשֶׁר קִדְּשָׁנוּ בְּמִצְוֹתָיו, וְצִוָּנוּ עַל נְטִילַת יָדָיִם.

---

themselves to a spiritual life, repudiating the hedonism of idolatry.

*Teshuvah* is a cornerstone of Judaism. The Talmud states that in confessing one's sins, one should say, "I was on a wrong path, and I was acting with a bad mind" (*Jerusalem Talmud,* end of *Yoma*). For this argument to be convincing, one must demonstrate that one has rejected the errant path of the past, and is living according to different principles and values.

According to all customs the cup is lifted and the matzos covered during the recitation of this blessing. (On Saturday night the phrase in parentheses substitutes for the preceding phrase.)

בָּרוּךְ Blessed are You, HASHEM, our God, King of the Universe, Who redeemed us and redeemed our ancestors from Egypt and enabled us to reach this night that we may eat matzah and *maror.* So, HASHEM, our God and God of our fathers, bring us also to future festivals and holidays in peace, gladdened in the rebuilding of Your city, and joyful at Your service. There we shall eat of the offerings and Passover sacrifices (of the Passover sacrifices and offerings) whose blood will gain the sides of Your altar for gracious acceptance. We shall then sing a new song of praise to You for our redemption and for the liberation of our souls. Blessed are You, HASHEM, Who has redeemed Israel.

בָּרוּךְ Bessed are You, HASHEM, our God, King of the Universe, Who creates the fruit of the vine.

The second cup is drunk while leaning on the left side — preferably the entire cup, but at least most of it.

## RACHTZAH

The hands are washed for matzah and the following blessing is recited. It is preferable to bring water and a basin to the head of the household at the *Seder* table.

בָּרוּךְ Blessed are You, HASHEM, our God, King of the Universe, Who has sanctified us with His commandments, and has commanded us concerning the washing of the hands.

---

When Moses asked God by what merit the Israelites would be delivered from Egypt, God answered, "They will serve Me at this mountain (Sinai)" (*Exodus* 3:12). The teaching of the Exodus is thus that simply repudiating the past is not enough. It is also essential to adopt a spiritual way of life.

# מוציא

The following two blessings are recited over matzah; the first is recited over matzah as food, and the second for the special *mitzvah* of eating matzah on the night of Passover. [The latter blessing is to be made with the intention that it also apply to the "sandwich" and the afikoman.]

The head of the household raises all the matzos on the *Seder* plate and recites the following blessing:

**בָּרוּךְ** אַתָּה יהוה אֱלֹהֵינוּ מֶלֶךְ הָעוֹלָם, הַמּוֹצִיא לֶחֶם מִן הָאָרֶץ.

The bottom matzah is put down and the following blessing is recited while the top (whole) matzah and the middle (broken) piece are still raised.

# מצה

**בָּרוּךְ** אַתָּה יהוה אֱלֹהֵינוּ מֶלֶךְ הָעוֹלָם, אֲשֶׁר קִדְּשָׁנוּ בְּמִצְוֹתָיו, וְצִוָּנוּ עַל אֲכִילַת מַצָּה.

Each participant is required to eat an amount of matzah equal in volume to an egg. Since it is impossible to provide a sufficient amount of matzah from the two matzos for all members of the household, the other matzos should be available at the head of the table from which to complete the required amounts. However, each participant should receive a piece from each of the top two matzos. The matzos are to be eaten while reclining on the left side and without delay; they need not be dipped in salt.

# מרור

The head of the household takes a half-egg volume of *maror,* dips it into *charoses,* shakes off the *charoses,* and gives each participant a like amount. The following blessing is recited with the intention that it also apply to the *maror* of the "sandwich." The *maror* is eaten without reclining, and without delay.

**בָּרוּךְ** אַתָּה יהוה אֱלֹהֵינוּ מֶלֶךְ הָעוֹלָם, אֲשֶׁר קִדְּשָׁנוּ בְּמִצְוֹתָיו, וְצִוָּנוּ עַל אֲכִילַת מָרוֹר.

### ◆§ מוֹצִיא מַצָּה — *Motzi Matzah*

*The chassidic master of Apt was extremely meticulous about the matzos he used for the Seder. He selected his three matzos carefully from among hundreds, and set them aside.*

*The day before Passover, a poor man came to the house asking for*

## MOTZI

The following two blessings are recited over matzah; the first is recited over matzah as food, and the second for the special *mitzvah* of eating matzah on the night of Passover. [The latter blessing is to be made with the intention that it also apply to the "sandwich" and the afikoman.]

The head of the household raises all the matzos on the *Seder* plate and recites the following blessing:

**בָּרוּךְ** Blessed are You, HASHEM, our God, King of the Universe, Who brings forth bread from the earth.

The bottom matzah is put down and the following blessing is recited while the top (whole) matzah and the middle (broken) piece are still raised.

## MATZAH

**בָּרוּךְ** Blessed are You, HASHEM, our God, King of the Universe, Who has sanctified us with His commandments, and has commanded us concerning the eating of matzah.

Each participant is required to eat an amount of matzah equal in volume to an egg. Since it is impossible to provide a sufficient amount of matzah from the two matzos for all members of the household, the other matzos should be available at the head of the table from which to complete the required amounts. However, each participant should receive a piece from each of the top two matzos. The matzos are to be eaten while reclining on the left side and without delay; they need not be dipped in salt.

## MAROR

The head of the household takes a half-egg volume of *maror,* dips it into *charoses,* shakes off the *charoses,* and gives each participant a like amount. The following blessing is recited with the intention that it also apply to the *maror* of the "sandwich." The *maror* is eaten without reclining, and without delay.

**בָּרוּךְ** Blessed are You, HASHEM, our God, King of the Universe, Who has sanctified us with His commandments, and has commanded us concerning the eating of *maror.*

---

*help with provisions for Passover. The Rabbi's wife gave him whatever she could, among which were the three matzos which the Rabbi had set aside for his personal Seder use. When she later discovered what she had done, she was very apprehensive in telling the rabbi of this, frightened that he might scold her for not having checked with him first.*

# כורך

The bottom (thus far unbroken) matzah is now taken. From it, with the addition of other matzos, each participant receives a half-egg volume of matzah along with an equal volume portion of *maror* (dipped into *charoses* which is shaken off). The following paragraph is recited and the "sandwich" is eaten while reclining.

**זֵכֶר** לְמִקְדָּשׁ כְּהִלֵּל. כֵּן עָשָׂה הִלֵּל בִּזְמַן שֶׁבֵּית הַמִּקְדָּשׁ הָיָה קַיָּם. הָיָה כּוֹרֵךְ (פֶּסַח) מַצָּה וּמָרוֹר וְאוֹכֵל בְּיַחַד. לְקַיֵּם מַה שֶּׁנֶּאֱמַר, עַל מַצּוֹת וּמְרֹרִים יֹאכְלֻהוּ.[1]

# שלחן עורך

The meal should be eaten in a combination of joy and solemnity, for the meal, too, is a part of the *Seder* service. While it is desirable that *zemiros* and discussion of the laws and events of Pesach be part of the meal, extraneous conversation should be avoided. It should be remembered that the *afikoman* must be eaten while there is still some appetite for it. In fact, if one is so sated that he must literally force himself to eat it, he is not credited with the performance of the *mitzvah* of *afikoman*. Therefore, it is unwise to eat more than a moderate amount during the meal.

# צפון

From the *afikoman* matzah (and from additional matzos to make up the required amount), a half-egg volume — according to some, a full egg's volume portion — is given to each participant. It should be eaten before midnight, while reclining, without delay, and uninterruptedly. Nothing may be eaten or drunk after the *afikoman* (with the exception of water and the like) except for the last two *Seder* cups of wine.

(1) *Numbers* 9:11.

*The Rabbi replied calmly, "I did have reason to choose these particular matzos in preference to others. However, if I use other matzos, I will still fulfill the mitzvah. On the other hand, if I were to become angry, I would be committing a gross transgression, because the Talmud states that allowing oneself to become enraged is equivalent to the sin of idolatry. Since Passover commemorates our repudiation of*

## KORECH

The bottom (thus far unbroken) matzah is now taken. From it, with the addition of other matzos, each participant receives a half-egg volume of matzah along with an equal volume portion of *maror* (dipped into *charoses* which is shaken off). The following paragraph is recited and the "sandwich" is eaten while reclining.

**זֵכֶר** In remembrance of the Beis HaMikdash, like Hillel: he would combine (meat of the Pesach offering) matzah and *maror* in a sandwich and eat them together, to fulfill what is written in the Torah: They shall eat it with matzos and bitter herbs.[1]

## SHULCHAN ORECH

The meal should be eaten in a combination of joy and solemnity, for the meal, too, is a part of the *Seder* service. While it is desirable that *zemiros* and discussion of the laws and events of Pesach be part of the meal, extraneous conversation should be avoided. It should be remembered that the *afikoman* must be eaten while there is still some appetite for it. In fact, if one is so sated that he must literally force himself to eat it, he is not credited with the performance of the *mitzvah* of *afikoman*. Therefore, it is unwise to eat more than a moderate amount during the meal.

## TZAFUN

From the *afikoman* matzah (and from additional matzos to make up the required amount), a half-egg volume — according to some, a full egg's volume portion — is given to each participant. It should be eaten before midnight, while reclining, without delay, and uninterruptedly. Nothing may be eaten or drunk after the *afikoman* (with the exception of water and the like) except for the last two *Seder* cups of wine.

---

*idolatry, what kind of mitzvah would I have by eating the matzos, while violating the spirit of Passover?"*

### ◆§ צָפוּן — *Tzafun*

We complete the *Seder* meal by removing the *afikoman* matzah from its hiding place. The matzah, which represents the redemption, was hidden for some time, and only at the end of the meal is it revealed. This symbolizes the ultimate Redemption. Once the latter is realized and is revealed, we will understand that it was with us all the time, throughout the centuries of suffering in the diaspora, although it was concealed from our view.

# ברך

The third cup is poured and *Bircas HaMazon* (Grace After Meals) is recited. According to some customs, the Cup of Elijah is poured at this point.

תהלים קכו

**שִׁיר הַמַּעֲלוֹת,** בְּשׁוּב יהוה אֶת שִׁיבַת צִיּוֹן, הָיִינוּ כְּחֹלְמִים. אָז יִמָּלֵא שְׂחוֹק פִּינוּ וּלְשׁוֹנֵנוּ רִנָּה, אָז יֹאמְרוּ בַגּוֹיִם, הִגְדִּיל יהוה לַעֲשׂוֹת עִם אֵלֶּה. הִגְדִּיל יהוה לַעֲשׂוֹת עִמָּנוּ, הָיִינוּ שְׂמֵחִים. שׁוּבָה יהוה אֶת שְׁבִיתֵנוּ, כַּאֲפִיקִים בַּנֶּגֶב. הַזֹּרְעִים בְּדִמְעָה בְּרִנָּה יִקְצֹרוּ. הָלוֹךְ יֵלֵךְ וּבָכֹה נֹשֵׂא מֶשֶׁךְ הַזָּרַע, בֹּא יָבֹא בְרִנָּה, נֹשֵׂא אֲלֻמֹּתָיו.

**תְּהִלַּת** יהוה יְדַבֶּר פִּי, וִיבָרֵךְ כָּל בָּשָׂר שֵׁם קָדְשׁוֹ לְעוֹלָם וָעֶד.[1] וַאֲנַחְנוּ נְבָרֵךְ יָהּ, מֵעַתָּה וְעַד עוֹלָם, הַלְלוּיָהּ.[2] הוֹדוּ לַיהוה כִּי טוֹב, כִּי לְעוֹלָם חַסְדּוֹ.[3] מִי יְמַלֵּל גְּבוּרוֹת יהוה, יַשְׁמִיעַ כָּל תְּהִלָּתוֹ.[4]

(1) *Psalms* 145:21. (2) 115:18. (3) 118:1. (4) 106:2.

**בְּשׁוּב יהוה אֶת שִׁיבַת צִיּוֹן — *When Hashem will return the captivity of Zion***

We chant the 126th Chapter of *Psalms* prior to the Blessing After the Meal, and the very first sentence of this psalm confirms the message of the *afikoman.* "When Hashem will return the captivity of Zion, we will be like dreamers." During a dream one may have frightening experiences, which upon awaking prove to have been only illusions. So it will be with the ultimate Redemption, when our salvation will be so great that the centuries of suffering in the diaspora will appear to have been as a dream.

**הַזֹּרְעִים בְּדִמְעָה בְּרִנָּה יִקְצֹרוּ — *Those who tearfully sow wiill reap in glad song***

A person who has never been exposed to any phase of the agricultural cycle and observes a farmer sowing his grain may say, "How foolish that man is. He is taking perfectly good grain and burying it in the ground." Not being

# BARECH

The third cup is poured and *Bircas HaMazon* (Grace After Meals) is recited. According to some customs, the Cup of Elijah is poured at this point.

Psalm 126

**שִׁיר הַמַּעֲלוֹת** A song of ascents. When HASHEM will return the captivity of Zion, we will be like dreamers. Then our mouth will be filled with laughter and our tongue with glad song. Then they will declare among the nations, "HASHEM has done greatly with these." HASHEM has done greatly with us, we were gladdened. O HASHEM — return our captivity like springs in the desert. Those who tearfully sow will reap in glad song. He who bears the measure of seeds walks along weeping, but will return in exultation, a bearer of his sheaves.

**תְּהִלַּת** May my mouth declare the praise of HASHEM and may all flesh bless His Holy Name forever.[1] We will bless HASHEM from this time and forever, Halleluyah![2] Give thanks to God for He is good, His kindness endures forever.[3] Who can express the mighty acts of HASHEM? Who can declare all His praise?[4]

---

aware of the process of planting, whereby each seed sprouts a whole stalk of grain, the observer views the farmer's actions as destructive.

One woman who recovered from years of excessive addictive behavior related her years of deterioration as a result of substance abuse. One listener asked, "How did you cope with all the losses you sustained during that period?"

The woman responded, "Very poorly. When I lost my job, I thought the world had come to an end for me. When my marriage broke up, I was angry at God. 'Why are You doing this to me? What did I ever do to You?'

"After seven years, I can look back and see that God was taking away those things that I lacked the good sense to give up on my own. I have now received my master's degree, which I never would have achieved had I stayed in the menial job. My marriage was detrimental but I did not know that. I am now happily married to a wonderful man."

There are times when we shed tears over very distressing happenings.

### זימון

If three or more males, aged thirteen or older, participate in a meal, the leader is appointed to formally invite the others to join him in the recitation of *Bircas HaMazon*. Following is the "*Zimun*," or formal invitation.

Leader – רַבּוֹתַי נְבָרֵךְ.

Others – יְהִי שֵׁם יהוה מְבֹרָךְ מֵעַתָּה וְעַד עוֹלָם.[1]

If ten men join in the *zimun* the words in parentheses are added.

Leader – יְהִי שֵׁם יהוה מְבֹרָךְ מֵעַתָּה וְעַד עוֹלָם.[1]
בִּרְשׁוּת מָרָנָן וְרַבָּנָן וְרַבּוֹתַי, נְבָרֵךְ (אֱלֹהֵינוּ) שֶׁאָכַלְנוּ מִשֶּׁלּוֹ.

Others – בָּרוּךְ (אֱלֹהֵינוּ) שֶׁאָכַלְנוּ מִשֶּׁלּוֹ וּבְטוּבוֹ חָיִינוּ.

Leader – בָּרוּךְ (אֱלֹהֵינוּ) שֶׁאָכַלְנוּ מִשֶּׁלּוֹ וּבְטוּבוֹ חָיִינוּ.
(בָּרוּךְ הוּא וּבָרוּךְ שְׁמוֹ.)

### ברכת הזן

**בָּרוּךְ** אַתָּה יהוה אֱלֹהֵינוּ מֶלֶךְ הָעוֹלָם, הַזָּן אֶת הָעוֹלָם כֻּלּוֹ, בְּטוּבוֹ, בְּחֵן בְּחֶסֶד וּבְרַחֲמִים, הוּא נֹתֵן לֶחֶם לְכָל בָּשָׂר, כִּי לְעוֹלָם חַסְדּוֹ.[2] וּבְטוּבוֹ הַגָּדוֹל, תָּמִיד לֹא חָסַר לָנוּ,

(1) *Psalms* 113:2. (2) 136:25.

---

Much like the seeds that are planted in the ground, and like the "losses" of the woman in the above account, our unpleasant happenings may be precursors to truly felicitous events.

When the ultimate Redemption comes about, we will rejoice and we will understand why the suffering was necessary. This faith should strengthen us and enable us to withstand adversity.

### ☙ *The Painful Investment*

*One of the elder citizens of Kovno falsely accused the great Rabbi Yitzchak Elchonon of having caused an economic crisis in town, and as a result, became his bitter enemy. One time, both were present at a local celebration, and when Rabbi Yitzchak Elchonon saw that the man was avoiding him, he went over to greet him. The man was taken aback by the Rabbi's self-effacement, going out of his way to acknowledge him publicly even though he had become his adversary. The Rabbi's*

## ZIMUN/INVITATION

If three or more males, aged thirteen or older, participate in a meal, the leader is appointed to formally invite the others to join him in the recitation of *Bircas HaMazon*. Following is the *"Zimun,"* or formal invitation.

Leader – Gentlemen, let us bless.

Others – Blessed be the Name of HASHEM from this time and forever![1]

If ten men join in the *zimun* the words in brackets are added.

Leader – Blessed be the Name of HASHEM from this time and forever![1] With the permission of the distinguished people present, let us bless [our God,] He of Whose we have eaten.

Others – Blessed is [our God,] He of Whose we have eaten and Whose goodness we live.

Leader – Blessed is [our God,] He of Whose we have eaten and Whose goodness we live.
[Blessed is He and Blessed is His Name.]

## FIRST BLESSING: FOR THE NOURISHMENT

**בָּרוּךְ** Blessed are You, HASHEM, our God, King of the Universe, Who nourishes the entire world, in His goodness — with grace, with kindness, and with mercy. He gives nourishment to all flesh, for His kindness is eternal.[2] And through His great goodness, we have never lacked,

---

*friends were outraged that he had humbled himself before so vile a person, who had unjustly behaved toward him with chutzpah.*

*Some time later, a committee from a nearby village consulted Rabbi Yitzchak Elchonon. Because of an anti-Semitic false charge, the Jewish community was under threat of expulsion. Rabbi Yitzchak Elchonon tried to intercede with the authorities, but all his efforts were in vain. He then learned that this elder citizen had some contacts with influential officials, and appealed to him to intercede on behalf of the Jewish community. The man honored the Rabbi's request, and the expulsion decree was revoked.*

*Rabbi Yitzchak Elchonon then said to his friends, "Suppose that I had done as you had wished, and had allowed a hostile relationship to persist. Whence would the community be saved? I made the investment of setting aside the indignities I had suffered, and the result was that Hashem designated him as the catalyst for the salvation of the Jewish community. Is this not what the Psalmist says, 'Those who sow in tears will reap with joy'? We sometimes must made a painful investment for the good that it will bring in the future."*

וְאַל יֶחְסַר לָנוּ מָזוֹן לְעוֹלָם וָעֶד. בַּעֲבוּר שְׁמוֹ הַגָּדוֹל, כִּי הוּא אֵל זָן וּמְפַרְנֵס לַכֹּל, וּמֵטִיב לַכֹּל, וּמֵכִין מָזוֹן לְכָל בְּרִיּוֹתָיו אֲשֶׁר בָּרָא. ❖ בָּרוּךְ אַתָּה יהוה, הַזָּן אֶת הַכֹּל. (Others – אָמֵן.)

ברכת הארץ

**נוֹדֶה** לְּךָ יהוה אֱלֹהֵינוּ, עַל שֶׁהִנְחַלְתָּ לַאֲבוֹתֵינוּ אֶרֶץ חֶמְדָּה טוֹבָה וּרְחָבָה. וְעַל שֶׁהוֹצֵאתָנוּ יהוה אֱלֹהֵינוּ מֵאֶרֶץ מִצְרַיִם, וּפְדִיתָנוּ מִבֵּית עֲבָדִים, וְעַל בְּרִיתְךָ שֶׁחָתַמְתָּ בִּבְשָׂרֵנוּ, וְעַל תּוֹרָתְךָ שֶׁלִּמַּדְתָּנוּ, וְעַל חֻקֶּיךָ שֶׁהוֹדַעְתָּנוּ, וְעַל חַיִּים חֵן וָחֶסֶד שֶׁחוֹנַנְתָּנוּ, וְעַל אֲכִילַת מָזוֹן שָׁאַתָּה זָן וּמְפַרְנֵס אוֹתָנוּ תָּמִיד, בְּכָל יוֹם וּבְכָל עֵת וּבְכָל שָׁעָה.

**וְעַל הַכֹּל** יהוה אֱלֹהֵינוּ אֲנַחְנוּ מוֹדִים לָךְ, וּמְבָרְכִים אוֹתָךְ, יִתְבָּרַךְ שִׁמְךָ בְּפִי כָּל חַי תָּמִיד לְעוֹלָם וָעֶד. כַּכָּתוּב, וְאָכַלְתָּ

---

**וּמֵכִין מָזוֹן לְכָל בְּרִיּוֹתָיו — *And He prepares food for all of His creatures***

The above phrase in the first paragraph of the Grace After Meals is more than just an expression of gratitude for the food we have eaten. It is also a profound statement of trust in God.

If you wish to take something to eat for yourself, you may open the refrigerator and take whatever happens to be available. However, if you have invited important guests, you prepare the food for them with great care. Also, if you are serving someone who has special dietary needs, you prepare the food so that it meets these particular requirements.

This concept is conveyed by the words "He prepares food for all of His creatures." Every one of us is an important guest in the world, and God relates to us as such. Furthermore, He prepares for our special needs as only He can understand them with His infinite wisdom. The Grace After Meals thus affirms our faith and trust in God, as well as being an expression of our self-esteem and feeling of worthiness.

and may we never lack, nourishment, for all eternity. For the sake of His great Name, because He is God Who nourishes and sustains all, and benefits all, and He prepares food for all of His creatures which He has created. Leader– Blessed are You, HASHEM, Who nourishes all. (Others– Amen.)

SECOND BLESSING: FOR THE LAND

**נוֹדֶה** We thank You, HASHEM, our God, because You have given to our forefathers as a heritage a desirable, good and spacious land; because You removed us, HASHEM, our God, from the land of Egypt and You redeemed us from the house of bondage; for Your covenant which You sealed in our flesh; for Your Torah which You taught us and for Your statutes which You made known to us; for life, grace, and lovingkindness which You granted us; and for the provision of food with which You nourish and sustain us constantly, in every day, in every season, and in every hour.

**וְעַל** For all, HASHEM, our God, we thank You and bless You. May Your Name be blessed by the mouth of all the living, continuously for all eternity. As it is written: "And you

---

### ◆§ וְעַל שֶׁהוֹצֵאתָנוּ ... מֵאֶרֶץ מִצְרַיִם ... וְעַל תּוֹרָתְךָ שֶׁלִּמַּדְתָּנוּ — *Because You removed us ... from the land of Egypt ...; for Your Torah which You taught us.*

This verse in the Grace After Meals is recited every day of the year, thus reinforcing the message of Passover. The liberation from Egypt was much more than a geographical remedy. Our removal from Egypt was also a redemption from bondage, not only the bondage of enslavement to a despot, but also a liberation from the tyranny of our own physical temptations, and a self-mastery which is achieved by the teachings of the Torah.

### ◆§ וְעַל הַכֹּל ה' אֱלֹהֵינוּ אֲנַחְנוּ מוֹדִים לָךְ — *For all, Hashem, our God, we thank You*

Over and above our gratitude for God's bounty, we are most grateful that we have the privilege of giving thanks to God. The capacity to be grateful is a uniquely human trait, hence it is a component of spirituality. We are thankful for the ability to be thankful.

וְשָׂבָעְתָּ, וּבֵרַכְתָּ אֶת יהוה אֱלֹהֶיךָ, עַל הָאָרֶץ הַטֹּבָה אֲשֶׁר נָתַן לָךְ.[1] ❖ בָּרוּךְ אַתָּה יהוה, עַל הָאָרֶץ וְעַל הַמָּזוֹן. (Others — אָמֵן.)

בנין ירושלים

**רַחֵם** יהוה אֱלֹהֵינוּ עַל יִשְׂרָאֵל עַמֶּךָ, וְעַל יְרוּשָׁלַיִם עִירֶךָ, וְעַל צִיּוֹן מִשְׁכַּן כְּבוֹדֶךָ, וְעַל מַלְכוּת בֵּית דָּוִד מְשִׁיחֶךָ, וְעַל הַבַּיִת הַגָּדוֹל וְהַקָּדוֹשׁ שֶׁנִּקְרָא שִׁמְךָ עָלָיו. אֱלֹהֵינוּ אָבִינוּ רְעֵנוּ זוּנֵנוּ פַּרְנְסֵנוּ וְכַלְכְּלֵנוּ וְהַרְוִיחֵנוּ, וְהַרְוַח לָנוּ יהוה אֱלֹהֵינוּ מְהֵרָה מִכָּל צָרוֹתֵינוּ. וְנָא אַל תַּצְרִיכֵנוּ יהוה אֱלֹהֵינוּ, לֹא לִידֵי מַתְּנַת בָּשָׂר וָדָם, וְלֹא לִידֵי הַלְוָאָתָם, כִּי אִם לְיָדְךָ הַמְּלֵאָה הַפְּתוּחָה הַקְּדוֹשָׁה וְהָרְחָבָה, שֶׁלֹּא נֵבוֹשׁ וְלֹא נִכָּלֵם לְעוֹלָם וָעֶד.

On the Sabbath add the following. [If forgotten, see box on page 164.]

**רְצֵה** וְהַחֲלִיצֵנוּ יהוה אֱלֹהֵינוּ בְּמִצְוֹתֶיךָ, וּבְמִצְוַת יוֹם הַשְּׁבִיעִי הַשַּׁבָּת הַגָּדוֹל וְהַקָּדוֹשׁ הַזֶּה, כִּי יוֹם זֶה גָּדוֹל וְקָדוֹשׁ הוּא לְפָנֶיךָ, לִשְׁבָּת בּוֹ וְלָנוּחַ בּוֹ בְּאַהֲבָה כְּמִצְוַת רְצוֹנֶךָ, וּבִרְצוֹנְךָ הָנִיחַ לָנוּ יהוה אֱלֹהֵינוּ, שֶׁלֹּא תְהֵא צָרָה וְיָגוֹן וַאֲנָחָה בְּיוֹם מְנוּחָתֵנוּ, וְהַרְאֵנוּ יהוה אֱלֹהֵינוּ בְּנֶחָמַת צִיּוֹן עִירֶךָ, וּבְבִנְיַן יְרוּשָׁלַיִם עִיר קָדְשֶׁךָ, כִּי אַתָּה הוּא בַּעַל הַיְשׁוּעוֹת וּבַעַל הַנֶּחָמוֹת.

**אֱלֹהֵינוּ** וֵאלֹהֵי אֲבוֹתֵינוּ, יַעֲלֶה, וְיָבֹא, וְיַגִּיעַ, וְיֵרָאֶה, וְיֵרָצֶה, וְיִשָּׁמַע, וְיִפָּקֵד, וְיִזָּכֵר זִכְרוֹנֵנוּ וּפִקְדּוֹנֵנוּ, וְזִכְרוֹן אֲבוֹתֵינוּ, וְזִכְרוֹן מָשִׁיחַ בֶּן

(1) *Deuteronomy* 8:10.

---

**יַעֲלֶה וְיָבֹא וְיַגִּיעַ וְיֵרָאֶה — *May there (our prayers) rise, come, reach, be noted***

There are so many ways in which our prayers can come before God! Some people complain that prayer is boring. We repeat the same words

shall eat and you shall be satisfied and you shall bless HASHEM, your God, for the good land which He gave you."[1]

Leader— Blessed are You, HASHEM, for the land and for the nourishment. (Others— Amen.)

THIRD BLESSING: FOR JERUSALEM

רַחֵם Have mercy, HASHEM, our God, on Israel Your people; on Jerusalem, Your city, on Zion, the resting place of Your Glory; on the monarchy of the house of David, Your anointed; and on the great and holy House upon which Your Name is called. Our God, our Father — tend us, nourish us, sustain us, support us, relieve us; HASHEM, our God, grant us speedy relief from all our troubles. Please, make us not needful — HASHEM, our God — of the gifts of human hands nor of their loans, but only of Your Hand that is full, open, holy, and generous, that we not feel inner shame nor be humiliated for ever and ever.

On the Sabbath add the following. [If forgotten, see box on page 164.]

רְצֵה May it please You, HASHEM, our God — give us rest through Your commandments and through the commandment of the seventh day, this great and holy Sabbath. For this day is great and holy before You to rest on it and be content on it in love, as ordained by Your will. May it be Your will, HASHEM, our God, that there be no distress, grief, or lament on this day of our contentment. And show us, HASHEM, our God, the consolation of Zion, Your city, and the rebuilding of Jerusalem, City of Your holiness, for You are the Master of salvations and Master of consolations.

אֱלֹהֵינוּ Our God and God of our forefathers, may there rise, come, reach, be noted, be favored, be heard, be considered, and be remembered — the remembrance and consideration of ourselves; the remembrance of our forefathers; the remembrance of Mashiach, son of

---

over and over again every day.

Perhaps if you were to hear a particular melody over and over again it might become boring, even if the melody is beautiful. However, if it is first played on a piano, then by a violin, and then again by a clarinet, and then by a flute, it has a freshness. The tune may indeed be the same,

דָּוִד עַבְדֶּךָ, וְזִכְרוֹן יְרוּשָׁלַיִם עִיר קָדְשֶׁךָ, וְזִכְרוֹן כָּל עַמְּךָ בֵּית יִשְׂרָאֵל לְפָנֶיךָ, לִפְלֵיטָה לְטוֹבָה לְחֵן וּלְחֶסֶד וּלְרַחֲמִים, לְחַיִּים וּלְשָׁלוֹם בְּיוֹם חַג הַמַּצּוֹת הַזֶּה. זָכְרֵנוּ יהוה אֱלֹהֵינוּ בּוֹ לְטוֹבָה, וּפָקְדֵנוּ בוֹ לִבְרָכָה, וְהוֹשִׁיעֵנוּ בוֹ לְחַיִּים. וּבִדְבַר יְשׁוּעָה וְרַחֲמִים, חוּס וְחָנֵּנוּ וְרַחֵם עָלֵינוּ וְהוֹשִׁיעֵנוּ, כִּי אֵלֶיךָ עֵינֵינוּ, כִּי אֵל חַנּוּן וְרַחוּם אָתָּה.[1]

❖ **וּבְנֵה** יְרוּשָׁלַיִם עִיר הַקֹּדֶשׁ בִּמְהֵרָה בְיָמֵינוּ. בָּרוּךְ אַתָּה יהוה, בּוֹנֵה (בְּרַחֲמָיו) יְרוּשָׁלָיִם. אָמֵן. (אָמֵן. – Others)

---

**If One Omitted רְצֵה or יַעֲלֶה וְיָבֹא**

If one omitted יַעֲלֶה וְיָבֹא on Pesach (and/or רְצֵה on Pesach that falls on the Sabbath):

(a) If he realizes his omission after having recited the word בּוֹנֵה, *Who rebuilds,* of the next paragraph, but has not yet begun the following blessing, he completes the blessing until אָמֵן, and then makes up for the omission by reciting the appropriate Compensatory Blessing (page 133).

(b) If he realizes his omission after reciting the words בָּרוּךְ אַתָּה ה׳, *Blessed are You,* HASHEM*,* but had not yet said the word בּוֹנֵה, *Who rebuilds,* he concludes with the phrase לַמְּדֵנִי חֻקֶּיךָ, *teach me Your statutes;* then recites the omitted paragraph and continues from there. [This ruling is based on the fact that בָּרוּךְ אַתָּה ה׳ לַמְּדֵנִי חֻקֶּיךָ, *Blessed are You,* HASHEM*; teach me Your statutes,* is a verse in *Psalms* (119:12) and not a blessing. Only if one has recited the next blessing of *Bircas HaMazon* is it forbidden to go back to a previous blessing, but if one has merely inserted a verse from *Psalms* he is still in the middle of the prayer and may go back to correct an omission.]

(c) If he realizes his omission after having recited the first six words of the fourth blessing, he may still switch immediately into the compensatory blessing since the words אַתָּה . . . הָעוֹלָם are identical in both blessings.

(d) If he realizes his omission after having recited the word הָאֵל, *the Almighty,* of the fourth blessing, it is too late for the compensatory blessing to be recited. In that case, at the first two meals of *Shabbos* and *Yom Tov* (but not *Chol HaMoed*), *Bircas HaMazon* must be repeated in its entirety; at the third meal, nothing need be done.

---

but it is presented in a new manner each time.

If our prayers are boring, it is not because of their content, but because of

David, Your servant; the remembrance of Jerusalem, the City of Your Holiness; the remembrance of Your entire people the Family of Israel — before You for deliverance, for goodness, for grace, for kindness, and for compassion, for life, and for peace on this Day of the Festival of Matzos. Remember us on it, HASHEM, our God, for goodness; consider us on it for blessing; and help us on it for life. In the matter of salvation and compassion, pity, be gracious and compassionate with us and help us, for our eyes are turned to You, because You are God, gracious and compassionate.[1]

✣ **וּבְנֵה** Rebuild Jerusalem, the Holy City, soon in our days. Blessed are You, HASHEM, Who rebuilds Jerusalem (in His mercy). Amen. (Others— Amen.)

**Compensatory Blessings**

If יַעֲלֶה וְיָבֹא was omitted on any day other than the Sabbath:

**בָּרוּךְ** אַתָּה יהוה אֱלֹהֵינוּ מֶלֶךְ הָעוֹלָם, אֲשֶׁר נָתַן יָמִים טוֹבִים לְעַמּוֹ יִשְׂרָאֵל לְשָׂשׂוֹן וּלְשִׂמְחָה, אֶת יוֹם חַג הַמַּצּוֹת הַזֶּה. בָּרוּךְ אַתָּה יהוה, מְקַדֵּשׁ יִשְׂרָאֵל וְהַזְּמַנִּים.

Blessed are You, HASHEM, our God, King of the Universe, Who gave festivals to His people Israel for happiness and gladness, this day of the Festival of Matzos. Blessed are You, HASHEM, Who sanctifies Israel and the seasons.

If both רְצֵה and יַעֲלֶה וְיָבֹא were omitted on Pesach that falls on the Sabbath:

**בָּרוּךְ** אַתָּה יהוה אֱלֹהֵינוּ מֶלֶךְ הָעוֹלָם, אֲשֶׁר נָתַן שַׁבָּתוֹת לִמְנוּחָה לְעַמּוֹ יִשְׂרָאֵל בְּאַהֲבָה, לְאוֹת וְלִבְרִית, וְיָמִים טוֹבִים לְשָׂשׂוֹן וּלְשִׂמְחָה, אֶת יוֹם חַג הַמַּצּוֹת הַזֶּה. בָּרוּךְ אַתָּה יהוה, מְקַדֵּשׁ הַשַּׁבָּת וְיִשְׂרָאֵל וְהַזְּמַנִּים.

Blessed are You, HASHEM, our God, King of the Universe, Who gave Sabbaths for contentment to His people Israel with love as a sign and as a covenant, and festivals for happiness and gladness, this day of the Festival of Matzos. Blessed are You, HASHEM, Who sanctifies the Sabbath, Israel, and the seasons.

If יַעֲלֶה וְיָבֹא was recited but רְצֵה was omitted on the Sabbath:

**בָּרוּךְ** אַתָּה יהוה אֱלֹהֵינוּ מֶלֶךְ הָעוֹלָם, אֲשֶׁר נָתַן שַׁבָּתוֹת לִמְנוּחָה לְעַמּוֹ יִשְׂרָאֵל בְּאַהֲבָה, לְאוֹת וְלִבְרִית. בָּרוּךְ אַתָּה יהוה, מְקַדֵּשׁ הַשַּׁבָּת.

Blessed are You, HASHEM, our God, King of the Universe, Who gave Sabbaths for contentment to His people Israel with love, as a sign and as a covenant. Blessed are You, HASHEM, Who sanctifies the Sabbath.

(1) Cf. *Nehemiah* 9:31.

---

the manner of our delivery. It is feasible to deliver the same words with a freshness that makes them new and exciting each time.

**בָּרוּךְ** אַתָּה יהוה אֱלֹהֵינוּ מֶלֶךְ הָעוֹלָם, הָאֵל אָבִינוּ מַלְכֵּנוּ אַדִּירֵנוּ בּוֹרְאֵנוּ גּוֹאֲלֵנוּ יוֹצְרֵנוּ קְדוֹשֵׁנוּ קְדוֹשׁ יַעֲקֹב, רוֹעֵנוּ רוֹעֵה יִשְׂרָאֵל, הַמֶּלֶךְ הַטּוֹב וְהַמֵּטִיב לַכֹּל, שֶׁבְּכָל יוֹם וָיוֹם הוּא הֵטִיב, הוּא מֵטִיב, הוּא יֵיטִיב לָנוּ. הוּא גְמָלָנוּ הוּא גוֹמְלֵנוּ הוּא יִגְמְלֵנוּ לָעַד, לְחֵן וּלְחֶסֶד וּלְרַחֲמִים וּלְרֶוַח הַצָּלָה וְהַצְלָחָה, בְּרָכָה וִישׁוּעָה נֶחָמָה פַּרְנָסָה וְכַלְכָּלָה ❖ וְרַחֲמִים וְחַיִּים וְשָׁלוֹם וְכָל טוֹב, וּמִכָּל טוּב לְעוֹלָם אַל יְחַסְּרֵנוּ. (—Others אָמֵן.)

**הָרַחֲמָן** הוּא יִמְלוֹךְ עָלֵינוּ לְעוֹלָם וָעֶד. הָרַחֲמָן הוּא יִתְבָּרַךְ בַּשָּׁמַיִם וּבָאָרֶץ. הָרַחֲמָן הוּא יִשְׁתַּבַּח לְדוֹר דּוֹרִים, וְיִתְפָּאַר בָּנוּ לָעַד וּלְנֵצַח נְצָחִים, וְיִתְהַדַּר בָּנוּ לָעַד וּלְעוֹלְמֵי עוֹלָמִים. הָרַחֲמָן הוּא יְפַרְנְסֵנוּ בְּכָבוֹד. הָרַחֲמָן הוּא יִשְׁבּוֹר עֻלֵּנוּ מֵעַל צַוָּארֵנוּ, וְהוּא יוֹלִיכֵנוּ קוֹמְמִיּוּת לְאַרְצֵנוּ. הָרַחֲמָן הוּא יִשְׁלַח לָנוּ בְּרָכָה מְרֻבָּה בַּבַּיִת הַזֶּה, וְעַל שֻׁלְחָן זֶה שֶׁאָכַלְנוּ עָלָיו. הָרַחֲמָן הוּא יִשְׁלַח לָנוּ אֶת אֵלִיָּהוּ הַנָּבִיא זָכוּר לַטּוֹב, וִיבַשֶּׂר לָנוּ בְּשׂוֹרוֹת טוֹבוֹת יְשׁוּעוֹת וְנֶחָמוֹת.

The Talmud (*Berachos* 46a) gives a rather lengthy text of the blessing that a guest inserts here for the host. It is quoted with minor variations in *Shulchan Aruch* (*Orach Chaim* 201) and many authorities are at a loss to explain why the prescribed text has fallen into disuse in favor of the briefer version commonly used. The text found in *Shulchan Aruch* is:

**יְהִי רָצוֹן** שֶׁלֹּא יֵבוֹשׁ וְלֹא יִכָּלֵם בַּעַל הַבַּיִת הַזֶּה, לֹא בָעוֹלָם הַזֶּה וְלֹא בָעוֹלָם הַבָּא, וְיַצְלִיחַ בְּכָל נְכָסָיו, וְיִהְיוּ נְכָסָיו מוּצְלָחִים וּקְרוֹבִים לָעִיר, וְאַל יִשְׁלוֹט שָׂטָן בְּמַעֲשֵׂה יָדָיו, וְאַל יִזְדַּקֵּק לְפָנָיו שׁוּם דְּבַר חֵטְא וְהִרְהוּר עָוֹן, מֵעַתָּה וְעַד עוֹלָם.

**בָּרוּךְ** Blessed are You, HASHEM, our God, King of the Universe, the Almighty, our Father, our King, our Sovereign, our Creator, our Redeemer, our Maker, our Holy One, Holy One of Yaakov, our Shepherd, the Shepherd of Israel, the King Who is good and Who does good for all. For every single day He did good, He does good, and He will do good to us. He was bountiful with us, He is bountiful with us, and He will forever be bountiful with us — with grace and with kindness and with mercy, with relief, salvation, success, blessing, help, consolation, sustenance, support, Leader— mercy, life, peace, and all good; and of all good things may He never deprive us. (Others— Amen.)

**הָרַחֲמָן** The compassionate One! May He reign over us forever. The compassionate One! May He be blessed in heaven and on earth. The compassionate One! May He be praised throughout all generations, may He be glorified through us forever to the ultimate ends, and be honored through us forever and for all eternity. The compassionate One! May He sustain us in honor. The compassionate One! May He break the yoke of oppression from our necks and guide us erect to our Land. The compassionate One! May He send us abundant blessing to this house and upon this table at which we have eaten. The compassionate One! May He send us Eliahu, the Prophet — he is remembered for good — to proclaim to us good tidings, salvations, and consolations.

The Talmud (*Berachos* 46a) gives a rather lengthy text of the blessing that a guest inserts here for the host. It is quoted with minor variations in *Shulchan Aruch* (*Orach Chaim* 201) and many authorities are at a loss to explain why the prescribed text has fallen into disuse in favor of the briefer version commonly used. The text found in *Shulchan Aruch* is:

**יְהִי רָצוֹן** May it be God's will that this host not be shamed nor humiliated in This World or in the World to Come. May he be successful in all his dealings. May his dealings be successful and conveniently close at hand. May no evil impediment reign over his handiwork, and may no semblance of sin or iniquitous thought attach itself to him from this time and forever.

Those eating at their own table recite (including the words in parentheses that apply):

הָרַחֲמָן הוּא יְבָרֵךְ אוֹתִי (וְאֶת אִשְׁתִּי/ בַּעְלִי וְאֶת זַרְעִי) וְאֶת כָּל אֲשֶׁר לִי.

Guests recite the following (children at their parents' table include the words in parentheses):

הָרַחֲמָן הוּא יְבָרֵךְ אֶת (אָבִי מוֹרִי) בַּעַל הַבַּיִת הַזֶּה, וְאֶת (אִמִּי מוֹרָתִי) בַּעֲלַת הַבַּיִת הַזֶּה, אוֹתָם וְאֶת בֵּיתָם וְאֶת זַרְעָם וְאֶת כָּל אֲשֶׁר לָהֶם.

אוֹתָנוּ וְאֶת כָּל אֲשֶׁר לָנוּ, כְּמוֹ שֶׁנִּתְבָּרְכוּ אֲבוֹתֵינוּ אַבְרָהָם יִצְחָק וְיַעֲקֹב בַּכֹּל מִכֹּל כֹּל,[1] כֵּן יְבָרֵךְ אוֹתָנוּ כֻּלָּנוּ יַחַד בִּבְרָכָה שְׁלֵמָה, וְנֹאמַר, אָמֵן.

**בַּמָּרוֹם** יְלַמְּדוּ עֲלֵיהֶם וְעָלֵינוּ זְכוּת, שֶׁתְּהֵא לְמִשְׁמֶרֶת שָׁלוֹם. וְנִשָּׂא בְרָכָה מֵאֵת יהוה, וּצְדָקָה מֵאֱלֹהֵי יִשְׁעֵנוּ, וְנִמְצָא חֵן וְשֵׂכֶל טוֹב בְּעֵינֵי אֱלֹהִים וְאָדָם.[2]

On the Sabbath add:

הָרַחֲמָן הוּא יַנְחִילֵנוּ יוֹם שֶׁכֻּלּוֹ שַׁבָּת וּמְנוּחָה לְחַיֵּי הָעוֹלָמִים.

Some add the words in parentheses on the two *Seder* nights.

**הָרַחֲמָן** הוּא יַנְחִילֵנוּ יוֹם שֶׁכֻּלּוֹ טוֹב. (יוֹם שֶׁכֻּלּוֹ אָרוּךְ, יוֹם שֶׁצַּדִּיקִים יוֹשְׁבִים וְעַטְרוֹתֵיהֶם בְּרָאשֵׁיהֶם וְנֶהֱנִים מִזִּיו הַשְּׁכִינָה, וִיהִי חֶלְקֵנוּ עִמָּהֶם.)

**הָרַחֲמָן** הוּא יְזַכֵּנוּ לִימוֹת הַמָּשִׁיחַ וּלְחַיֵּי הָעוֹלָם הַבָּא. מִגְדּוֹל יְשׁוּעוֹת מַלְכּוֹ וְעֹשֶׂה חֶסֶד לִמְשִׁיחוֹ לְדָוִד וּלְזַרְעוֹ עַד עוֹלָם.[3] עֹשֶׂה שָׁלוֹם בִּמְרוֹמָיו, הוּא יַעֲשֶׂה שָׁלוֹם עָלֵינוּ וְעַל כָּל יִשְׂרָאֵל. וְאִמְרוּ, אָמֵן.

Those eating at their own table recite (including the words in parentheses that apply):

The compassionate One! May He bless me (my wife/husband and my children) and all that is mine.

Guests recite the following (children at their parents' table include the words in parentheses):

The compassionate One! May He bless (my father, my teacher) the master of this house, and (my mother, my teacher) lady of this house, them, their house, their family, and all that is theirs.

Ours and all that is ours — just as our forefathers Avraham, Yitzchak, and Yaakov were blessed in everything, from everything, with everything.[1] So may He bless us all together with a perfect blessing. And let us say: Amen!

**בַּמָּרוֹם** On high, may merit be pleaded upon them and upon us, for a safeguard of peace. May we receive a blessing from HASHEM and just kindness from the God of our salvation, and find favor and good understanding in the eyes of God and man.[2]

On the Sabbath add:

The compassionate One! May He cause us to inherit the day which will be completely a Sabbath and rest day for eternal life.

Some add the words in parentheses on the two *Seder* nights.

**הָרַחֲמָן** The compassionate One! May He cause us to inherit the day which is completely good (that everlasting day, the day when the just will sit with crowns on their heads, enjoying the reflection of God's majesty — and may our portion be with them!).

**הָרַחֲמָן** The compassionate One! May He make us worthy of the days of Mashiach and the life of the World to Come. He Who is a tower of salvations to His king and does kindness for His anointed, to David and to his descendants forever.[3] He Who makes peace in His heights, may He make peace upon us and upon all Israel. Now respond: Amen!

---

(1) Cf. *Genesis* 24:1; 27:33; 33:11. (2) Cf. *Proverbs* 3:4. (3) *Psalms* 18:51.

**יִרְאוּ** אֶת יהוה קְדֹשָׁיו, כִּי אֵין מַחְסוֹר לִירֵאָיו.
כְּפִירִים רָשׁוּ וְרָעֵבוּ, וְדֹרְשֵׁי יהוה לֹא יַחְסְרוּ
כָל טוֹב.[1] הוֹדוּ לַיהוה כִּי טוֹב, כִּי לְעוֹלָם חַסְדּוֹ.[2]
פּוֹתֵחַ אֶת יָדֶךָ, וּמַשְׂבִּיעַ לְכָל חַי רָצוֹן.[3] בָּרוּךְ הַגֶּבֶר
אֲשֶׁר יִבְטַח בַּיהוה, וְהָיָה יהוה מִבְטַחוֹ.[4] נַעַר הָיִיתִי
גַּם זָקַנְתִּי, וְלֹא רָאִיתִי צַדִּיק נֶעֱזָב, וְזַרְעוֹ מְבַקֶּשׁ
לָחֶם.[5] יהוה עֹז לְעַמּוֹ יִתֵּן, יהוה יְבָרֵךְ אֶת עַמּוֹ
בַשָּׁלוֹם.[6]

Upon completion of *Bircas HaMazon* the blessing over wine is recited and the third cup is drunk while reclining on the left side. It is preferable to drink the entire cup, but at the very least, most of the cup should be drained.

**בָּרוּךְ** אַתָּה יהוה אֱלֹהֵינוּ מֶלֶךְ הָעוֹלָם, בּוֹרֵא
פְּרִי הַגָּפֶן.

The fourth cup is poured. According to most customs, the Cup of Elijah is poured at this point, after which the door is opened in accordance with the verse 'It is a guarded night,' and the following paragraph is recited:

**שְׁפֹךְ** חֲמָתְךָ אֶל הַגּוֹיִם אֲשֶׁר לֹא יְדָעוּךָ וְעַל
מַמְלָכוֹת אֲשֶׁר בְּשִׁמְךָ לֹא קָרָאוּ. כִּי אָכַל אֶת
יַעֲקֹב וְאֶת נָוֵהוּ הֵשַׁמּוּ.[7] שְׁפָךְ עֲלֵיהֶם זַעְמֶךָ וַחֲרוֹן
אַפְּךָ יַשִּׂיגֵם.[8] תִּרְדֹּף בְּאַף וְתַשְׁמִידֵם מִתַּחַת שְׁמֵי
יהוה.[9]

---

### ◆§ *The Cup of Elijah*

Whereas each participant in the *Seder* drinks from his own cup, the cup of Elijah is traditionally a large chalice, and many have the custom that it is shared by all.

Once the cup of Elijah is filled to the brim, the door of the house is thrown open, perhaps to symbolize our inviting the spirit of the prophet who is to be the harbinger of the ultimate Redemption. Tradition has it that Elijah drinks from this cup, whose contents is then distributed among all *Seder* participants.

**יִרְאוּ** Fear HASHEM, you — His holy ones — for there is no deprivation for His reverent ones. Young lions may want and hunger, but those who seek HASHEM will not lack any good.[1] Give thanks to God for He is good; His kindness endures forever.[2] You open Your hand and satisfy the desire of every living thing.[3] Blessed is the man who trusts in HASHEM, then HASHEM will be his security.[4] I was a youth and also have aged, and I have not seen a righteous man forsaken, with his children begging for bread.[5] HASHEM will give might to His people; HASHEM will bless His people with peace.[6]

Upon completion of *Bircas HaMazon* the blessing over wine is recited and the third cup is drunk while reclining on the left side. It is preferable to drink the entire cup, but at the very least, most of the cup should be drained.

**בָּרוּךְ** Blessed are You, HASHEM, our God, King of the Universe, Who creates the fruit of the vine.

The fourth cup is poured. According to most customs, the Cup of Elijah is poured at this point, after which the door is opened in accordance with the verse 'It is a guarded night,' and the following paragraph is recited:

**שְׁפֹךְ** Pour Your wrath upon the nations that do not recognize You and upon the kingdoms that do not invoke Your Name. For they have devoured Yaakov and destroyed His habitation.[7] Pour Your anger upon them and let Your fiery wrath overtake them.[8] Pursue them with wrath and annihilate them from beneath the heavens of HASHEM.[9]

---

(1) *Psalms* 34:10-11. (2) 136:1 et al. (3) 145:16. (4) *Jeremiah* 17:7. (5) *Psalms* 37:25. (6) 29:11. (7) 79:6-7. (8) 69:25. (9) *Lamentations* 3:66.

---

Our individual cups of life may differ, some being more fortunate, some less so. If we remain totally distinct, we are not bringing ourselves closer to the ultimate Redemption. When we drink of a single cup, sharing with each other both the joys and sorrows of life, rejoicing in each other's moments of happiness and strengthening one another in moments of distress, we are then bringing ourselves and all mankind nearer to the Redemption of mankind.

# הלל

The door is closed and the recitation of the Haggadah is continued.

**לֹא לָנוּ** יהוה לֹא לָנוּ, כִּי לְשִׁמְךָ תֵּן כָּבוֹד, עַל חַסְדְּךָ עַל אֲמִתֶּךָ. לָמָּה יֹאמְרוּ הַגּוֹיִם, אַיֵּה נָא אֱלֹהֵיהֶם. וֵאלֹהֵינוּ בַשָּׁמָיִם, כֹּל אֲשֶׁר חָפֵץ עָשָׂה. עֲצַבֵּיהֶם כֶּסֶף וְזָהָב, מַעֲשֵׂה יְדֵי אָדָם. פֶּה לָהֶם וְלֹא יְדַבֵּרוּ, עֵינַיִם לָהֶם וְלֹא יִרְאוּ. אָזְנַיִם לָהֶם וְלֹא יִשְׁמָעוּ, אַף לָהֶם וְלֹא יְרִיחוּן. יְדֵיהֶם וְלֹא יְמִישׁוּן, רַגְלֵיהֶם וְלֹא יְהַלֵּכוּ, לֹא יֶהְגּוּ בִּגְרוֹנָם. כְּמוֹהֶם יִהְיוּ עֹשֵׂיהֶם, כֹּל אֲשֶׁר בֹּטֵחַ בָּהֶם. יִשְׂרָאֵל

### ⁂ לֹא לָנוּ יהוה לֹא לָנוּ, כִּי לְשִׁמְךָ — *Not for our sake, HASHEM, not for our sake, but for Your Name's sake*

Sometimes we find ourselves feeling unworthy, lacking positive feelings, or even feeling frankly worthless. When we think of ourselves as undeserving of God's blessing or attention, we may feel incapable of asking God for anything.

Logical arguments may not budge a person from his negative feelings. He may think, "If you knew the real me, you would agree that I am undeserving." The psalmist provides an approach that cannot be thwarted by this self-destructive perception.

"Not for us, God, but for You. You created each person in Your image, with a spark of Yourself embedded in each of us. Perhaps I am worthless and deserve nothing. But Your Godliness that You have placed within me certainly merits Your love.

"When my self-esteem is at an all-time low, I don't dare ask for Your favor for my sake. But for Your Name, Your essence that lies within me, for Your sake, give me Your blessing."

### ⁂ *The Ultimate Goal*

The hallmark of the spiritual person is that he can set aside personal gain and sacrifice his own comfort and convenience in the interest of an ultimate goal.

When the campaign "Just say no to drugs" was launched, some research

## HALLEL

The door is closed and the recitation of the Haggadah is continued.

**לֹא לָנוּ** Not for our sake, HASHEM, not for our sake, but for Your Name's sake give glory, for Your kindness and for Your truth! Why should the nations say, "Where is their God now?" Our God is in the heavens; whatever He pleases, He does! Their idols are silver and gold, the handiwork of man. They have a mouth, but cannot speak; they have eyes, but cannot see. They have ears, but cannot hear; they have a nose, but cannot smell. Their hands — they cannot feel; their feet — they cannot walk; they cannot utter a sound from their throat.Those who make them should become like them, whoever trusts in them! O Israel,

---

psychologists interviewed young people for their reaction to this, and some responded, "Why? What else is there?"

The goal in life for the majority of western civilization has become pleasure-seeking. When attainment of pleasure is the ultimate goal, it is difficult to convince young people, who consider themselves immune to the dangers of drugs, to forego the euphoria of drugs. It appears to them an absurdity to deny themselves pleasure now for the sake of achieving pleasure in the future.

A spiritual way of life requires adopting a goal of something other than self-gratification. Even the prayers for deliverance from the oppression of hostile rulers should not be primarily for self-seeking interests, but to enable us to bring greater glory to God. This is therefore the clarion call of the Haggadah, and a prayer for redemption: "Not for our sake, Hashem, but for Your Name's sake give glory."

### כְּמוֹהֶם יִהְיוּ עֹשֵׂיהֶם — *Those who make them should become like them*

Because man was created in the image of God, there is an inborn yearning to emulate one's Creator. We must thus be very careful about whom we "choose" as our God. If I choose a molten "god of silver or gold," then, like the mute inanimate idol, I too will lack the aspirations to communicate and empathize with my fellow man.

בְּטַח בַּיהוה, עֶזְרָם וּמָגִנָּם הוּא. בֵּית אַהֲרֹן בִּטְחוּ בַיהוה, עֶזְרָם וּמָגִנָּם הוּא. יִרְאֵי יהוה בִּטְחוּ בַיהוה, עֶזְרָם וּמָגִנָּם הוּא.

**יהוה** זְכָרָנוּ יְבָרֵךְ, יְבָרֵךְ אֶת בֵּית יִשְׂרָאֵל, יְבָרֵךְ אֶת בֵּית אַהֲרֹן. יְבָרֵךְ יִרְאֵי יהוה, הַקְּטַנִּים עִם הַגְּדֹלִים. יֹסֵף יהוה עֲלֵיכֶם, עֲלֵיכֶם וְעַל בְּנֵיכֶם. בְּרוּכִים אַתֶּם לַיהוה, עֹשֵׂה שָׁמַיִם וָאָרֶץ. הַשָּׁמַיִם שָׁמַיִם לַיהוה, וְהָאָרֶץ נָתַן לִבְנֵי אָדָם. לֹא הַמֵּתִים יְהַלְלוּ יָהּ, וְלֹא כָּל יֹרְדֵי דוּמָה. וַאֲנַחְנוּ נְבָרֵךְ יָהּ, מֵעַתָּה וְעַד עוֹלָם, הַלְלוּיָהּ.

---

Israel is therefore reminded to place its trust in Hashem, the true God. By doing this, the desire to emulate the Divine Being enhances our spiritual nature. "As He is merciful, you too shall be merciful." We fashion our character traits after His, and we become better people.

**יהוה זְכָרָנוּ יְבָרֵךְ, יְבָרֵךְ אֶת בֵּית יִשְׂרָאֵל, יְבָרֵךְ אֶת בֵּית אַהֲרֹן. יְבָרֵךְ יִרְאֵי יהוה, הַקְּטַנִּים עִם הַגְּדֹלִים — *Hashem Who has remembered us will bless — He will bless the House of Israel; He will bless the House of Aharon; He will bless those who fear Hashem, the small as well as the great.***

How can one recognize those that truly fear God? It is when the great associate with the small, and do not consider themselves superior to them.

*Rabbi Yisrael of Salant, the great Torah scholar who was the founder of the school of mussar (formal teaching of ethics), spent several weeks at a health resort, and befriended one of the residents, who was unaware of his identity. Since they were some distance from the shochet (ritual slaughterer) in the village, this man asked Rabbi Yisrael if he would alternate days taking chickens to the shochet, to which Rabbi Yisrael gladly consented.*

*Two weeks later the man received a letter from a relative asking whether he had the opportunity to meet the great Rabbi Yisrael at the*

trust in HASHEM; — their help and their shield is He! House of Aaron, trust in HASHEM; their help and their shield is He! You who fear HASHEM, trust in HASHEM; their help and their shield is He!

**יהוה** HASHEM Who has remembered us will bless — He will bless the House of Israel; He will bless the House of Aharon; He will bless those who fear HASHEM, the small as well as the great. May HASHEM increase upon you, upon you and upon your children! You are blessed of HASHEM, maker of heaven and earth. As for the heavens — the heavens are HASHEM's, but the earth He has given to mankind. Neither the dead can praise God, nor any who descend into silence; but we will bless God from this time and forever. Halleluyah!

---

*resort. It was only after some investigation that he confirmed that the friend with whom he sent the chickens to the shochet was the renowned Rabbi Yisrael.*

There are countless stories of Torah personalities who did not let their greatness go to their heads, and remained in touch with the average person. They emulated the Almighty Himself, of whom the Talmud says, "Wherever you find the greatness of God, there also will you find His humility" (*Megillah* 31a).

### לֹא הַמֵּתִים יְהַלְלוּ יָהּ — *Neither the dead can praise God*

When something is lifeless, it no longer has the opportunity or the possibility to develop or improve. After death we only have "what I've done" but no longer "what I will do." If we are left only with our past, we might feel that our actions or intentions were often less than honorable, and we are doomed by our past. "Judged solely on my past, my case may be hopeless! How dare I show my face! 'The dead cannot praise God.' "

On the other hand, if I have the capacity to say, "As of now I am making a commitment toward improvement," then I am alive. I have hope for a future.

"But we will bless God." We do not have to mourn for an unchangeable past, because from now on, "I can develop and I can grow. I have potential."

**אָהַבְתִּי** כִּי יִשְׁמַע יהוה, אֶת קוֹלִי תַּחֲנוּנָי. כִּי הִטָּה אָזְנוֹ לִי, וּבְיָמַי אֶקְרָא. אֲפָפוּנִי חֶבְלֵי מָוֶת, וּמְצָרֵי שְׁאוֹל מְצָאוּנִי, צָרָה וְיָגוֹן אֶמְצָא. וּבְשֵׁם יהוה אֶקְרָא, אָנָּה יהוה מַלְּטָה נַפְשִׁי. חַנּוּן יהוה וְצַדִּיק, וֵאלֹהֵינוּ מְרַחֵם. שֹׁמֵר פְּתָאִים יהוה, דַּלּוֹתִי וְלִי יְהוֹשִׁיעַ. שׁוּבִי נַפְשִׁי לִמְנוּחָיְכִי, כִּי יהוה גָּמַל עָלָיְכִי. כִּי חִלַּצְתָּ נַפְשִׁי מִמָּוֶת, אֶת עֵינִי מִן דִּמְעָה, אֶת רַגְלִי מִדֶּחִי. אֶתְהַלֵּךְ לִפְנֵי יהוה, בְּאַרְצוֹת הַחַיִּים. הֶאֱמַנְתִּי כִּי אֲדַבֵּר, אֲנִי עָנִיתִי מְאֹד. אֲנִי אָמַרְתִּי בְחָפְזִי, כָּל הָאָדָם כֹּזֵב.

**מָה אָשִׁיב** לַיהוה, כָּל תַּגְמוּלוֹהִי עָלָי. כּוֹס

---

**אָהַבְתִּי כִּי יִשְׁמַע יהוה, אֶת קוֹלִי תַּחֲנוּנָי — *I love Him, for HASHEM hears my voice, my supplications.***

Who is unable to identify with this beautiful prayer? Who has not cried out to God in moments of anguish? Who cannot recognize how often God has saved one from the consequences of one's foolish deeds?

The Talmud states that we are the beneficiaries of countless miracles, but that we are often unaware that God has intervened in our behalf. We sometimes attribute our salvation to a "lucky break" or to coincidence. One recovering alcoholic said, "I came to the conclusion that coincidences are nothing other than miracles where God has chosen to remain anonymous."

It is possible to find peace even in the midst of torment. We can rest securely in the knowledge that at all times God is at the helm.

❦ ❦ ❦

How comforting to find someone who really listens. I'm not asking anyone to do anything nor even to say anything. I can gain comfort because someone listens to me.

God, my Beloved, You listen not to my fine oratory or poetic hymns. No, You listen to קוֹלִי, *my voice,* though it might just be the sound of my sobbing or the cry of my confusion. There may be no words that accompany this sound, and even if there are inappropriate words, you nevertheless hear the

**אָהַבְתִּי** I love Him, for HASHEM hears my voice, my supplications. As He has inclined His ear to me, so in my days shall I call. The pains of death encircled me; the confines of the grave have found me; trouble and sorrow I would find. Then I would invoke the Name of HASHEM: "Please HASHEM, save my soul." Gracious is HASHEM and righteous, our God is merciful. HASHEM protects the simple; I was brought low, but He saved me. Return, my soul, to your rest; for HASHEM has been kind to you. For You have delivered my soul from death, my eyes from tears, my feet from stumbling. I shall walk before HASHEM in the lands of the living. I have kept faith although I say: "I suffer exceedingly." I said in my haste: "All mankind is deceitful."

**מָה אָשִׁיב** How can I repay HASHEM for all His kindness to me?

---

voice behind it. It is my sound You listen to. The words might be those of King David or one of the prophets, but the sound is me. You are listening to me, and I am comforted.

### ◆§ הֶאֱמַנְתִּי כִּי אֲדַבֵּר, אֲנִי עָנִיתִי מְאֹד — *I have kept faith although I say: "I suffer exceedingly."*

The Rabbi of Slonim translated this verse to read, "I believed that I will speak, I have suffered greatly," and explained the confusion in the tenses as follows:

The psalmist reflects back to a time of anguish and says, "I believed, even then while I suffered so intensely, that one day I will speak. I believed that there would be a time in the future when I would be able to look back at my distress and say, 'Yes, I suffered then, but today I am a survivor.' " This is the Jewish hope, that today I know that tomorrow I will be able to reflect on yesterday.

### ◆§ מָה אָשִׁיב לַיהוה, כָּל תַּגְמוּלוֹהִי עָלָי — *How can I repay HASHEM for all His kindness to me?*

*One of the chassidic masters, who lived in abject poverty, did not have enough money for food. Initially the pangs of hunger distressed him, but then he thought, "Think of how many people with grave illnesses spend fortunes on medical treatment because they have no appetite. How fortunate you are that you are hungry and that God has*

יְשׁוּעוֹת אֶשָּׂא, וּבְשֵׁם יהוה אֶקְרָא. נְדָרַי לַיהוה אֲשַׁלֵּם, נֶגְדָה נָּא לְכָל עַמּוֹ. יָקָר בְּעֵינֵי יהוה, הַמָּוְתָה לַחֲסִידָיו. אָנָּה יהוה כִּי אֲנִי עַבְדֶּךָ, אֲנִי עַבְדְּךָ, בֶּן אֲמָתֶךָ, פִּתַּחְתָּ לְמוֹסֵרָי. לְךָ אֶזְבַּח זֶבַח תּוֹדָה, וּבְשֵׁם יהוה אֶקְרָא. נְדָרַי לַיהוה אֲשַׁלֵּם, נֶגְדָה נָּא לְכָל עַמּוֹ. בְּחַצְרוֹת בֵּית יהוה, בְּתוֹכֵכִי יְרוּשָׁלָיִם הַלְלוּיָהּ.

**הַלְלוּ** אֶת יהוה, כָּל גּוֹיִם, שַׁבְּחוּהוּ כָּל הָאֻמִּים. כִּי גָבַר עָלֵינוּ חַסְדּוֹ, וֶאֱמֶת יהוה לְעוֹלָם, הַלְלוּיָהּ.

**הוֹדוּ** לַיהוה כִּי טוֹב, כִּי לְעוֹלָם חַסְדּוֹ.

---

*given you an appetite!" He began to dance with joy celebrating his hunger.*

*Another chassidic master said, "I was never in want for anything. If I really needed something, God would have provided it for me. Since He did not, then I must not need it. Why should I want something I do not need?"*

We are often dissatisfied with what we have. We sometimes act like juveniles, who demand something and cry until it is given to them, only to discard it shortly afterward. A healthy spiritual attitude is to accept with equanimity whatever we have, and if we feel deprived of something, to carefully analyze whether it is truly a need. As parents, we try to impress our young children that we know better what their wholesome needs are. As children of God, we should accord Him that wisdom.

### ⁂ כּוֹס יְשׁוּעוֹת אֶשָּׂא — *I will raise the cup of salvations*

It is of interest that this verse is included in the *Havdalah* service, concluding the Shabbos. It is not recited at the entrance of Shabbos, but at its completion, as we prepare to enter another week of challenge.

The Shabbos itself is not a challenge. To the contrary, it is a period of respite from our struggle with life. On Shabbos we gather spiritual strength to enable us to continue our mission on earth. God has sanctified the Shabbos

I will raise the cup of salvations and the Name of HASHEM I will invoke. My vows to HASHEM I will pay, in the presence, now, of His entire people. Difficult in the eyes of HASHEM is the death of His devout ones. Please, HASHEM — for I am Your servant, I am Your servant, son of Your handmaid — You have released my bonds. To You I will sacrifice thanksgiving offerings, and the name of HASHEM I will invoke. My vows to HASHEM I will pay, in the presence, now, of His entire people. In the courtyards of the House of HASHEM, in your midst, O Jerusalem, Halleluyah!

**הַלְלוּ** Praise HASHEM, all nations; praise Him, all the states! For His kindness has overwhelmed us, and the truth of HASHEM is eternal, Halleluyah!

**הוֹדוּ** Give thanks to HASHEM for He is good;
His kindness endures forever!

---

and made it holy. We must take this sanctity with us and make the workweek holy as well.

### ◆§ אֲנִי עַבְדְּךָ . . . פִּתַּחְתָּ לְמוֹסֵרָי — *I am Your servant . . . You have released my bonds.*

I serve God by choice, not because I am compelled to do so. There are no shackles around my wrists or ankles that prevent me from running away. Not only am I free of such restraints, but serving God has removed other restraints from me. I can be free of the tyranny of my temptations and impulses. I am not a brute beast that is a slave to its bodily desires. Serving human masters can make a person into a slave. Serving God makes a person free.

### ◆§ הוֹדוּ לַיהוה כִּי טוֹב, כִּי לְעוֹלָם חַסְדּוֹ — *Give thanks to Hashem, for He is good, His kindness endures forever!*

Why do these two phrases go together? We seem to be saying that we should be grateful to God because His kindness is *always* with us. But should one not be grateful for any and all kindnesses? Suppose a person does me a kindness only once, am I not supposed to be thankful to him? Why do we seem to be qualifying that our gratitude is contingent on God always being kind?

This verse contains an important message. We must understand that the Hebrew word *hoda'ah* has two meanings: (1) gratitude and (2) confession.

יֹאמַר נָא יִשְׂרָאֵל, כִּי לְעוֹלָם חַסְדּוֹ.
יֹאמְרוּ נָא בֵית אַהֲרֹן, כִּי לְעוֹלָם חַסְדּוֹ.
יֹאמְרוּ נָא יִרְאֵי יהוה, כִּי לְעוֹלָם חַסְדּוֹ.

**מִן הַמֵּצַר** קָרָאתִי יָּהּ, עָנָנִי בַמֶּרְחָב יָהּ. יהוה לִי לֹא אִירָא, מַה יַּעֲשֶׂה לִי אָדָם. יהוה לִי בְּעֹזְרָי, וַאֲנִי אֶרְאֶה בְשֹׂנְאָי. טוֹב לַחֲסוֹת בַּיהוה, מִבְּטֹחַ בָּאָדָם. טוֹב לַחֲסוֹת בַּיהוה, מִבְּטֹחַ בִּנְדִיבִים. כָּל גּוֹיִם סְבָבוּנִי, בְּשֵׁם יהוה כִּי אֲמִילַם. סַבּוּנִי גַם סְבָבוּנִי, בְּשֵׁם יהוה כִּי אֲמִילַם. סַבּוּנִי כִדְבֹרִים דֹּעֲכוּ כְּאֵשׁ קוֹצִים, בְּשֵׁם יהוה כִּי אֲמִילַם. דַּחֹה דְחִיתַנִי לִנְפֹּל, וַיהוה עֲזָרָנִי. עָזִּי וְזִמְרָת יָהּ,

---

There are times that we experience unpleasant things in life and we are not in the least grateful for them. On the contrary, we are resentful, and we may feel angry towards God, but out of reverence, we say nothing. Then time goes by, months, perhaps years, and we see that what we had thought to be detrimental was actually to our own advantage, but we were not able to see it as such at that time. We now admit that God was indeed wiser than we, and we now thank Him not only for the current benevolence, but for what He did back then that enabled the present kindness to occur.

When we were infants, our mothers took us to the doctor to be immunized. We hardly appreciated the painful injections then, but now as mature adults, when we recognize that we were spared from crippling diseases, we admit that our mothers were right, and we thank them for acting in our behalf.

*Hodu LaShem* means admit to God, and also *Hodu LaShem,* thank Him, *ki tov,* because He is good, and His kindness is always with us. Admit to Him now that what you failed to recognize as a kindness back then, was indeed such, and thank Him for it.

### ☙ *Expressing Gratitude*

Is it not strange that people refer only to earthquakes, volcanic eruptions, and tidal waves as "acts of God"? Why do we not refer to it as an act of God when the earth produces grain, when trees bear delicious fruit, and when a

Let Israel say: His kindness endures forever!

Let the House of Aharon say:

His kindness endures forever!

Let those who fear HASHEM say:

His kindness endures forever!

**מִן הַמֵּצַר** From the straits did I call upon God; He answered me in the broad places of HASHEM. HASHEM is with me, I have no fear; how can man affect me? HASHEM is with me through my helpers; therefore I can face my foes. It is better to take refuge in HASHEM than to rely on man. It is better to take refuge in HASHEM than to rely on nobles. All the nations surround me; in the Name of HASHEM I cut them down! They encircle me, they also surround me; in the Name of HASHEM I cut them down! They encircle me like bees, but they are extinguished as a fire on thorns; in the Name of HASHEM I cut them down! You pushed me constantly that I might fall, but HASHEM assisted me. God is my might and my praise,

---

beautifully formed child emerges from its mother's womb? True, the Talmud requires that we always express our gratitude to God, even when we experience distress. Like the infant who feels the pain of the injection which will protect him from dreaded diseases, but who cannot understand that the pain he is experiencing is to his ultimate advantage, we may not appreciate the Divine beneficence that is sometimes clothed in suffering. There is still a great deal of good and kindness evident even in such Divine blessings, but altogether too frequently we are derelict in expressing our gratitude to God for His manifest blessings.

### ◆§ מִן הַמֵּצַר קָרָאתִי יָּהּ — *From the straits did I call upon God*

Having just stated that we should always express our gratitude to God, the psalmist acknowledges human nature. Sometimes we do not turn to God until we are in dire straits, only when we have hit "rock bottom."

But as long as we turn to Him, God responds. Some people deny their anguish, or drown in addictive behavior. Some people run away and try a change of venue. None of these work. The psalmist tells us to allow ourselves to feel the pain, and call upon God for help.

וַיְהִי לִי לִישׁוּעָה. קוֹל רִנָּה וִישׁוּעָה, בְּאָהֳלֵי צַדִּיקִים, יְמִין יהוה עֹשָׂה חָיִל. יְמִין יהוה רוֹמֵמָה, יְמִין יהוה עֹשָׂה חָיִל. לֹא אָמוּת כִּי אֶחְיֶה, וַאֲסַפֵּר מַעֲשֵׂי יָהּ. יַסֹּר יִסְּרַנִּי יָּהּ, וְלַמָּוֶת לֹא נְתָנָנִי. פִּתְחוּ לִי שַׁעֲרֵי צֶדֶק, אָבֹא בָם אוֹדֶה יָהּ. זֶה הַשַּׁעַר לַיהוה, צַדִּיקִים יָבֹאוּ בוֹ. אוֹדְךָ כִּי עֲנִיתָנִי, וַתְּהִי לִי לִישׁוּעָה. אוֹדְךָ כִּי עֲנִיתָנִי, וַתְּהִי לִי לִישׁוּעָה. אֶבֶן מָאֲסוּ הַבּוֹנִים, הָיְתָה לְרֹאשׁ פִּנָּה. אֶבֶן מָאֲסוּ הַבּוֹנִים, הָיְתָה לְרֹאשׁ פִּנָּה. מֵאֵת יהוה הָיְתָה זֹּאת, הִיא נִפְלָאת בְּעֵינֵינוּ. מֵאֵת יהוה הָיְתָה זֹּאת, הִיא נִפְלָאת בְּעֵינֵינוּ.

---

**לֹא אָמוּת כִּי אֶחְיֶה, וַאֲסַפֵּר מַעֲשֵׂי יָהּ — *I shall not die! But I shall live and relate the deeds of God.***

What does the psalmist mean, "I shall not die"? No human being is eternal, no one escapes death.

No, we may not escape death when we die, but we can avoid dying while we are alive. Some people lose their dreams and ambitions, and their spirit dies while their body still lingers. Although they go through the motions of life, they have suffered a spiritual death.

True, God has put me through tests. I have suffered, but I have grown with the sufferings. I see God's handiwork in everything, and this enables me to rise through my sufferings to higher spiritual levels. I may be mortal, but I can defy spiritual death.

**אוֹדְךָ כִּי עֲנִיתָנִי, וַתְּהִי לִי לִישׁוּעָה — *I thank You for You have answered me and become my salvation.***

In this psalm King David relates his anguish and suffering, and closes with gratitude to God for his salvation. An understanding of this psalm requires some biographical data provided by the Midrash.

King David is one of the greatest of all figures in the tradition of Judaism — a spiritual giant who is ranked with Abraham, Isaac, Jacob and Moses — but no one suffered greater distress and humiliation. His older brothers, noble men themselves, considered him an upstart and an outcast. When God commissioned the prophet Samuel to anoint one of Yishai's sons as the King

and He will be a salvation for me. The sound of rejoicing and salvation is in the tents of the righteous: "HASHEM's right hand does valiantly. HASHEM's right hand is raised triumphantly; HASHEM's right hand does valiantly!" I shall not die! But I shall live and relate the deeds of God. God has chastened me exceedingly, but He did not let me die. Open for me the gates of righteousness, I will enter them and thank God. This is the gate of HASHEM; the righteous shall enter through it. I thank You for You have answered me and become my salvation. I thank You for You have answered me and become my salvation. The stone the builders despised has become the cornerstone. The stone the builders despised has become the cornerstone. This emanated from HASHEM; it is wondrous in our eyes. This emanated from HASHEM; it is wondrous in our eyes.

---

of Israel, Yishai brought his seven older sons to the prophet; David was left in the field with the sheep. His own family did not even consider him a candidate. When Samuel rejected all the sons brought before him, he asked, "Is there not yet another?" When he laid eyes on David, he said, "This is the one chosen by God."

Later, a member of the Sanhedrin, Doeg the Edomite, cast aspersions on David's ancestry, claiming that he was ineligible to become king. Incredible as it seems in the light of history, the Davidic dynasty, which is so central to the history of our people, was almost stillborn.

Yet David survived years of calumny and rejection. Ultimately he was elevated to the highest position in Jewish history. With his psalms he earned the title "the sweet minstrel of Israel." David gives hope to the suffering and downtrodden, and as they find courage and strength in his psalms, he is perpetuated in their lives. Of no other personality in Jewish history is it said, "David, King of Israel, lives forever."

### ◆§ אוֹדְךָ כִּי עֲנִיתָנִי — *I thank You for having given me suffering*

The Midrash interprets this verse a bit differently, translating the word עניתני to mean "having given me suffering," and the phrase then reads, "I give thanks to You for giving me suffering and being my salvation." But how are we to understand anyone being grateful for suffering?

When I began to work with people recovering from various addictions, I

זֶה הַיּוֹם עָשָׂה יהוה, נָגִילָה וְנִשְׂמְחָה בוֹ. זֶה הַיּוֹם עָשָׂה יהוה, נָגִילָה וְנִשְׂמְחָה בוֹ.

**אָנָּא** יהוה הוֹשִׁיעָה נָּא. אָנָּא יהוה הוֹשִׁיעָה נָּא. אָנָּא יהוה הַצְלִיחָה נָא. אָנָּא יהוה הַצְלִיחָה נָא.

**בָּרוּךְ** הַבָּא בְּשֵׁם יהוה, בֵּרַכְנוּכֶם מִבֵּית יהוה. בָּרוּךְ הַבָּא בְּשֵׁם יהוה, בֵּרַכְנוּכֶם מִבֵּית יהוה. אֵל יהוה וַיָּאֶר לָנוּ, אִסְרוּ חַג בַּעֲבֹתִים, עַד קַרְנוֹת הַמִּזְבֵּחַ. אֵל יהוה וַיָּאֶר לָנוּ, אִסְרוּ חַג בַּעֲבֹתִים, עַד קַרְנוֹת הַמִּזְבֵּחַ. אֵלִי אַתָּה וְאוֹדֶךָּ, אֱלֹהַי אֲרוֹמְמֶךָּ. אֵלִי אַתָּה וְאוֹדֶךָּ, אֱלֹהַי אֲרוֹמְמֶךָּ. הוֹדוּ לַיהוה כִּי טוֹב, כִּי לְעוֹלָם חַסְדּוֹ. הוֹדוּ לַיהוה כִּי טוֹב, כִּי לְעוֹלָם חַסְדּוֹ.

**יְהַלְלוּךָ** יהוה אֱלֹהֵינוּ כָּל מַעֲשֶׂיךָ, וַחֲסִידֶיךָ צַדִּיקִים עוֹשֵׂי רְצוֹנֶךָ, וְכָל עַמְּךָ בֵּית יִשְׂרָאֵל בְּרִנָּה יוֹדוּ וִיבָרְכוּ וִישַׁבְּחוּ וִיפָאֲרוּ וִירוֹמְמוּ וְיַעֲרִיצוּ וְיַקְדִּישׁוּ וְיַמְלִיכוּ אֶת שִׁמְךָ מַלְכֵּנוּ, כִּי לְךָ טוֹב לְהוֹדוֹת וּלְשִׁמְךָ נָאֶה לְזַמֵּר, כִּי מֵעוֹלָם וְעַד עוֹלָם אַתָּה אֵל.

---

would hear someone say, "Thank God I was addictive. I never could have been what I am now if I had not gone through that suffering." I was perplexed. Why would anyone be thankful for suffering?

As I watched these people grow in spirituality, I began to understand. Spiritual growth is not easy. It calls for self-sacrifice and for denying oneself many of the things that people consider to be the pleasures of life. Spiritual growth may be where the colloquial "growing pains" occur.

People instinctively avoid pain, and may avoid spiritual growth because of the discomfort it entails. The addict has no choice. If he is to recover, he must improve the quality of his spirituality, otherwise he will relapse.

This is why recovered addicts may be grateful for their suffering, because it was the only stimulus that could bring them to spirituality.

This phenomenon is not restricted to addicts. We may all plod along in life,

This is the day HASHEM has made; let us rejoice and be glad on it. This is the day HASHEM has made; let us rejoice and be glad on it.

**אָנָּא** Please, HASHEM, save now! Please, HASHEM, save now! Please, HASHEM, bring success now! Please, HASHEM, bring success now!

**בָּרוּךְ** Blessed is he who comes in the Name of HASHEM; we bless you from the House of HASHEM. Blessed is he who comes in the Name of HASHEM; we bless you from the House of HASHEM. HASHEM is God, He illuminated for us; bind the festival offering with cords until the corners of the Altar. HASHEM is God, He illuminated for us; bind the festival offering with cords until the corners of the Altar. You are my God, and I will thank You; my God, I will exalt You. You are my God, and I will thank You; my God, I will exalt You. Give thanks to HASHEM, for He is good; His kindness endures forever. Give thanks to HASHEM, for He is good; His kindness endures forever.

**יְהַלְלוּךָ** All Your works shall praise You, HASHEM our God. And Your devout ones, the righteous, who do Your will, and Your entire people, the House of Israel, with glad song will thank, bless, praise, glorify, exalt, extol, sanctify, and proclaim the sovereignty of Your Name, our King. For to You it is fitting to give thanks, and unto Your Name it is proper to sing praises, for from This World to the World to Come You are God.

---

and we may neglect our spirituality unless we are forced into it. When God gives and stimulates us to spiritual growth, we should be grateful.

### אֵלִי אַתָּה וְאוֹדֶךָּ — *You are my God, and I will thank You*

The word אוֹדֶךָּ has a two-fold meaning. It can be translated as "I will praise you," or "I will acknowledge you." To acknowledge God means to proclaim, "God is my Father. I am a child of God."

To be children of God places a responsibility upon us. A child may behave

**הוֹדוּ** לַיהוה כִּי טוֹב כִּי לְעוֹלָם חַסְדּוֹ.
הוֹדוּ לֵאלֹהֵי הָאֱלֹהִים כִּי לְעוֹלָם חַסְדּוֹ.
הוֹדוּ לַאֲדֹנֵי הָאֲדֹנִים כִּי לְעוֹלָם חַסְדּוֹ.
לְעֹשֵׂה נִפְלָאוֹת גְּדֹלוֹת לְבַדּוֹ כִּי לְעוֹלָם חַסְדּוֹ.
לְעֹשֵׂה הַשָּׁמַיִם בִּתְבוּנָה כִּי לְעוֹלָם חַסְדּוֹ.
לְרֹקַע הָאָרֶץ עַל הַמָּיִם כִּי לְעוֹלָם חַסְדּוֹ.
לְעֹשֵׂה אוֹרִים גְּדֹלִים כִּי לְעוֹלָם חַסְדּוֹ.
אֶת הַשֶּׁמֶשׁ לְמֶמְשֶׁלֶת בַּיּוֹם כִּי לְעוֹלָם חַסְדּוֹ.
אֶת הַיָּרֵחַ וְכוֹכָבִים לְמֶמְשְׁלוֹת בַּלָּיְלָה
כִּי לְעוֹלָם חַסְדּוֹ.
לְמַכֵּה מִצְרַיִם בִּבְכוֹרֵיהֶם כִּי לְעוֹלָם חַסְדּוֹ.
וַיּוֹצֵא יִשְׂרָאֵל מִתּוֹכָם כִּי לְעוֹלָם חַסְדּוֹ.
בְּיָד חֲזָקָה וּבִזְרוֹעַ נְטוּיָה כִּי לְעוֹלָם חַסְדּוֹ.
לְגֹזֵר יַם סוּף לִגְזָרִים כִּי לְעוֹלָם חַסְדּוֹ.
וְהֶעֱבִיר יִשְׂרָאֵל בְּתוֹכוֹ כִּי לְעוֹלָם חַסְדּוֹ.
וְנִעֵר פַּרְעֹה וְחֵילוֹ בְיַם סוּף כִּי לְעוֹלָם חַסְדּוֹ.
לְמוֹלִיךְ עַמּוֹ בַּמִּדְבָּר כִּי לְעוֹלָם חַסְדּוֹ.
לְמַכֵּה מְלָכִים גְּדֹלִים כִּי לְעוֹלָם חַסְדּוֹ.
וַיַּהֲרֹג מְלָכִים אַדִּירִים כִּי לְעוֹלָם חַסְדּוֹ.

---

in a manner that may bring shame to the parents, and parents may wish to avoid embarrassment by denying that this is their child.

To acknowledge God as our Father, we must live so that our actions praise Him and bring honor to His Name. We are indeed proud to say, "This (You) are my God," and we must behave in such a fashion that God will be proud to say, "That is My child."

הודו Give thanks to HASHEM for He is good,
for His kindness endures forever.
Give thanks to the God of the heavenly powers,
for His kindness endures forever.
Give thanks to the Lord of the lords,
for His kindness endures forever.
To Him Who alone performs great wonders,
for His kindness endures forever.
To Him Who made the heavens with understanding,
for His kindness endures forever.
To Him Who spread out the earth upon the waters,
for His kindness endures forever.
To Him Who made great lights,
for His kindness endures forever.
The sun for the reign of the day,
for His kindness endures forever.
The moon and the stars for the reign of the night,
for His kindness endures forever.
To Him Who smote Egypt through their firstborn,
for His kindness endures forever.
And brought Israel forth from their midst,
for His kindness endures forever.
With strong hand and outstretched arm,
for His kindness endures forever.
To Him Who divided the Sea of Reeds into parts,
for His kindness endures forever.
And caused Israel to pass through it,
for His kindness endures forever.
And threw Pharaoh and his army into the Sea of Reeds,
for His kindness endures forever.
To Him Who led His people through the wilderness,
for His kindness endures forever.
To Him Who smote great kings,
for His kindness endures forever.
And slew mighty kings, for His kindness endures forever.

לְסִיחוֹן מֶלֶךְ הָאֱמֹרִי כִּי לְעוֹלָם חַסְדּוֹ.
וּלְעוֹג מֶלֶךְ הַבָּשָׁן כִּי לְעוֹלָם חַסְדּוֹ.
וְנָתַן אַרְצָם לְנַחֲלָה כִּי לְעוֹלָם חַסְדּוֹ.
נַחֲלָה לְיִשְׂרָאֵל עַבְדּוֹ כִּי לְעוֹלָם חַסְדּוֹ.
שֶׁבְּשִׁפְלֵנוּ זָכַר לָנוּ כִּי לְעוֹלָם חַסְדּוֹ.
וַיִּפְרְקֵנוּ מִצָּרֵינוּ כִּי לְעוֹלָם חַסְדּוֹ.
נֹתֵן לֶחֶם לְכָל בָּשָׂר כִּי לְעוֹלָם חַסְדּוֹ.
הוֹדוּ לְאֵל הַשָּׁמָיִם כִּי לְעוֹלָם חַסְדּוֹ.

**נִשְׁמַת** כָּל חַי תְּבָרֵךְ אֶת שִׁמְךָ יהוה אֱלֹהֵינוּ וְרוּחַ כָּל בָּשָׂר תְּפָאֵר וּתְרוֹמֵם זִכְרְךָ מַלְכֵּנוּ תָּמִיד. מִן הָעוֹלָם וְעַד הָעוֹלָם אַתָּה אֵל וּמִבַּלְעָדֶיךָ אֵין לָנוּ מֶלֶךְ גּוֹאֵל וּמוֹשִׁיעַ פּוֹדֶה וּמַצִּיל וּמְפַרְנֵס וּמְרַחֵם בְּכָל עֵת צָרָה וְצוּקָה. אֵין לָנוּ מֶלֶךְ אֶלָּא אָתָּה. אֱלֹהֵי הָרִאשׁוֹנִים וְהָאַחֲרוֹנִים אֱלוֹהַּ כָּל בְּרִיּוֹת אֲדוֹן כָּל תּוֹלָדוֹת הַמְּהֻלָּל בְּרֹב הַתִּשְׁבָּחוֹת הַמְנַהֵג עוֹלָמוֹ בְּחֶסֶד וּבְרִיּוֹתָיו בְּרַחֲמִים

---

### *Nishmas*

It is almost criminal to comment on the *Nishmas* prayer. It is the "prayer of prayers," complete with every possible aspect of prayer: praise of God; expression of faith, trust, and hope; man's humility and at the very same time his greatness. All one should do with *Nishmas* is roll over every single word on one's tongue, savoring it as one would each bite of an exquisite delicacy. To try to comment on *Nishmas* is like trying to improve on a breathtaking sunset or a majestic waterfall.

Yet, if one is standing alongside a person who has lost his vision, one would try as best as possible to describe the colors and cloud formations of the sunset or the falling, foaming water of the cascade. Similarly, someone may be reciting *Nishmas,* and be oblivious of its beauty. I know, because it happened to me.

Sichon, king of the Emorites,
for His kindness endures forever.
And Og, king of Bashan, for His kindness endures forever.
And presented their land as a heritage,
for His kindness endures forever.
A heritage for Israel, His servant,
for His kindness endures forever.
In our lowliness He remembered us,
for His kindness endures forever.
And released us from our tormentors,
for His kindness endures forever.
He gives nourishment to all flesh,
for His kindness endures forever.
Praise to the God of heaven,
for His kindness endures forever.

**נִשְׁמַת** The soul of every living being shall bless Your Name, HASHEM our God; the spirit of all flesh shall always glorify and exalt Your remembrance, our King. From This World to the World to Come, You are God, and other than You we have no king, redeemer or savior. Liberator, Rescuer, Sustainer and Merciful One in every time of distress and anguish, we have no king but You! — God of the first and of the last, God of all creatures, Master of all generations, Who is extolled through a multitude of praises, Who guides His world with kindness and His creatures with mercy.

---

I once attended a meeting of Alcoholics Anonymous at which a number of people expressed their gratitude on being sober and how wonderful life had become for them. It was a day on which I was definitely not in a euphoric state of mind. One person rose and said, "I'm now sober for four years, and I wish I could say it has all been good. Two years ago my plant closed down and I haven't been able to find a job since. My wife is suing me for divorce. My house is up for sheriff's sale and my car has been repossessed. But I can't believe that God has brought me through everything only to walk out on me now."

I was buoyed by this statement, and my hope was strengthened. On the following Shabbos I noted for the first time the words of *Nishmas* that I had been reciting for fifty years. "You redeemed us from Egypt . . . In famine You

וַיהוה לֹא יָנוּם וְלֹא יִישָׁן הַמְּעוֹרֵר יְשֵׁנִים וְהַמֵּקִיץ נִרְדָּמִים וְהַמֵּשִׂיחַ אִלְּמִים וְהַמַּתִּיר אֲסוּרִים וְהַסּוֹמֵךְ נוֹפְלִים וְהַזּוֹקֵף כְּפוּפִים לְךָ לְבַדְּךָ אֲנַחְנוּ מוֹדִים. אִלּוּ פִינוּ מָלֵא שִׁירָה כַּיָּם וּלְשׁוֹנֵנוּ רִנָּה כַּהֲמוֹן גַּלָּיו וְשִׂפְתוֹתֵינוּ שֶׁבַח כְּמֶרְחֲבֵי רָקִיעַ וְעֵינֵינוּ מְאִירוֹת כַּשֶּׁמֶשׁ וְכַיָּרֵחַ וְיָדֵינוּ פְרוּשׂוֹת כְּנִשְׂרֵי שָׁמָיִם וְרַגְלֵינוּ קַלּוֹת כָּאַיָּלוֹת אֵין אֲנַחְנוּ מַסְפִּיקִים לְהוֹדוֹת לְךָ יהוה אֱלֹהֵינוּ וֵאלֹהֵי אֲבוֹתֵינוּ וּלְבָרֵךְ אֶת שְׁמֶךָ עַל אַחַת מֵאָלֶף אֶלֶף אַלְפֵי אֲלָפִים וְרִבֵּי רְבָבוֹת פְּעָמִים הַטּוֹבוֹת שֶׁעָשִׂיתָ עִם אֲבוֹתֵינוּ וְעִמָּנוּ. מִמִּצְרַיִם גְּאַלְתָּנוּ יהוה אֱלֹהֵינוּ וּמִבֵּית עֲבָדִים פְּדִיתָנוּ בְּרָעָב זַנְתָּנוּ וּבְשָׂבָע כִּלְכַּלְתָּנוּ מֵחֶרֶב הִצַּלְתָּנוּ וּמִדֶּבֶר מִלַּטְתָּנוּ וּמֵחֳלָיִם רָעִים וְנֶאֱמָנִים דִּלִּיתָנוּ. עַד הֵנָּה עֲזָרוּנוּ רַחֲמֶיךָ וְלֹא עֲזָבוּנוּ חֲסָדֶיךָ וְאַל תִּטְּשֵׁנוּ יהוה אֱלֹהֵינוּ לָנֶצַח. עַל כֵּן אֵבָרִים שֶׁפִּלַּגְתָּ בָּנוּ וְרוּחַ וּנְשָׁמָה שֶׁנָּפַחְתָּ בְּאַפֵּינוּ וְלָשׁוֹן אֲשֶׁר שַׂמְתָּ בְּפִינוּ הֵן הֵם יוֹדוּ וִיבָרְכוּ וִישַׁבְּחוּ וִיפָאֲרוּ וִירוֹמְמוּ וְיַעֲרִיצוּ וְיַקְדִּישׁוּ וְיַמְלִיכוּ אֶת שִׁמְךָ מַלְכֵּנוּ. כִּי כָל פֶּה לְךָ יוֹדֶה וְכָל לָשׁוֹן לְךָ תִשָּׁבַע

---

nourished us . . . from sword You saved us . . . and from severe and enduring diseases You spared us. **Until now Your mercy has helped us, and Your kindness has not forsaken us. Do not abandon us, Hashem, our God, forever."** How strange! I had been saying these words, but had never really heard them.

The reconciliation of self-esteem and humility could not be better done. "Were our mouths as full of song as the sea, and our tongues full of joyous song as its multitude of waves, and our lips as full of praise as the breadth of the heavens, and our eyes as brilliant as the sun . . . we still could not thank You sifficiently." How is that for humility? "Therefore, the organs that You set

HASHEM neither slumbers nor sleeps. He Who rouses the sleepers and awakens the slumberers, Who makes the mute speak and releases the bound; Who supports the fallen and straightens the bent. To You alone we give thanks. Were our mouth as full of song as the sea, and our tongue as full of joyous song as its multitude of waves, and our lips as full of praise as the breadth of the heavens, and our eyes as brilliant as the sun and the moon, and our hands as outspread as eagles of the sky and our feet as swift as hinds — we still could not thank You sufficiently, HASHEM our God and God of our forefathers, and to bless Your Name for even one of the thousand thousand, thousands of thousands and myriad myriads of favors that You performed for our ancestors and for us. You redeemed us from Egypt, HASHEM our God, and liberated us from the house of bondage. In famine You nourished us and in plenty You sustained us. From sword You saved us; from plague You let us escape; and from severe and enduring diseases You spared us. Until now Your mercy has helped us, and Your kindness has not forsaken us. Do not abandon us, HASHEM our God, forever. Therefore, the organs that You set within us, and the spirit and soul that You breathed into our nostrils, and the tongue that You placed in our mouth — all of them shall thank and bless, praise and glorify, exalt and revere, sanctify and proclaim the sovereignty of Your Name, our King. For every mouth shall offer thanks to You; every tongue shall vow allegiance to You;

---

within us, and the spirit and soul that You breathed into our nostrils, and the tongue that You placed in our mouth . . . all of them shall praise and glorify Your great Name." In other words, we ourselves are nothing, but with the greatness that God has instilled within us, we can approach the Infinite.

As I write, I realize that I am accusing the reader of being oblivious to the exquisite beauty of this prayer, similar to the sightless person who can- not see the sunset. I have no right to pass judgment and perhaps insult you. Let me therefore assume that some people may just not have noticed the western sky at dusk, and all I need to say is, "Just look at that gorgeous sunset."

❧ ❧ ❧

וְכָל בֶּרֶךְ לְךָ תִכְרַע וְכָל קוֹמָה לְפָנֶיךָ תִשְׁתַּחֲוֶה וְכָל לְבָבוֹת יִירָאוּךָ וְכָל קֶרֶב וּכְלָיוֹת יְזַמְּרוּ לִשְׁמֶךָ. כַּדָּבָר שֶׁכָּתוּב כָּל עַצְמֹתַי תֹּאמַרְנָה יהוה מִי כָמוֹךָ מַצִּיל עָנִי מֵחָזָק מִמֶּנּוּ וְעָנִי וְאֶבְיוֹן מִגֹּזְלוֹ. מִי יִדְמֶה לָּךְ וּמִי יִשְׁוֶה לָּךְ וּמִי יַעֲרָךְ לָךְ הָאֵל הַגָּדוֹל הַגִּבּוֹר וְהַנּוֹרָא אֵל עֶלְיוֹן קֹנֵה שָׁמַיִם וָאָרֶץ. נְהַלֶּלְךָ וּנְשַׁבֵּחֲךָ וּנְפָאֶרְךָ וּנְבָרֵךְ אֶת שֵׁם קָדְשֶׁךָ כָּאָמוּר לְדָוִד בָּרְכִי נַפְשִׁי אֶת יהוה וְכָל קְרָבַי אֶת שֵׁם קָדְשׁוֹ:

**הָאֵל** בְּתַעֲצֻמוֹת עֻזֶּךָ הַגָּדוֹל בִּכְבוֹד שְׁמֶךָ הַגִּבּוֹר לָנֶצַח וְהַנּוֹרָא בְּנוֹרְאוֹתֶיךָ הַמֶּלֶךְ הַיּוֹשֵׁב עַל כִּסֵּא רָם וְנִשָּׂא:

**שׁוֹכֵן עַד** מָרוֹם וְקָדוֹשׁ שְׁמוֹ. וְכָתוּב רַנְּנוּ צַדִּיקִים בַּיהוה לַיְשָׁרִים נָאוָה תְהִלָּה: בְּפִי יְשָׁרִים תִּתְהַלָּל וּבְדִבְרֵי צַדִּיקִים תִּתְבָּרַךְ וּבִלְשׁוֹן חֲסִידִים תִּתְרוֹמָם וּבְקֶרֶב קְדוֹשִׁים תִּתְקַדָּשׁ:

**וּבְמַקְהֲלוֹת** רִבְבוֹת עַמְּךָ בֵּית יִשְׂרָאֵל בְּרִנָּה יִתְפָּאַר שִׁמְךָ מַלְכֵּנוּ בְּכָל דּוֹר וָדוֹר שֶׁכֵּן חוֹבַת כָּל הַיְצוּרִים לְפָנֶיךָ יהוה אֱלֹהֵינוּ וֵאלֹהֵי אֲבוֹתֵינוּ לְהוֹדוֹת לְהַלֵּל לְשַׁבֵּחַ לְפָאֵר לְרוֹמֵם לְהַדֵּר לְבָרֵךְ לְעַלֵּה וּלְקַלֵּס עַל כָּל דִּבְרֵי שִׁירוֹת וְתִשְׁבְּחוֹת דָּוִד בֶּן יִשַׁי עַבְדְּךָ מְשִׁיחֶךָ:

---

*One man who suffered from insomnia stated that his salvation was reading the Prayer of "Nishmas." Why? "Because," he said, "I would lie awake worrying about so many things. When I read the Prayer of*

every knee shall bend to You; every erect spine shall prostrate itself before You; all hearts shall fear You, and all innermost feelings and thoughts shall sing praises to Your Name, as it is written: "All my bones shall say: 'HASHEM, who is like You?' You save the poor man from one stronger than he, the poor and destitute from one who would rob him." Who is like unto You? Who is equal to You? Who can be compared to You? O great, mighty, and awesome God, the supreme God, Creator of heaven and earth. We shall laud, praise, and glorify You and bless Your holy Name, as it is said: "Of David: Bless HASHEM, O my soul, and let all my innermost being bless His holy Name!"

**הָאֵל** O God, in the omnipotence of Your strength, great in the glory of Your Name, mighty forever and awesome through Your awesome deeds, O King enthroned upon a high and lofty throne!

**שׁוֹכֵן עַד** He Who abides forever, exalted and holy is His Name. And it is written: "Sing joyfully, O righteous, before HASHEM; for the upright, praise is fitting." By the mouth of the upright shall You be lauded; by the words of the righteous shall You be blessed; by the tongue of the devout shall You be exalted; and amid the holy shall You be sanctified.

**וּבְמַקְהֲלוֹת** And in the assemblies of the myriads of Your people, the House of Israel, with joyous song shall Your Name be glorified, our King, throughout every generation. For such is the duty of all creatures — before You, HASHEM, our God, God of our forefathers, to thank, laud, praise, glorify, exalt, adore, bless, raise high, and sing praises — even beyond all expressions of the songs and praises of David the son of Yishai, Your servant, Your anointed.

---

*"Nishmas," that God is always awake and never sleeps, it occurred to me that since God is awake anyway, there is no need for both of us to be up. Knowing that God is always alert allows me to sleep."*

**יִשְׁתַּבַּח** שִׁמְךָ לָעַד מַלְכֵּנוּ הָאֵל הַמֶּלֶךְ הַגָּדוֹל וְהַקָּדוֹשׁ בַּשָּׁמַיִם וּבָאָרֶץ כִּי לְךָ נָאֶה יהוה אֱלֹהֵינוּ וֵאלֹהֵי אֲבוֹתֵינוּ שִׁיר וּשְׁבָחָה הַלֵּל וְזִמְרָה עֹז וּמֶמְשָׁלָה נֶצַח גְּדֻלָּה וּגְבוּרָה תְּהִלָּה וְתִפְאֶרֶת קְדֻשָּׁה וּמַלְכוּת בְּרָכוֹת וְהוֹדָאוֹת מֵעַתָּה וְעַד עוֹלָם: בָּרוּךְ אַתָּה יהוה אֵל מֶלֶךְ גָּדוֹל בַּתִּשְׁבָּחוֹת אֵל הַהוֹדָאוֹת אֲדוֹן הַנִּפְלָאוֹת הַבּוֹחֵר בְּשִׁירֵי זִמְרָה מֶלֶךְ אֵל חֵי הָעוֹלָמִים.

The blessing over wine is recited and the fourth cup is drunk while reclining to the left side. It is preferable that the entire cup be drunk.

**בָּרוּךְ** אַתָּה יהוה אֱלֹהֵינוּ מֶלֶךְ הָעוֹלָם בּוֹרֵא פְּרִי הַגָּפֶן:

After drinking the fourth cup, the concluding blessing is recited. On Shabbos include the passage in brackets.

**בָּרוּךְ** אַתָּה יהוה אֱלֹהֵינוּ מֶלֶךְ הָעוֹלָם עַל הַגֶּפֶן וְעַל פְּרִי הַגֶּפֶן וְעַל תְּנוּבַת הַשָּׂדֶה וְעַל אֶרֶץ חֶמְדָּה טוֹבָה וּרְחָבָה שֶׁרָצִיתָ וְהִנְחַלְתָּ לַאֲבוֹתֵינוּ לֶאֱכוֹל מִפִּרְיָהּ וְלִשְׂבּוֹעַ מִטּוּבָהּ. רַחֵם נָא יהוה אֱלֹהֵינוּ עַל יִשְׂרָאֵל עַמֶּךָ וְעַל יְרוּשָׁלַיִם עִירֶךָ וְעַל צִיּוֹן מִשְׁכַּן כְּבוֹדֶךָ וְעַל מִזְבְּחֶךָ וְעַל הֵיכָלֶךָ. וּבְנֵה יְרוּשָׁלַיִם עִיר הַקֹּדֶשׁ בִּמְהֵרָה בְיָמֵינוּ וְהַעֲלֵנוּ לְתוֹכָהּ וְשַׂמְּחֵנוּ בְּבִנְיָנָהּ וְנֹאכַל מִפִּרְיָהּ וְנִשְׂבַּע מִטּוּבָהּ וּנְבָרֶכְךָ עָלֶיהָ בִּקְדֻשָּׁה וּבְטָהֳרָה. [וּרְצֵה וְהַחֲלִיצֵנוּ בְּיוֹם הַשַּׁבָּת הַזֶּה] וְשַׂמְּחֵנוּ בְּיוֹם חַג הַמַּצּוֹת הַזֶּה. כִּי אַתָּה יהוה טוֹב וּמֵטִיב לַכֹּל וְנוֹדֶה לְּךָ עַל הָאָרֶץ וְעַל פְּרִי הַגָּפֶן: בָּרוּךְ אַתָּה יהוה עַל הָאָרֶץ וְעַל פְּרִי הַגָּפֶן:

**יִשְׁתַּבַּח** May Your Name be praised forever — our King, the God, the great and holy King — in heaven and on earth. Because for You is fitting — O HASHEM, our God, and the God of our forefathers — song and praise, lauding and hymns, power and dominion, triumph, greatness and strength, praise and splendor, holiness and sovereignty, blessings and thanksgivings from this time and forever. Blessed are You, HASHEM, God, King exalted through praises, God of thanksgivings, Master of wonders, Who chooses musical songs of praise — King, God, Life-giver of the world.

The blessing over wine is recited and the fourth cup is drunk while reclining to the left side. It is preferable that the entire cup be drunk.

**בָּרוּךְ** Blessed are You, HASHEM, our God, King of the Universe, Who creates the fruit of the vine.

After drinking the fourth cup, the concluding blessing is recited. On Shabbos include the passage in brackets.

**בָּרוּךְ** Blessed are You, HASHEM, our God, King of the Universe, for the vine and the fruit of the vine, and for the produce of the field. For the desirable, good, and spacious land that You were pleased to give our forefathers as a heritage, to eat of its fruit and to be satisfied with its goodness. Have mercy, we beg You, HASHEM, our God, on Israel Your people; on Jerusalem, Your city; on Zion, resting place of Your glory; Your Altar, and Your Temple. Rebuild Jerusalem the city of holiness, speedily in our days. Bring us up into it and gladden us in its rebuilding and let us eat from its fruit and be satisfied with its goodness and bless You upon it in holiness and purity. [Favor us and strengthen us on this Shabbos day] and grant us happiness on this Festival of Matzos; for You, HASHEM, are good and do good to all, and we thank You for the land and for the fruit of the vine. Blessed are You, HASHEM, for the land and for the fruit of the vine.

# נרצה

**חֲסַל** סִדּוּר פֶּסַח כְּהִלְכָתוֹ. כְּכָל מִשְׁפָּטוֹ וְחֻקָּתוֹ. כַּאֲשֶׁר זָכִינוּ לְסַדֵּר אוֹתוֹ. כֵּן נִזְכֶּה לַעֲשׂוֹתוֹ: זָךְ שׁוֹכֵן מְעוֹנָה. קוֹמֵם קְהַל עֲדַת מִי מָנָה. בְּקָרוֹב נַהֵל נִטְעֵי כַנָּה. פְּדוּיִם לְצִיּוֹן בְּרִנָּה:

## לְשָׁנָה הַבָּאָה בִּירוּשָׁלָיִם:

On the first night recite the following. On the second night continue on page 168.

**וּבְכֵן וַיְהִי בַּחֲצִי הַלַּיְלָה:**

אָז רוֹב נִסִּים הִפְלֵאתָ בַּלַּיְלָה.
בְּרֹאשׁ אַשְׁמוֹרֶת זֶה הַלַּיְלָה.
גֵּר צֶדֶק נִצַּחְתּוֹ כְּנֶחֱלַק לוֹ לַיְלָה.
וַיְהִי בַּחֲצִי הַלַּיְלָה.
דַּנְתָּ מֶלֶךְ גְּרָר בַּחֲלוֹם הַלַּיְלָה.

---

### חֲסַל סִדּוּר פֶּסַח — *The Seder is now concluded*

In some Haggadahs this paragraph is omitted, because the process of the Passover ritual should never be considered as "concluded" i.e., over and done with. Rather, as was stated in the Introduction, the Passover message should accompany us all year round.

Given the interpretations we have provided, we can well understand this viewpoint. Passover is the festival of the liberation of the human spirit, and one cannot afford a single day of one's life spent in spiritual captivity.

Those who do include this paragraph in the Haggadah should be aware of its closing phrase: the aspiration for the ultimate Redemption, when there will be a true liberation of the human spirit and the universal acknowledgment of the sovereignty of God.

### לְשָׁנָה הַבָּאָה בִּירוּשָׁלָיִם — *Next year in Jerusalem*

*One man invited a friend to the Seder year after year. When the host recited the prayer, "Next year in Jerusalem," his guest asked,*

## NIRTZAH

**חֲסַל** The *Seder* is now concluded in accordance with its laws, with all its ordinances and statutes. Just as we were privileged to arrange it, so may we merit to perform it. O Pure One, Who dwells on high, raise up the countless congregation, soon — guide the offshoots of Your plants, redeemed, to Zion with glad song.

## NEXT YEAR IN JERUSALEM

On the first night recite the following. On the second night continue on page 169.

### It came to pass at midnight.

You have, of old, performed many wonders by night.
At the head of the watches of this night.
To the righteous convert (Avraham),
You gave triumph by dividing for him the night.
It came to pass at midnight.
You judged the king of Gerar (Avimelech), in a dream by night.

---

*"But you said that last year, yet you are still here."*

*The host explained that indeed last year's prayer was not fulfilled, but that he was hopeful that the coming year would bring the Redemption.*

*The following year, as they approached this portion of the Seder, the host turned his eyes toward Heaven. "Please God," he said, "don't put me through this humiliation again. I cannot keep on explaining why we are not being taken back to Jerusalem."*

Perhaps if we were all a bit more genuinely ashamed of remaining in the diaspora, our prayers to be returned to our homeland might be more sincere.

**◆§ דַּנְתָּ מֶלֶךְ גְּרָר בַּחֲלוֹם — *You judged the king of Gerar, (Avimelech) in a dream***

In the ballad "It came to pass at midnight," one of the occurrences refers to the episode described in *Genesis* chapter 20, where the matriarch Sarah was taken captive into the palace of Abimelech, and the entire palace household was punished by God until Sarah was released.

הִפְחַדְתָּ אֲרַמִּי בְּאֶמֶשׁ לַיְלָה.

וַיָּשַׂר יִשְׂרָאֵל לְמַלְאָךְ וַיּוּכַל לוֹ לַיְלָה.

וַיְהִי בַּחֲצִי הַלַּיְלָה.

זֶרַע בְּכוֹרֵי פַּתְרוֹס מָחַצְתָּ בַּחֲצִי הַלַּיְלָה.

חֵילָם לֹא מָצְאוּ בְּקוּמָם בַּלַּיְלָה.

טִיסַת נְגִיד חֲרוֹשֶׁת סִלִּיתָ בְּכוֹכְּבֵי לַיְלָה.

וַיְהִי בַּחֲצִי הַלַּיְלָה.

יָעַץ מְחָרֵף לְנוֹפֵף אִוּי הוֹבַשְׁתָּ פְּגָרָיו בַּלַּיְלָה.

כָּרַע בֵּל וּמַצָּבוֹ בְּאִישׁוֹן לַיְלָה.

לְאִישׁ חֲמוּדוֹת נִגְלָה רָז חֲזוֹת לַיְלָה.

וַיְהִי בַּחֲצִי הַלַּיְלָה.

מִשְׁתַּכֵּר בִּכְלֵי קֹדֶשׁ נֶהֱרַג בּוֹ בַּלַּיְלָה.

נוֹשַׁע מִבּוֹר אֲרָיוֹת פּוֹתֵר בִּעֲתוּתֵי לַיְלָה.

שִׂנְאָה נָטַר אֲגָגִי וְכָתַב סְפָרִים בַּלַּיְלָה.

וַיְהִי בַּחֲצִי הַלַּיְלָה.

עוֹרַרְתָּ נִצְחֲךָ עָלָיו בְּנֶדֶד שְׁנַת לַיְלָה.

פּוּרָה תִדְרוֹךְ לְשֹׁמֵר מַה מִּלַּיְלָה.

---

*This incident led to an interesting decision rendered by Rabbi Yaakov Shamson. A woman delivered a child twelve months after the death of her husband, and the community accused her of promiscuity. She was known to be a devout person, and she protested bitterly that the child was that of her late husband. The community refused to believe her, claiming that there is no such thing as a twelve-month pregnancy.*

*Rabbi Yaakov Shamson did believe the woman, and in a lecture to the community, quoted the Midrash that because some people attributed the paternity of Isaac to Abimelech rather than to Abraham, God made Isaac's appearance identical to Abraham, so that all would*

You frightened the Aramean (Lavan), in the dark of night.
Israel (Yaakov) fought with an angel and overcame him
by night.
It came to pass at midnight.
Egypt's firstborn You crushed at midnight.
Their host they found not upon arising at night.
The army of the prince of Charoshes (Sisera)
You swept away with stars of the night.
It came to pass at midnight.
The blasphemer (Sancherib) planned to raise his hand against
Jerusalem — but You withered his corpses by night.
Bel was overturned with its pedestal, in the darkness
of night.
To the man of Your delights (Daniel)
was revealed the mystery of the visions of night.
It came to pass at midnight.
He (Belshazzar) who became intoxicated
from the holy vessels was killed that very night.
From the lions' den was rescued he (Daniel)
who interpreted the "terrors" of the night.
The Aggagite (Haman) nursed hatred
and wrote decrees at night.
It came to pass at midnight.
You began Your triumph over him when You disturbed
(Ahaseurus') sleep at night.
Trample the wine press to help those who ask the
watchman, "What of the long night?"

---

*know that he was Abraham's son.*

*"Now then," said Rabbi Yaakov Shamson, "we know from the Talmud that Isaac was born on Passover. Since this ballad tells us that Sarah was taken captive by Abimelech on the night of Passover, how could anyone claim that she had conceived from Abimelech, since that would indicate a twelve-month gestation period?*

*"The only conclusion," said Rabbi Yaakov Shamson, "is that a twelve-month pregnancy is indeed a possibility."*

*This ballad saved the woman's honor and reputation.*

צָרַח כַּשּׁוֹמֵר וְשָׂח אָתָא בֹקֶר וְגַם לַיְלָה.
וַיְהִי בַּחֲצִי הַלַּיְלָה.
קָרֵב יוֹם אֲשֶׁר הוּא לֹא יוֹם וְלֹא לַיְלָה.
רָם הוֹדַע כִּי לְךָ הַיּוֹם אַף לְךָ הַלַּיְלָה.
שׁוֹמְרִים הַפְקֵד לְעִירְךָ כָּל הַיּוֹם וְכָל הַלַּיְלָה.
תָּאִיר כְּאוֹר יוֹם חֶשְׁכַּת לַיְלָה.
וַיְהִי בַּחֲצִי הַלַּיְלָה.

On the second night recite the following. On the first night continue on page 174.

**וּבְכֵן וַאֲמַרְתֶּם זֶבַח פֶּסַח:**

אֹמֶץ גְּבוּרוֹתֶיךָ הִפְלֵאתָ בַּפֶּסַח.
בְּרֹאשׁ כָּל מוֹעֲדוֹת נִשֵּׂאתָ פֶּסַח.

---

**קָרֵב יוֹם אֲשֶׁר הוּא לֹא יוֹם וְלֹא לַיְלָה — *Hasten the day (of Messiah) that is neither day nor night***

In Torah literature "light" is often used to indicate truth, wisdom, clarity of vision, and reality; whereas "darkness" refers to the sinister, to folly, and to the distortion of reality. *Ecclesiastes* states, "The superiority of wisdom over folly is like that of light over darkness. . .the fool walks in darkness" (2:13-14). As important as physical vision is to a person, wisdom is yet more important. It is possible for a person with healthy vision to distort reality and walk through life, as it were, in total darkness, stumbling into obstacles that one does not perceive.

*A story is related of a tzaddik who was teaching his disciples one Friday night, and when he left the room, the wind extinguished the candle. One of his disciples asked a non-Jewish neighbor to light the candle, something which is not permitted, since other than for health reasons or other unusual circumstances, it is forbidden to ask a non-Jew to perform a restricted act on Shabbos.*

*A bit later, the tzaddik returned to the room, and groped around as if in the dark, saying, "Oh, the candle must have gone out." The disciples said, "But Rabbi, there is a light in the room!" The tzaddik continued to feel his way around. "I see nothing," he said. "It is totally dark."*

He will shout, like a watchman, and say:
"Morning shall come and also night."
It came to pass at midnight.
Hasten the day (of Mashiach), that is neither day nor night.
Most High — make known that Yours are day and night.
Appoint guards for Your city, all the day and all the night.
Brighten like the light of day the darkness of night.
It came to pass at midnight.

On the second night recite the following. On the first night continue on page 175.

**And you shall say: This is the feast of Pesach.**

You displayed wondrously Your mighty powers on Pesach.
Above all festivals You elevated Pesach.

---

The explanation? A light which came about through a violation of Shabbos did not provide illumination for him. The *tzaddik's* spirituality was so advanced that it dominated his physical senses. That which was not permissible did not exist for him. A brightness resulting from a candle which was lit on Shabbos was darker than dark.

In my practice of psychiatry, I regularly see people who engage in self-destructive practices, fully convinced that what they are doing is right. Often it is not their logic that is distorted, but their perception. They are deluded into thinking that what is harmful is actually good for them.

On this festival of liberation, we pray for the ultimate Redemption, for a day when there will be a Divine revelation, when all evil will be eradicated, and humanity will be privileged to see the truth. With this Divine light, there will be no difference between day and night.

### ◆§ וּבְכֵן וַיְהִי בַּחֲצִי הַלַּיְלָה . . . וּבְכֵן וַאֲמַרְתֶּם זֶבַח פֶּסַח — *It came to pass at midnight . . . And you shall say: This is the feast of Passover*

These two ballads enumerate many of the miracles that occurred precisely at midnight. One might ask, "So what? What difference does it really make at what time of day or night a miracle occurred? Furthermore, of what significance is it for us to know that all these events occurred at midnight?" And why are we instructed to say, "Tihs is the feast of Passover" as a refrain when we are referring to miracles that do not appear to even be remotely related to the Exodus?

גִּלִּיתָ לְאֶזְרָחִי חֲצוֹת לֵיל פֶּסַח.

וַאֲמַרְתֶּם זֶבַח פֶּסַח.

דְּלָתָיו דָּפַקְתָּ כְּחֹם הַיּוֹם בַּפֶּסַח.

הִסְעִיד נוֹצְצִים עֻגוֹת מַצּוֹת בַּפֶּסַח.

וְאֶל הַבָּקָר רָץ זֵכֶר לְשׁוֹר עֵרֶךְ פֶּסַח.

וַאֲמַרְתֶּם זֶבַח פֶּסַח.

---

Both of these ballads begin with the miraculous triumph of the patriarch Abraham in his battle with the kings who had taken his nephew, Lot, into captivity, as is related in the Scriptures (*Genesis* 14:14-16). The Midrash modifies this Scriptural account, explaining that Abraham and his trusted servant, Eliezer, miraculously subdued the enemy without the aid of an army.

Let us preface a possible explanation with two additional questions. The Talmud states that a person should be particularly diligent when reciting *Minchah* (Afternoon Prayer), because the prophet Elijah received a favorable Divine response to his prayer of *Minchah.* But why does this give the *Minchah* prayer special significance? Perhaps if Elijah's prayers had been uttered in the morning or evening they would have been equally effective. Secondly, the Torah gives prominence to the miracle of the matriarch, Sarah, who bore Isaac at the advanced age of ninety. According to the Midrash, however, Moses was conceived by Yocheved at the age of one hundred and thirty-seven. Yet this clearly miraculous event is not even mentioned in the Scriptures. Why is this apparently greater miracle totally overlooked?

If we give it some thought, we will note that an unusual event is unique only the first time it occurs. Thus, when the first human being set foot on the moon, millions of people sat glued to television screens, watching this unprecedented, breathtaking phenomenon. Today, if an entire regiment of soldiers marched on the moon's surface, it would probably not cause more than a few individuals to switch channels away from the football game. Walking on the moon was unique only once.

Similarly, conception at an advanced age was a unique phenomenon only once. After Sarah gave birth to Isaac at ninety, the breakthrough had been achieved, and beyond that, even if such events could not be considered commonplace, they no longer attracted much attention. Yocheved's pregnancy at age one hundred and thirty-seven was simply

To the Oriental (Avraham) You revealed
the future midnight of Pesach.
And you shall say: This is the feast of Pesach.
At his door You knocked in the heat of the day on Pesach;
He satiated the angels with matzah-cakes on Pesach.
And he ran to the herd — symbolic of the sacrificial beast of Pesach.
And you shall say: This is the feast of Pesach.

---

seen as another manifestation of Sarah's miracle, and to use the vernacular, was "old hat."

The "breakthrough" principle can be applied to all miraculous events. Hence, because Elijah made a "breakthrough" at the *Minchah* prayer, this service is now propitious for receiving a favorable Divine response. Certainly Elijah would have been granted his wish had he prayed at any other time of the day, but inasmuch as it did occur during *Minchah,* he had paved the way for further miraculous Divine responses at the *Minchah* prayer.

Turning to our ballads, we learn that the patriarch Abraham made a breakthrough at midnight. Upon hearing that his kin had been taken captive, Abraham placed himself in great personal danger in order to rescue him. His nephew, Lot, was not exactly a virtuous person, and indeed, Abraham was forced to part company from him because he could not tolerate his corrupt behavior. The Midrash states that the Divine spirit did not visit Abraham until he had separated himself from the degenerate nephew. There was therefore abundant reason for Abraham to justify doing nothing to rescue this scoundrel who had been taken into captivity, yet Abraham placed himself in a gravely perilous position in order to do so. This attribute of coming to the aid of a person who is in need, without considering whether that individual was deserving or non-deserving, emulates the Divine attribute, since God grants his benevolence to the non-deserving as well as to the deserving. Abraham was therefore rewarded with the miraculous triumph over an entire army (*Bereishes Rabbah* 43:1).

In making the breakthrough by virtue of the merit of unconditional love, Abraham thereby set a precedent for his descendants. Future miracles would occur at a propitious time for Divine favor, and this first miracle, which occurred at midnight, should serve as a reminder to us that even when we are critical of a person's behavior, we should not withhold our help in his time of need.

Indeed, the Midrash states that the final plague that compelled Pharaoh to

זוֹעֲמוּ סְדוֹמִים וְלוֹהֲטוּ בָּאֵשׁ בַּפֶּסַח.
חֻלַּץ לוֹט מֵהֶם וּמַצּוֹת אָפָה בְּקֵץ פֶּסַח.
טִאטֵאתָ אַדְמַת מוֹף וְנוֹף בְּעָבְרְךָ בַּפֶּסַח.
וַאֲמַרְתֶּם זֶבַח פֶּסַח.

יָהּ רֹאשׁ כָּל אוֹן מָחַצְתָּ בְּלֵיל שִׁמּוּר פֶּסַח.
כַּבִּיר עַל בֵּן בְּכוֹר פָּסַחְתָּ בְּדַם פֶּסַח.
לְבִלְתִּי תֵּת מַשְׁחִית לָבֹא בִּפְתָחַי בַּפֶּסַח.
וַאֲמַרְתֶּם זֶבַח פֶּסַח.

מְסֻגֶּרֶת סֻגָּרָה בְּעִתּוֹתֵי פֶּסַח.
נִשְׁמְדָה מִדְיָן בִּצְלִיל שְׂעוֹרֵי עֹמֶר פֶּסַח.
שׂוֹרְפוּ מִשְׁמַנֵּי פּוּל וְלוּד בִּיקַד יְקוֹד פֶּסַח.
וַאֲמַרְתֶּם זֶבַח פֶּסַח.

עוֹד הַיּוֹם בְּנֹב לַעֲמוֹד עַד גָּעָה עוֹנַת פֶּסַח.
פַּס יַד כָּתְבָה לְקַעֲקֵעַ צוּל בַּפֶּסַח.
צָפֹה הַצָּפִית עָרוֹךְ הַשֻּׁלְחָן בַּפֶּסַח.
וַאֲמַרְתֶּם זֶבַח פֶּסַח.

קָהָל כִּנְּסָה הֲדַסָּה צוֹם לְשַׁלֵּשׁ בַּפֶּסַח.
רֹאשׁ מִבֵּית רָשָׁע מָחַצְתָּ בְּעֵץ חֲמִשִּׁים בַּפֶּסַח.

---

free the Israelites occurred at the stroke of midnight on the fifteenth day of Nissan, because that was the very same night on which Abraham risked his life to rescue Lot from his captors. Earlier we have noted that the Passover offering represented a rejection of paganism, since the lamb was an Egyptian totem, and that paganism is nothing but self-indulgence legitimized by an idol, which was fashioned by man to give positive sanction to fulfilling one's desires. Hedonism and self-sacrifice are irreconcilable polar opposites. Self-sacrifice can only occur in an individual whose spirituality has overcome the innate tendency toward gratification of one's desires.

Both ballads now take on a new meaning. The night of Passover was preordained as a propitious time for miraculous salvation because the

The Sodomites provoked (God) and were devoured by fire on Pesach;
Lot was withdrawn from them — he had baked matzos at the time of Pesach.
You swept clean the soil of Moph and Noph (in Egypt) when You passed through on Pesach.
And you shall say: This is the feast of Pesach.

God, You crushed every firstborn of On (in Egypt) on the watchful night of Pesach.
But Master — Your own firstborn, You skipped by merit of the blood of Pesach,
Not to allow the Destroyer to enter my doors on Pesach.
And you shall say: This is the feast of Pesach.

The beleaguered (Yericho) was besieged on Pesach.
Midian was destroyed with a barley cake, from the Omer of Pesach.
The princes of Pul and Lud (Assyria) were consumed in a great conflagration on Pesach.
And you shall say: This is the feast of Pesach.

He (Sancherib) would have stood that day at Nob, but for the advent of Pesach.
A hand inscribed the destruction of Zul (Babylon) on Pesach.
As the watch was set, and the royal table decked on Pesach.
And you shall say: This is the feast of Pesach.

Hadassah (Esther) gathered her people for a three-day fast on Pesach.
You caused the head of the evil clan (Haman) to be hanged on a fifty-cubit gallows on Pesach.

---

patriarch Abraham, Father of the Israelites, established the precedent not only of self-sacrifice, but of doing so even for someone of questionable worth. This event was commemorated and perpetuated by a ritual that represented repudiation of paganism and its inherent hedonism. It is by virtue of these spiritual achievements that the Israelites merited all subsequent Divine miracles.

שְׁתֵּי אֵלֶּה רֶגַע תָּבִיא לְעוּצִית בַּפֶּסַח.
תָּעֹז יָדְךָ וְתָרוּם יְמִינְךָ כְּלֵיל הִתְקַדֵּשׁ חַג פֶּסַח.
וַאֲמַרְתֶּם זֶבַח פֶּסַח.

On both nights continue here:

**כִּי לוֹ נָאֶה, כִּי לוֹ יָאֶה:**

**אַדִּיר** בִּמְלוּכָה, **בָּ**חוּר כַּהֲלָכָה, **גְּ**דוּדָיו יֹאמְרוּ לוֹ,
לְךָ וּלְךָ, לְךָ כִּי לְךָ, לְךָ אַף לְךָ, לְךָ יהוה
הַמַּמְלָכָה, כִּי לוֹ נָאֶה, כִּי לוֹ יָאֶה.
**דָּ**גוּל בִּמְלוּכָה, **הָ**דוּר כַּהֲלָכָה, **וָ**תִיקָיו יֹאמְרוּ לוֹ,
לְךָ וּלְךָ, לְךָ כִּי לְךָ, לְךָ אַף לְךָ, לְךָ יהוה הַמַּמְלָכָה,
כִּי לוֹ נָאֶה, כִּי לוֹ יָאֶה.
**זַ**כַּאי בִּמְלוּכָה, **חָ**סִין כַּהֲלָכָה, **טַ**פְסְרָיו יֹאמְרוּ לוֹ,
לְךָ וּלְךָ,לְךָ כִּי לְךָ, לְךָ אַף לְךָ, לְךָ יהוה הַמַּמְלָכָה, כִּי
לוֹ נָאֶה, כִּי לוֹ יָאֶה.

---

### ⁂ אַדִּיר בִּמְלוּכָה — *Powerful in Kingship*

When we approach God in prayer, we must reflect on His infinite greatness and acknowledge His sovereignty over the universe. Regretfully we must admit that our prayer is often lacking in appropriate fervor. We often recite prayers as rote, without the requisite *kavanah* (concentration).

If a person entered a contest, and knew that several of the contestants who were to follow him were outstanding and far surpassed him in their talents, he would make a concerted effort to prepare himself adequately for the performance, knowing that he would be judged in comparison to the others. The Midrash states that God receives the prayers of Israel prior to the chanting of the heavenly angels. We must know, then, that our prayers will be followed by those of the heavenly host. If we do not exert ourselves to greater *kavanah,* and merely rattle off the words of prayer without the requisite thought and concentration, how anemic our prayers will appear to be when compared to the songs of the heavenly angels.

Doubly, will You bring in an instant
upon Utsis (Edom) on Pesach.
Let Your hand be strong, and Your right arm exalted, as on
that night when You hallowed the festival of Pesach.
And you shall say: This is the feast of Pesach.

On both nights continue here:

**To Him praise is due! To Him praise is fitting!**

Powerful in kingship, perfectly distinguished, His companies of angels say to Him: Yours and only Yours; Yours, yes Yours; Yours, surely Yours; Yours, HASHEM, is the sovereignty. To Him praise is due! To Him praise is fitting!

Supreme in kingship, perfectly glorious, His faithful say to Him: Yours and only Yours; Yours, yes Yours; Yours, surely Yours; Yours, HASHEM, is the sovereignty. To Him praise is due! To Him praise is fitting!

Pure in kingship, perfectly mighty, His angels say to Him: Yours and only Yours; Yours, yes Yours; Yours, surely Yours; Yours, HASHEM, is the sovereignty. To Him praise is due! To Him praise is fitting!

---

Many prayer books contain an admonition as an introduction to prayer: "Know before Whom you stand." While "before" means that one should think of oneself spatially in the Divine presence, "before" may also refer to time sequence; i.e., whom we precede. We submit our praises to God "before" the angels do, and the knowledge that the hymns that will follow ours will be of angelic purity and quality should stimulate us to greater *kavannah.*

Yet, the very fact that our prayers are received prior to those of the heavenly host indicates the Divine preference for being worshiped by humans. On Yom Kippur we chant a beautiful hymn that specifically states that God values the prayers of mere mortals above those of the angels. This is because man, precisely because he is mortal and must overcome a base physical nature to achieve spirituality, actually stands on a higher plain than the heavenly angels, who are created perfect and spiritual, and who do not have to make any effort to achieve spirituality.

Our very struggle to achieve spirituality should therefore infuse us with *simchah* (joy), that we have the capacity to surpass the *kedushah* (sanctity) of the heavenly host.

יָחִיד בִּמְלוּכָה, כַּבִּיר כַּהֲלָכָה, לִמּוּדָיו יֹאמְרוּ לוֹ,
לְךָ וּלְךָ, לְךָ כִּי לְךָ, לְךָ אַף לְךָ, לְךָ יהוה הַמַּמְלָכָה,
כִּי לוֹ נָאֶה, כִּי לוֹ יָאֶה.

מוֹשֵׁל בִּמְלוּכָה, נוֹרָא כַּהֲלָכָה, סְבִיבָיו יֹאמְרוּ לוֹ,
לְךָ וּלְךָ, לְךָ כִּי לְךָ, לְךָ אַף לְךָ, לְךָ יהוה הַמַּמְלָכָה,
כִּי לוֹ נָאֶה, כִּי לוֹ יָאֶה.

עָנָיו בִּמְלוּכָה, פּוֹדֶה כַּהֲלָכָה, צַדִּיקָיו יֹאמְרוּ לוֹ,
לְךָ וּלְךָ, לְךָ כִּי לְךָ, לְךָ אַף לְךָ, לְךָ יהוה הַמַּמְלָכָה,
כִּי לוֹ נָאֶה, כִּי לוֹ יָאֶה.

קָדוֹשׁ בִּמְלוּכָה, רַחוּם כַּהֲלָכָה, שִׁנְאַנָּיו יֹאמְרוּ לוֹ,
לְךָ וּלְךָ, לְךָ כִּי לְךָ, לְךָ אַף לְךָ, לְךָ יהוה הַמַּמְלָכָה,
כִּי לוֹ נָאֶה, כִּי לוֹ יָאֶה.

תַּקִּיף בִּמְלוּכָה, תּוֹמֵךְ כַּהֲלָכָה, תְּמִימָיו יֹאמְרוּ לוֹ,
לְךָ וּלְךָ, לְךָ כִּי לְךָ, לְךָ אַף לְךָ, לְךָ יהוה הַמַּמְלָכָה,
כִּי לוֹ נָאֶה, כִּי לוֹ יָאֶה.

**אַדִּיר הוּא** יִבְנֶה בֵיתוֹ בְּקָרוֹב, בִּמְהֵרָה, בִּמְהֵרָה,
בְּיָמֵינוּ בְּקָרוֹב. אֵל בְּנֵה, אֵל בְּנֵה,
בְּנֵה בֵיתְךָ בְּקָרוֹב.

---

**☙ יִבְנֶה בֵיתוֹ בְּקָרוֹב — *May He soon rebuild His House***

Why is there a need for a Sanctuary? Can one not pray everywhere? Does the Torah not state, "Wherever My Name is mentioned, I will come to you and bless you"? (*Exodus* 20:21).

The Temple in Jerusalem was a powerful unifying force. Three times a year all Israelites would gather from all corners of the land to celebrate the festivals. The various offerings and the first-ripened fruits were brought to the Temple, and some of the tithes were also brought to Jerusalem. Following the seventh year of the cycle, all Israelites, including infants, were brought to hear the king of Israel read the Book of Deuteronomy at the great assembly in one of the Temple Courtyards (*Deuteronomy* 31:2). Even today, if one

Alone in kingship, perfectly omnipotent, His scholars say to Him: Yours and only Yours; Yours, yes Yours; Yours, surely Yours; Yours, HASHEM, is the sovereignty. To Him praise is due! To Him praise is fitting!

Commanding in kingship, perfectly wondrous, His surrounding (angels) say to Him: Yours and only Yours; Yours, yes Yours; Yours, surely Yours; Yours, HASHEM, is the sovereignty. To Him praise is due! To Him praise is fitting!

Gentle in kingship, perfectly the Redeemer, His righteous say to Him: Yours and only Yours; Yours, yes Yours; Yours, surely Yours; Yours, HASHEM, is the sovereignty. To Him praise is due! To Him praise is fitting!

Holy in kingship, perfectly merciful, His troops of angels say to Him: Yours and only Yours; Yours, yes Yours; Yours, surely Yours; Yours, HASHEM, is the sovereignty. To Him praise is due! To Him praise is fitting.

Almighty in kingship, perfectly sustaining, His perfect ones say to Him: Yours and only Yours; Yours, yes Yours; Yours, surely Yours; Yours, HASHEM, is the sovereignty. To Him praise is due! To Him praise is fitting!

**אַדִּיר הוּא** He is most mighty. May He soon rebuild His House, speedily, yes speedily, in our days, soon. God, rebuild, God, rebuild, rebuild Your House soon!

---

visits the *Kotel* on a festival, where Jews from the six continents get together, and people meet distant relatives or friends of their friends, one can have a taste of what Jerusalem must have been like in the days of the Temple.

"Israel, God, and the Torah are one" (*Zohar Vayikra* 73). We are an absolute unity only when all three components are united. Separation of a Jew from a fellow Jew results in separation from God.

For a Jew to be fully spiritual, one must identify with God and with the Torah. This identification cannot be complete unless we also identify with every other Jew.

As we pray for the restoration of the Temple, we must demonstrate our commitment to unity. We must make every effort to overcome the factionalism that has plagued our people since time immemorial, and try to truly become: one with each other, with the Torah, and with the Almighty.

בָּחוּר הוּא. גָּדוֹל הוּא. דָּגוּל הוּא. יִבְנֶה בֵיתוֹ בְּקָרוֹב, בִּמְהֵרָה, בִּמְהֵרָה, בְּיָמֵינוּ בְּקָרוֹב. אֵל בְּנֵה, אֵל בְּנֵה, בְּנֵה בֵיתְךָ בְּקָרוֹב.

הָדוּר הוּא. וָתִיק הוּא. זַכַּאי הוּא. חָסִיד הוּא. יִבְנֶה בֵיתוֹ בְּקָרוֹב, בִּמְהֵרָה, בִּמְהֵרָה, בְּיָמֵינוּ בְּקָרוֹב. אֵל בְּנֵה, אֵל בְּנֵה, בְּנֵה בֵיתְךָ בְּקָרוֹב.

טָהוֹר הוּא. יָחִיד הוּא. כַּבִּיר הוּא. לָמוּד הוּא. מֶלֶךְ הוּא. נוֹרָא הוּא. סַגִּיב הוּא. עִזּוּז הוּא. פּוֹדֶה הוּא. צַדִּיק הוּא. יִבְנֶה בֵיתוֹ בְּקָרוֹב, בִּמְהֵרָה, בִּמְהֵרָה, בְּיָמֵינוּ בְּקָרוֹב. אֵל בְּנֵה, אֵל בְּנֵה, בְּנֵה בֵיתְךָ בְּקָרוֹב.

קָדוֹשׁ הוּא. רַחוּם הוּא. שַׁדַּי הוּא. תַּקִּיף הוּא. יִבְנֶה בֵיתוֹ בְּקָרוֹב, בִּמְהֵרָה, בִּמְהֵרָה, בְּיָמֵינוּ בְּקָרוֹב. אֵל בְּנֵה, אֵל בְּנֵה, בְּנֵה בֵיתְךָ בְּקָרוֹב.

**אֶחָד מִי יוֹדֵעַ?** אֶחָד אֲנִי יוֹדֵעַ. אֶחָד אֱלֹהֵינוּ שֶׁבַּשָּׁמַיִם וּבָאָרֶץ.

---

### ❧ **אֶחָד מִי יוֹדֵעַ** — *Who Knows One?*

Who knows one? Who knows two? Who knows three?

The Torah states, "You shall know this day, and take to your heart that Hashem, He is the God, in heaven above and on the earth below, there is none other" (*Deuteronomy* 4:39).

The chassidic works translate this verse a bit differently. *Ein od* does not mean merely that there are no other gods. Rejecting a plurality of gods is a matter of simple logic and hardly requires profound reflection. Rather, *ein od* means "There is nothing else," i.e, the only true existence in the entire universe, both in all physical worlds and celestial spheres, is God.

Rabbi Shneur Zalman explains in *Tanya* that creation, or bringing something into being out of nothingness, is far different than the crafting of an item from existing substances, as when an artisan fashions something out of wood or metal. In the latter case, the substance preexisted the artisan, and

He is distinguished, He is great, He is exalted. May He soon rebuild His House, speedily, yes speedily, in our days, soon. God, rebuild, God, rebuild, rebuild Your House soon!

He is all glorious, He is faithful, He is faultless, He is righteous. May He soon rebuild His House, speedily, yes speedily, in our days, soon. God, rebuild, God, rebuild, rebuild Your House soon!

He is pure, He is unique, He is powerful, He is all-wise, He is King, He is awesome, He is sublime, He is all-powerful, He is the Redeemer, He is the all-righteous. May He soon rebuild His House, speedily, yes speedily, in our days, soon. God, rebuild, God, rebuild, rebuild Your House soon!

He is holy, He is compassionate, He is Almighty, He is omnipotent. May He soon rebuild His House, speedily, yes speedily, in our days, soon. God, rebuild, God, rebuild, rebuild Your House soon!

**אֶחָד מִי יוֹדֵעַ?** Who knows one? I know one: One is our God, in heaven and on earth.

---

he merely alters its form. The item which the artisan fashioned can thus continue to exist after it leaves the hands of the artisan.

Not so with creation. Prior to creation there was absolute nothingness, and in creating matter, God brought basic substance into being. Prior to this act of creation, then, the natural state of being was nothingness. Bringing something out of nothingness is much different than shaping an existing substance, as happens with the work of the artisan.

Changing a natural state, says Rabbi Shneur Zalman, requires ongoing energy to maintain this change. For example, the natural state of an object lying on the ground is that it is at rest, held to the ground by the force of gravity. Moving an object from its natural state therefore requires energy, and when one throws an item high into the air, there is a force of energy that exceeds the pull of gravity, and the object is lifted into the air. When the force of the thrower dissipates, the force of gravity then attracts the object back to earth, and it comes to rest in its natural state. To maintain the object in the air, which would be against its natural state of rest, would require an ongoing exertion of energy.

Similarly, reasons Rabbi Shneur Zalman, bringing something out of nothing is in defiance of the natural state of nothingness, and maintaining something in existence therefore requires ongoing energy. Creation was thus not a one-time incident, but is an ongoing process, to prevent all that exists from returning to the natural state of nothingness. This maintenance is achieved by the presence of a Divine spark or nucleus, which is the source of energy in every bit of existence. This Divine nucleus is the true essence of everything in existence, but since the Divine spark is invisible to our visual sense, we see only the object in which it is contained. Our intellectual perception, however, should exceed our visual perception, and we should understand that all existence is really but an external manifestation of the Godliness contained within it. This concept indeed requires profound thought, and much "reflection of the heart" is necessary for us to realize that "in the heavens above and on the earth below there is nothing else."

This, then, is the answer to "Who knows One?" What is the Oneness that comprises the entire universe, both spiritual and physical? This Oneness is God.

This profound philosophical concept, the primary principle of existence, is not easily grasped. Furthermore, how there can be a relationship of man to the Creator of the Universe? A relationship between a finite being to the Eternal and Infinite Being is something which unaided human logic cannot fathom. We were therefore given the Divine word, the *two* Tablets of the law at Sinai, as a bridge between finite man and Infinite God.

There is a system of Divinely revealed laws which allows man to relate to the Divine presence and to unite with God. Hence, the two Tablets contain the *Ten* Commandments, and there are the *five* Books of the written Torah as well as the *six* Orders of the Mishnah, which are all vehicles to enable us to grasp the concept of the Oneness of God as interpreted above, and to relate to Him.

We also have the *three* Patriarchs and *four* Matriarchs, whose lives served as models for us to emulate and to permit a union with God. We have the *seven* days of the week, representing the *six* days in which God brought the universe into being, and the *seventh* day of Shabbos, a day of spirituality and holiness, provided by God as a day of contemplation, and blessed by Him with a special charm that permits us to better grasp the abstract truth of existence. We have the covenant of circumcision on the *eighth* day, whereby the patriarch Abraham brought all his descendants into an eternal pact with God. The *nine* months of gestation and the *eleven* stars of great

Who knows two? I know two: two are the Tablets of the Covenant; One is our God, in heaven and on earth.

---

magnitude are included here in order to teach us that even "natural" phenomena are no less Divinely ordained than those more readily defined as religious, and that they are all a manifestation of Godliness. Judaism categorically rejects "giving to God what is to God and to Caesar what is to Caesar," because *everything* is to God, the mundane as well as the celestial. The *twelve* tribes represent the destiny of Israel, the children of the patriarch Jacob, who, in contrast to the sons of Abraham and Isaac, were *all* dedicated to the belief in the One true God. Finally, the *thirteen* Divine attributes are the models of character traits which we are to adopt in our lives, and achieve a spirituality akin to that of God Himself.

Judaism is thus an inverted pyramid, with the entire superstructure resting on the single item of faith, the Omnipresence of God as the essence of all existence. Only when we know the "One" is all other knowledge valid, and failure to know "What is One" renders all other knowledge meaningless.

Inasmuch as the true essence of the universe is spiritual rather than physical, we can experience the true essence of life only if the focus of our lives is primarily spiritual rather than material.

### ☙ אֶחָד מִי יוֹדֵעַ — *Who Knows One?*

I know, dear reader, that by now you may have become weary of my bringing you into my treatment center to observe the features of alcoholism and other chemical addictions, but I must ask you to bear with me just a bit more.

A lasting recovery from addiction generally requires participation in the Twelve Step programs of Alcoholics Anonymous and Narcotics Anonymous. The First of the Twelve Steps is an acknowledgment that one is powerless over a chemical, and that recourse to chemicals has made one's life unmanageable. The subsequent eleven steps are those which one must take to bring about recovery. The First Step is thus a statement of the awareness of the true nature of one's problem, and the remaining steps contain the methodology for healing and restoration of health.

It is axiomatic among recovering people that if at any point in recovery, whether in the first month or the fortieth year, they find themselves encountering difficulties which are amenable to the program's methodology, the first thing to do is to reexamine the First Step. The delusions of omnipotence and the denial of the real problem can recur to any degree and

**שְׁלֹשָׁה מִי יוֹדֵעַ?** שְׁלֹשָׁה אֲנִי יוֹדֵעַ. שְׁלֹשָׁה אָבוֹת, שְׁנֵי לֻחוֹת הַבְּרִית, אֶחָד אֱלֹהֵינוּ שֶׁבַּשָּׁמַיִם וּבָאָרֶץ.

**אַרְבַּע מִי יוֹדֵעַ?** אַרְבַּע אֲנִי יוֹדֵעַ. אַרְבַּע אִמָּהוֹת, שְׁלֹשָׁה אָבוֹת, שְׁנֵי לֻחוֹת הַבְּרִית, אֶחָד אֱלֹהֵינוּ שֶׁבַּשָּׁמַיִם וּבָאָרֶץ.

**חֲמִשָּׁה מִי יוֹדֵעַ?** חֲמִשָּׁה אֲנִי יוֹדֵעַ. חֲמִשָּׁה חֻמְשֵׁי תוֹרָה, אַרְבַּע אִמָּהוֹת, שְׁלֹשָׁה אָבוֹת, שְׁנֵי לֻחוֹת הַבְּרִית, אֶחָד אֱלֹהֵינוּ שֶׁבַּשָּׁמַיִם וּבָאָרֶץ.

**שִׁשָּׁה מִי יוֹדֵעַ?** שִׁשָּׁה אֲנִי יוֹדֵעַ. שִׁשָּׁה סִדְרֵי מִשְׁנָה, חֲמִשָּׁה חֻמְשֵׁי תוֹרָה, אַרְבַּע אִמָּהוֹת, שְׁלֹשָׁה אָבוֹת, שְׁנֵי לֻחוֹת הַבְּרִית, אֶחָד אֱלֹהֵינוּ שֶׁבַּשָּׁמַיִם וּבָאָרֶץ.

**שִׁבְעָה מִי יוֹדֵעַ?** שִׁבְעָה אֲנִי יוֹדֵעַ. שִׁבְעָה יְמֵי שַׁבַּתָּא, שִׁשָּׁה סִדְרֵי מִשְׁנָה, חֲמִשָּׁה חֻמְשֵׁי תוֹרָה, אַרְבַּע אִמָּהוֹת, שְׁלֹשָׁה אָבוֹת, שְׁנֵי לֻחוֹת הַבְּרִית, אֶחָד אֱלֹהֵינוּ שֶׁבַּשָּׁמַיִם וּבָאָרֶץ.

---

at any point in the recovering person's life, and the first thing one must therefore do is to recheck whether one has not fallen victim to these self-deceptions. Only after one has thoroughly reexamined the adequacy of one's compliance with the First Step can one go on to check one's application of the restorative steps of recovery.

The Talmud states that Moses gave us the six hundred and thirteen Divine precepts. To simplify our grasp of them, David condensed and categorized them under eleven headings. Isaiah provided a scheme of six categories, Micah provided three, and Habbakuk subsumed everything under a single principle: "The righteous person lives with faith and trust in God" (*Makkos* 23b). In other words, Habbakuk states that a firm faith and trust in God is the foundation upon which the six hundred and thirteen Torah *mitzvos* rest, and that furthermore, all are derivative of this single basic principle.

Who knows three? I know three: three are the Patriarchs; two are the Tablets of the Covenant; One is our God, in heaven and on earth.

Who knows four? I know four: four are the Matriarchs; three are the Patriarchs; two are the Tablets of the Covenant; One is our God, in heaven and on earth.

Who knows five? I know five: five are the Books of the Torah; four are the Matriarchs; three are the Patriarchs; two are the Tablets of the Covenant; One is our God, in heaven and on earth.

Who knows six? I know six: six are the Orders of the Mishnah; five are the Books of the Torah; four are the Matriarchs; three are the Patriarchs; two are the Tablets of the Covenant; One is our God, in heaven and on earth.

Who knows seven? I know seven: seven are the days of the week; six are the Orders of the Mishnah; five are the Books of the Torah; four are the Matriarchs; three are the Patriarchs; two are the Tablets of the Covenant; One is our God, in heaven and on earth.

---

Just as a recovering person is advised to recheck his acceptance of the First Step, anyone encountering any difficulty in wholesome Torah observance should recheck this first principle stated by Habbakuk, and reexamine how sincere and firm is one's faith and trust in God. Often this will reveal a less-than-perfect faith, in which case the correction must be made at the very source.

Confusion or uncertainty about one's faith may be the result of distorted understanding of God. Our Torah literature provides guidance in developing a concept of God. An excellent resource is *The Way of God* by Luzatto.

A rabbi entered into a discussion of faith with a young man who said, "Look, Rabbi, I am an atheist. I don't believe in God." The rabbi responded, "Don't let that interfere. The god that you don't believe in, I don't believe in either." It makes little sense to assert that one does or does not believe, unless one understands at least something about the object of the belief.

It is likely that a person who encounters difficulty in living a Torah life may reflect, "What is it that I am not doing properly?" and examine his current behavior. The hymn *Who Knows One* begins with the principle of Habbakuk,

**שְׁמוֹנָה מִי יוֹדֵעַ?** שְׁמוֹנָה אֲנִי יוֹדֵעַ. שְׁמוֹנָה יְמֵי מִילָה, שִׁבְעָה יְמֵי שַׁבַּתָּא, שִׁשָּׁה סִדְרֵי מִשְׁנָה, חֲמִשָּׁה חֻמְשֵׁי תוֹרָה, אַרְבַּע אִמָּהוֹת, שְׁלֹשָׁה אָבוֹת, שְׁנֵי לֻחוֹת הַבְּרִית, אֶחָד אֱלֹהֵינוּ שֶׁבַּשָּׁמַיִם וּבָאָרֶץ.

**תִּשְׁעָה מִי יוֹדֵעַ?** תִּשְׁעָה אֲנִי יוֹדֵעַ. תִּשְׁעָה יַרְחֵי לֵדָה, שְׁמוֹנָה יְמֵי מִילָה, שִׁבְעָה יְמֵי שַׁבַּתָּא, שִׁשָּׁה סִדְרֵי מִשְׁנָה, חֲמִשָּׁה חֻמְשֵׁי תוֹרָה, אַרְבַּע אִמָּהוֹת, שְׁלֹשָׁה אָבוֹת, שְׁנֵי לֻחוֹת הַבְּרִית, אֶחָד אֱלֹהֵינוּ שֶׁבַּשָּׁמַיִם וּבָאָרֶץ.

**עֲשָׂרָה מִי יוֹדֵעַ?** עֲשָׂרָה אֲנִי יוֹדֵעַ. עֲשָׂרָה דִבְּרַיָּא, תִּשְׁעָה יַרְחֵי לֵדָה, שְׁמוֹנָה יְמֵי מִילָה, שִׁבְעָה יְמֵי שַׁבַּתָּא, שִׁשָּׁה סִדְרֵי מִשְׁנָה, חֲמִשָּׁה חֻמְשֵׁי תוֹרָה, אַרְבַּע אִמָּהוֹת, שְׁלֹשָׁה אָבוֹת, שְׁנֵי לֻחוֹת הַבְּרִית, אֶחָד אֱלֹהֵינוּ שֶׁבַּשָּׁמַיִם וּבָאָרֶץ.

**אַחַד עָשָׂר מִי יוֹדֵעַ?** אַחַד עָשָׂר אֲנִי יוֹדֵעַ. אַחַד עָשָׂר כּוֹכְבַיָּא, עֲשָׂרָה דִבְּרַיָּא, תִּשְׁעָה יַרְחֵי לֵדָה, שְׁמוֹנָה יְמֵי מִילָה, שִׁבְעָה יְמֵי שַׁבַּתָּא, שִׁשָּׁה סִדְרֵי מִשְׁנָה, חֲמִשָּׁה חֻמְשֵׁי תוֹרָה, אַרְבַּע אִמָּהוֹת, שְׁלֹשָׁה אָבוֹת, שְׁנֵי לֻחוֹת הַבְּרִית, אֶחָד אֱלֹהֵינוּ שֶׁבַּשָּׁמַיִם וּבָאָרֶץ.

**שְׁנֵים עָשָׂר מִי יוֹדֵעַ?** שְׁנֵים עָשָׂר אֲנִי יוֹדֵעַ. שְׁנֵים עָשָׂר שִׁבְטַיָּא, אַחַד עָשָׂר כּוֹכְבַיָּא, עֲשָׂרָה דִבְּרַיָּא, תִּשְׁעָה יַרְחֵי לֵדָה, שְׁמוֹנָה יְמֵי מִילָה, שִׁבְעָה יְמֵי

---

and the following twelve verses are all derivatives of this fundamental belief of the Oneness of God, particularly as it has been explained in *Who Knows One (I).* The repeated pattern of the hymn, which continually refers back from thirteen to twelve to eleven, etc., teaches us that wherever we may be in our

Who knows eight? I know eight: eight are the days of circumcision; seven are the days of the week; six are the Orders of the Mishnah; five are the Books of the Torah; four are the Matriarchs; three are the Patriarchs; two are the Tablets of the Covenant; One is our God, in heaven and on earth.

Who knows nine? I know nine: nine are the months of gestation; eight are the days of circumcision; seven are the days of the week; six are the Orders of the Mishnah; five are the Books of the Torah; four are the Matriarchs; three are the Patriarchs; two are the Tablets of the Covenant; One is our God, in heaven and on earth.

Who knows ten? I know ten: ten are the Ten Commandments; nine are the months of gestation; eight are the days of circumcision; seven are the days of the week; six are the Orders of the Mishnah; five are the Books of the Torah; four are the Matriarchs; three are the Patriarchs; two are the Tablets of the Covenant; One is our God, in heaven and on earth.

Who knows eleven? I know eleven: eleven are the stars (in Yosef's dream); ten are the Ten Commandments; nine are the months of gestation; eight are the days of circumcision; seven are the days of the week; six are the Orders of the Mishnah; five are the Books of the Torah; four are the Matriarchs; three are the Patriarchs; two are the Tablets of the Covenant; One is our God, in heaven and on earth.

Who knows twelve? I know twelve: twelve are the tribes; eleven are the stars (in Yosef's dream); ten are the Ten Commandments; nine are the months of gestation; eight are the days of circumcision; seven are the days

---

course of living a Torah life, we should always refer back to the adequacy of the steps we have taken up to the present time, and ultimately to reinvestigate the wholesomeness of our faith in God. Once the necessary corrections are made to reaffirm our faith, we can then proceed to take other corrective steps.

שַׁבַּתָּא, שִׁשָּׁה סִדְרֵי מִשְׁנָה, חֲמִשָּׁה חֻמְשֵׁי תוֹרָה, אַרְבַּע אִמָּהוֹת, שְׁלֹשָׁה אָבוֹת, שְׁנֵי לֻחוֹת הַבְּרִית, אֶחָד אֱלֹהֵינוּ שֶׁבַּשָּׁמַיִם וּבָאָרֶץ.

**שְׁלֹשָׁה עָשָׂר מִי יוֹדֵעַ?** שְׁלֹשָׁה עָשָׂר אֲנִי יוֹדֵעַ. שְׁלֹשָׁה עָשָׂר מִדַּיָּא, שְׁנֵים עָשָׂר שִׁבְטַיָּא, אַחַד עָשָׂר כּוֹכְבַיָּא, עֲשָׂרָה דִבְּרַיָּא, תִּשְׁעָה יַרְחֵי לֵדָה, שְׁמוֹנָה יְמֵי מִילָה, שִׁבְעָה יְמֵי שַׁבַּתָּא, שִׁשָּׁה סִדְרֵי מִשְׁנָה, חֲמִשָּׁה חֻמְשֵׁי תוֹרָה, אַרְבַּע אִמָּהוֹת, שְׁלֹשָׁה אָבוֹת, שְׁנֵי לֻחוֹת הַבְּרִית, אֶחָד אֱלֹהֵינוּ שֶׁבַּשָּׁמַיִם וּבָאָרֶץ.

**חַד גַּדְיָא,** חַד גַּדְיָא, דְּזַבִּין אַבָּא בִּתְרֵי זוּזֵי, חַד גַּדְיָא חַד גַּדְיָא.

---

**שְׁלֹשָׁה עָשָׂר מִי יוֹדֵעַ? . . . שְׁלֹשָׁה עָשָׂר מִדַּיָּא — *Who knows thirteen? . . . thirteen are the attributes of God.***

Why does this hymn end with thirteen? Why not stop it at an even number of ten? Are there no items of fourteen and fifteen that could have been added?

The hymn begins with one and ends with thirteen because these two items embrace the entirety of Judaism. The number one refers to the unity of God, the fundamental principle of Jewish faith.The number thirteen refers to the Divine attributes which a person is required to emulate.

The Torah states, "You shall follow after God" (*Deuteronomy* 13:5), which the Talmud explains means to adopt the traits of mercy, care, kindness, and the other attributes by which God is characterized. "Just as God clothes the naked, so you shall provide clothes for the needy. Just as God comforts the sick, so you should visit and comfort the sick" (*Sotah* 14a). All other components of Judaism, which have been enumerated in this hymn, are elaborations on these fundamental principles and provide the methodology whereby a person can bring himself to emulate God.

The purpose of the Exodus and the formation of the Jewish nation was to establish a spiritual people (*Exodus* 19:4-6). It is only proper that the Haggadah come to a close with a hymn which incorporates this goal, beginning with the belief in the Oneness of God, and closing with the requirement to fashion oneself after Him.

of the week; six are the Orders of the Mishnah; five are the Books of the Torah; four are the Matriarchs; three are the Patriarchs; two are the Tablets of the Covenant; One is our God, in heaven and on earth.

Who knows thirteen? I know thirteen: thirteen are the attributes of God; twelve are the tribes; eleven are the stars (in Yosef's dream); ten are the Ten Commandments; nine are the months of gestation eight are the days of circumcision; seven are the days of the week; six are the Orders of the Mishnah; five are the Books of the Torah; four are the Matriarchs; three are the Patriarchs; two are the Tablets of the Covenant; One is our God, in heaven and on earth.

**חַד גַּדְיָא,** A kid, a kid, that father bought for two zuzim, a kid, a kid.

---

### ◆§ חַד גַּדְיָא, חַד גַּדְיָא — *A kid, a kid*

In *Ethics of the Fathers* (2:6) it is related that Hillel once saw a head floating upon the water, and addressed it saying, "You drowned in retribution for your having drowned others, but those who drowned you will ultimately be drowned themselves." The question this raises is obvious. There cannot be an infinite regress. The first person to have been drowned must have been an innocent victim, and if so, whoever drowned this murderer was actually performing an act of justice. Why, then, did this person deserve to be drowned?

The answer is that meting out punishment must be left to the judges who are authorized and competent to carry out justice. An individual who takes the law into his own hands, even if he is zealous in the cause of righteousness, is nevertheless vulnerable to being wrongly influenced by his personal interests. For example, if he harbors any resentments towards the criminal, he may be motivated by a thirst for revenge rather than by pure pursuit of fairness. Emotions are powerful motivating forces, and a person may think he is acting in the interest of justice, whereas he is in fact succumbing to his passions.

A spiritual person should be aware of the pitfalls of being misled by emotions, and should refrain from overzealous behavior. Hillel's message was therefore, "The person whom you drowned may well have been guilty of a capital crime for which he should have been put to death. Nevertheless, it was not your function to act as executioner. Your act was possibly motivated by a personal grudge you held against the murderer rather than by your desire to

וְאָתָא **שׁוּנְרָא** וְאָכְלָה לְגַדְיָא, דְּזַבִּין אַבָּא בִּתְרֵי זוּזֵי, חַד גַּדְיָא חַד גַּדְיָא.

וְאָתָא **כַלְבָּא** וְנָשַׁךְ לְשׁוּנְרָא, דְּאָכְלָא לְגַדְיָא, דְּזַבִּין אַבָּא בִּתְרֵי זוּזֵי, חַד גַּדְיָא חַד גַּדְיָא.

וְאָתָא **חוּטְרָא** וְהִכָּה לְכַלְבָּא, דְּנָשַׁךְ לְשׁוּנְרָא, דְּאָכְלָה לְגַדְיָא, דְּזַבִּין אַבָּא בִּתְרֵי זוּזֵי, חַד גַּדְיָא חַד גַּדְיָא.

וְאָתָא **נוּרָא** וְשָׂרַף לְחוּטְרָא, דְּהִכָּה לְכַלְבָּא, דְּנָשַׁךְ לְשׁוּנְרָא, דְּאָכְלָה לְגַדְיָא, דְּזַבִּין אַבָּא בִּתְרֵי זוּזֵי, חַד גַּדְיָא חַד גַּדְיָא.

וְאָתָא **מַיָּא** וְכָבָה לְנוּרָא, דְּשָׂרַף לְחוּטְרָא, דְּהִכָּה לְכַלְבָּא, דְּנָשַׁךְ לְשׁוּנְרָא, דְּאָכְלָה לְגַדְיָא, דְּזַבִּין אַבָּא בִּתְרֵי זוּזֵי, חַד גַּדְיָא חַד גַּדְיָא.

וְאָתָא **תוֹרָא** וְשָׁתָה לְמַיָּא, דְּכָבָה לְנוּרָא, דְּשָׂרַף לְחוּטְרָא, דְּהִכָּה לְכַלְבָּא, דְּנָשַׁךְ לְשׁוּנְרָא,

---

see justice triumph, and you rationalized your behavior by claiming to be acting in the interest of justice. That is why you were punished." Dogs attack cats because of an inherent enmity towards them. Even if the cat had committed a crime, the dog's action was not to avenge the innocent victim, but rather to assuage his hatred for cats. Although the criminal may have deserved his due fate, none but the established authorities of the law have the prerogative of exacting justice. The motives of an individual who takes the law into his own hands are suspect.

Even people of great spirituality must exert caution when motivated by zeal. The Torah states that Phineas was handsomely rewarded for avenging the desecration of the Divine honor when he slew an adulterer who publicly profaned the Torah. Years later in his other identity as Elijah, he fled into the desert because he could not tolerate the Israelites' idolatrous behavior, but the Midrash states that this time God rebuked him for his zeal. The commentaries ask: Why was he rewarded for his initial zealousness but chastised for its repetition?

A cat then came and devoured the kid, that father bought for two zuzim, a kid, a kid.

A dog then came and bit the cat, that devoured the kid, that father bought for two zuzim, a kid, a kid.

A stick then came and beat the dog, that bit the cat, that devoured the kid, that father bought for two zuzim, a kid, a kid.

A fire then came and burnt the stick, that beat the dog, that bit the cat, that devoured the kid, that father bought for two zuzim, a kid, a kid.

Water then came and quenched the fire, that burnt the stick, that beat the dog, that bit the cat, that devoured the kid, that father bought for two zuzim, a kid, a kid.

An ox then came and drank the water, that quenched the fire, that burnt the stick, that beat the dog, that bit the cat,

---

The answer, they say, is that a single act of zeal may be assumed to be genuine, and a person who overcomes his natural passivity to avenge injustice is praiseworthy. However, if he commits repetitious acts of zealousness, it must be suspected that his motives are not purely in the interest of righteousness and justice, but are tainted by a trait of intolerance. Phineas's first act of zealousness was therefore considered virtuous, but a repetition thereof was suspect as being less than one hundred-percent unadulterated zeal.

In the *Had Gadya* hymn, the first offender, the cat, is the real villain, having attacked the innocent kid, and all subsequent characters can be seen as heroes, each one meting out just punishment for what it saw as an evil act. Why are they then all punished, and why does God intervene at the end to punish the Angel of Death? It is because no one is beyond acting out of personal interest, and even the Angel of Death, a totally spiritual being, is considered to be acting sadistically rather than carrying out the mission for which he was created.

Spirituality requires that we be extremely cautious in doing anything which may be injurious to others, even when we think our actions to be fully justified. It is obvious that we must have a court system to deal with anti-social behavior, but beyond that, we should leave judgment of others, and particularly punitive action, to the one and only true Judge.

דְּאָכְלָה לְגַדְיָא, דְּזַבִּין אַבָּא בִּתְרֵי זוּזֵי, חַד גַּדְיָא חַד גַּדְיָא.

וְאָתָא **הַשּׁוֹחֵט** וְשָׁחַט לְתוֹרָא, דְּשָׁתָא לְמַיָּא, דְּכָבָה לְנוּרָא, דְּשָׂרַף לְחוּטְרָא, דְּהִכָּה לְכַלְבָּא, דְּנָשַׁךְ לְשׁוּנְרָא, דְּאָכְלָה לְגַדְיָא, דְּזַבִּין אַבָּא בִּתְרֵי זוּזֵי, חַד גַּדְיָא חַד גַּדְיָא.

וְאָתָא **מַלְאַךְ הַמָּוֶת** וְשָׁחַט לְשׁוֹחֵט, דְּשָׁחַט לְתוֹרָא, דְּשָׁתָה לְמַיָּא, דְּכָבָה לְנוּרָא, דְּשָׂרַף לְחוּטְרָא, דְּהִכָּה לְכַלְבָּא, דְּנָשַׁךְ לְשׁוּנְרָא, דְּאָכְלָה לְגַדְיָא, דְּזַבִּין אַבָּא בִּתְרֵי זוּזֵי, חַד גַּדְיָא חַד גַּדְיָא.

וְאָתָא **הַקָּדוֹשׁ בָּרוּךְ הוּא** וְשָׁחַט לְמַלְאַךְ הַמָּוֶת, דְּשָׁחַט לְשׁוֹחֵט, דְּשָׁחַט לְתוֹרָא, דְּשָׁתָה לְמַיָּא, דְּכָבָה לְנוּרָא, דְּשָׂרַף לְחוּטְרָא, דְּהִכָּה לְכַלְבָּא, דְּנָשַׁךְ לְשׁוּנְרָא, דְּאָכְלָה לְגַדְיָא, דְּזַבִּין אַבָּא בִּתְרֵי זוּזֵי, חַד גַּדְיָא חַד גַּדְיָא.

Although the Haggadah formally ends at this point, one should continue to occupy himself with the story of the Exodus, and the laws of Pesach, until sleep overtakes him. Many recite שִׁיר הַשִּׁירִים, *Song of Songs* (page 196), after the Haggadah.

that devoured the kid, that father bought for two zuzim, a kid, a kid.

A slaughterer then came and slaughtered the ox, that drank the water, that quenched the fire, that burnt the stick, that beat the dog, that bit the cat, that devoured the kid, that father bought for two zuzim, a kid, a kid.

The angel of death then came and killed the slaughterer, who slaughtered the ox, that drank the water, that quenched the fire, that burnt the stick, that beat the dog, that bit the cat, that devoured the kid, that father bought for two zuzim, a kid, a kid.

The Holy One, Blessed is He, then came and slew the angel of death, who killed the slaughterer, who slaughtered the ox, that drank the water, that quenched the fire, that burnt the stick, that beat the dog, that bit the cat, that devoured the kid, that father bought for two zuzim, a kid, a kid.

Although the Haggadah formally ends at this point, one should continue to occupy himself with the story of the Exodus, and the laws of Pesach, until sleep overtakes him. Many recite שִׁיר הַשִּׁירִים, *Song of Songs* (page 197), after the Haggadah.

## קריאת שמע על המטה
## לשני לילות הראשונים של פסח

**בָּרוּךְ** אַתָּה יהוה אֱלֹהֵינוּ מֶלֶךְ הָעוֹלָם, הַמַּפִּיל חֶבְלֵי שֵׁנָה עַל עֵינָי, וּתְנוּמָה עַל עַפְעַפָּי. וִיהִי רָצוֹן מִלְּפָנֶיךָ יהוה אֱלֹהַי וֵאלֹהֵי אֲבוֹתַי, שֶׁתַּשְׁכִּיבֵנִי לְשָׁלוֹם וְתַעֲמִידֵנִי לְשָׁלוֹם. וְאַל יְבַהֲלוּנִי רַעְיוֹנַי, וַחֲלוֹמוֹת רָעִים, וְהַרְהוֹרִים רָעִים. וּתְהֵא מִטָּתִי שְׁלֵמָה לְפָנֶיךָ. וְהָאֵר עֵינַי פֶּן אִישַׁן הַמָּוֶת.[1] כִּי אַתָּה הַמֵּאִיר לְאִישׁוֹן בַּת עָיִן. בָּרוּךְ אַתָּה יהוה, הַמֵּאִיר לָעוֹלָם כֻּלּוֹ בִּכְבוֹדוֹ.

אֵל מֶלֶךְ נֶאֱמָן.

Recite the first verse aloud, with the right hand covering the eyes, and concentrate intently upon accepting God's absolute sovereignty.

**שְׁמַע** ׀ **יִשְׂרָאֵל, יהוה** ׀ **אֱלֹהֵינוּ, יהוה** ׀ **אֶחָד**:[2]

In an undertone – בָּרוּךְ שֵׁם כְּבוֹד מַלְכוּתוֹ לְעוֹלָם וָעֶד.

דברים ו:ה-ט

**וְאָהַבְתָּ** אֵת ׀ יהוה ׀ אֱלֹהֶיךָ, בְּכָל־לְבָבְךָ, וּבְכָל־נַפְשְׁךָ, וּבְכָל־מְאֹדֶךָ: וְהָיוּ הַדְּבָרִים הָאֵלֶּה, אֲשֶׁר ׀ אָנֹכִי מְצַוְּךָ הַיּוֹם, עַל־לְבָבֶךָ: וְשִׁנַּנְתָּם לְבָנֶיךָ, וְדִבַּרְתָּ בָּם, בְּשִׁבְתְּךָ בְּבֵיתֶךָ, וּבְלֶכְתְּךָ בַדֶּרֶךְ, וּבְשָׁכְבְּךָ וּבְקוּמֶךָ: וּקְשַׁרְתָּם לְאוֹת ׀ עַל־יָדֶךָ, וְהָיוּ לְטֹטָפֹת בֵּין ׀ עֵינֶיךָ: וּכְתַבְתָּם ׀ עַל־מְזֻזוֹת בֵּיתֶךָ, וּבִשְׁעָרֶיךָ:

# THE BEDTIME SHEMA FOR THE FIRST TWO NIGHTS OF PESACH

**בָּרוּךְ** *Blessed are You, HASHEM, our God, King of the Universe, Who casts the bonds of sleep upon my eyes and slumber upon my eyelids. May it be Your will, HASHEM, my God and the God of my forefathers, that You lay me down to sleep in peace and raise me erect in peace. May my ideas, bad dreams, and bad notions not confound me; may my offspring be perfect before You, and may You illuminate my eyes lest I die in sleep,*[1] *for it is You Who illuminates the pupil of the eye. Blessed are You, HASHEM, Who illuminates the entire world with His glory.*

*God, trustworthy King.*

Recite the first verse aloud, with the right hand covering the eyes, and concentrate intently upon accepting God's absolute sovereignty.

**Hear, O Israel: HASHEM is our God, HASHEM, the One and Only.**[2]

In an undertone—

*Blessed is the Name of His glorious kingdom for all eternity.*

*Deuteronomy* 6:5-9

**וְאָהַבְתָּ** *You shall love HASHEM, your God, with all your heart, with all your soul and with all your resources. Let these matters that I command you today be upon your heart. Teach them thoroughly to your children and speak of them while you sit in your home, while you walk on the way, when you retire and when you arise. Bind them as a sign upon your arm and let them be tefillin between your eyes. And write them on the doorposts of your house and upon your gates.*

---

(1) Cf. *Psalms* 13:4. (2) *Deuteronomy* 6:4.

# שיר השירים

# Shir HaShirim / Song of Songs

# שיר השירים

## פרק א

א שִׁ֥יר הַשִּׁירִ֖ים אֲשֶׁ֥ר לִשְׁלֹמֹֽה׃ ב יִשָּׁקֵ֙נִי֙ מִנְּשִׁיק֣וֹת
פִּ֔יהוּ כִּֽי־טוֹבִ֥ים דֹּדֶ֖יךָ מִיָּֽיִן׃ ג לְרֵ֙יחַ֙ שְׁמָנֶ֣יךָ טוֹבִ֔ים
שֶׁ֖מֶן תּוּרַ֣ק שְׁמֶ֑ךָ עַל־כֵּ֖ן עֲלָמ֥וֹת אֲהֵבֽוּךָ׃ ד מָשְׁכֵ֕נִי
אַחֲרֶ֖יךָ נָּר֑וּצָה הֱבִיאַ֨נִי הַמֶּ֜לֶךְ חֲדָרָ֗יו נָגִ֤ילָה וְנִשְׂמְחָה֙
בָּ֔ךְ נַזְכִּ֤ירָה דֹדֶ֙יךָ֙ מִיַּ֔יִן מֵישָׁרִ֖ים אֲהֵבֽוּךָ׃ ה שְׁחוֹרָ֤ה
אֲנִי֙ וְֽנָאוָ֔ה בְּנ֖וֹת יְרוּשָׁלִָ֑ם כְּאָהֳלֵ֣י קֵדָ֔ר כִּירִיע֖וֹת
שְׁלֹמֹֽה׃ ו אַל־תִּרְא֙וּנִי֙ שֶׁאֲנִ֣י שְׁחַרְחֹ֔רֶת שֶׁשֱּׁזָפַ֖תְנִי הַשָּׁ֑מֶשׁ
בְּנֵ֧י אִמִּ֣י נִֽחֲרוּ־בִ֗י שָׂמֻ֙נִי֙ נֹטֵרָ֣ה אֶת־הַכְּרָמִ֔ים כַּרְמִ֥י
שֶׁלִּ֖י לֹ֥א נָטָֽרְתִּי׃ ז הַגִּ֣ידָה לִּ֗י שֶׁאָֽהֲבָה֙ נַפְשִׁ֔י אֵיכָ֣ה
תִרְעֶ֔ה אֵיכָ֖ה תַּרְבִּ֣יץ בַּֽצָּהֳרָ֑יִם שַׁלָּמָ֤ה אֶֽהְיֶה֙ כְּעֹ֣טְיָ֔ה
עַ֖ל עֶדְרֵ֥י חֲבֵרֶֽיךָ׃ ח אִם־לֹ֤א תֵֽדְעִי֙ לָ֔ךְ הַיָּפָ֖ה בַּנָּשִׁ֑ים
צְאִי־לָ֞ךְ בְּעִקְבֵ֣י הַצֹּ֗אן וּרְעִי֙ אֶת־גְּדִיֹּתַ֔יִךְ עַ֖ל מִשְׁכְּנ֥וֹת
הָרֹעִֽים׃ ט לְסֻסָתִי֙ בְּרִכְבֵ֣י פַרְעֹ֔ה דִּמִּיתִ֖יךְ רַעְיָתִֽי׃
י נָאו֤וּ לְחָיַ֙יִךְ֙ בַּתֹּרִ֔ים צַוָּארֵ֖ךְ בַּחֲרוּזִֽים׃ יא תּוֹרֵ֤י זָהָב֙
נַֽעֲשֶׂה־לָּ֔ךְ עִ֖ם נְקֻדּ֥וֹת הַכָּֽסֶף׃ יב עַד־שֶׁהַמֶּ֙לֶךְ֙ בִּמְסִבּ֔וֹ
נִרְדִּ֖י נָתַ֥ן רֵיחֽוֹ׃ יג צְר֨וֹר הַמֹּ֤ר ׀ דּוֹדִי֙ לִ֔י בֵּ֥ין שָׁדַ֖י
יָלִֽין׃ יד אֶשְׁכֹּ֨ל הַכֹּ֤פֶר ׀ דּוֹדִי֙ לִ֔י בְּכַרְמֵ֖י עֵ֥ין גֶּֽדִי׃ טו הִנָּ֤ךְ
יָפָה֙ רַעְיָתִ֔י הִנָּ֥ךְ יָפָ֖ה עֵינַ֥יִךְ יוֹנִֽים׃ טז הִנְּךָ֨ יָפֶ֤ה דוֹדִי֙
אַ֣ף נָעִ֔ים אַף־עַרְשֵׂ֖נוּ רַֽעֲנָנָֽה׃ יז קֹר֤וֹת בָּתֵּ֙ינוּ֙ אֲרָזִ֔ים
רַֽהִיטֵ֖נוּ בְּרוֹתִֽים׃

## פרק ב

א אֲנִי֙ חֲבַצֶּ֣לֶת הַשָּׁר֔וֹן שֽׁוֹשַׁנַּ֖ת הָעֲמָקִֽים׃ ב כְּשֽׁוֹשַׁנָּה֙
בֵּ֣ין הַחוֹחִ֔ים כֵּ֥ן רַעְיָתִ֖י בֵּ֥ין הַבָּנֽוֹת׃ ג כְּתַפּ֙וּחַ֙ בַּעֲצֵ֣י הַיַּ֔עַר
כֵּ֥ן דּוֹדִ֖י בֵּ֣ין הַבָּנִ֑ים בְּצִלּוֹ֙ חִמַּ֣דְתִּי וְיָשַׁ֔בְתִּי וּפִרְי֖וֹ
מָת֥וֹק לְחִכִּֽי׃ ד הֱבִיאַ֙נִי֙ אֶל־בֵּ֣ית הַיָּ֔יִן וְדִגְל֥וֹ עָלַ֖י אַהֲבָֽה׃

# ⁂ SHIR HASHIRIM / SONG OF SONGS ⁂
# ⁂ ALLEGORICAL TRANSLATION ⁂

## CHAPTER ONE

1 The song that excels all songs dedicated to God, Him to Whom peace belongs.
2 Communicate Your innermost wisdom to me again in loving closeness, for Your friendship is dearer than all earthly delights. 3 Like the scent of goodly oils is the spreading fame of Your great deeds; Your very name is Flowing Oil, therefore have nations loved You.

**[Israel in Exile to God:]** 4 Upon perceiving a mere hint that You wished to draw me, we rushed with perfect faith after You into the wilderness. The King brought me into His cloud-pillared chamber; whatever our travail we shall always be glad and rejoice in Your Torah. We recall Your love more than earthly delights, unrestrainedly do they love You.

**[Israel to the nations:]** 5 Though I am black with sin, I am comely with virtue, O nations who are destined to ascend to Jerusalem; though sullied as the tents of Kedar, I will be immaculate as the draperies of Him to Whom peace belongs. 6 Do not view me with contempt despite my swarthiness, for it is but the sun which has glared upon me. The alien children of my mother were incensed with me and made me a keeper of the vineyards of idols, but the vineyard of my own true God I did not keep.

**[Israel to God:]** 7 Tell me, You Whom my soul loves: Where will You graze Your flock? Where will You rest them under the fiercest sun of harshest Exile? Why shall I be like one veiled in mourning among the flocks of Your fellow shepherds?

**[God responds to Israel:]** 8 If you know not where to graze, O fairest of nations, follow the footsteps of the sheep — your forefathers who traced a straight, unswerving path after My Torah. Then you can graze your tender kids even among the dwellings of foreign shepherds.

9 With My mighty steeds who battled Pharaoh's riders I revealed that you are My beloved. 10 Your cheeks are lovely with rows of gems, your neck with necklaces — My gifts to you from the splitting sea, 11 by inducing Pharaoh to engage in pursuit, to add circlets of gold to your spangles of silver.

**[Israel about God:]** 12 While the King was yet at Sinai my malodorous deed gave forth its scent as my Golden Calf defiled the covenant. 13 But my Beloved responded with a bundle of myrrh — the fragrant atonement of erecting a Tabernacle where His Presence would dwell amid the Holy Ark's staves. 14 Like a cluster of henna in Ein Gedi vineyards has my Beloved multiplied his forgiveness to me.

15 He said, 'I forgive you, My friend, for you are lovely in deed and lovely in resolve. The righteous among you are loyal as a dove.'

**[Israel to God:]** 16 It is You Who are lovely, my Beloved, so pleasant that You pardoned my sin enabling our Temple to make me ever fresh. 17 The beams of our House are cedar, our panels are cypress.

## CHAPTER TWO

1 I am but a rose of Sharon, even an ever-fresh rose of the valleys.

**[God to Israel:]** 2 Like the rose maintaining its beauty among the thorns, so is My faithful beloved among the nations.

**[Israel reminisces . . .:]** 3 Like the fruitful, fragrant apple tree among the barren trees of the forest, so is my Beloved among the gods. In His shade I delighted and there I sat, and the fruit of His Torah was sweet to my palate. 4 He brought me to the chamber of Torah delights and clustered my encampments about Him in love.

ה סַמְּכוּנִי בָּאֲשִׁישׁוֹת רַפְּדוּנִי בַּתַּפּוּחִים כִּי־חוֹלַת אַהֲבָה
אָנִי: ו שְׂמֹאלוֹ תַּחַת לְרֹאשִׁי וִימִינוֹ תְּחַבְּקֵנִי: ז הִשְׁבַּעְתִּי
אֶתְכֶם בְּנוֹת יְרוּשָׁלִַם בִּצְבָאוֹת אוֹ בְּאַיְלוֹת הַשָּׂדֶה אִם־
תָּעִירוּ | וְאִם־תְּעוֹרְרוּ אֶת־הָאַהֲבָה עַד שֶׁתֶּחְפָּץ: ח קוֹל
דּוֹדִי הִנֵּה־זֶה בָּא מְדַלֵּג עַל־הֶהָרִים מְקַפֵּץ עַל־הַגְּבָעוֹת:
ט דּוֹמֶה דוֹדִי לִצְבִי אוֹ לְעֹפֶר הָאַיָּלִים הִנֵּה־זֶה עוֹמֵד אַחַר
כָּתְלֵנוּ מַשְׁגִּיחַ מִן־הַחַלֹּנוֹת מֵצִיץ מִן־הַחֲרַכִּים: י עָנָה דוֹדִי
וְאָמַר לִי קוּמִי לָךְ רַעְיָתִי יָפָתִי וּלְכִי־לָךְ: יא כִּי־הִנֵּה הַסְּתָו
עָבָר הַגֶּשֶׁם חָלַף הָלַךְ לוֹ: יב הַנִּצָּנִים נִרְאוּ בָאָרֶץ עֵת הַזָּמִיר
הִגִּיעַ וְקוֹל הַתּוֹר נִשְׁמַע בְּאַרְצֵנוּ: יג הַתְּאֵנָה חָנְטָה פַגֶּיהָ
וְהַגְּפָנִים | סְמָדַר נָתְנוּ רֵיחַ קוּמִי לָךְ רַעְיָתִי יָפָתִי וּלְכִי־לָךְ:
יד יוֹנָתִי בְּחַגְוֵי הַסֶּלַע בְּסֵתֶר הַמַּדְרֵגָה הַרְאִינִי אֶת־מַרְאַיִךְ
הַשְׁמִיעִנִי אֶת־קוֹלֵךְ כִּי־קוֹלֵךְ עָרֵב וּמַרְאֵיךְ נָאוֶה: טו אֶחֱזוּ־
לָנוּ שֻׁעָלִים שֻׁעָלִים קְטַנִּים מְחַבְּלִים כְּרָמִים וּכְרָמֵינוּ
סְמָדַר: טז דּוֹדִי לִי וַאֲנִי לוֹ הָרֹעֶה בַּשּׁוֹשַׁנִּים: יז עַד שֶׁיָּפוּחַ
הַיּוֹם וְנָסוּ הַצְּלָלִים סֹב דְּמֵה־לְךָ דוֹדִי לִצְבִי אוֹ לְעֹפֶר
הָאַיָּלִים עַל־הָרֵי בָתֶר:

## פרק ג

א עַל־מִשְׁכָּבִי בַּלֵּילוֹת בִּקַּשְׁתִּי אֵת שֶׁאָהֲבָה נַפְשִׁי
בִּקַּשְׁתִּיו וְלֹא מְצָאתִיו: ב אָקוּמָה נָּא וַאֲסוֹבְבָה בָעִיר
בַּשְּׁוָקִים וּבָרְחֹבוֹת אֲבַקְשָׁה אֵת שֶׁאָהֲבָה נַפְשִׁי בִּקַּשְׁתִּיו
וְלֹא מְצָאתִיו: ג מְצָאוּנִי הַשֹּׁמְרִים הַסֹּבְבִים בָּעִיר אֵת
שֶׁאָהֲבָה נַפְשִׁי רְאִיתֶם: ד כִּמְעַט שֶׁעָבַרְתִּי מֵהֶם עַד
שֶׁמָּצָאתִי אֵת שֶׁאָהֲבָה נַפְשִׁי אֲחַזְתִּיו וְלֹא אַרְפֶּנּוּ
עַד־שֶׁהֲבֵיאתִיו אֶל־בֵּית אִמִּי וְאֶל־חֶדֶר הוֹרָתִי:
ה הִשְׁבַּעְתִּי אֶתְכֶם בְּנוֹת יְרוּשָׁלִַם בִּצְבָאוֹת אוֹ בְּאַיְלוֹת
הַשָּׂדֶה אִם־תָּעִירוּ | וְאִם־תְּעוֹרְרוּ אֶת־הָאַהֲבָה עַד
שֶׁתֶּחְפָּץ: ו מִי זֹאת עֹלָה מִן־הַמִּדְבָּר כְּתִימֲרוֹת עָשָׁן

5 I say to Him, 'Sustain me in exile with dainty cakes, spread fragrant apples about me to comfort my dispersion — for, bereft of Your Presence, I am sick with love.' 6 With memories of His loving support in the desert, of His left hand under my head, of His right hand enveloping me.

**[Turns to the nations:]** 7 I adjure you, O nations who are destined to ascend to Jerusalem — for if you violate your oath you will become as defenseless as gazelles or hinds of the field — if you dare provoke God to hate me or disturb His love for me while He still desires it.

**[Then reminisces further:]** 8 The voice of my Beloved! Behold — it came suddenly to redeem me, as if leaping over mountains, skipping over hills. 9 In His swiftness to redeem me, my Beloved is like a gazelle or a young hart. I thought I would be forever alone, but behold! He was standing behind our wall, observing through the windows, peering through the lattices.

10 When He redeemed me from Egypt, my Beloved called out and said to me, 'Arise My love, My fair one, and go forth. 11 For the winter of bondage has passed, the deluge of suffering is over and gone. 12 The righteous blossoms are seen in the land, the time of your song has arrived, and the voice of your guide is heard in the land. 13 The fig tree has formed its first small figs, ready for ascent to the Temple. The vines are in blossom, their fragrance declaring they are ready for libation. Arise, My love, My fair one, and go forth!'

14 At the sea, He said to me, 'O My dove, trapped at the sea as if in the clefts of the rock, the concealment of the terrace. Show Me your prayerful gaze, let Me hear your supplicating voice, for your voice is sweet and your countenance comely.' 15 Then He told the sea, 'Seize for us the Egyptian foxes, even the small foxes who spoiled Israel's vineyards while our vineyards had just begun to blossom.'

16 My Beloved is mine, He fills all my needs and I seek from Him and none other. He grazes me in roselike bounty. 17 Until my sin blows His friendship away and sears me like the midday sun and His protection departs, my sin caused Him to turn away.

I say to him, 'My Beloved, You became like a gazelle or a young hart on the distant mountains.'

## CHAPTER THREE

**[Israel to the nations:]** 1 As I lay on my bed in the night of my desert travail, I sought Him Whom my soul loves. I sought Him but I found Him not, for He maintained His aloofness. 2 I resolved to arise then, and roam through the city, in the streets and squares; that through Moses I would seek Him Whom my soul loved. I sought Him, but I found Him not. 3 They found me, Moses and Aaron, the watchmen patrolling the city. 'You have seen Him Whom my soul loves — what has He said?' 4 Scarcely had I departed from them when, in the days of Joshua, I found Him Whom my soul loves. I grasped Him, determined that my deeds would never again cause me to lose hold of Him, until I brought His Presence to the Tabernacle of my mother and to the chamber of the one who conceived me. 5 I adjure you, O nations who are destined to ascend to Jerusalem — for if you violate your oath you will become as defenseless as gazelles or hinds of the field — if you dare provoke God to hate me or disturb His love for me while He still desires it.

6 You nations have asked, 'Who is this ascending from the desert, its way secured and smoothed by palmlike pillars of smoke, burning fragrant myrrh and frankincense, of all the perfumer's powders?' 7 Behold the resting place of Him

שֶׁלִּשְׁלֹמֹה שִׁשִּׁים גִּבֹּרִים סָבִיב לָהּ מִגִּבֹּרֵי יִשְׂרָאֵל׃ ח כֻּלָּם
אֲחֻזֵי חֶרֶב מְלֻמְּדֵי מִלְחָמָה אִישׁ חַרְבּוֹ עַל־יְרֵכוֹ מִפַּחַד
בַּלֵּילוֹת׃ ט אַפִּרְיוֹן עָשָׂה לוֹ הַמֶּלֶךְ שְׁלֹמֹה מֵעֲצֵי הַלְּבָנוֹן׃
י עַמּוּדָיו עָשָׂה כֶסֶף רְפִידָתוֹ זָהָב מֶרְכָּבוֹ אַרְגָּמָן תּוֹכוֹ רָצוּף
אַהֲבָה מִבְּנוֹת יְרוּשָׁלָםִ׃ יא צְאֶינָה ׀ וּרְאֶינָה בְּנוֹת צִיּוֹן בַּמֶּלֶךְ
שְׁלֹמֹה בָּעֲטָרָה שֶׁעִטְּרָה־לּוֹ אִמּוֹ בְּיוֹם חֲתֻנָּתוֹ וּבְיוֹם
שִׂמְחַת לִבּוֹ׃

פרק ד

א הִנָּךְ יָפָה רַעְיָתִי הִנָּךְ יָפָה עֵינַיִךְ יוֹנִים מִבַּעַד לְצַמָּתֵךְ
שַׂעְרֵךְ כְּעֵדֶר הָעִזִּים שֶׁגָּלְשׁוּ מֵהַר גִּלְעָד׃ ב שִׁנַּיִךְ כְּעֵדֶר
הַקְּצוּבוֹת שֶׁעָלוּ מִן־הָרַחְצָה שֶׁכֻּלָּם מַתְאִימוֹת וְשַׁכֻּלָה אֵין
בָּהֶם׃ ג כְּחוּט הַשָּׁנִי שִׂפְתוֹתַיִךְ וּמִדְבָּרֵיךְ נָאוֶה כְּפֶלַח הָרִמּוֹן
רַקָּתֵךְ מִבַּעַד לְצַמָּתֵךְ׃ ד כְּמִגְדַּל דָּוִיד צַוָּארֵךְ בָּנוּי
לְתַלְפִּיּוֹת אֶלֶף הַמָּגֵן תָּלוּי עָלָיו כֹּל שִׁלְטֵי הַגִּבֹּרִים׃ ה שְׁנֵי
שָׁדַיִךְ כִּשְׁנֵי עֳפָרִים תְּאוֹמֵי צְבִיָּה הָרוֹעִים בַּשּׁוֹשַׁנִּים׃ ו עַד
שֶׁיָּפוּחַ הַיּוֹם וְנָסוּ הַצְּלָלִים אֵלֶךְ לִי אֶל־הַר הַמּוֹר
וְאֶל־גִּבְעַת הַלְּבוֹנָה׃ ז כֻּלָּךְ יָפָה רַעְיָתִי וּמוּם אֵין בָּךְ׃ ח אִתִּי
מִלְּבָנוֹן כַּלָּה אִתִּי מִלְּבָנוֹן תָּבוֹאִי תָּשׁוּרִי ׀ מֵרֹאשׁ אֲמָנָה
מֵרֹאשׁ שְׂנִיר וְחֶרְמוֹן מִמְּעֹנוֹת אֲרָיוֹת מֵהַרְרֵי נְמֵרִים׃
ט לִבַּבְתִּנִי אֲחֹתִי כַלָּה לִבַּבְתִּנִי בְּאַחַת מֵעֵינַיִךְ בְּאַחַד עֲנָק
מִצַּוְּרֹנָיִךְ׃ י מַה־יָּפוּ דֹדַיִךְ אֲחֹתִי כַלָּה מַה־טֹּבוּ דֹדַיִךְ מִיַּיִן
וְרֵיחַ שְׁמָנַיִךְ מִכָּל־בְּשָׂמִים׃ יא נֹפֶת תִּטֹּפְנָה שִׂפְתוֹתַיִךְ כַּלָּה
דְּבַשׁ וְחָלָב תַּחַת לְשׁוֹנֵךְ וְרֵיחַ שַׂלְמֹתַיִךְ כְּרֵיחַ לְבָנוֹן׃ יב גַּן ׀
נָעוּל אֲחֹתִי כַלָּה גַּל נָעוּל מַעְיָן חָתוּם׃ יג שְׁלָחַיִךְ פַּרְדֵּס
רִמּוֹנִים עִם פְּרִי מְגָדִים כְּפָרִים עִם־נְרָדִים׃ יד נֵרְדְּ ׀ וְכַרְכֹּם
קָנֶה וְקִנָּמוֹן עִם כָּל־עֲצֵי לְבוֹנָה מֹר וַאֲהָלוֹת עִם כָּל־רָאשֵׁי
בְשָׂמִים׃ טו מַעְיַן גַּנִּים בְּאֵר מַיִם חַיִּים וְנֹזְלִים מִן־לְבָנוֹן׃
טז עוּרִי צָפוֹן וּבוֹאִי תֵימָן הָפִיחִי גַנִּי יִזְּלוּ בְשָׂמָיו יָבֹא דוֹדִי
לְגַנּוֹ וְיֹאכַל פְּרִי מְגָדָיו׃

to Whom peace belongs, with sixty myriads of Israel's mighty encircling it. 8 All of
them gripping the sword of tradition, skilled in the battle of Torah, each with his
sword ready at his side, lest he succumb in the nights of exile. 9 A Tabernacle for His
presence has the King to Whom peace belongs made of the wood of Lebanon. 10 Its
pillars He made of silver, His resting place was gold, its suspended curtain was
purple wool, its midst was decked with implements bespeaking love by the
daughters of Jerusalem. 11 Go forth and gaze, O daughters distinguished by loyalty
to God, upon the King to Whom peace belongs adorned with the crown His nation
made for Him, on the day His Law was given and He became one with Israel, and on
the day His heart was gladdened by His Tabernacle's consecration.

## CHAPTER FOUR

**[God to Israel:]** 1 Behold, you are lovely, My friend, behold you are lovely, your
very appearance radiates dovelike constancy. The most common sons within your
encampments are as dearly beloved as the children of Jacob in the goatlike
procession descending the slopes of Mount Gilead. 2 Accountable in deed are your
fiercest warriors like a well-numbered flock come up from the washing, all of them
unblemished with no miscarriage of action in them.

3 Like the scarlet thread, guarantor of Rachav's safety, is the sincerity of your lips,
and your word is unfeigned. As many as a pomegranate's seeds are the merits of
your unworthiest within your modest veil. 4 As stately as the Tower of David is the
site of your Sanhedrin built as a model to emulate, with a thousand shields of Torah
armor hung upon it, all the disciple-filled quivers of the mighty. 5 Moses and Aaron,
your two sustainers, are like two fawns, twins of the gazelle, who graze their sheep in
roselike bounty.

6 Until My sunny benevolence was withdrawn from Shiloh and the protective
shadows were dispersed by your sin. I will go to Mount Moriah and the hill of
frankincense — 7 where you will be completely fair, My beloved, and no blemish will
be in you.

8 With Me will you be exiled from the Temple, O bride, with Me from the Temple
until you return; then to contemplate the fruits of your faith from its earliest
beginnings from your first arrival at the summits of Snir and of Hermon, the lands of
mighty Sichon and Og, as impregnable as dens of lions, and as mountains of
leopards.

9 You captured My heart, My sister, O bride; you captured My heart with but one of
your virtues, with but one of the precepts that adorn you like beads of a necklace
resplendent. 10 How fair was your love in so many settings, My sister, O bride; so
superior is your love to wine and your spreading fame to all perfumes.

11 The sweetness of Torah drops from your lips, like honey and milk it lies under
your tongue; your very garments are scented with precepts like the scent of
Lebanon. 12 As chaste as a garden locked, My sister, O bride; a spring locked up, a
fountain sealed. 13 Your least gifted ones are a pomegranate orchard with luscious
fruit; henna with nard; 14 nard and saffron, calamus and cinnamon, with all trees of
frankincense, myrrh and aloes with all the chief spices; 15 purified in a garden spring,
a well of waters alive and flowing clean from Lebanon.

16 Awake from the north and come from the south! Like the winds let My exiles
return to My garden, let their fragrant goodness flow in Jerusalem.

**[Israel responds:]** Let but my Beloved come to His garden and enjoy His precious
people.

## פרק ה

א בָּ֣אתִי לְגַנִּי֮ אֲחֹתִ֣י כַלָּה֒ אָרִ֤יתִי מוֹרִי֙ עִם־בְּשָׂמִ֔י אָכַ֤לְתִּי
יַעְרִי֙ עִם־דִּבְשִׁ֔י שָׁתִ֥יתִי יֵינִ֖י עִם־חֲלָבִ֑י אִכְל֣וּ רֵעִ֔ים
שְׁת֥וּ וְשִׁכְר֖וּ דּוֹדִֽים׃ ב אֲנִ֥י יְשֵׁנָ֖ה וְלִבִּ֣י עֵ֑ר ק֣וֹל ׀ דּוֹדִ֣י
דוֹפֵ֗ק פִּתְחִי־לִ֞י אֲחֹתִ֤י רַעְיָתִי֙ יוֹנָתִ֣י תַמָּתִ֔י שֶׁרֹּאשִׁי֙
נִמְלָא־טָ֔ל קְוֻצּוֹתַ֖י רְסִ֥יסֵי לָֽיְלָה׃ ג פָּשַׁ֙טְתִּי֙ אֶת־כֻּתָּנְתִּ֔י
אֵיכָ֖כָה אֶלְבָּשֶׁ֑נָּה רָחַ֥צְתִּי אֶת־רַגְלַ֖י אֵיכָ֥כָה אֲטַנְּפֵֽם׃
ד דּוֹדִ֗י שָׁלַ֤ח יָדוֹ֙ מִן־הַחֹ֔ר וּמֵעַ֖י הָמ֥וּ עָלָֽיו׃ ה קַ֥מְתִּֽי
אֲנִ֖י לִפְתֹּ֣חַ לְדוֹדִ֑י וְיָדַ֣י נָֽטְפוּ־מ֗וֹר וְאֶצְבְּעֹתַי֙ מ֣וֹר עֹבֵ֔ר
עַ֖ל כַּפּ֥וֹת הַמַּנְעֽוּל׃ ו פָּתַ֤חְתִּֽי אֲנִי֙ לְדוֹדִ֔י וְדוֹדִ֖י חָמַ֣ק
עָבָ֑ר נַפְשִׁי֙ יָֽצְאָ֣ה בְדַבְּר֔וֹ בִּקַּשְׁתִּ֙יהוּ֙ וְלֹ֣א מְצָאתִ֔יהוּ
קְרָאתִ֖יו וְלֹ֥א עָנָֽנִי׃ ז מְצָאֻ֧נִי הַשֹּׁמְרִ֛ים הַסֹּבְבִ֥ים בָּעִ֖יר
הִכּ֣וּנִי פְצָע֑וּנִי נָשְׂא֤וּ אֶת־רְדִידִי֙ מֵעָלַ֔י שֹׁמְרֵ֖י הַחֹמֽוֹת׃
ח הִשְׁבַּ֥עְתִּי אֶתְכֶ֖ם בְּנ֣וֹת יְרוּשָׁלִָ֑ם אִֽם־תִּמְצְאוּ֙ אֶת־
דּוֹדִ֔י מַה־תַּגִּ֣ידוּ ל֔וֹ שֶׁחוֹלַ֥ת אַהֲבָ֖ה אָֽנִי׃ ט מַה־דּוֹדֵ֣ךְ
מִדּ֔וֹד הַיָּפָ֖ה בַּנָּשִׁ֑ים מַה־דּוֹדֵ֣ךְ מִדּ֔וֹד שֶׁכָּ֖כָה הִשְׁבַּעְתָּֽנוּ׃
י דּוֹדִ֥י צַח֙ וְאָד֔וֹם דָּג֖וּל מֵרְבָבָֽה׃ יא רֹאשׁ֖וֹ כֶּ֣תֶם פָּ֑ז
קְוֻצּוֹתָיו֙ תַּלְתַּלִּ֔ים שְׁחֹר֖וֹת כָּעוֹרֵֽב׃ יב עֵינָ֕יו כְּיוֹנִ֖ים עַל־
אֲפִ֣יקֵי מָ֑יִם רֹֽחֲצוֹת֙ בֶּֽחָלָ֔ב יֹשְׁב֖וֹת עַל־מִלֵּֽאת׃ יג לְחָיָו֙
כַּעֲרוּגַ֣ת הַבֹּ֔שֶׂם מִגְדְּל֖וֹת מֶרְקָחִ֑ים שִׂפְתוֹתָיו֙ שֽׁוֹשַׁנִּ֔ים
נֹטְפ֖וֹת מ֥וֹר עֹבֵֽר׃ יד יָדָיו֙ גְּלִילֵ֣י זָהָ֔ב מְמֻלָּאִ֖ים בַּתַּרְשִׁ֑ישׁ
מֵעָיו֙ עֶ֣שֶׁת שֵׁ֔ן מְעֻלֶּ֖פֶת סַפִּירִֽים׃ טו שׁוֹקָיו֙ עַמּ֣וּדֵי שֵׁ֔שׁ
מְיֻסָּדִ֖ים עַל־אַדְנֵי־פָ֑ז מַרְאֵ֙הוּ֙ כַּלְּבָנ֔וֹן בָּח֖וּר כָּאֲרָזִֽים׃
טז חִכּוֹ֙ מַֽמְתַקִּ֔ים וְכֻלּ֖וֹ מַחֲמַדִּ֑ים זֶ֤ה דוֹדִי֙ וְזֶ֣ה רֵעִ֔י בְּנ֖וֹת
יְרוּשָׁלִָֽם׃

## פרק ו

א אָ֤נָה הָלַךְ֙ דּוֹדֵ֔ךְ הַיָּפָ֖ה בַּנָּשִׁ֑ים אָ֚נָה פָּנָ֣ה דוֹדֵ֔ךְ
וּנְבַקְשֶׁ֖נּוּ עִמָּֽךְ׃ ב דּוֹדִי֙ יָרַ֣ד לְגַנּ֔וֹ לַעֲרוּג֖וֹת הַבֹּ֑שֶׂם
לִרְעוֹת֙ בַּגַּנִּ֔ים וְלִלְקֹ֖ט שֽׁוֹשַׁנִּֽים׃ ג אֲנִ֤י לְדוֹדִי֙ וְדוֹדִ֣י לִ֔י

## CHAPTER FIVE

**[God replies:]** [1] To your Tabernacle Dedication, My sister, O bride, I came as if to My garden. I gathered My myrrh with My spice from your princely incense; I accepted your unbidden as well as your bidden offerings to Me; I drank your libations pure as milk. Eat, My beloved priests! Drink and become God-intoxicated, O friends!

**[Israel reminisces regretfully:]** [2] I let my devotion slumber, but the God of my heart was awake! A sound! My Beloved knocks!

He said, 'Open your heart to Me, My sister, My love, My dove, My perfection; admit Me and My head is filled with dewlike memories of Abraham; spurn Me and I bear collections of punishing rains in exile-nights.'

[3] And I responded, 'I have doffed my robe of devotion; how can I don it? I have washed my feet that trod Your path; how can I soil them?'

[4] In anger at my recalcitrance, my Beloved sent forth His Hand from the portal in wrath, and my intestines churned with longing for Him. [5] I arose to open for my Beloved and my hands dripped myrrh of repentant devotion to Torah and God, and my fingers flowing with myrrh to remove the traces of my foolish rebuke from the handles of the lock. [6] I opened for my Beloved; but, alas, my Beloved had turned His back on my plea and was gone. My soul departed at His decree! I sought His closeness but could not find it; I beseeched Him but He would not answer.

[7] They found me, the enemy watchmen patrolling the city; they struck me, they bloodied me wreaking God's revenge on me. They stripped my mantle of holiness from me, the angelic watchmen of the wall.

**[Israel to the nations:]** [8] I adjure you, O nations who are destined to ascend to Jerusalem, when you see my Beloved on the future Day of Judgment, won't you tell Him that I bore all travails for love of Him?

**[The nations ask Israel:]** [9] With what does your beloved God excel all others that you suffer for His Name, O fairest of nations? With what does your beloved God excel all others that you dare to adjure us?

**[Israel responds:]** [10] My Beloved is pure and purifies sin, and ruddy with vengeance to punish betrayers, surrounded with myriad angels. [11] His opening words were finest gold, His crowns hold mounds of statutes written in raven-black flame.

[12] Like the gaze of doves toward their cotes, His eyes are fixed on the waters of Torah, bathing all things in clarity, established upon creation's fullness. [13] Like a bed of spices are His words at Sinai, like towers of perfume. His comforting words from the Tabernacle are roses dripping flowing myrrh. [14] The Tablets, His handiwork, are desirable above even rolls of gold; they are studded with commandments precious as gems, the Torah's innards are sparkling as ivory intricately overlaid with precious stone. [15] The Torah's columns are marble set in contexts of finest gold, its contemplation flowers like Lebanon, it is sturdy as cedars. [16] The words of His palate are sweet and He is all delight.

This is my Beloved and this is my Friend, O nations who are destined to ascend to Jerusalem.

## CHAPTER SIX

**[The nations derisively, to Israel:]** [1] Where has your Beloved gone, O forsaken fairest among women? Where has your Beloved turned to rejoin you? Let us seek Him with you and build His Temple with you.

**[Israel responds:]** [2] My Beloved has descended to His Temple garden, to His incense altar, yet still He grazes my brethren remaining in gardens of exile to gather the roseate fragrance of their words of Torah. [3] I alone am my Beloved's and my

הָרֹעֶה בַּשּׁוֹשַׁנִּים׃ ד יָפָה אַתְּ רַעְיָתִי כְּתִרְצָה נָאוָה
כִּירוּשָׁלָםִ אֲיֻמָּה כַּנִּדְגָּלוֹת׃ ה הָסֵבִּי עֵינַיִךְ מִנֶּגְדִּי שֶׁהֵם
הִרְהִיבֻנִי שַׂעְרֵךְ כְּעֵדֶר הָעִזִּים שֶׁגָּלְשׁוּ מִן־הַגִּלְעָד׃
ו שִׁנַּיִךְ כְּעֵדֶר הָרְחֵלִים שֶׁעָלוּ מִן־הָרַחְצָה שֶׁכֻּלָּם
מַתְאִימוֹת וְשַׁכֻּלָה אֵין בָּהֶם׃ ז כְּפֶלַח הָרִמּוֹן רַקָּתֵךְ
מִבַּעַד לְצַמָּתֵךְ׃ ח שִׁשִּׁים הֵמָּה מְלָכוֹת וּשְׁמֹנִים פִּילַגְשִׁים
וַעֲלָמוֹת אֵין מִסְפָּר׃ ט אַחַת הִיא יוֹנָתִי תַמָּתִי אַחַת
הִיא לְאִמָּהּ בָּרָה הִיא לְיוֹלַדְתָּהּ רָאוּהָ בָנוֹת וַיְאַשְּׁרוּהָ
מְלָכוֹת וּפִילַגְשִׁים וַיְהַלְלוּהָ׃ י מִי־זֹאת הַנִּשְׁקָפָה כְּמוֹ־
שָׁחַר יָפָה כַלְּבָנָה בָּרָה כַּחַמָּה אֲיֻמָּה כַּנִּדְגָּלוֹת׃ יא אֶל־
גִּנַּת אֱגוֹז יָרַדְתִּי לִרְאוֹת בְּאִבֵּי הַנָּחַל לִרְאוֹת הֲפָרְחָה
הַגֶּפֶן הֵנֵצוּ הָרִמֹּנִים׃ יב לֹא יָדַעְתִּי נַפְשִׁי שָׂמַתְנִי מַרְכְּבוֹת
עַמִּי נָדִיב׃

## פרק ז

א שׁוּבִי שׁוּבִי הַשּׁוּלַמִּית שׁוּבִי שׁוּבִי וְנֶחֱזֶה־בָּךְ מַה־
תֶּחֱזוּ בַּשּׁוּלַמִּית כִּמְחֹלַת הַמַּחֲנָיִם׃ ב מַה־יָּפוּ פְעָמַיִךְ
בַּנְּעָלִים בַּת־נָדִיב חַמּוּקֵי יְרֵכַיִךְ כְּמוֹ חֲלָאִים מַעֲשֵׂה יְדֵי
אָמָּן׃ ג שָׁרְרֵךְ אַגַּן הַסַּהַר אַל־יֶחְסַר הַמָּזֶג בִּטְנֵךְ עֲרֵמַת
חִטִּים סוּגָה בַּשּׁוֹשַׁנִּים׃ ד שְׁנֵי שָׁדַיִךְ כִּשְׁנֵי עֳפָרִים תָּאֳמֵי
צְבִיָּה׃ ה צַוָּארֵךְ כְּמִגְדַּל הַשֵּׁן עֵינַיִךְ בְּרֵכוֹת בְּחֶשְׁבּוֹן
עַל־שַׁעַר בַּת־רַבִּים אַפֵּךְ כְּמִגְדַּל הַלְּבָנוֹן צוֹפֶה פְּנֵי
דַמָּשֶׂק׃ ו רֹאשֵׁךְ עָלַיִךְ כַּכַּרְמֶל וְדַלַּת רֹאשֵׁךְ כָּאַרְגָּמָן
מֶלֶךְ אָסוּר בָּרְהָטִים׃ ז מַה־יָּפִית וּמַה־נָּעַמְתְּ אַהֲבָה
בַּתַּעֲנוּגִים׃ ח זֹאת קוֹמָתֵךְ דָּמְתָה לְתָמָר וְשָׁדַיִךְ לְאַשְׁכֹּלוֹת׃
ט אָמַרְתִּי אֶעֱלֶה בְתָמָר אֹחֲזָה בְּסַנְסִנָּיו וְיִהְיוּ־נָא שָׁדַיִךְ
כְּאֶשְׁכְּלוֹת הַגֶּפֶן וְרֵיחַ אַפֵּךְ כַּתַּפּוּחִים׃ י וְחִכֵּךְ כְּיֵין
הַטּוֹב הוֹלֵךְ לְדוֹדִי לְמֵישָׁרִים דּוֹבֵב שִׂפְתֵי יְשֵׁנִים׃ יא אֲנִי
לְדוֹדִי וְעָלַי תְּשׁוּקָתוֹ׃ יב לְכָה דוֹדִי נֵצֵא הַשָּׂדֶה נָלִינָה
בַּכְּפָרִים׃ יג נַשְׁכִּימָה לַכְּרָמִים נִרְאֶה אִם־פָּרְחָה הַגֶּפֶן

Beloved is mine, He Who grazes His sheep in roselike pastures.

**[God to Israel:]** [4] You are beautiful, My love, when your deeds are pleasing, as comely now as once you were in Jerusalem of old, hosts of angels stand in awe of you. [5] Turn your pleading eyes from Me lest I be tempted to bestow upon you holiness more than you can bear. But with all your flaws, your most common sons are as dearly beloved as the children of Jacob in the goatlike procession descending the slopes of Mount Gilead. [6] Your mighty leaders are perfect, as a flock of ewes come up from the washing, all of them unblemished with no miscarriage of action in them. [7] As many as a pomegranate's seeds are the merits of your unworthiest within your modest veil. [8] The queenly offspring of Abraham are sixty, compared to whom the eighty Noachides and all their countless nations are like mere concubines.

[9] Unique is she, My constant dove, My perfect one. Unique is she, this nation striving for the truth; pure is she to Jacob who begot her. Nations saw her and acclaimed her; queens and concubines, and they praised her: [10] 'Who is this that gazes down from atop the Temple Mount, brightening like the dawn, beautiful as the moon, brilliant as the sun, awesome as the bannered hosts of kings?'

[11] I descended upon the deceptively simple holiness of the Second Temple to see your moisture-laden deeds in valleys. Had your Torah scholars budded on the vine, had your merit-laden righteous flowered like the pomegranates filled with seeds?

**[Israel responds:]** [12] Alas, I knew not how to guard myself from sin! My own devices harnessed me, like chariots subject to a foreign nation's mercies.

## CHAPTER SEVEN

[1] The nations have said to me, 'Turn away, turn away from God, O nation whose faith in Him is perfect, turn away, turn away, and we shall choose nobility from you.'

But I replied to them, 'What can you bestow upon a nation whole in faith to Him commensurate even with the desert camps encircling?'

**[The nations to Israel:]** [2] But your footsteps were so lovely when shod in pilgrim's sandals, O daughter of nobles. The rounded shafts for your libations' abysslike trenches, handiwork of the Master Craftsman. [3] At earth's very center your Sanhedrin site is an ivory basin of ceaseless, flowing teaching; your national center an indispensable heap of nourishing knowledge hedged about with roses. [4] Your twin sustainers, the Tablets of the Law, are like two fawns, twins of the gazelle. [5] Your altar and Temple, erect and stately as an ivory tower; your wise men aflow with springs of complex wisdom at the gate of the many-peopled city; your face, like a Lebanese tower, looks to your future boundary as far as Damascus.

[6] The Godly name on your head is as mighty as Carmel; your crowning braid is royal purple, your King is bound in nazaritic tresses. [7] How beautiful and pleasant are you, befitting the pleasures of spiritual love. [8] Such is your stature, likened to a towering palm tree, from your teachers flow sustenance like wine-filled clusters.

**[God to Israel:]** [9] I boast on High that your deeds cause Me to ascend on your palm tree, I grasp onto your branches. I beg now your teachers that they may remain like clusters of grapes from which flow strength to your weakest ones, and the fragrance of your face like apples. **[Israel interjects:]** [10] and may your utterance be like finest wine.

I shall heed Your plea to uphold my faith before my Beloved in love so upright and honest that my slumbering fathers will move their lips in approval.

[11] I say to the nations, 'I am my Beloved's and He longs for my perfection.'

[12] Come, my Beloved, let us go to the fields where Your children serve You in want, there let us lodge with Esau's children who are blessed with plenty yet still deny.

[13] Let us wake at dawn in vineyards of prayer and study. Let us see if students of Writ

פֹּתַח הַסְּמָדַר הֵנֵצוּ הָרִמּוֹנִים שָׁם אֶתֵּן אֶת־דֹּדַי לָךְ׃
יד הַֽדּוּדָאִים נָֽתְנוּ־רֵיחַ וְעַל־פְּתָחֵינוּ כָּל־מְגָדִים חֲדָשִׁים
גַּם־יְשָׁנִים דּוֹדִי צָפַנְתִּי לָךְ׃

פרק ח

א מִי יִתֶּנְךָ כְּאָח לִי יוֹנֵק שְׁדֵי אִמִּי אֶמְצָאֲךָ בַחוּץ אֶשָּׁקְךָ
גַּם לֹא־יָבֻזוּ לִי׃ ב אֶנְהָגְךָ אֲבִיאֲךָ אֶל־בֵּית אִמִּי תְּלַמְּדֵנִי
אַשְׁקְךָ מִיַּיִן הָרֶקַח מֵעֲסִיס רִמֹּנִי׃ ג שְׂמֹאלוֹ תַּחַת
רֹאשִׁי וִימִינוֹ תְּחַבְּקֵנִי׃ ד הִשְׁבַּעְתִּי אֶתְכֶם בְּנוֹת יְרוּשָׁלָםִ
מַה־תָּעִירוּ ׀ וּמַה־תְּעֹרְרוּ אֶת־הָאַהֲבָה עַד שֶׁתֶּחְפָּץ׃
ה מִי זֹאת עֹלָה מִן־הַמִּדְבָּר מִתְרַפֶּקֶת עַל־דּוֹדָהּ תַּחַת
הַתַּפּוּחַ עוֹרַרְתִּיךָ שָׁמָּה חִבְּלַתְךָ אִמֶּךָ שָׁמָּה חִבְּלָה
יְלָדַתְךָ׃ ו שִׂימֵנִי כַחוֹתָם עַל־לִבֶּךָ כַּחוֹתָם עַל־זְרוֹעֶךָ
כִּי־עַזָּה כַמָּוֶת אַהֲבָה קָשָׁה כִשְׁאוֹל קִנְאָה, רְשָׁפֶיהָ רִשְׁפֵּי
אֵשׁ, שַׁלְהֶבֶתְיָה. ז מַיִם רַבִּים לֹא יוּכְלוּ לְכַבּוֹת אֶת־
הָאַהֲבָה, וּנְהָרוֹת לֹא יִשְׁטְפוּהָ, אִם יִתֵּן אִישׁ אֶת כָּל־הוֹן
בֵּיתוֹ בָּאַהֲבָה, בּוֹז יָבוּזוּ לוֹ. ח אָחוֹת לָנוּ קְטַנָּה, וְשָׁדַיִם אֵין
לָהּ, מַה־נַּעֲשֶׂה לַאֲחֹתֵנוּ בַּיּוֹם שֶׁיְּדֻבַּר־בָּהּ. ט אִם־חוֹמָה
הִיא, נִבְנֶה עָלֶיהָ טִירַת כָּסֶף, וְאִם־דֶּלֶת הִיא, נָצוּר עָלֶיהָ
לוּחַ אָרֶז. י אֲנִי חוֹמָה, וְשָׁדַי כַּמִּגְדָּלוֹת, אָז הָיִיתִי בְעֵינָיו
כְּמוֹצְאֵת שָׁלוֹם. יא כֶּרֶם הָיָה לִשְׁלֹמֹה בְּבַעַל הָמוֹן, נָתַן אֶת
הַכֶּרֶם לַנֹּטְרִים, אִישׁ יָבִא בְּפִרְיוֹ אֶלֶף כָּסֶף. יב כַּרְמִי
שֶׁלִּי לְפָנָי, הָאֶלֶף לְךָ שְׁלֹמֹה, וּמָאתַיִם לְנֹטְרִים אֶת־
פִּרְיוֹ. יג הַיּוֹשֶׁבֶת בַּגַּנִּים, חֲבֵרִים מַקְשִׁיבִים לְקוֹלֵךְ,
הַשְׁמִיעִנִי. יד בְּרַח דּוֹדִי, וּדְמֵה לְךָ לִצְבִי, אוֹ לְעֹפֶר
הָאַיָּלִים, עַל הָרֵי בְשָׂמִים.

have budded, if students of Oral Law have blossomed, if ripened scholars have bloomed — there I will display my finest products to You.

[14] All my baskets, good and bad, emit a fragrance, all at our doors have the precious fruits of comely deeds — those the Scribes have newly ordained and Your Torah's timeless wisdom, for You, Beloved, has my heart stored them.

## CHAPTER EIGHT

[1] If only, despite my wrongs, You could comfort me as Joseph did, like a brother nurtured at the bosom of my mother, if in the streets I found Your prophets I would kiss You and embrace You through them, nor could anyone despise me for it. [2] I would lead You, I would bring You to my mother's Temple for You to teach me as You did in Moses' Tent; to drink I'd give You spiced libations, wines like pomegranate nectar.

**[Israel to the nations:]** [3] Despite my laments in Exile, His left hand supports my head and His right hand embraces me in support. [4] I adjure you, O nations destined to ascend to Jerusalem — for if you violate your oath you will become defenseless — if you dare provoke God to hate me or disturb His love for me while He still desires it.

**[God and the Heavenly Tribunal:]** [5] How worthy she is who rises from the desert bearing Torah and His Presence, clinging to her Beloved!

**[Israel interjects:]** Under Sinai suspended above me, there I roused Your love, there was Your people born; a mother to other nations, there she endured the travail of her birth. [6] For the sake of my love, place me like a seal on Your heart, like a seal to dedicate Your strength for me, for strong till the death is my love; though their zeal for vengeance is hard as the grave, its flashes are flashes of fire from the flame of God. [7] Many waters of heathen tribulation cannot extinguish the fire of this love, nor rivers of royal seduction or torture wash it away.

**[God replies to Israel:]** Were any man to offer all the treasure of his home to entice you away from your love, they would scorn him to extreme.

**[The Heavenly Tribunal reflects:]** [8] Israel desires to cleave to us, the small and humble one, but her time of spiritual maturity has not come. What shall we do for our cleaving one on the day the nations plot against her?

[9] If her faith and belief are strong as a wall withstanding incursions from without, we shall become her fortress and beauty; building her City and Holy Temple; but if she wavers like a door, succumbing to every alien knock, with fragile cedar panels shall we then enclose her.

**[Israel replies proudly:]** [10] My faith is firm as a wall, and my nourishing synagogues and study halls are strong as towers! Then, having said so, I become in His eyes like a bride found perfect.

**[. . . and reminisces:]** [11] Israel was vineyard of Him to Whom peace belongs in populous Jerusalem. He gave His vineyard to harsh, cruel guardians; each one came to extort his fruit, even a thousand silver pieces.

**[God to the nations, on the Day of Judgment:]** [12] The vineyard is Mine! Your iniquities are before Me!

**[The nations will reply:]** The thousand silver pieces are Yours, You to Whom peace belongs, and two hundred more to the Sages who guarded the fruit of Torah from our designs.

**[God to Israel:]** [13] O My beloved, dwelling in far-flung gardens, your fellows, the angels hearken to your voice of Torah and prayer. Let Me hear it that they may then sanctify Me.

**[Israel to God:]** [14] Flee, my Beloved, from our common Exile and be like a gazelle or a young hart in Your swiftness to redeem and rest your Presence among us on the fragrant Mount Moriah, site of Your Temple.

Val Mitchell, Sally Moon and Alison Head

# About this book

## Purpose of the book

This book provides structured practice in the final weeks leading up to the 11+ tests, focusing on the most important English skills.

Because your time is valuable this book will…

1 help you to identify the skills where you are weakest
2 help plan your time to target these skills and recap skills where you are more confident
3 provide a clear explanation of what you need to be able to do
4 lead you through typical questions
5 give you opportunities to practise your skills
6 provide test practice at the end of each stage
7 direct you back to the skills where you are less confident for your final practice.

The book is designed to help you complete your practice in **four weeks**, once you have assessed your current skills.

**You are provided with the following tools to help you plan how much time to spend on each skill:**

- **The Placement test**, covering the most important 11+ skills. The questions are designed to be challenging and are of a similar standard to the more difficult questions in the 11+ tests. *The Placement test* is timed so that you can check you are working at the speed expected for the 11+ tests.
- **The Placement test answer grid** directs you to the relevant skills pages in the book, covering all the areas you have been tested on.
- **A Practice planner** (built into the *Placement test answer grid*) enables you to plan your time efficiently, based on the feedback from your *Placement test*. It allows more time for skills you have highlighted for further practice and a short amount of time for skills that simply need refreshing.
- **The skills practice** pages (Sections 1–3) are designed to build confidence in the key English skills needed in the 11+ tests. Each topic covers a set of skills with step-by-step instructions on how to tackle related questions with Skills practice boxes to test your understanding.
- **Practice tests** at the end of each chapter cover the skills you have just worked through. The questions are challenging and represent difficult problems you may face in the 11+ tests. The tests are timed so that you can check you are working at the speed expected; in the actual tests you will have, on average, one minute per question.
- **Practice tests answer grids** are provided for you to record your scores from the *Practice tests* and to help you decide which skills you may need to look at again in your final preparation for the 11+ tests.
- **A Countdown grid** is provided for you to record the skills you want to practise again before the 11+ tests, so that you can plan your time effectively.

## Timing the Practice tests

You should time the *Practice tests* yourself (aiming for the 'Target time' at the top of each test) to make sure you are working at the speed expected for the 11+ tests. If you feel that you need more time, complete the tests and make a note of the time you have taken.

Plan to retake any tests that you didn't complete in the suggested time as part of your final practice. Because these tests are challenging, you are allocated approximately one minute 15 seconds per question but are likely to have only one minute in the 11+ tests.

**Countdown *grid***

*Follow the instructions on page 5 to fill in and use this grid.*

| *Skill* | *Page* | *Review ✕* | *Time (mins)* | *Completed ✓* |
|---|---|---|---|---|
| **1 Understanding fiction and non-fiction** | | | | |
| **Understanding fiction, plays and poetry** | | | | |
| Stories | 6 | | 15 | ✓ |
| Plays | 8 | ✕ | 10 | ✓ |
| Poetry | 9 | | 10 | ✓ |
| **Comprehension *test 1*** | 10 | Retake | 20 | ✓ |
| **Understanding non-fiction** | | | | |

# Contents

# Taking the *Placement test*...

**Take the *Placement test* in this book to help you identify the skills you need to concentrate on and plan your practice time effectively. Follow the instructions below to take the test.**

## 1 Begin by taking the Placement test

- Find a quiet place to work.
- Assemble the materials you will need before beginning: a pen, pencil, eraser, pencil sharpener, ruler, timer and spare paper.
- Turn to the *Placement test* on pages 52–57.
- Allow **55** minutes to take the test.

## 2 Mark the Placement test

- Go to the *Placement test answers* on page 62 and score your completed paper by filling in the blank boxes in the 'Mark' column on your test paper:
  - There is one mark per question.
  - **There are no half marks.**
- Now turn to the *Placement test answer grid* on page 58 and fill in the blue *Test score* section for Section 2 of the grid, 'Test skills':
  - Put a cross in the 'Error' column for each question you answered **incorrectly**.

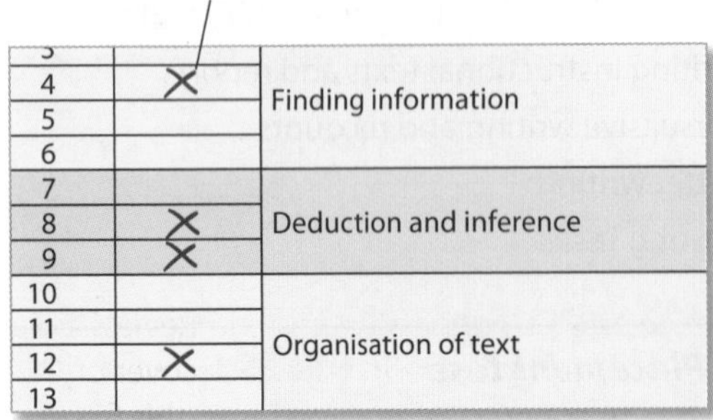

| | | |
|---|---|---|
| 4 | X | Finding information |
| 5 | | |
| 6 | | |
| 7 | | Deduction and inference |
| 8 | X | |
| 9 | X | |
| 10 | | Organisation of text |
| 11 | | |
| 12 | X | |
| 13 | | |

- Count up the boxes **without** crosses in, and put this number in the blue 'Total' box.

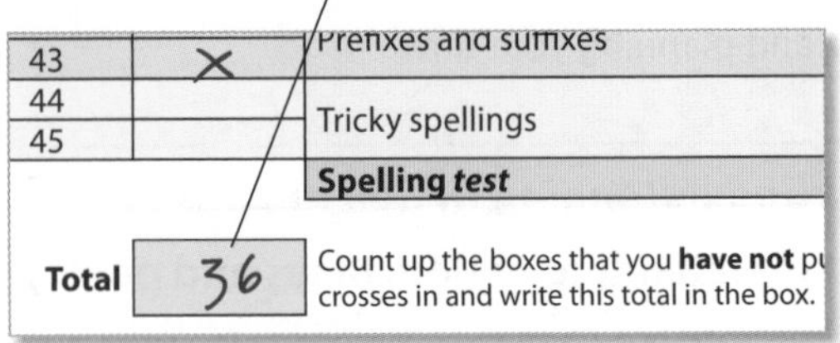

| | | |
|---|---|---|
| 43 | X | Prefixes and suffixes |
| 44 | | Tricky spellings |
| 45 | | |
| | | **Spelling *test*** |
| **Total** | 36 | Count up the boxes that you **have not** put crosses in and write this total in the box. |

- Calculate your percentage score as directed and write this in the red box provided.

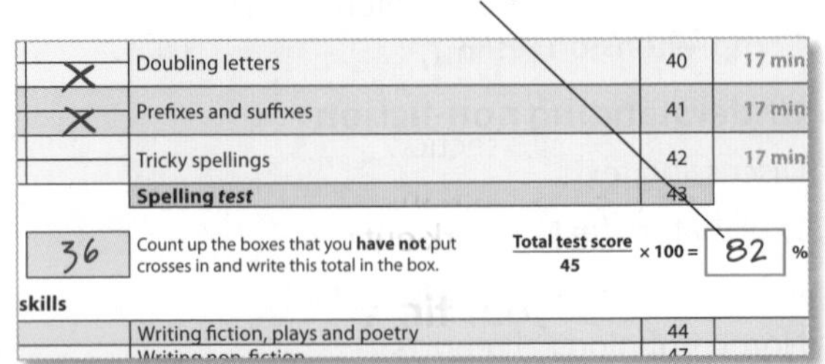

| | | | |
|---|---|---|---|
| X | Doubling letters | 40 | 17 mins |
| X | Prefixes and suffixes | 41 | 17 mins |
| | Tricky spellings | 42 | 17 mins |
| | **Spelling *test*** | 43 | |
| 36 | Count up the boxes that you **have not** put crosses in and write this total in the box. | Total test score / 45 × 100 = 82 % | |
| **skills** | | | |
| | Writing fiction, plays and poetry | 44 | |

Although the *Placement test* is designed to test your ability to answer the more difficult questions in the 11+ tests, it is also a useful indicator of your progress. A score of 70% or above should give you confidence for the 11+ tests.

**Now you have the results, you can begin to plan your time.**

## 1 Fill in the Practice planner

The *Practice planner* forms the right-hand section of the *Placement test answer grid* on page 58. The time needed to completely review each skill is listed in the 'To do' column; the time needed to recap skills already mastered is listed in the 'Achieved' column.

The following instructions explain how to work out the time you should allow to practise these skills:

- Use a highlighter to mark every skill that you have put a cross against.
- Transfer the time needed to complete these skills from the 'To do' column to the 'Time' column.

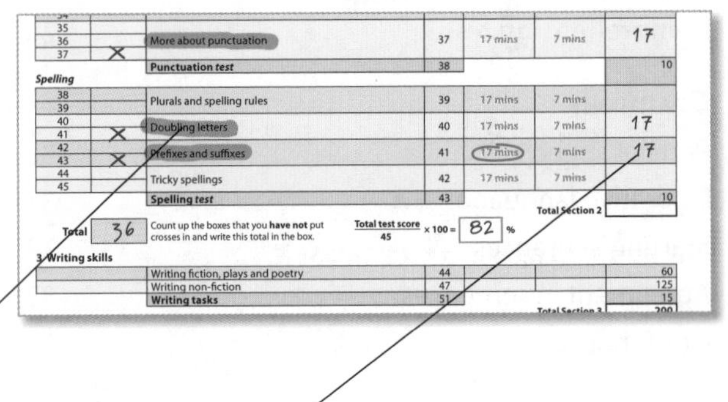

| | | | | | | |
|---|---|---|---|---|---|---|
| 35 | | | | | | |
| 36 | | More about punctuation | 37 | 17 mins | 7 mins | 17 |
| 37 | X | | | | | |
| | | **Punctuation *test*** | 38 | | | 10 |
| ***Spelling*** | | | | | | |
| 38 | | Plurals and spelling rules | 39 | 17 mins | 7 mins | |
| 39 | | | | | | |
| 40 | | Doubling letters | 40 | 17 mins | 7 mins | 17 |
| 41 | X | | | | | |
| 42 | | Prefixes and suffixes | 41 | 17 mins | 7 mins | 17 |
| 43 | X | | | | | |
| 44 | | Tricky spellings | 42 | 17 mins | 7 mins | |
| 45 | | | | | | |
| | | **Spelling *test*** | 43 | | | 10 |
| | | | | | Total Section 2 | |
| Total | 36 | Count up the boxes that you **have not** put crosses in and write this total in the box. | Total test score / 45 × 100 = 82 % | | | |
| **3 Writing skills** | | | | | | |
| | | Writing fiction, plays and poetry | 44 | | | 60 |
| | | Writing non-fiction | 47 | | | 125 |
| | | **Writing tasks** | 51 | | | 15 |
| | | | | | Total Section 3 | 200 |

- Work down the 'Achieved' column to transfer the time needed to complete the remaining skills (the skills where you have answered the questions correctly) to the 'Time' column.

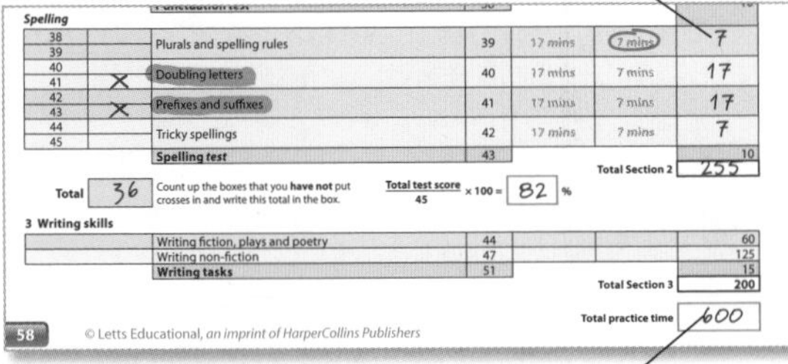

Spelling

| Question | Error | Skill | Page | | | Time |
|---|---|---|---|---|---|---|
| 38, 39 | | Plurals and spelling rules | 39 | 17 mins | 7 mins | 7 |
| 40, 41 | X | Doubling letters | 40 | 17 mins | 7 mins | 17 |
| 42, 43 | X | Prefixes and suffixes | 41 | 17 mins | 7 mins | 17 |
| 44, 45 | | Tricky spellings | 42 | 17 mins | 7 mins | 7 |
| | | **Spelling test** | 43 | | | 10 |
| | | | | | Total Section 2 | 255 |

Total 36 Count up the boxes that you **have not** put crosses in and write this total in the box. Total test score / 45 × 100 = 82 %

3 Writing skills

| Skill | Page | Time |
|---|---|---|
| Writing fiction, plays and poetry | 44 | 60 |
| Writing non-fiction | 47 | 125 |
| **Writing tasks** | 51 | 15 |
| Total Section 3 | | 200 |
| Total practice time | | 600 |

58 © Letts Educational, *an imprint of HarperCollins Publishers*

- Add up the times you have written down for Section 2, including the *Practice tests*. (The suggested times for these tests are already recorded in the 'Time' column.) Add this time to the total for Section 1, 'Understanding fiction and non-fiction'. (You are advised to work through all the pages in this section.) If your 11+ test includes a Writing task, add in the times for Section 3, 'Writing skills', to work out your total practice time.

## 2 Planning your time

You now know the total number of minutes you will need to work through the skills in this book.

- Divide the number of minutes by 60 to find the number of hours.
- Work out how many hours you need to spend each week:
  - Split your time between the number of weeks you have available.
  - Aim to complete your practice at least one week before the 11+ tests to give you time to go over any skills you feel you would like to look at again.
- Monitor your time to make sure that you are working to the suggested timings and adjust the amount of time you allow if you are working a little slower.

## 3 Practising the skills

Work through your practice using your *Practice planner* in the following way:

- Go through Section 1 of the book, read the text and answer the *Skills practice* questions, then complete the *Practice tests* at the end of each chapter.
- Complete each chapter in Section 2 by…
  - working through the highlighted skills thoroughly and answering the *Skills practice* questions. (The answers are on page 62–63.)
  - quickly reading through the remaining skills and answering these *Skills practice* questions as well.
- Complete the *Practice test* at the end of the chapter to double-check that you are confident in the skills.
- Mark your answers to the *Practice tests* using the answers on pages 63–64.
- Complete the *Practice tests answer grids* on pages 59–60 (and review your writing task against the *Writing tasks checklist* on page 61) to help you plan your remaining practice time:
  - Make notes about any of the questions you found challenging in the 'Notes' column.
  - Complete the 'Review' and 'Achieved' columns to indicate whether you want to revisit the skills.
  - Add up your score and work out your percentage.
- A score of 70% or above in these challenging tests should give you confidence for the 11+ tests.

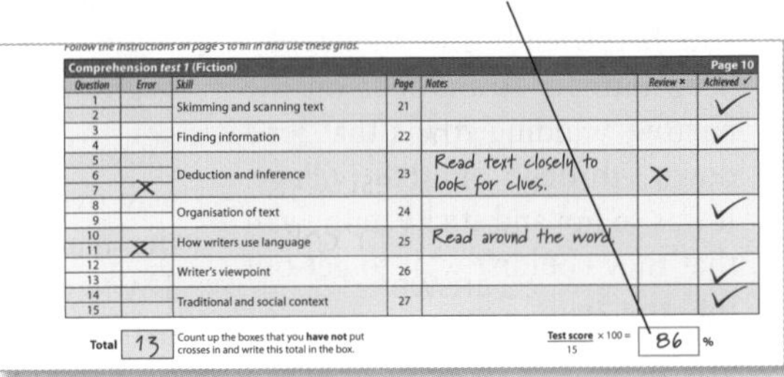

Follow the instructions on page 5 to fill in and use these grids.

Comprehension *test 1* (Fiction) — Page 10

| Question | Error | Skill | Page | Notes | Review × | Achieved ✓ |
|---|---|---|---|---|---|---|
| 1, 2 | | Skimming and scanning text | 21 | | | ✓ |
| 3, 4 | | Finding information | 22 | | | ✓ |
| 5, 6, 7 | X (7) | Deduction and inference | 23 | Read text closely to look for clues. | X | |
| 8, 9 | | Organisation of text | 24 | | | ✓ |
| 10, 11 | X (11) | How writers use language | 25 | Read around the word. | | |
| 12, 13 | | Writer's viewpoint | 26 | | | ✓ |
| 14, 15 | | Traditional and social context | 27 | | | ✓ |

Total 13 Count up the boxes that you **have not** put crosses in and write this total in the box. Test score / 15 × 100 = 86 %

## 4 Completing your practice

After you have completed all your planned practice, you will probably have a few skills that you want to go back to. You should have recorded these skills on the *Practice tests answer grids* in the 'Review' column. The *Countdown grid* inside the back cover of this book is provided to help you to plan this final review:

- From reviewing your *Practice tests answer grids*, put a cross in the *Countdown grid* 'Review' column to indicate the skills you are going to look at again.
- Highlight 'Retake' in the 'Review' column for any *Practice tests* you would like to take again.
- Fill in the 'Time' column for these skills and tests with the amount of time printed in grey; the *Practice test* timings are a guide to the speed you should now be achieving.
- Add up your total time to plan your final practice.
- Complete your final practice programme and tick the 'Completed' column for each skill as you finish it.
- Plan a break before your 11+ tests so that you are feeling awake and ready to face the challenge.

Feel confident that you are well prepared, and stay positive. **This is your chance to shine!**

**You must be able to...**

- identify the genre, setting and characters
- trace the plot and progression of events
- interpret the language used.

**Examples:** adventure, mystery, historical fiction, science fiction, fantasy, contemporary fiction, dilemma stories, myths and legends.

# A festival of experiences

Jack and Jill arrived in their camper van at E19 on the blue route. It was their fourth trip to Glastonbury with Mum and her friend. The traffic had been bumper to bumper on the narrow, winding roads that lead down through Pilton village. It was so hot and sticky in the van that they couldn't wait to get out into the fields.

The twins had strawberry blond hair, freckles and piercing blue eyes with surprisingly dark lashes. Jill had spent the first week of her holidays customising her jeans and T-shirts with applique flowers and animals. As they slid open the door and breathed in the hot afternoon air the smell of sandalwood rose to greet them.

While Jill was collecting the containers, Jack rummaged around under the bench seat for their wellies. As usual, there was very little grass and wide expanses of furrowed mud. Parking in the north corner of E19 meant peace and quiet but also walking a long way to get the water from back near the blue route. Jack was very thirsty and beginning to get a bit grumpy!

Carefully, the twins picked their way over the guy ropes between the tents and vans towards the TW sign. Jill's wellies began to make a slurping sound as she trudged through the sludgy mire. The plastic containers bumped their legs annoyingly and Jill complained she would get bruises.

Finally, they reached the standpipes and filled their containers as the thunder began to roll over the Glastonbury hillside.

They ran, heads down, weaving in and out of the tents, under and over the guy ropes like a purple snake weaving across the field.

Jill was panting as she struggled to drag the water weighing heavier and heavier on her arms. Pulling her feet frantically from the gripping earth, she wasn't watching Jack up ahead whose eyes were on their blue camper van in the distance. Unaware of the half folded chair blocking his path, Jack tumbled head first into a Harley Davidson belonging to a middle-aged rocker, sending it crashing to the ground, wheels spinning. Jill struggled to keep her feet steady but it was too late. She slipped forward, falling on top of Jack, sending water and mud in all directions!

## 1 Identifying the key elements

### *Skimming and scanning*

Fiction texts belong to the genres (types of story) listed at the top of this page and explained on page 44. The genre will establish the type of characters and setting that are likely to be described and these can be found by a quick review of the text.

*Skim the text before you begin, looking at the first and last paragraph and the beginning of the remaining paragraphs to identify the genre.*

*Next, scan the text for character names (these usually have capital letters) and setting. Be careful to read around the text to check the words in context.*

*Make some notes about what you have found and then read the questions that relate to it.*

## Watch out!

Not all characters in texts are referred to using proper nouns. There are five characters mentioned in 'A festival of experiences': Jack, Jill, Mum, Mum's friend and a middle-aged rocker.

Sometimes a word may look like a name, such as 'Harley Davidson', but when you read around the text to check you may find that it isn't (in this case it is clear that a Harley Davidson is a motorcycle).

### *Deduction and inference*

Deduction means finding information by looking at a collection of facts.

Inference is the prediction of feelings and events where direct information is not provided.

By looking for clues in the text, you can find out about the characters' feelings and personalities; you can also get an idea about what the setting is like.

*A typical deduction question would be: 'What is a Harley Davidson?'*

*A typical inference question would be: 'How would you expect the middle-aged rocker to react when Jack knocks over his motorcycle?' You can infer that the middle-aged rocker would be angry but there is no evidence to support it.*

## 2 Tracing the plot and progression of events

### *Skimming and scanning*

Skimming and scanning are also useful skills to help you trace the plot and progression of events.

*Make notes next to each paragraph about these features, as you did for the characters and setting.*

### *Deduction and inference*

Deduction questions can be answered by reviewing a collection of facts in the text. Inference questions will expect you to make predictions based on the events in the text but without direct information.

*A typical deduction question would be: 'Is Dad on the trip to Glastonbury?' You would scan the text for clue words about characters. Because the text states that the twins have come with 'Mum and her friend', you can deduce that Dad wasn't there.*

*A typical inference question would be: 'Do the family like popular music?' There is no mention of this in the text but the fact that they are at a music festival suggests that they do.*

### *Organisation of text*

As fiction texts usually don't have headings, the skill in understanding the organisation of fiction texts is to identify key events and what needs to be resolved.

*Identify when events happen, look for connectives of time (a connective is something that links one set of words to another).*

*Underline the connectives to trace the events as you review the paragraphs. The connectives in this story are 'While' and 'finally'. If you don't see any connectives, jot down the basic events in each paragraph.*

## Watch out!

Stories that include flashbacks and dual storylines do not follow a clear progression of time.

## 3 Interpreting the language

### *Writer's language and viewpoint*

The writer's use of description creates the mood of the text and conveys the characters' feelings.

*Scan the text for descriptive words, such as adjectives and adverbs, when asked questions about language. Highlighting the words helps you to visualise the emotions involved.*

*For example, the descriptive words in the first paragraph, 'bumper to bumper', 'narrow, winding', 'hot and sticky', suggest the children didn't enjoy their journey.*

### *Traditional and social context*

Grammar is a key aspect of the text to review when considering its traditional and social context. Consider whether it is written in a familiar everyday style or if the grammar is more old-fashioned. The theme of a story may also contain clues to the context.

*The grammar in 'A festival of experiences' is written in an everyday style, although the theme behind the story is the nursery rhyme 'Jack and Jill'.*

## Skills practice

1. What is the genre of the text 'A festival of experiences'?
2. What was the weather like in the village in the days leading up to the children's arrival?
3. Why does the author describe the earth as 'gripping' in the final paragraph?
   - **A** to show that it is muddy
   - **B** because the earth holds on to her wellies
   - **C** because it has been raining
   - **D** because Jill dislikes the mud
   - **E** because Jack has fallen over.

### You must be able to...

- identify the genre, setting and characters
- trace the plot and progression of events
- interpret the language used.

**Examples:** adventure, mystery, historical fiction, science fiction, fantasy, contemporary fiction, dilemma stories, myths and legends.

## The Wolves and the Moon

(An old man is sitting on a garden bench in the twilight, banging his walking stick on the wooden slats. A young girl walks up to greet him.)

*Nina* Why are you banging your stick Granddad?

*Granddad* There is an eclipse tomorrow so I have to send the great wolf packing!

*Nina* What are you talking about?

*Granddad* It's an old, old story told to me by your Great Granddad when I was a lad. He lived in the lands of the north where the nights are long and stories were told to pass the dark, cold evenings. I loved to sit by the open fire and listen to his spine-chilling tales.

*Nina* (climbing on to Granddad's knee) Please tell me the story Granddad! (aside) I hope it's not too scary.

*Granddad* Well, the old poem says...

*Skoll the Wolf will follow the Moon*
*when he flies to the wood of woe.*
*Hati the Wolf will chase the Sun*
*'til the light of the day must go.*

*Nina* But that doesn't make sense!

*Granddad* The Vikings believed that two great wolves lived in the skies and played by chasing the Sun and Moon. Skoll the Wolf chased the Moon and Hati, his sister, chased the Sun. An eclipse happens when the wolves catch the globes so people need to make as much noise as they can to scare the wolves away. ...Otherwise, we might not get our day out at the seaside tomorrow because there won't be any sunlight!

## 1 Identifying the key elements

### Skimming and scanning

Play scripts can belong to the same genres as stories (listed at the top of this page, and explained on page 44). The genre determines the type of characters and setting.

*Skim the characters' names (from a cast list, or from the names on the left of the text). Next skim the text for stage directions to find out about the setting. Make some notes and then read the related questions.*

### Deduction and inference

Deduction means finding information in a collection of facts. Inference is the prediction of feelings and events where direct information is not provided.

*The stage directions are a good place to start to look for clues for the setting. Look for dialogue that is marked 'aside' as such comments show what the character is thinking or feeling.*

## 2 Tracing the plot and progression of events

### Skimming and scanning

Reading the text quickly can help you to work out the order in which things happen. The stage directions and asides give additional information.

### Deduction and inference

Prior knowledge about what different characters know can help you to infer events to come.

*Again, stage directions are a good place to start. They often give information about events that have happened off-stage.*

### Organisation of text

As play scripts don't have headings, the skill in understanding the organisation of the script is to identify key events and what needs to be resolved.

*Look for change of scenes or stage directions to identify the action. You may need to read the dialogue to check the order of events.*

## 3 Interpreting the language

### Writer's language and viewpoint

The writer's use of words and dialogue creates the mood of the play, conveying the characters' feelings.

*Scan the text for verbs and phrases that show opinion ('Hope it's not too scary'). These give a clue as to how the characters are feeling.*

### Traditional and social context

As with fiction stories, the sentence structure is a key aspect. Think about whether it is written in an everyday style or if the grammar seems old-fashioned. The theme of a story may also contain clues to the context.

*In 'The Wolves and the Moon', the older character speaks differently from the younger character. Also look at the theme. The poem indicates a link with the past, but the girl's language suggests it is set in the present.*

### Skills practice

1 Why is Granddad banging his stick?
2 What happens to daylight when a wolf catches the Sun or Moon?

## You must be able to...

 identify the poetry style

 identify the rhyme or syllable pattern

 interpret the language used.

**Examples:** structured poems (haiku, tanka, cinquain, rap, limerick, sonnet, ballad, verse), free verse, visual poems (concrete, acrostic).

### Let's celebrate!

Excitement buzzes in the air
Players darting here and there
Take your seats and settle down
Nature's show has come to town!

Sunbeams flash, the curtain rises
Trees shake off their winter guises
Buds burst out in rainbow shades
Nature's show is on parade!

Somersaulting lambs perform
Swooping swallows dance at dawn
Jackdaws juggle, building nests
Nature's show is far the best!

Valentines and violets
Maypole ribbons, amulets
Easter eggs and simnel cake
Spring is here, LET'S CELEBRATE!

## 1 Identifying the poetry style

Poems can be based on the same genres used for stories and play scripts or can focus on one aspect, such as the description of a setting. Features of the most common genres are listed on page 46.

## 2 Identifying the rhyme or syllable pattern

### Skimming and scanning

Some poems are rhyming and some contain blank verse. Skimming poems is an easier task than skimming fiction texts and play scripts since they are shorter and rhyming patterns are easy to find.

*Skim the poem before you begin, looking at the rhyming pattern. Look at the end of each line to find out where the rhyming words occur.*

### Organisation of text

The style of the poem will determine the rhythm, rhyme or syllable structure.

*Having skimmed the poem to determine the rhyming pattern, count the syllables (or beats) in each line to try to match the poem to the familiar styles.*

## 3 Interpreting the language

### Deduction and inference

Poems use description and imagery to put across a subject in a new way. Deduction and inference questions about poetry usually ask you to interpret these descriptions.

*Look at the descriptive words in the poem.*
*A deduction question about 'Let's celebrate!' could be: 'What is the subject?' The last line makes it clear that the poem is about Spring.*

*A typical inference question would be: 'What is Spring being compared to?' This information is not provided but it is clear from the imagery that Spring is being compared to a circus.*

### Writer's language and viewpoint

Alliteration (words beginning with the same initial letter for effect), assonance (repeating internal vowel sounds) and onomatopoeia (words that imitate a sound) are used frequently in poetry to create sound and emotional effect. These are combined with metaphors, similes and other descriptive devices to paint pictures with words.

*Scan for words that begin with the same letters to find alliteration; look for repeated vowel sounds to locate uses of assonance; look for action words which might be examples of onomatopoeia.*

Be aware of the use of metaphor and simile in poems as these help to identify the writer's viewpoint.

### Traditional and social context

Looking at the language in a poem will give you clues to the traditional and social context, even though more unusual language is often used. Spelling can also be a clue to the age of a text.

*Look at grammar as you would for a fiction text or play script. If there are a number of unfamiliar words the text is likely to be a historical text.*

### Skills practice

1 What type of poem is 'Let's celebrate!'?
2 What is the rhyming pattern in each verse?
   **A** A, B, B, A  **B** A, A, B, A  **C** A, B, A, B
   **D** A, A, B, B  **E** no rhyme
3 Give an example of onomatopoeia in verse 1.

# Comprehension *test* 1

**Write your answers on the lines provided. When you are given a choice of answers, you will need to write the correct option (A, B, C, D or E). *Do not write answers in the 'Mark' column.***

TARGET TIME
**20 minutes**

**!** Note: the questions in this test are challenging, and are intended to find out which skills you may need to develop to achieve success in the 11+ tests.

---

**Read this text carefully before answering the questions below.**

Tom and Max heard it take the stairs three at a time then skitter down the tiled hallway towards the kitchen, and followed in hot pursuit. As they reached the bottom of the stairs, the sound of rustling packaging and loud chewing could already be heard from the kitchen. Inside, the boys found a scene of devastation. The floor was littered with spilt flour, pasta and dried fruit, and under the kitchen table cowered Barney, the family dog, who was suspiciously eyeing the sinister creature chewing plastic bags greedily in the corner.

'What do you think it is?' whispered Max.

'Ian told me it's a goblin, or a pixie,' said Tom.

'Don't be daft,' retorted Max. 'There's no such thing. It *must* be an alien!'

Tom reached for a large glass mixing bowl and deftly popped it over the creature, trapping it beneath. 'Well, whatever it is, we've got to get it out of here,' he said. 'Mum will be furious!'

As the creature hammered furiously on the glass bowl with small, slimy fists they heard the scrunch of gravel on their driveway.

'Too late,' said Max, gloomily. 'Now you're for it!'

**Mark**

**1** How was the creature captured?

_______________________________________________

**2** What was the creature eating?

**A** pasta **B** plastic bags **C** dried fruit **D** flour **E** flooring ________

**3** What is on the floor in the hallway?

**A** flour **B** carpet **C** pasta **D** dried fruit **E** tiles ________

**4** Who or what is Barney?

_______________________________________________

**5** Who or what do you think Max and Tom are?

**A** aliens **B** father and son **C** friends **D** brothers **E** dogs ________

**Mark**

**6** What makes the 'scrunch of gravel on their driveway'?

**A** an alien spaceship **B** Mum's car **C** a pixie **D** Barney
**E** we never find out

**7** Who do you think is to blame for the creature being in the boys' house? Give a reason for your answer.

**8** What effect is the writer trying to achieve by calling the creature 'it' in line 1, instead of describing it?

**9** Why does the writer use italics for the word 'must' in line 11?

**A** to confirm that the creature is definitely an alien

**B** to stress that Max believes it must be an alien

**C** to suggest that finding a pixie or goblin in your house would be very surprising

**D** because we all know that aliens exist but goblins and pixies do not

**E** to suggest that Tom and Max often have aliens in their house.

**10** Why do you think the author used the word 'skitter' in line 1 to describe the way the creature moved?

**11** What do you think the word 'devastation' means in line 4?

**A** havoc **B** sorrow **C** danger **D** mystery **E** dirty

**12** Which of these words best describes the way the creature is portrayed by the writer?

**A** cute **B** menacing **C** frightened **D** funny **E** dangerous

**13** Why do you think the writer never tells us exactly what the creature is?

**14** When do you think this story is set? Give a reason for your answer.

**15** Choose the correct option to complete this statement about the boys' opinion of the creature:

If this story had been written 200 years ago, the boys would have been…

**A** very likely to think it was an alien rather than a goblin or a pixie

**B** very unlikely to think it was an alien rather than a goblin or a pixie

**C** just as likely to think it was an alien as a pixie or a goblin

**D** most likely to think it was a pixie rather than an alien or a goblin

**E** most likely to think it was a goblin rather than an alien or a pixie

**TEST ENDS**

### You must be able to...

 identify the main issue in the text

 identify different points of view

understand the structure, purpose and context.

**Examples:** newspaper articles, leaflets, debate and interview transcripts.

# Laptops for all

There is a growing campaign amongst parents, known as 'Kidstech', for schools to provide laptops for each child. Computer use has been rising for the past 20 years and this technology is now widely used for both recreation and business. Because of these continuing trends, the computer is now seen as an essential tool for learning.

Although this is a popular crusade, there is convincing evidence to counteract this view: some doctors believe that exercise and outdoor games are more important for a child's development, and computers are known to be a contributing factor in the decline of children's fitness. Furthermore, the expense of providing computers for all students would cut into school budgets and so reduce standards in education.

On the other hand, the 'Kidstech' lobbyists brandish the figures released in the 2011 Higgins report, which stated that school leavers with restricted access to computers were 30 per cent less likely to find skilled employment and spent longer on state benefits.

In conclusion, while there are benefits in providing computers for all students, until the price of computers comes down, this would be impossible for the government to fund.

## 1 Identifying the main issue

Discussion texts usually have a question that is used to debate the issue concerned. Otherwise they should contain a title, an introduction that explains the topic and a conclusion at the end.

*Read the title and any initial questions in the text that give clues to the issue being discussed. If this is not clear, skim the first paragraph to be sure you are right.*

## 2 Identifying different points of view

Although discussion texts provide a balanced point of view, by looking at the weighting of the arguments and the language used you can often predict the views and background of the writer.

*Review the remaining paragraphs, jotting down the point of view put forward in each one.*

*Look for persuasive words and the style of language in the text to find clues when answering deduction and inference questions.*

*The answer will be included in the text when you are asked to deduce something, as in question 2 in the Skills practice below.*

## 3 Understanding the structure, purpose and context

### *Organisation of text*

There are unlikely to be headings in discussion texts but the arguments should be structured into paragraphs. These texts will always contain…

- an introduction
- points for and against (structured into paragraphs, which can alternate)
- a conclusion.

*Summarise the content of each paragraph to help you retrieve information quickly.*

### *Writer's language and viewpoint*

The purpose of a discussion text and the writer's viewpoint can be understood by examining the writer's use of language.

*Scan for descriptive words the writer has used to put across their thoughts on the issue. For example, the word 'brandish' in paragraph 3 suggests the writer doesn't agree with the parents' campaign. ('Brandish', in the way the writer has used the word here, suggests the lobbyists are spouting figures to prove a point they don't completely understand.)*

### Watch out!

Although discussion texts put both points of view, authors may be selective in the information included and so the discussion may be biased.

### *Traditional and social context*

The style of language and the information given, such as dates and events, help to place a discussion text in its historical context. The style of language can give clues to the author's social status.

*Look at dates, events and organisations mentioned to help you decide when a text is written.*

### Skills practice

1 What issue is raised in the discussion text about laptops?

2 Which point of view do you think the author is most sympathetic to?

3 What sort of person could the author be?

**A** a government representative

**B** a parent  **C** a computer salesman

**D** a doctor  **E** a child

### You must be able to...

- identify the subject

- identify the stages in the process or explanation

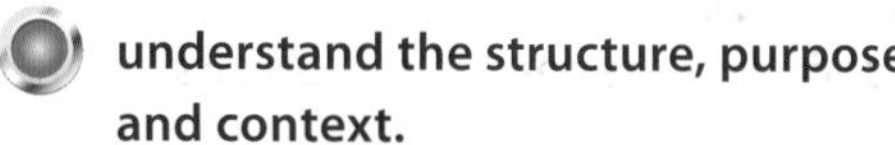

- understand the structure, purpose and context.

**Examples:** encyclopedia entry, non-fiction educational text.

# Tides

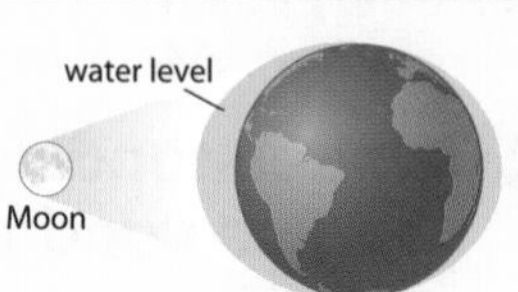


Tides are the alternate rising and falling of the sea level, usually twice in each lunar day at a particular place, due to the attraction of the Moon and Sun. The gravitational pull of the Moon draws the water in the oceans upwards, causing high tides; as the Moon moves away the water level falls, leading to low tides.

Tides are caused by the positions of the Earth, Moon and Sun. As these follow a known pattern, the times of tides can be predicted and planned for in advance. Account has to be taken of rising sea levels as these will affect how high the tides are. There are tide timetables published for coastal areas on the Internet and by local councils. The times of the high and low tide vary around the coast.

When the Earth, Moon and Sun are in line and when the Moon is new or full, the bulges of water caused by the Moon and Sun happen in the same area. The lunar tide and the solar tide are working together so this leads to higher high tides and lower than average low tides. These are called spring tides.

When the Earth, Moon and Sun are perpendicular to each other and the high water caused by the lunar tide is cancelled out by the solar tide, this produces lower tidal levels. These are called neap tides.

Knowing when the highest tides are likely to occur can help coastal areas prepare for possible flooding. High tides follow a day or two after a full or new moon that is nearest to the equinoxes. The spring equinox is around 21st March and the autumn equinox is 23rd September, so these are the times that local authorities will need to prepare for possible problems.

## 1 Identifying the subject

Explanatory texts are factual, often scientific and provide reasons why something happens. The subject is described in the opening paragraph and the text sometimes has headings.

*Read the title and the opening paragraph to identify the topic and the subject area the text would fit into. If this is not clear, skim each paragraph to find additional information and any headings.*

## 2 Identifying the stages in the process

Explanatory texts should be written in an impersonal style and the information should be clearly organised into paragraphs. There are sometimes headings and subheadings to help locate specific stages of information. There will be...

- an introduction
- stages described in a logical order
- a conclusion.

*Summarise the content of each paragraph to help you retrieve information quickly.*

## 3 Understanding the structure, purpose and context

### *Deduction and inference*

Explanatory texts should not express personal opinions. However, the writer's choice of facts, and how they structure them, can sometimes give clues to the sort of publication that the text is written for.

*Look for clues in the language used and the amount of technical vocabulary. If the text is aimed at a younger audience there may be glossaries or diagrams to help with the explanation. The language used in 'Tides' contains some technical terms and challenging words so is likely to have been written for a general audience, possibly an adult encyclopedia. As the technical terms are not very complex it is unlikely to have been written for a specialist publication.*

### *Writer's language and viewpoint*

The purpose of an explanatory text is to explain technical, historical, scientific or mechanical phenomena or events. The language used will reflect this.

*Look for specific vocabulary linked to the topic. Look out for glossaries or diagrams to support the explanation or vocabulary.*

### *Traditional and social context*

Specific information given, such as dates and events, places an explanatory text in its historical context.

*Look at dates, events and organisations mentioned to help you decide when a text is written. The 'Tides' text mentions the Internet and local authorities so this tells you it was written within the last 20 years.*

### Skills practice

1. What happens to tides, according to the text, when the Earth, Moon and Sun are in line?
2. Which paragraph would help you prepare for flooding if you lived near the coast?

### You must be able to...

 identify the types of text

 identify the stages in instructions

 understand the structure, purpose and context.

**Examples:** recipes, craft ideas, instruction manuals, directions

## Flapjack recipe

**Ingredients**

200g butter

200g golden syrup

200g sugar

400g porridge oats or 380g porridge oats and 20g dried fruit

finely grated zest of $\frac{1}{2}$ lemon

pinch of ginger and pinch of salt

**Preparation method**

1 Preheat the oven to 150°C/300°F/Gas Mark 2 and line a 20cm/8 inch-square baking tin with baking paper.

2 Melt the butter in a medium pan over a low heat. Dip a brush in the butter and brush the baking tin to grease it.

3 Add the golden syrup and sugar to the butter and heat gently. Once the sugar is dissolved and the butter is melted, remove the pan from the heat and stir in the porridge oats, lemon zest and ginger.

4 Pack the mixture into the baking tin and squash down. Bake in the oven for 40 minutes.

5 Remove from the oven, leave to cool for 15 minutes, then turn out on to a chopping board and cut into squares.

## 1 Identifying the types of text

Instructional and procedural texts often contain different formats such as lists, numbered points, illustrations and captions.

*Read the title and look for lists or illustrations to identify the subject. If this is not clear, skim the lists or numbered points and review any captions.*

## 2 Identifying the stages in instructions

Instructional texts should be organised into lists to indicate equipment or materials needed and instructions to explain what to do with the materials. They will include...

1 a title, such as 'How to make...'

2 details of equipment or materials

3 bullet pointed or numbered list to explain how to complete the task.

*Look for a range of different text types to identify this sort of non-fiction text. Numbered points indicate that you must complete the instructions in a given order.*

## 3 Understanding the structure, purpose and context

### *Organisation of text*

The structure of instructional texts is built around what you need and what you do.

*The bulleted or numbered section of any instructional text is the main body of the text.*

### *Writer's language and viewpoint*

The purpose of instructional or procedural text is to explain how to make or assemble something. The language used will reflect this with the instructions written using imperative verbs. This means in a style that tells someone what to do. Each sentence begins with a verb such as:

Put Mix Weigh Cut Measure

*Look for the imperative verbs that begin each instruction to identify the style of the text (such as the red words in the flapjack recipe).*

### *Traditional and social context*

Technical language in instructional or procedural texts help to place a text in its historical context. Materials and measures help to locate it geographically or historically.

### Skills practice 

1 What text type associated with instructional texts is not present in the flapjack recipe?

A numbered list B bulleted list

C paragraphs D glossary E index

2 List the equipment, utensils and materials (apart from ingredients) needed to complete this recipe.

3 How many processes are there in point 5?

# Non-chronological reports

**You must be able to...**

 identify the subject

 understand the structure of non-chronological reports

 understand the purpose and context of non-chronological reports.

**Examples:** encyclopedias, reference books.

## Bows and arrows

Archery is a popular activity around the world and is also an Olympic sport. The equipment used may differ in size and shape but always consists of a bow, arrow and target. Rules can also vary as well as the techniques taught and used. In some countries bows and arrows are still used for hunting food.

Bows and arrows come in a variety of designs. Bows consist of a string that can be used to store energy and a wooden or metal limb in a characteristic D shape. Arrows are made in three parts: an arrow head, a shaft and fletchings. The arrow head is the sharp point that is used to pierce the target. The shaft is the long stick that carries the arrow head in flight. Fletchings, made from feathers, add stability to the arrow in its path to the target.

As with any sport, the aim is to beat your competitors. Archery has a clear set of rules that involve shooting at a stationary target from set distances. The targets are usually made from straw with a gold bullseye in the centre.

Although target archery is a popular sport, in developing countries bows and arrows are essential tools for survival. Hunting prey, such as small mammals and fish, involves the skills of stalking and understanding the habits of prey. Fishermen using this method have keen vision and calculate the position of the fish, accounting for how water distorts the visual image.

The increasing popularity of archery in the 21st century is mainly due to the rising number of outdoor activity centres for children and adults. Bows and arrows have fascinated children for centuries, stimulating legends of heroes from Robin Hood to Hiawatha! Archery appeals to adults and children alike in both competitive and recreational situations.

## 1 Identifying the subject

Non-chronological means that texts are not structured by time and are unlikely to have headings, so identifying the subject of the key paragraphs is vital.

*Review the first and last paragraphs, which, if well written, should explain what the subject is about.*

## 2 Understanding the structure

### *Organisation of text*

The first and last paragraphs introduce and sum up the subject; the remaining paragraphs provide themed information (information with a common idea running through them) split into groups.

*Summarise each paragraph in a few words to speed up information retrieval before working through your comprehension questions.*

*Identify any other features present, even a small illustration, as in the 'Bows and arrows' text. You may also see a glossary or additional references. Questions often relate to these additional elements.*

## Understanding the purpose and context

### *Deduction and inference*

These reports are full of facts as their purpose is to convey information, not to express opinions.

*Look for key technical words linked to the question you are asked and look at the language level when deducing the audience the text is written for.*

### *Writer's language and viewpoint*

Because non-chronological reports are designed to convey factual, technical or scientific information, they are written in the third person to give the text weight and authority.

These texts should not show a bias (so should be reliably factual). It is therefore unlikely that personal opinions will be included, so save time by making this assumption.

### *Traditional and social context*

Historical facts in this genre are generally included for background information. Facts within the text often give clues to when the text was written.

### Skills practice

1 Summarise paragraphs 2 and 4 of 'Bows and arrows' in one short sentence for each.

2 List three features of non-chronological reports.

3 What is the purpose of this text?

**A** to help you make a bow and arrow

**B** to tell you about Robin Hood and Hiawatha

**C** to describe an Olympic sport

**D** to provide general information about bows and arrows

**E** to persuade you to buy a bow and arrow.

## You must be able to...

 identify the point of view

 identify bias in the text

 understand the structure, purpose and context.

**Examples:** adverts, balloon debates, speech transcripts, campaign articles, leaflets.

## Language louts

What is happening to our beautiful language? The constant and relentless 'layzee' slang, abbreviations and meaningless phrases pervading our culture is nothing short of linguistic vandalism.

Aside from the detritus of smartphone jargonese, there are two loathsome phrases that I rate as the most objectionable: 'going forward', and 'see you later'. I am sure that you'll agree with my choices.

Firstly, as you are not able to move back in time, the phrase *'going forward'* is totally redundant in any context. It creates extra verbal waffle and irritates the listener. Take a phrase I heard last week: 'Going forward, our plan is to cut out unnecessary waste.' Cut out the first two words and you have already started on the plan! A complete ban on the phrase would lead to shorter meetings, more productivity and higher profits for British business. It is widely acknowledged in linguistics that over 20 per cent of the words used in current business language are superfluous.

Secondly, there is the dreaded 'see you later'. The worst recorded culprit of this linguistic crime being a girl at the pet crematorium I visited last week: having come to collect the sad little urn containing my beloved pet guinea pig's ashes I was horrified to hear the phrase, 'see you later' as I departed.

Unless we all make a point of thinking before we speak and discipline the offenders, this disease will infect our entire nation!

## 1 Identifying the point of view

Persuasive texts are written with the purpose of getting you to agree with the point of view of the author. The descriptive language is the clue to working out the message quickly.

*To find the viewpoint of the author, read the heading, then first and last paragraphs, looking closely at the descriptions.*

## 2 Identifying bias

### *Deduction and inference*

Bias is very common in persuasive texts so finding where it occurs helps you to analyse the content.

*Review the text to decide whether the facts given are reliable. Is it based on fact or opinion? Look for descriptive language (verbs are often used to provoke an emotional response), quotes and statistics.*

**Watch out!**

Identify personal pronouns that show the author's opinion: I (believe/think), me, my.

## 3 Understanding the structure, purpose and context

### *Organisation of text*

Persuasive texts can come in a range of forms, both audio and visual. The title may range from intriguing to persuasive to encourage you to read on. There may be headings and boxed features with additional information and references.

Ideas are often arranged in groups of three, for effect.

*When other navigation features are not present, look for subject clues within each paragraph.*

### *Writer's language and viewpoint*

The writer's choice of language creates the tone of the text and should clearly show what the author is thinking. It may be stirring, provocative or uplifting. Repetition is often used, as well as direct questions that encourage the reader to agree with the author.

*Highlight descriptive words, repetition and phrases that draw out a direct response from the reader.*

### *Traditional and social context*

There are some famous examples of persuasive texts in history, especially among political and campaign speeches. The subject often gives a clue to the historical context as well as the choice of language.

*Look for events and facts in the text for clues to the historical context. Look at the grammar to find out more about the social context.*

**Skills practice**

1 Look at paragraph 2 of 'Language louts'. Which words reflect the negative tone of the text?

1 detritus 2 jargonese 3 going forward
4 achieve 5 agree

**A** 1 and 5 **B** 2 and 3 **C** 1 and 2
**D** 4 and 5 **E** none of the above

2 What are the three reasons given by the author that suggest banning the phrase 'going forward' would improve working life?

# Recount texts

## You must be able to…

 **answer what?, when?, where? and who?**

 **identify the writer's viewpoint**

 **understand the traditional and social context.**

**Examples:** diary entries, journals, reports, newspaper articles.

### Phoebe

As I look at the little statue in the courtyard I remember the day I first saw her with affection. The statue is called Phoebe; she holds a basket of flowers and has bare feet. Now she is covered in lichens that give the stone a lacy covering, but back then she was warm and golden in the summer light. I brush the grey hair from my eyes and remember.

It only seems like yesterday; the sun was beating down and it must have been the summer holidays. Just after the war, my Dad and Uncle had bought the garden statues from the owner of the large lodge, to which the garden belonged. The lodge had burnt down, hit by a stray *doodlebug*, and everything was to be sold. I wandered around looking at the alabaster statues and then, coming round a tall hedge I saw her, positioned in the formal garden, a small figure bathed in a warm glow.

I ran back to my Dad and asked if the list he was carrying included the little girl. He smiled and said, 'Show me the one you mean.' I grabbed his hand and skipped towards the beech hedge, dragging him with me.

'Can we keep her?' I asked.

'We'll see,' was the thoughtful reply.

'You had better ask your Uncle, he may have already sold it,' he added as he moved away.

I ran around the garden hunting for my Uncle, but I knew she would be coming home to our garden. My Uncle always indulged his favourite niece.

## 1 Answering what?, when?, where? and who?

### Skimming and scanning

Recount texts are written in the past tense, often in the first person. They report events that have happened in the past and they describe events in the sequence in which they have happened (in other words, chronologically).

The first paragraph should identify…

- what the text is about
- when it may have been set
- where it may have been set
- who the text is about.

*Skim the remaining paragraphs to check for further information that might confirm your views.*

### Organisation of text

Recounts should be clearly structured into paragraphs. These texts will contain…

- an introduction
- chronological paragraphs
- a summary or overview.

*Summarise the content of each paragraph to help you retrieve information quickly.*

##  Identifying the writer's point of view

### Deduction and inference

Although recount texts report events that have happened, by looking at the word choices and the language used you can often predict the hidden views and background of the writer.

*Look for verbs that reveal emotions and the style of language to find clues when answering deduction and inference questions.*

*The answer will be included in the text when you are asked to deduce something. For inference questions you will need to think of possible reasons and make predictions.*

### Writer's language and viewpoint

The purpose of a recount and the writer's viewpoint can be understood by examining the writer's use of language.

*Scan for descriptive words the writer has used to convey their thoughts on the evidence.*

##  Understanding the traditional and social context

Being aware of when and where recounts are written gives you a better insight into the thoughts and motivations of the writer. Dates and events described in recounts help to place the text historically.

*Look at dates, events and organisations mentioned to help you decide when a text is written. Review the style of language used by the author to discover more about their age, viewpoint and social position.*

### Skills practice 

1. How old is the writer of 'Phoebe'?
2. Why did the writer think the statue would be coming home with her?
3. What are we told about the lodge?
   - **A** It was bathed in a warm glow.
   - **B** It belonged to the author's Dad.
   - **C** It had been bombed.
   - **D** It was small. **E** It was built after the war.

### You must be able to...

 decide if the letter is formal or informal

 identify the subject, the sender and addressee

 understand the structure, purpose and context.

**Examples:** formal letters, informal letters, postcards.

Dr M Plume PhD
Headteacher
Parkway Primary
The Green, Pilchester
Devon EX40 7EJ

Mr and Mrs B A Fleece
55 Aries Lane
Ovis Bridge
Devon EX41 5LW

7th May 2012

**Ref: Health and safety**

Dear Mr and Mrs Fleece

It is with regret that I am writing to you today but I am at the end of my tether. For the third day running, Mary has arrived at school with an unruly lamb.

On Monday the animal was accommodated in the reception play area until the end of school. On Tuesday it took two members of staff 30 minutes to coax the creature into the bicycle shed, where it could be secured. Mary was informed that the animal should not be brought to Parkway again.

Despite our clear instructions, Mary arrived with the lamb in tow on Wednesday morning, causing chaos at morning break. We have now had numerous complaints from parents, staff and the governors.

Today, adding insult to injury, the health and safety inspector arrived and has made a damning report of our kitchen facilities, where a small puddle was found by the fridge.

Consequently, I will have no alternative but to suspend your daughter from school should our rules be flouted again and contact the RSPCA regarding the animal's welfare.

Yours sincerely

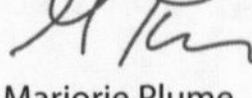

Marjorie Plume

## 1 Deciding on the formality of the letter

Letters can be formal, for example to a newspaper, business or council, or informal, to a friend or relative.

The start and ending will also help to identify the type of letter. Look at the table on page 50 for more details on the structure of formal letters.

*Check the layout and beginning and ending to see whether the letter is formal or informal.*

*Skim the letter to check the information and style. Review the remaining paragraphs to find out the main point being put across.*

##  Identifying the subject, sender and addressee

Finding these three key facts will give you an overview of the letter before you begin to look at the text more closely.

*Look at the top of formal letters to find the subject and the two addresses: the address on the left is the person it is being sent to; the one on the right the person it is being sent from.*

*Look at the top of informal letters for the address of the sender and scan the text to discover the subject and the details of who it is being sent to.*

##  Understanding the structure, purpose and context

### *Deduction and inference*

Look at the layout of the main content of formal letters (the length, key facts and points) to work out the message the writer is conveying to the reader.

Short informal letters are often 'thank you' letters, with longer letters written to keep in touch with a friend.

*Look at the length of the letter and paragraphs to get a general impression of the structure and make notes about the key facts in each paragraph to build a picture of the writer and recipient.*

### *Writer's language and viewpoint*

The purpose of the letter and the writer's viewpoint can be understood by examining the language used.

*Scan for challenging vocabulary that can indicate the letter is formal. Scan for descriptive words to convey thoughts and feelings that suggest an informal letter.*

### *Traditional and social context*

Dates and events described in letters help to place a text historically. The language used by the author also gives clues to their age and viewpoint.

### Skills practice 

1 Pick out the phrase at the start of the letter from Marjorie Plume that is more suited to an informal letter.

- **A** It is with regret
- **B** I am at the end of my tether
- **C** For the third day running
- **D** Mary has arrived at school with an unruly lamb

2 What is the purpose of the letter?

# Comprehension *test 2*

**Write your answers on the lines provided. When you are given a choice of answers, you will need to write the correct option (A, B, C, D or E).** ***Do not write answers in the 'Mark' column.***

TARGET TIME
:20
**20 minutes**

**!** Note: the questions in this test are challenging, and are intended to find out which skills you may need to develop to achieve success in the 11+ tests.

**Read this text carefully before answering the questions below.**

## Toilets through time

We take toilets for granted, but did you know that until as recently as the 1960s many people in Britain **still** did not have an indoor toilet?

Toilets have a long history; the oldest known plumbed-in loo was discovered by archaeologists in India and is thought to be 4000 years old. It did not have a flushing mechanism but people poured water down it to wash away the contents, which were flushed into pipes that led to drains beneath the streets.

Two thousand years ago, the Romans had quite sophisticated plumbing. They built large communal toilets and people would go there to meet friends and socialise: not very private!

Things took a turn for the worse in medieval times when most people used potties, which were emptied directly into open drains in the streets. Some rich people had special rooms for going to the toilet, but the waste simply dropped through the floor to the street below. In castles, the stench of these rooms was so overpowering that people kept their clothes in them to keep away the moths and body lice.

The flushing toilet was invented in the 18$^{th}$ century but it took another century for us Brits to sort out proper sewers. So next time you use the smallest room in the house, spare a thought for your ancestors who had to do without. And don't forget to wash your hands!

**Mark**

**1** When did the Romans build their toilets?

______________________________

**2** What did medieval people keep in the same room as their toilets?

**A** potties **B** moths **C** toilet paper **D** clothes **E** bleach ______

**3** What were medieval drains like?

**A** sewers **B** open **C** pipes **D** under the street
**E** in the floor ______

**4** Why did the Romans build large communal toilets?

______________________________

______________________________

Mark

**5** When were British sewers mainly built?

**A** 4000 years ago **B** in the medieval period **C** 19th century
**D** 18th century **E** 1960s ______

**6** Why does the writer say we 'take toilets for granted' (line 2)?

**A** because toilets are boring **B** because we all have to go to the toilet

**C** because almost all houses in the UK have indoor toilets today

**D** because we all know about toilets **E** because we have proper sewers now. ______

**7** Why do you think the drains which led away from the ancient Indian toilet were buried beneath the streets?

______________________________________________

**8** Why do you think the writer chose the title 'Toilets through time'?

______________________________________________

**9** If you were to add information about Roman drains to this text, which paragraph would you put it in?

**A** paragraph 1 **B** paragraph 2 **C** paragraph 3
**D** paragraph 4 **E** paragraph 5 ______

**10** Why do you think the author used the word 'stench' to describe the smell in medieval castle toilets (line 14)?

______________________________________________

______________________________________________

**11** What do you think the word 'sophisticated' means in this text (line 8)?

**A** complex **B** large **C** expensive **D** clean **E** ancient ______

**12** The writer describes toilets in several historical periods. Which period do you think the writer feels is the worst?

**A** 1960s **B** medieval **C** 18th century **D** 19th century **E** ancient India ______

**13** Give a reason for your answer to question 12.

______________________________________________

______________________________________________

**14** Why does the idea of the Roman communal toilet seem strange to us today?

______________________________________________

**15** What do you think a Roman person reading about medieval toilet arrangements would be most likely to think?

**A** They would think that having a private toilet was a good idea.
**B** They would think that hanging clothes in a smelly toilet was a good idea.
**C** They would think that disposing of toilet waste in the streets was a bad idea.
**D** They would think that toilets had improved since Roman times.
**E** They would think that using potties was a good idea. ______

**TEST ENDS**

# Skimming and scanning text

## Non-fiction

### You must be able to…

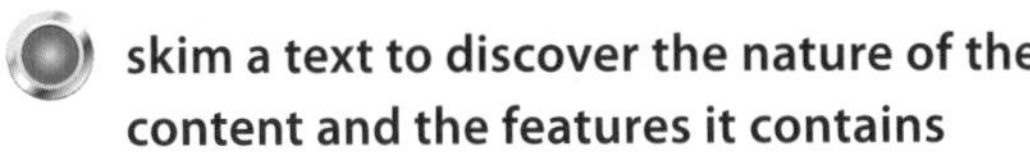

- skim a text to discover the nature of the content and the features it contains

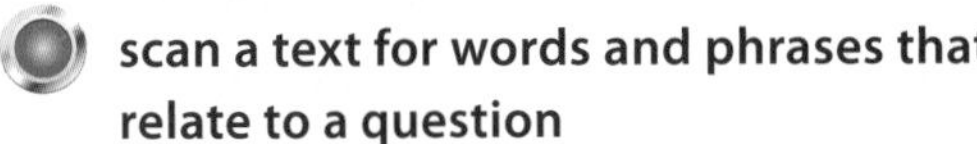

- scan a text for words and phrases that relate to a question

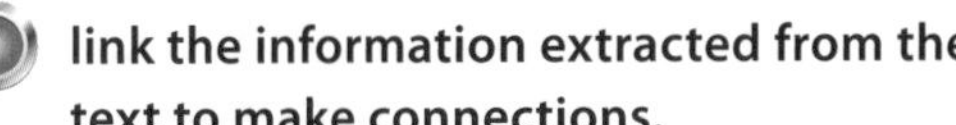

- link the information extracted from the text to make connections.

### 1 Skimming for nature of content

Skimming means quickly searching through a text to gain an idea of the content. Skim the text to…

- discover the type of text
- identify what the text is about
- summarise introductions and conclusions
- understand how the text is organised (e.g. use of features like subheadings, boxes and glossaries).

### 2 Scanning for words and phrases

Scanning involves more detailed analysis of the words and phrases in the text.

*Looking for word families that relate to a question is a quick way to scan a text effectively. For example, when answering the question below you could look for nouns linked to cooking:*

What utensils were used in the Victorian kitchen?

For other questions, you may find that the text structure is more helpful.

*For example, if a question asks about the ingredients in a recipe, look at the list at the top.*

*Check for glossaries as these often contain answers!*

### 3 Linking information

After deciding on an area of text that is likely to contain an answer, look more closely at the text to make sure your selection is correct.

*Read around the words or sections you have highlighted to get a clearer idea of the context.*

### Skills practice ›››

Read the extract commenting on the content of a newspaper, below. What programmes are going to be shown on the new TV channel?

*The newspaper was full of adverts for celebrity programmes but the main theme was the start of the new TV Games channel.*

## Fiction

### You must be able to…

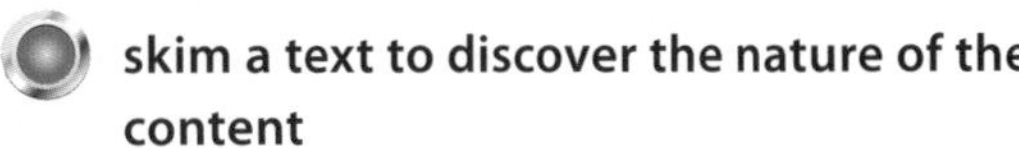

- skim a text to discover the nature of the content

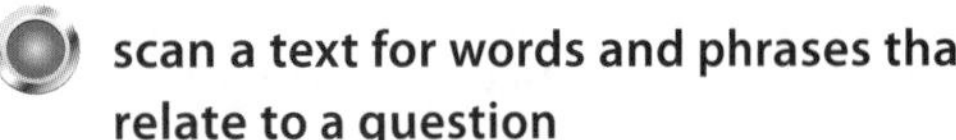

- scan a text for words and phrases that relate to a question
- link the information extracted from the text to make connections.

### 1 Skimming for nature of content

Skimming in fiction has the same function as in non-fiction. Understanding how an author has organised the text will help you to answer questions more effectively. Skim the text to…

- discover the genre
- understand what the chapters are about
- summarise introductions and conclusions
- summarise the plot
- summarise the paragraph content.

### 2 Scanning for words and phrases

Scanning fiction texts can be more challenging than non-fiction as there are generally less features to break up the text. You need to be confident that you know the content of each paragraph.

*Looking for word families is also useful in fiction texts.*

*When looking for words that describe a particular character, pronouns (such as he, she, the boy) can help you track down information quickly.*

*Highlighting the verbs and adverbs can help you find out about the action.*

When answering questions about figurative language (see page 31), scan for…

- 'as' and 'like' to pick out similes
- repeated initial letters for alliteration
- descriptive words for metaphors.

### 3 Linking information

You should be reasonably confident that the words you have highlighted are relevant if you have skimmed the text effectively first and understood the content of each paragraph.

*Not all the key words from the question will be in the text: you may need to read around the words you have found to check those most relevant to the subject.*

# Finding information

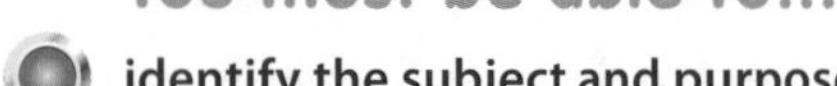

## Non-fiction

**You must be able to...**

- identify the subject and purpose of texts
- find the main points of the text
- find words and phrases relating to specific information.

### 1 Identifying subject and purpose

***Text with headings and subheadings***

If the text has a title or headings, then finding the subject is often straightforward (exceptions to this rule include advertisements and tabloid headlines).

***Text with no headings***

If there are no headings, skim the text quickly to find the subjects covered in each paragraph, then read the entire first and last paragraphs.

### 2 Finding the main points

***Text with headings and subheadings***

Look at the subheadings to identify main points. Subheadings will give you the skeleton (outline) of the text.

***Text with no headings***

Text with no headings is more difficult to work with. You will need to look more closely at the text and paragraph structure.

*The first and last sentence of each paragraph should provide a quick overview of the main points.*

### 3 Finding specific information

When searching for specific words or phrases, scan the text and underline these words and phrases and those close in meaning.

*For example, when looking for answers about areas of water in a text about global geography, underline the names of seas and oceans. Also underline any other words linked to water such as 'river' or 'lake'.*

**Skills practice >>>**

Read the heading and subheadings below. Summarise in one paragraph what you would expect to be contained in this text.

**Athens Alive!**

The Acropolis, Eating and drinking, Entertainment, Getting about

## Fiction

**You must be able to...**

- identify the storyline
- identify the characters and setting
- find words and phrases that convey mood and atmosphere.

### 1 Identifying the storyline

***Text with chapters or scenes***

Longer texts may have chapters or scenes that can indicate how the story progresses. For example...

Chapter 1 The problem

Chapter 2 The chase

Chapter 3 All is revealed

The titles may help to locate information.

***Shorter texts***

Read the first and last sentence of each paragraph to get an overview of the storyline. Then read carefully, jotting down key events in each paragraph.

### 2 Identifying the characters and setting

***Finding information about characters***

First scan the text for proper nouns (these will indicate some of the characters). Look for specific information linked to the questions.

What does the girl look like?

*Scan for adjectives linked to peoples' appearance.*

What does the boy do?

*Scan for verbs and adverbs linked to his actions.*

***Finding information about setting***

These questions can be more difficult as descriptions of setting are often woven into the text. Scan for words relating to the place or time in which the text is set, then adverbs and adjectives linked to these words.

What was unusual about the room?

*Look for all the text that mentions aspects of the room. Scan for adjectives describing the contents or layout.*

### 3 Identifying the mood

Look for phrases, adjectives and adverbs that describe the action, characters, setting and events. These can quickly identify the mood.

The sunlit forest spread before the smiling couple.

The forbidding forest spread out before the frightened couple.

## Non-fiction

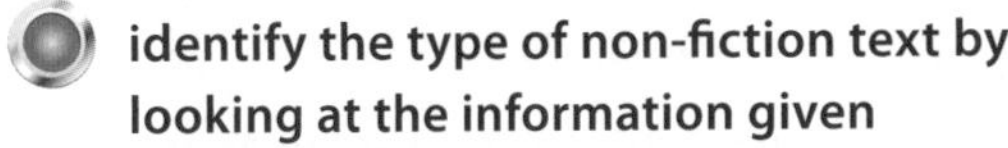

You must be able to...

- identify the type of non-fiction text by looking at the information given

- review technical language to understand who the text is written for and its purpose
- review descriptive language to find the writer's intent and factual accuracy.

### 1 Identifying the type of non-fiction text

*Deduction* is about reaching a conclusion based on information that is given in the text. *Inference* involves using clues from the text as well as your own general knowledge, unrelated to the text, to think about what is most likely to be true.

*Use your knowledge of different types of text to decide on the type of text you are working with. This will help you to understand its purpose.*

### 2 Reviewing technical language

If you are working with an informative text, you are likely to be asked to deduce information from the technical language.

*The difficulty of the technical terms can also provide clues as to the intended audience. Glossaries suggest a general audience.*

### 3 Reviewing descriptive language

Descriptive language in non-fiction can be used to persuade and influence the reader.

*For example, a discussion text may express different viewpoints, but you can deduce the writer's opinion from the weight of argument and use of language.*

When searching for bias or viewpoint, scan the text and underline the descriptive words. These can indicate how the author feels about the subject.

### Skills practice

These texts are written for two different audiences. How could these audiences differ?

1. The molecular formula is a way to clearly record information about the atoms that constitute a specific chemical compound.
2. Objects are made from very small particles. Everything that you can see around you is made up of these tiny pieces of matter.

## Fiction

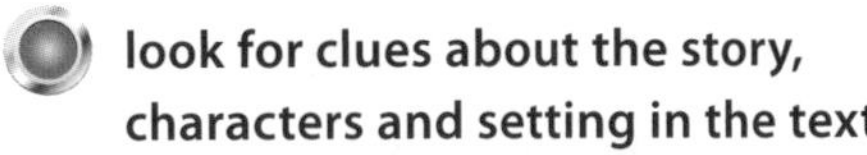

You must be able to...

- look for clues about the story, characters and setting in the text

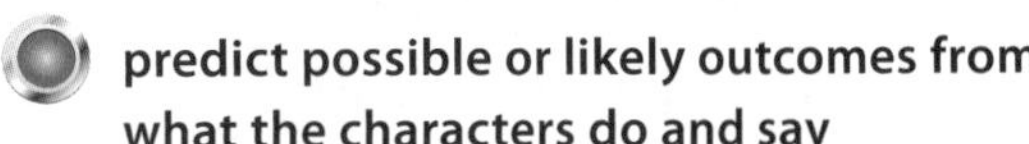

- predict possible or likely outcomes from what the characters do and say
- pick out how the characters are feeling and the mood and atmosphere created.

### 1 Looking for clues

To answer deduction questions in fiction texts you will need to collect all the information in the text linked to the question. For example...

How old is Charlie?

*Search for descriptions that suggest his age. Perhaps there is information linked to the senses...*

visual: grey hair, wrinkled skin, false teeth

sound: gurgling, babbling

smell: talcum powder, violet scent

touch: dry paper-thin skin

### 2 Predicting outcomes

To answer inference questions in fiction texts you have to think about what might happen in the story, using your own knowledge and evidence from the text. For example...

What was the weather like?

There may not be a sentence or phrase that actually tells you but there may be something that hints at the weather. The information in this example suggests it was raining.

The girl dropped her wet umbrella.

*Watch out for additional information that can hint at things that may happen in the future.*

She eyed up the height of the wall, looking behind her to make sure Mum wasn't watching.

### 3 Picking out feelings and moods

What the characters say is not always what they feel. For example...

How did Idra really feel?

*Look for language revealing emotions.*

'It's fine, Dad,' said Idra, shooting an anxious glance at Mum.

## Non-fiction

**You must be able to...**

- quickly identify each text style
- list the variations in different text types
- identify the purpose of the text.

### 1 Identifying text style

Identify the text type before answering questions on text organisation. This will give you a clue to the area of text where information is likely to be found. The table at the base of the page is a helpful summary.

***Text without headings***

Read the first and last paragraphs and then the opening sentence of the rest to consider the purpose of the text. For example, does the text discuss a topic from different viewpoints? If so, it is likely to be a discussion text.

***Text with headings and subheadings***

Read the headings and subheadings first. These will give you a quick summary of the content and narrow down the style of text you are looking at.

### 2 Text variations

Once you have identified the possible type of text, use your knowledge of text types to identify all the features where information might be located.

*Letters fall outside these categories. Find out about writing letters and their structure on page 50.*

### 3 Purpose of the text

Identifying the way a text is organised also enables you to understand its purpose. This is very useful in questions about a writer's viewpoint.

| | Without headings | With headings | Enclosed features | Bullet points | Numbered lists | Additional information | Illustrations |
|---|---|---|---|---|---|---|---|
| Discussion texts | • | | | | | references | illustrative |
| Explanatory texts | • | • | • | • | • | glossary, index | technical |
| Instructional and procedural texts | | • | • | • | • | references | technical |
| Non-chronological reports | • | | | • | | glossary, references | illustrative |
| Persuasive writing | • | • | • | • | • | references | illustrative |
| Recount texts | • | • | | | | dates | illustrative |

## Fiction

**You must be able to...**

- quickly identify the text type
- list the key features for the given genre
- pick out the key points of the plot.

### 1 Identifying the text type

Fiction falls into three main categories.
The layout will help you decide the category:

1 Is it written in paragraphs?

*It is likely to be a story.*

2 Is it made up exclusively from dialogue and stage directions?

*It is likely to be a play script.*

3 Is there evidence of rhyme or verses in the text structure?

*It is likely to be a poem.*

### 2 Listing the key features

Now you have identified the text form, you need to understand the genre.

A table detailing the features of each genre can be found on page 44. These features will help you to predict where to find specific information.

### 3 Picking out the key points

Story and play script texts almost always have an identifiable plot and this is the key structure you should aim to identify.

*In stories, summarise the paragraphs, read highlighted words (bold, italic) and review unusual sentence structures used to add impact. In play scripts, review the stage directions.*

In poems that tell a story, the plot is usually included in the structure of the verses.

### Skills practice

Identify the genre and text type.

(The Queen beckons the knight towards her.)

*Elizabeth 1:* Tell me Sir Walter, this new vegetable – how should one prepare it?

*Sir Walter:* I have observed the sailors boiling them until they are quite broken and then smashing them into tiny pieces.

# How writers use language

## Non-fiction

**You must be able to...**

 identify specialist vocabulary and language techniques

 identify the sentence structure

 identify the purpose and audience.

### 1 Identifying language features

***Factual texts***

Look out for specialist vocabulary. If the text is aimed at a general audience there will usually be a glossary or explanation of the technical language.

***Persuasive texts***

Look out for rhetorical questions (questions that are asked in order to make a point rather than require an answer) and words that are intended to flatter or suggest you are foolish if you do not agree.

> Chewing gum is disgusting, only a fool would disagree with this. Have you looked at the horrendous state of our streets?

*The writer is addressing the reader using words to provoke a response such as 'disgusting' and 'horrendous'.*

### 2 Identifying the sentence structure

Look at the writer's use of sentence structure and the length of the sentences.

*Longer sentences suggest an older audience. Shorter sentences suggest a younger audience.*

*Short sentences are often used to create impact in persuasive texts for audiences of any age.*

> The paths are filthy. The streets are crime-ridden. Our taxes are being squandered by an irresponsible government.

### 3 Identifying the purpose and audience

By looking at both word use and sentence structure, you can often work out who the intended audience is.

*Is the writing aimed at children, parents, pensioners or experts? Does the text favour men or women?*

Lastly check on the tone of the text.

*Look at the word choices to identify whether the mood is enthusiastic, angry, questioning, knowledgeable, humorous or neutral.*

## Fiction

**You must be able to...**

 identify language techniques

 identify the sentence structure

 identify the genre and tone of the text.

### 1 Identifying language techniques

Apart from descriptive language, the use of figurative language in fiction adds another layer to the overall tone and effect. Look out for the use of...

- similes – comparing two things using 'as' or 'like'
- metaphors – comparing one thing to another as if it is a reality, i.e. without 'as' or 'like'
- personification – when animals or objects are described as having human characteristics
- alliteration – when a pair or group of words all begin with the same sound or letter
- onomatopoeia – the use of words that sound like what they describe
- assonance – when the same vowel sound occurs in a pair or group of words.

### 2 Identifying sentence structure

The writer's use of active or passive sentences can add a sense of mystery to a story. For example:

> The aliens invaded the planet. (active)
>
> The planet was invaded. (passive)

By changing the sentence around and leaving out the subject in this way, the reader is left with a question:

> Who invaded the planet?

### 3 Identifying the genre and tone

The writer's choice of language can indicate the genre and traditional or social context.

Looking at the adjectives and adverbs can help identify the tone of a piece and answer questions about feelings.

> The sulky child slouched off petulantly.

### Skills practice 

Identify the language techniques used here:

1 The Midnight Stallion

2 The daylight beckoned and it was time to get up.

# Writer's viewpoint

## Non-fiction

You must be able to...

- distinguish between fact and opinion
- identify whether a text is objective or subjective
- identify the writer's viewpoint.

### 1 Distinguishing between fact and opinion

It is important to be able to tell the difference between facts and opinion when answering questions about the writer's viewpoint. These differences can be tricky to spot.

> Most cat owners say that their cats prefer Catlicks catfood to any other. It is made from pure meat and has no additives. Don't risk your cat's health. It's the best cat food you can buy.

*The only facts in this text are that Catlicks is made from pure meat and has no additives.*

### 2 Identifying objective texts

An objective text is impartial and tries to include all viewpoints. A subjective text promotes the writer's view. Objective texts are based on clear facts that can be checked. Subjective texts are based on opinions and so are always biased.

*When answering writer's viewpoint questions, check whether the text is balanced or one-sided.*

### 3 Identifying the writer's viewpoint

The writer's point of view is not always obvious. Especially in the case of persuasive texts, the bias is often disguised as fact rather than opinion.

***Vocabulary***

Adjective choice can give a clue to the writer's viewpoint. The use of positive adjectives can give away the fact that the text is trying to persuade you of something. For example...

> The amazing, new, intelligent toy for three-year-olds.

***Sentence structure***

Rhetorical questions can also indicate persuasive text. When the reader is spoken to directly this can be convincing, both because it flatters the reader and because is assumes the reader will agree with the point of view expressed. For example...

> I'm sure you, as a discerning parent, will agree.

## Fiction

You must be able to...

- identify the narrator or 'I' character
- identify how the writer wants the reader to react to characters, settings or events
- identify the writer's viewpoint.

### 1 Identifying the narrator

***First person***

When a text is written in the first person (I, me, mine) it is told from that one person's viewpoint: the reader can only know what this character experiences.

***Third person***

When the story or play is written in the third person (he, she, it) it is told through descriptions of what happens. Third person narrative can therefore be used to convey the viewpoint of more than one character, or the author's viewpoint as if they are looking at all the characters remotely.

*Sometimes the third person can be used when the reader can see everyone's thoughts.*

> 'What do you mean?' James asked, knowing exactly what had been implied.
>
> 'There were six sweets left and now there are two', stated Ann, hoping he would own up.

The writer's choice of narrator can develop the reader's understanding of, and help them share, the character's point of view, or it can limit their understanding of the plot or storyline.

### 2 Identifying expected reactions

The choice of narrator can change how the reader feels about characters and the plot.

*When the story is written in the first person, the reader is likely to identify with a particular character as they are able to find out about their inner thoughts and feelings.*

Mystery can be added to the plot when it is written in the first person as the character has only one point of view, so parts of the storyline can be hidden.

### 3 Identifying the writer's viewpoint

Some writers use multiple narrators to present an event from differing perspectives.

**Skills practice >>>**

Rewrite the blue extract above in the first person, from James's point of view.

# Traditional and social context

## Non-fiction

### You must be able to...

- identify when a text was written
- identify where a text was written
- understand the social context of the writing.

### 1 Identifying when a text was written

Understanding when a text was written gives you an insight into the content and context of the writing.

*First look for obvious clues about when the text was written (such as a date at the bottom!). Look out for known historical events, and weights and measures.*

### 2 Identifying where a text was written

Information texts can be written about or from different locations.

*Obvious clues can be references to a text being translated, words from different languages in glossaries and place descriptions.*

### 3 Understanding the social context

You can find clues to the social context of persuasive writing by looking at the grammar.

What position do you think this person holds?

> I seek to preserve property and to respect order, and I equally decry the appeal to the passions of the many or the prejudices of the few.

**A** Prime Minister **B** butler **C** miner
**D** school pupil **E** teacher

The grammar in this text suggests it is from a formal speech, hence the answer is A.

### Skills practice 

This text was produced by a travel journalist on location. Where is it likely to have been written?

The reef stretches more than 2000km along the east coast from the mainland town of Port Douglas to Bundaberg. Swimming, snorkelling, diving and sailing offer the gap-year student an amazing experience.

## Fiction

### You must be able to...

- identify when a text was written
- identify where a text was written
- understand the social context of the writing.

### 1 Identifying when a text was written

Dating a fiction text is more challenging as the author may have chosen to set their story in the past and used old-fashioned language. Look for obvious clues first. For example, the writers name and the date of the text may be given at the end.

In what historical period could this text have been written?

> The gaslight flickered dimly in the pea soup fog as the horse and carriage thundered off into the cloak of darkness. *Alan Marsh 1999*

The text is set in a time before cars and electricity, however it has been written by a modern author creating an historical text.

*If you are asked to decide when a text is written and there is no date given, look for clues in the formality of the language and how objects are described.*

### 2 Identifying where a text was written

Being aware of the place a text was written enables you to answer questions about social context more easily.

*Look at the structure of sentences for texts written by people with English as an additional language.*

Other less obvious clues can be names, foods and customs. Where could this text have been written?

> Mother and Sangita chatted in the afternoon sun as they prepared the sweets for Holi, unaware of the mongoose lurking on the porch behind them.

The girl's name, festival, the weather and the mongoose suggest this text is set in Asia.

### 3 Understanding the social context

The social context relates to class, religion and political positioning.

> The housemaid was completely unreliable and, yet again, had left smuts on the carpet.

This text suggests the writer is of a higher social position than the housemaid.

# Comprehension *test 3*

**Write your answers on the lines provided. When you are given a choice of answers, you will need to write the correct option (A, B, C, D, E or X).** ***Do not write answers in the 'Mark' column.***

TARGET TIME
18 minutes

! Note: the questions in this test are challenging, and are intended to find out which skills you may need to develop to achieve success in the 11+ tests.

## Fiction

**Read this text carefully before answering the questions below.**

### Sky dancers

Hovering, like kestrels, watching avidly for prey,
They flit across the tropical sapphire sky like exotic butterflies,
Nylon strings tugging their twin owners across the salt pans.
Crayoned tails draw sketches in the castle cloud world,
Zigzagging crazily above the water buffalo and bright, upturned faces.

'Watch out, Parvati, it's falling!'
'No it's swooping and diving.'
Excited voices in sing-song cadences harmonise in the wind,
Caught in a moment but embedded in the memory for always.

Mark

1 Where are the castles?

________________________________________

2 How many people are mentioned in the poem?

________________________________________

3 What are the 'Sky dancers'?

**A** birds of prey **B** butterflies **C** aeroplanes **D** swallows **E** kites ______

4 How does the subject of the poem change between the first and the last parts?

________________________________________

5 Which of these sets of three words, taken from the poem, suggests an image of birds?

**A** tugging, zigzagging, harmonise **B** excited, embedded, hovering
**C** soar, swoop, hovering **D** hovering, swooping, diving
**E** falling, diving, caught ______

6 Does the author disapprove of this activity? Give your reasons.

________________________________________

________________________________________

7 Which part of the world do you think this poem is most likely to be set in?

**A** Europe **B** Asia **C** Antarctica **D** Australia **E** North America ______

# Non-fiction

Mark

**Read this text carefully before answering the questions below.**

To: Neil Van

NVX Marketing Inc.

Re: Termination of contract

It has been brought to the management's attention that the advertising campaign we commissioned you to produce and distribute has contravened the Trade Descriptions Act. The toys are not suitable for children under three, a requirement we specifically explained to you in both our initial and three subsequent meetings (minutes of the meetings are attached).

As you did not clearly advise parents that these toys were designed for older children, we are now facing a number of legal actions.

It is therefore with regret that we have to inform you that we are cancelling our agreement and terminating your contract forthwith. We will not be reimbursing you for your costs. Should NVX Marketing Inc. wish to dispute our position, please contact Russell and Russell, our solicitors.

**8** What age of children would the toys in the email be suitable for?

______________________

**9** How many meetings were held altogether?

______________________

**10** What is the purpose of this email?

**A** to cancel a contract with NVX Marketing Inc. **B** to start an advertising campaign

**C** to discuss the Trade Descriptions Act **D** to inform Neil Van about the company's toys

**E** to give information about the company's solicitor ______

**11** Which choice of three words best describes the content of each paragraph?

**A** pleasure, concern, delight **B** dissatisfaction, consequence, action

**C** management, parents, Russell and Russell **D** children, parents, grandparents

**X** none of the above ______

**12** How would you describe the writer's use of language?

______________________

**13** Which phrase suggests the writer is anticipating a response?

**A** It has been brought to the management's attention…

**B** The toys are not suitable for children under three…

**C** As you did not clearly advise parents…

**D** We are now facing a number of legal actions.

**E** Should NVX Marketing Inc. wish to dispute our position… ______

**14** What is the context of this email?

**A** educational **B** political **C** business **D** traditional **E** humour ______

**TEST ENDS**

### You must be able to…

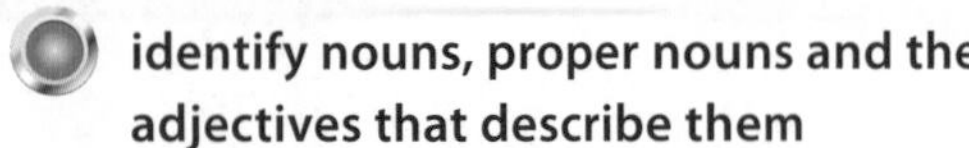

- identify nouns, proper nouns and the adjectives that describe them

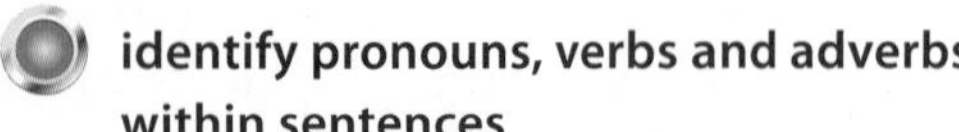

- identify pronouns, verbs and adverbs within sentences
- identify prepositions and conjunctions within a given text.

## 1 Identifying nouns, proper nouns and adjectives

Being able to identify nouns, proper nouns and adjectives helps the reader to understand the structure of sentences:

- A *noun* is the name of a thing or idea (the red words in the text below).

  Cold soup was delivered to Mrs Hardman in a ward of the Seeland General Hospital.

- A *proper noun* is the name of a person or place and begins with a capital letter (the purple words).
- *Adjectives* are the words used to describe nouns (the green word).
- *Comparatives* and *superlatives* are types of adjectives that compare one thing with another.

  Comparative: larger, heavier, kinder

  Superlative: largest, heaviest, kindest

## 2 Identifying pronouns, verbs and adverbs

Being able to identify pronouns, verbs and adverbs helps the reader to understand who or what is performing the action in sentences:

- *Pronouns* tell you who is doing the action or verb. Use this table to refresh your knowledge of personal and possessive pronouns.

| Personal Pronouns | | | | | | | |
|---|---|---|---|---|---|---|---|
| I | you | he | she | it | we | you | they |
| me | | | | | us | | them |

| Possessive pronouns | | | | | | | |
|---|---|---|---|---|---|---|---|
| my | whose | what | her | its | our | your | theirs |
| mine | yours | his | hers | | ours | yours | theirs |

- *Verbs* tell you about the action that is taking place or what is happening.

  to jump, to run, to talk, to be

- *Adverbs* tell you more about the verb.

  The boy ran enthusiastically towards the ice-cream van.

The action or verb is to run (the red word in the sentence above).

The way the boy ran is the adverb (the green word in the sentence above).

## 3 Identifying prepositions and conjunctions

### *Prepositions*

Prepositions tell you about *when* or *where* something happens:

- Time prepositions help you to understand when something happened.

  **at** three o'clock

  **in** two months

  **on** Friday, **last** Friday, **next** Friday, **every** Friday, **this** Friday

  after, ago, before, between, by, from… until, since, up to, within

- Place prepositions help you to visualise where things happen.

  above, across, around, behind, below, by, down, from, into, near, next to, off, on to, opposite, outside, towards, under, up

### *Conjunctions*

Conjunctions are words that join parts of a sentence together. They are sometimes called connectives.

although, and, as, because, but, either, if, however, neither, or, otherwise, since, unless, what, when, whether

### Skills practice

1 Identify the nouns and adjectives in this sentence.

*Sylvie went shopping and bought some green gloves, some blue tights and a bobble hat.*

2 Identify the pronouns, verbs and adverbs in this sentence.

*He played quietly on his game console on Saturday morning.*

3 Identify the prepositions and connectives in this sentence.

*The mouse raced across the room, under the piano and into his hole, which infuriated the cat.*

# Figurative language

### You must be able to...

 identify similes and metaphors in sentences

 identify personification in sentences

 identify alliteration, onomatopoeia, assonance, repetition and rhyme and explain the purpose of each.

## 1 Identifying similes and metaphors

Figurative language means using different techniques to add interest for the reader by...

- comparing two things in a new way (similes, metaphors or personification)
- using repetition of sounds or words to give imaginative effects (assonance, alliteration and onomatopoeia).

### *Similes*

Similes are used to make *connections* or *comparisons* between two nouns so that the reader can imagine what they are like. These are often used in text that tries to persuade (persuasive text) you to agree with a particular point of view, particularly adverts.

Two words are linked with *as* or *like*.

For sale: a beautiful evening dress *as* black *as* night and *as* smooth *as* silk.

Do you want water, cold *like* a mountain stream? Then buy the water clarifying system at HGF's.

### *Metaphors*

Metaphors compare nouns directly without using any linking words.

Dewdrop Diamond earrings for that special evening out.

Lion-hearted men fight the evil wizards. Watch at 9.30 on Wednesday.

Lollipop trees copied from your child's drawing on to tea towels for all the family.

*For instance, the diamonds look like dewdrops but the comparatives have been removed for a more poetic effect.*

## 2 Identifying personification

Personification means giving human characteristics to everyday objects or things.

He was late! The alarm clock shouted at him, the light glared at him. The bed groaned as he got up and the carpet tickled his toes.

*An alarm clock cannot shout, but this suggests to the reader that the noise is loud and the clock is trying to wake him up.*

## 3 Identifying additional language features

### *Alliteration*

Alliteration means using words that begin with the same letter and so catch the eye. It is often used for adverts or headlines.

Fumes fill family flat

### *Onomatopoeia*

When a word sounds like the sound it is describing it is called onomatopoeia.

meows, woofs, clucks, baas, crash, bang, wallop!

### *Assonance*

Assonance is when words have internal repetition of vowels.

Dining time for the nine white lions.

This is an amazing attraction for the whole family.

### *Repetition and rhyme*

Repetition and rhyme are often used in speeches to engage the listener.

A familiar face, a familiar voice, a familiar emotion...

Rhyming also helps the listener to remember and is often used in slogans at the end of commercials.

A spill, a slip, a hospital trip.

## Skills practice 

1 Underline any similes and circle any metaphors in this sentence.

*The poisonous mushroom looked like a sinister umbrella dripping black blood on to the emerald grass it grew from.*

2 Identify the figurative language techniques in these sentences from the list below. Write the correct option on the lines provided.

**A** personification **B** assonance
**C** alliteration **D** onomatopoeia **E** rhyme

***a*** *The curtains blinked and the front door yawned.* ______

***b*** *A cough, a sneeze – I've caught a disease!* ______

***c*** *The crack of thunder overhead made Danny sprint rapidly into the barn.* ______

3 What type of word is 'thump'?

**A** personification **B** assonance
**C** alliteration **D** onomatopoeia **E** rhyme

# Starting sentences

## You must be able to...

 identify appropriate words to open sentences

 construct opening sentences

 vary the structure of sentences.

## 1 Identifying appropriate words to open sentences

To help keep the interest of the reader, authors start sentences in a variety of ways. If all sentences started with the same part of speech, the writing would become boring.

Sentences can start with verbs, adverbs, nouns, adjectives and prepositions, as well as pronouns.

Particular nouns are referred to with the definite article ('the') and non-particular nouns by the indefinite article ('a').

the house, the girl, a dog, a person

*Look at how the following examples are structured to make the sentence more interesting:*

Shuffling through the autumn leaves, the small child laughed quietly. *verb*

Quietly, laughing, the child shuffled through the autumn leaves. *adverb*

The child laughed quietly, as he shuffled through the autumn leaves. *definite article and noun*

Autumn leaves crunched beneath the laughing child's feet. *adjective*

Under the child's feet, autumn leaves crunched like cornflakes. *preposition*

## 2 Constructing opening sentences

Opening sentences need to catch the reader's attention and make them want to read on! This technique is used in many different genres.

### *Historical text*

Charles Dickens began *The Old Curiosity Shop* with...

The reader must not expect to know where I live.

This immediately makes the reader wonder why.

### *Mystery*

It can be effective to use opposites to catch attention:

The victim was dead: the case was very much alive and kicking.

In certain genres, the first sentence can also indicate the type of text you are reading.

### *Fantasy*

Once upon a time...

Long, long ago in the lands of the north...

### *Adventure*

Everything had been boringly normal until I visited Great Aunt Ethel...

### *Science fiction*

The aliens flashed their antennae and started to walk towards us...

## 3 Varying the structure of sentences

Varying the structure of your sentences also helps to keep the reader interested.

*Beginning a sentence with speech can make action seem more realistic.*

'Hurry up!' shouted Sam, flying out of the door as the coffin lid slowly began to move.

## Skills practice

1 Identify the part of speech that each of these sentences start with.

*a* *Dancing through the poppies created waves of colour that radiated from her painted toes.*

**A** a verb **B** an adverb **C** a noun **D** an adjective **E** a preposition

*b* *Under the rugby posts, not over them, why did it happen to him?*

**A** a verb **B** an adverb **C** a noun **D** an adjective **E** a preposition

*c* *Slowly she walked away, leaving a trail of sweets from the hole in her pocket.*

**A** a verb **B** an adverb **C** a noun **D** an adjective **E** a preposition

2 Choose the most appropriate word to start these sentences from the list below.

*a* *...down, the sun shone fiercely on the desert.*

**A** Beating **B** Fierce **C** Dripping **D** Eider **E** The

*b* *...the children tip-toed past the sleeping giant.*

**A** Under **B** Quiet **C** If **D** It **E** Gingerly

# Agreement in sentences

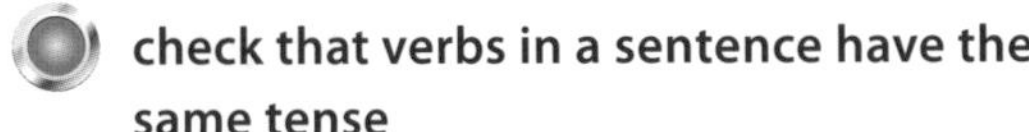

**You must be able to…**

- check that verbs in a sentence have the same tense
- check that the verbs are singular when the subject is singular and plural when the subject is plural
- check that pronouns and possession are consistent.

## 1 Checking verbs in a sentence have the same tense

Make sure that you can identify the verbs in a sentence. Verbs are the words that describe the action.

Eliza rushed home through the driving rain.

Raindrops, like cannon balls, hit the roof of the conservatory.

I will meet you at twelve outside the dry cleaners.

To help pick out the verb and the tense, think about when the action happened.

Yesterday I played in the park.

Today I am playing in the park.

Tomorrow I will play in the park.

If the sentence is extended the tenses must still be in the appropriate tense.

Yesterday I ***played*** in the park, although I had ***planned*** to go shopping in town.

Today I ***am playing*** in the park and ***paddling*** in the new pool.

Tomorrow I ***will play*** in the park and ***feed*** the ducks.

*It is important to keep in the same tense when you are writing. Don't swap from one tense to the other within the same paragraph.*

## 2 Checking that verbs are singular or plural

If the subject of a sentence is singular, the verb must be in the singular form too.

The child ***lies*** on the grass watching the ants.
singular

The children ***lie*** on the grass watching the ants.
plural

Paul ***enjoys*** playing computer games.
singular

People ***enjoy*** playing computer games.
plural

## 3 Checking pronouns and possession are consistent

Pronouns can be used to prevent the repetition of nouns, but they need to agree! For example…

The magical cat leapt across the canyon; she left a trail of sparks behind her.

The naughty boy hid his football behind the cricket pavilion; he wanted to play with it later.

The irate neighbours complained continually about the quadbikes being driven over their lawn, especially as they had just reseeded it.

### Skills practice

1 Pick out the verbs in this sentence.

*The snow drifted across the rooftops, covering everything in a white crystal blanket.*

2 Change this sentence into the past tense.

*I drive to the shop and buy a carton of milk.*

3 Spot the difference between these two sentence starts and fill in the missing word in the second sentence.

*The cat tries to balance along the fence at the end of the garden.*

*The cats ________ to balance along the fence at the end of the garden.*

4 Pick out the correct words to fill the gaps in this sentence.

*The children wanted to have ________ presents at 6.30pm on Christmas eve; ________ Mother said no!*

**A** she **B** children **C** their **D** they're **E** there

# Grammar *test*

**Write your answers on the lines provided. When you are given a choice of answers, you will need to write the correct option (A, B, C, D or E).** ***Do not write answers in the 'Mark' column.***

TARGET TIME 18 minutes

! Note: the questions in this test are challenging, and are intended to find out which skills you may need to develop to achieve success in the 11+ tests.

---

**Read this text carefully before answering the questions below.**

## Sam scoops story prize

Local schoolboy Sam Pickett is celebrating after winning first prize in a national competition for young writers. High-flyer Sam beat 340 hopeful authors to win the prize with his short story entitled *Boys of the Battlements*. The story, inspired by a visit to a castle on a family holiday, tells the tale of a pair of ghostly knaves who delight in frightening visitors to the castle. Children's author and competition judge Crispin Blake explains what gave Sam's entry the edge over his competitors. 'The standard of entries becomes more impressive every year and we were really spoilt with the quality of the stories submitted, but the originality of Sam's piece snatched our attention like a ghostly hand!' Sam himself has enjoyed being the centre of attention but admits to being shocked by his win. 'I'm as pleased as punch but totally gob-smacked,' he said.

**Mark**

1 **Sam beat 340 hopeful authors to win the prize with his short story entitled *Boys of the Battlements.***

What part of speech is the word '*Battlements*' in the above sentence?

**A** verb **B** adjective **C** definite article **D** adverb **E** noun ______ ☐

2 **The story, inspired by a visit to a castle…**

What part of speech is the word 'inspired' in the above sentence?

**A** adverb **B** adjective **C** noun **D** verb **E** pronoun ______ ☐

3 **…the originality of Sam's piece snatched our attention…**

What part of speech is the word 'originality' in the above sentence?

**A** preposition **B** noun **C** adjective **D** adverb **E** verb ______ ☐

4 What sort of language technique has the writer used in the headline 'Sam scoops story prize'?

**A** onomatopoeia **B** alliteration **C** assonance **D** simile **E** metaphor ______ ☐

5 What sort of language technique has the author used when describing Sam as a 'High-flyer'?

**A** metaphor **B** simile **C** personification **D** onomatopoeia **E** alliteration ______ ☐

6 What sort of technique has been used when describing how Sam's entry snatched the judges' attention 'like a ghostly hand'?

**A** personification **B** alliteration **C** simile **D** metaphor **E** onomatopoeia ______ ☐

# Grammar *test*

Choose the word that will fit best at the beginning of these sentences.
Write the letter for the answer on the lines provided.

**Mark**

**7 ...like winning writing competitions can help budding authors to become well known.**

**A** Judges **B** Writing **C** Stories
**D** Opportunities **E** Writers ______

**8 ...language techniques can make stories seem more realistic and believable.**

**A** Vocabulary **B** Creative **C** Correct **D** Careful **E** New ______

**9 ...you are careful about spelling and punctuation your writing will turn out better.**

**A** So **B** Unless **C** But **D** If **E** For ______

Circle a verb from each of the pairs so that the text makes sense and the verbs agree.

**10 Sam enjoy/enjoys writing stories, because it gives/given him the chance to captures/capture his ideas in words for other people to experiences/experience.** ______

**11 Like Sam, many writers gathers/gather ideas from real places and, use/using them, creates/create fantastic work that are/is a joy to read.** ______

**12 The judges, including Crispin Blake, believe/believes that writers like Sam has/have a real future in writing fiction, because they understand/understands the books children like to reads/read.** ______

Choose the correct word to complete these sentences so that they make sense.

**13 When Sam**

| goes | go | wanted | went | want |
|---|---|---|---|---|
| A | B | C | D | E |

**to the castle, he did not expect to find it so fascinating.** ______

**14 The runners-up collected**

| his | they | their | he | her |
|---|---|---|---|---|
| A | B | C | D | E |

**prizes from the judge.** ______

**15 Judges**

| are | is | was | were | was |
|---|---|---|---|---|
| A | B | C | D | E |

**often particularly pleased to receive entries based on real events.** ______

**TEST ENDS**

# Basic punctuation

## You must be able to...

 use punctuation in simple sentences

 use commas to separate information in sentences

 identify missing or incorrect punctuation.

## 1 Using punctuation in simple sentences

Sentences begin with a capital letter and end with a final punctuation mark, such as a full stop, question mark or exclamation mark.

A sentence consists of a group of words that contain a *subject*, a *verb* and (usually) an *object*. Sentences convey a statement, question, exclamation or command.

Many sentences also have commas that break up parts of the sentence to make it easier to read.

### Capital letters

Capital letters are used for...

- the first word in a sentence
- proper nouns, people's names and place names
- days of the week and months of the year
- first person singular (I).

### Full stops

Full stops are used to end a complete sentence.

### Question marks

Question marks show that the sentence is a question.

*Check for question indicator words.*

What?, Where?, When?, Who?, How?

*Check for reversed verbs.*

You can – can you?

### Exclamation marks

Exclamation marks indicate extreme happiness, shouting or surprise.

*Check speech for exclamations.*

Hurrah! Brilliant! (happiness)

Help! Goal! Ahhh! (shouting)

It was a real dinosaur! (surprise)

## 2 Using commas to separate information

Commas are used to separate information within sentences and are used for different purposes.

### Clauses and phrases

All sentences include a main clause and some also contain subordinate clauses:

- A main clause always contains a subject and a verb and can make sense on its own:

  The wolf crept across the room,
- A phrase doesn't contain both a subject and a verb, nor does it make sense on its own:

  step by step,
- A subordinate clause doesn't make sense on its own but does contain a subject and a verb:

  then he ate grandma.
- Sometimes subordinate clauses can be 'parachuted' into a sentence. These clauses are separated by commas and are easy to spot as the sentence makes sense without them.

  The wolf, seeing the tasty snack through the window, opened the door and ate grandma.

### Lists and descriptions

Some sentences contain smaller pieces of information that commas help to organise:

- They can be used to separate items in a list...

  For her birthday, Jo received a glass polar bear, a small teddy, a bear hat, and bear earmuffs.
- They can be used to separate adjectives...

  The long, sunny summer days were over.

...but not if you can't replace the comma with 'and'.

The dark brown bear.

## 3 Spotting errors in text

Punctuation marks are like traffic lights: they tell the reader when to pause and stop, and they add expression and meaning to a text:

- When correcting punctuation, it helps to read the sentences quietly so that you get a clear idea of where to stop to make the writing make sense.
- Reading the text in different ways and pausing in different places can help you to decide where punctuation marks should go.
- Check proper nouns and the first person singular ('I') have capital letters.

### Skills practice

Rewrite these sentences with the punctuation corrected.

1 stop where are you going i want to know

2 on tuesday abeshek kylie and yang were playing monopoly in the kitchen

# More about punctuation

## You must be able to...

 use speech conventions

 use colons and semicolons in texts

 use apostrophes, dashes, ellipses and brackets in text and correct errors.

## 1 Using speech conventions

Speech marks are used in text to show the words that a person or character is speaking or thinking:

- When text is handwritten, speech marks generally occur in pairs.

  "Hello!"

  In printed texts, speech marks mostly occur singularly.

  'Where are you going?'

- The first mark(s) are followed by a capital letter and the final mark(s) follow the punctuation mark.
- A new line begins every time a new person speaks.

## 2 Using colons and semicolons

### Colons

Colons are used to indicate additional information:

- They are used to introduce explanations.

  There is no need to rush: the school council meeting has been cancelled.

- They are used to introduce lists of information (although lists of one or two words are usually separated by commas).

  There are three away-day choices for Year 6: an activity day at James' Centre, a visit to the Tower of London, or a day at Rapley Zoo.

- They are used to introduce speech.

  She stood up and announced loudly: 'Ladies and gentlemen, dinner is served.'

Colons are also used in play scripts where they are often used after the character's name and before the dialogue.

Gary: It really was the butler!

### Semicolons

A semicolon is often used instead of a full stop to show that the following information is closely linked:

He worked very hard; I hope he passes the exam.

- A semicolon can often be replaced with a connective. The semicolon in this example could be replaced by 'because'.

  We bought Dad a London Irish season ticket for his birthday; he loves rugby.

## 3 Using apostrophes, dashes, ellipses and brackets

### Apostrophes

Apostrophes are used to show that a letter or letters have been missed out.

Why can't I go out tonight?

Possessive apostrophes are used to show that something belongs to somebody or something.

The alien's leg was covered in green pimples.

If the apostrophe comes after the 's' it shows there is more than one.

The aliens' home was beyond the Milky Way.

### Dashes

Dashes are used to make a sentence stand out in a text. Sometimes they are used to draw attention to a cliffhanger ending.

They lived happily ever after – or did they?

They can also be used to separate a clause, in the same way that commas can.

They all went to the cinema – although it was still raining – because they wanted to see the film.

### Ellipses

The use of ellipses (…) can indicate a range of things:

- something has been missed out
- the passage of time.

The headteacher congratulated the team, 'What an amazing performance… you ran incredibly.'

Time passed… The next Jed knew the sun was rising and the sand was growing hotter.

### Brackets

Brackets are often used in play scripts to separate the stage directions from the dialogue.

Kim: I'll never come here again.

(She stands up and runs off the stage left.)

These brackets ( ) are known as parenthesis.

## Skills practice

Which of these sentences are punctuated correctly? Rewrite any that are badly punctuated.

1 I collected the things for my school pencil case: pencils, crayons, a rubber, a sharpener.

2 It was an amazing match; a score line of seven clear goals didn't come that often for the Magpies.

3 Hannah: I don't want to come to your party starting to snivel.

# Punctuation *test*

**Write your answers on the lines provided. When you are given a choice of answers, you will need to write the correct option (A, B, C, D, E or X).** ***Do not write answers in the 'Mark' column.***

**!** Note: the questions in this test are challenging, and are intended to find out which skills you may need to develop to achieve success in the 11+ tests.

Pick out the section with the punctuation error. If they are all correct, choose X.

**Mark**

**1** **Can you imagine the** (A) **harsh conditions faced** (B) **by workers, especially** (C) **children, in Victorian factories.** (D) **X** ______ ☐

**2** **Some children were expected to clean the** (A) **machines in textile mills while the machines** (B) **were still running, As a result,** (C) **many suffered terrible injuries or were killed.** (D) **X** ______ ☐

**3** Rewrite this sentence with the punctuation corrected.

**Others worked in match factories dipping, matchsticks in a chemical called, phosphorus that can cause lung disease tooth decay and other illnesses.**

______

______ ☐

**4** Pick out the section with the punctuation error. If they are all correct, choose X.

**Often employing children from** (A) **orphanages factory owners paid** (B) **their child workers little,** (C) **so they were cheaper than adults.** (D) **X** ______ ☐

**5** Rewrite this sentence with the punctuation corrected.

**First-hand accounts from Victorian children have survived, with one nine-year-old girl explaining I work from five in the morning until after dark every day but Sunday.**

______

______ ☐

Pick out the section with the punctuation error. If they are all correct, choose X.

**6** **However, factories were not** (A) **the only places where children** (B) **worked they were also** (C) **employed as chimney sweeps and in coal mines.** (D) **X** ______ ☐

**7** **Its hard to imagine how much children** (A) **suffered, but things began to improve in the** (B) **middle of the 19th century, when laws** (C) **started to be passed to protect children.** (D) **X** ______ ☐

**8** **Understanding what life was like for** (A) **poor Victorian children helps us to appreciate** (B) **what we have; suddenly school** (C) **doesn't seem so bad after all!** (D) **X** ______ ☐

**TEST ENDS**

# Plurals and spelling rules

## You must be able to...

spell plurals using the correct endings

spell common words that follow general rules

identify incorrect spellings in a set text.

## 1 Spelling plurals

You need to know the common spelling rules for creating plurals:

- The most common plural ending is just adding 's'.
  cats, broomsticks, wizards
- When the singular word ends with 'ess', 'ch', 'sh', or 'x', add 'es' to make the plural.
  dresses, witches, crashes, boxes
- For words ending in 'y' you need to check the letter in front of the 'y'...
  - if the letter is a vowel, just add 's'
    keys, turkeys, buys
  - if the letter is a consonant then change the 'y' to an 'i' and add 'es'.
    carries, parties, flies
- For words that end in 'f', change the 'f', to a 'v' and add 'es'.
  elves, halves, hooves, scarves
- Some words stay the same for their plural.
  sheep, deer, salmon

### Watch out!

There are exceptions to the above rules. For instance, the plural of 'roof' is most commonly spelt 'roofs' and the plural of fish can be either 'fish' or 'fishes'. Some plurals you just have to learn, including...

man – men
woman – women
tooth – teeth
mouse – mice
louse – lice

## 2 Spelling common words that follow general rules

### *-ing endings*

When adding 'ing' to a word that ends in 'e', remember to drop the 'e'.

hope – hoping
hide – hiding
like – liking

### *-ly endings*

To make an adverb, 'ly' is often added:

- If the word ends with 'e', leave the 'e' in place and add 'ly'.
  rude – rudely, pure – purely
- If the word ends in 'y', change the 'y' to an 'i' and add 'ly'.
  merry – merrily, cosy – cosily

### *-full endings*

When adding 'full' to the end of a word, drop the second 'l'. However, keep it when adding 'fully'.

care + full – careful – carefully
hope + full – hopeful – hopefully

### *-age endings*

When adding 'age' to a word, if the word ends with 'e' you generally drop the 'e'.

use – usage

You can find further spelling rules involving word endings on page 41.

## 3 Spotting errors in text

Spotting errors in text can be tricky. It is best to take one word at a time.

If you are allowed to write on the paper, cross out all the words that you are sure are correct. Then concentrate on the others:

- Check for plurals with incorrect endings.
- Check for plurals that don't follow the normal rules.
- Check for words that end in 'ful'.

### Skills practice

Change all the nouns in these sentences to plurals. You may need to alter some of the other words too so that they agree.

1 The witch collected a frog, a leaf, a tooth, an elf and a deer, ready for the mystery quiz.
2 The ox carried the child to the field where the sheep were grazing.

Rewrite these sentences using correct spelling.

3 The beutifull maiden happyly skipped gracfully down the castle steps.
4 Hoping across the field the hair enjoyed the autumn whether.

# Doubling letters

**You must be able to...**

 **identify short and long vowels within words**

 **spell common words that involve double letters**

 **identify incorrect spellings in a text.**

## 1 Identifying long and short vowels

*How a vowel sounds* in a word affects how endings are added.

*Short vowels sound like the letters of the alphabet when you are first taught them…*

pat, pet, pin, pot, cut

*Long vowels sound like the name of the letter when reciting the alphabet, as in…*

bake, swede, like, bone, cube

The final 'e', sometimes called the *magic 'e'*, makes the vowel 'say' its name rather than its short vowel sound.

*Identify the short and long vowels in these words. Think about how they sound when read aloud.*

trip, hay, play, tripe, kick, hope, key, sat, lot, but

*The short vowel sounds are trip, kick, sat, lot, but. The long vowel sounds are hay, play, tripe, hope, key.*

## 2 Spelling common words with double letters

### *Short vowels*

To ensure the vowel keeps a *short* sound, you need to *double* the following consonant.

*When adding **-ing** to a word that contains a short vowel you need to double the consonant to preserve the short sound. This also applies when adding **-ed**.*

pat – patting, pin – pinning, shop – shopping

pat – patted, pin – pinned, shop – shopped

### *Long vowels*

Long vowels do not need double letters but there are other rules:

- For **-ing** endings you do need to drop the final 'e' to keep the long vowel sound.

  bake – baking, hope – hoping

- For **-er** and **-ed** endings it depends on where the stress is placed:
  - When the stress is on the main part of the word, such as *prefer,* you need to double the 'r' to keep the stress on the second syllable.

  prefer – preferred, infer – inferring

  - Where the stress is on the first syllable, the double 'r' is not needed.

  whisper – whispered

  - When there are more than two syllables and no prefix, you do not need to double the final letter.

  interrupt – interrupted (single 't')

  - When a prefix has been added to a two-part word with the stress on the second syllable, keep the double letter.

  *un*transmitted (double 't')

- For **-ly** endings when the word ends in 'l', remember you will need a double letter.

  magical – magically

  occasional – occasionally

## 3 Identifying incorrect spellings

Spotting doubling errors in text can be tricky. It is best to think of how the word sounds:

Concentrate on the sound of the vowel to check for words that need double letters.

Underline words ending in '-er', '-ed', '-ing' and '-ly' and circle the vowels in the root word.

Think about whether the vowels are short or long.

**Skills practice** 

Find the words that need double letters in these sentences and correct those that don't.

1 I was hopping for a new bike for my birthday but I got swiming lesons instead.

2 I was feelling hungry so my Mum brought me some broccolli quiche.

3 Generaly I go shoping with Mum but this weekend I went with Grandma.

4 Occasionaly I misspel words when I am not concentratting.

# Prefixes and suffixes

## You must be able to...

 identify and spell common prefixes

 identify and spell common suffixes

 modify spellings when using prefixes and suffixes.

## 1 Spelling common prefixes

Prefixes come at the start of a word. (There is a table of common prefixes in the column opposite.)

*When the prefix ends with the same letter as the word you are adding it to you get double letters.*

u**nn**atural, u**nn**ourished

Sometimes the double letters are hyphenated to make the spellings clearer, but there is no simple rule to tell you which words should have a hyphen.

under-paid, over-resourced

Double vowels often have hyphens added because the letters are pronounced differently.

Pre-elections, pre-empts

... but not always.

cooperate, coordinate

Just look at how the word reads and decide for yourself.

## 2 Spelling common suffixes

A suffix is a group of letters added to the end of a word to form a new word. It often changes its function. (You may already have looked at some of the common spelling rules when adding suffixes on page 39.)

### *Changing parts of speech*

Verbs can be changed to adjectives by adding different endings:

to fall – fallen, to cheer – cheerful

Adding the suffix -ly changes an adjective to an adverb.

sad – sadly, careful – carefully

### *Verb suffixes*

Suffixes at the end of verbs can change the person the verb is being used with or make the verb a noun:

to read – reader, to become – becoming

### *Noun suffixes*

Suffixes at the end of nouns can change the meaning:

duke – dukedom, free – freedom, train – trainer, protect – protector

### *Adjective suffixes*

Adding suffixes to adjectives can make the adjective mean the opposite:

hope – hopeless, defence – defenceless

## 3 Modifying spellings

### *Words ending in 'y'*

If a word ends in a 'y', you will need to change the 'y' to an 'i' when adding the suffix.

happy – happily, funny – funniest

### *Words ending in 'e'*

If a word ends in an 'e', check the suffix to see if it begins with a vowel.

*If the suffix starts with a vowel ('est' for example), drop the 'e'.*

pure – purest, fine – finest

*If the suffix starts with a consonant ('less' for example), keep the 'e'.*

care – careless, shame – shameful

*If the word ends in a double 'e', keep the 'e' unless the suffix starts with an 'e'.*

free – freedom, agree – agreed

| Prefix | Basic Meanings | Examples of words |
|---|---|---|
| anti | opposed to, against, not | antiseptic, anti-aircraft |
| auto | same, self | automatic, autobiography |
| bi | two, twin | bicycle, bisect |
| co | joined together | co-author, co-education, co-exist |
| dis | not, absence of | disbelief, discomfort, discredit, disrespect, disjoint |
| ex | former, out of | ex-wife, extract |
| hex | six | hexagon, hexagonal |
| inter | among, between | intertwine, international, interject |
| micro | small | microscopic, microbes |
| mono | one, single | monocycle, monochrome |
| non | not | nonstop, non-violent, non-resident |
| pre | before | pre-pay, premeditate, predetermine |
| quad | four | quadrilateral, quadrant |
| re | again, back | return, rearrange, recall |
| trans | across, beyond, through | transport, transatlantic |
| tri | three | triangle, tricycle, tripod |
| un | not | unable, un-American |

## Skills practice 

Pick out the incorrect spelling of words with prefixes and suffixes.

1 The hamburger restaurant was overrpriced.

2 The bicyclist was thinking of purchassing a unnicycle.

### You must be able to...

 spell common irregular spellings

 spell and use correctly words that sound the same

 identify incorrect irregular spellings.

## 1 Spelling common irregular spellings

There are groups of letters that you will often see together, and the way they sound when spoken does not help with their spelling.

***-ght endings***

These words sound as if they end in 't'.

fight, light, bright, weight, eight

***-tion and -sion endings***

These words sound as if they end with 'shun'.

station, action, addition, audition, conjunction, correction, dilution, abrasion, confusion, session, revision, tension, vision

***Silent letters***

Some words have silent letters, such as...

knit, knock, gnat, comb, tongue, queue

*Look out for...*

'kn', 'gn', 'wr', 'mn', 'gh', 'wh'

*These combinations often indicate silent letters.*

kneel, gnome, wren, solemn, high, what

***Very tricky spellings***

These are words that have been identified as being frequently misspelt.

absence, achievement, advice, advise, beginning, believe, calendar, changeable, committee, definite, disease, embarrass, fluorescent, grateful, hygiene, independent, investigate, laboratory, license, malice, miscellaneous, misspelled, necessary, noticeable, previous, professor, questionnaire, rhyme, rhythm, separate, skiing, sergeant, twelfth, usable, vacuum, weird, yacht

## 2 Spelling and using words that sound the same

***Homophones***

Homophones are generally words that sound the same but have different meanings and spellings.

| Homophones | | | |
|---|---|---|---|
| air | heir | morning | mourning |
| aisle | isle | pair | pear |
| bare | bear | peace | piece |
| cent | scent | pray | prey |
| cereal | serial | principal | principle |
| coarse | course | profit | prophet |
| dear | deer | right | write |
| die | dye | sail | sale |
| flour | flower | shore | sure |
| hair | hare | stationary | stationery |
| him | hymn | suite | sweet |
| hole | whole | their | there |
| knight | night | waist | waste |
| know | no | wear | where |
| made | maid | weather | whether |

Look at this list of homophones and think about the different meaning of each pair of words.
For example...

'air' is what we breathe in, 'heir' is somebody who will inherit something.

***Homonyms***

Homonyms are words that have the same spelling but can sound different and mean different things.

wind – meaning air movement

wind – meaning to turn a key, to store energy.

## 3 Identifying incorrect irregular spellings

Irregular spelling errors are the hardest to spot. It is best to take one word at a time. Check for...

- common irregular spellings
- words where silent letters have been left out
- homophones, words spelt correctly but used in the wrong place.

Remember, the more you read, the better your spelling skills are likely to become!

### Skills practice

Rewrite these sentences, correcting the spelling.

1 The buoy was not aloud to sea his birthday present.

2 The prophet from the bisness deal was less than the bored was expecting.

3 The nitting pattern required a pear of size ate needles.

# Spelling test

**Write your answers on the lines provided. When you are given a choice of answers, you will need to write the correct option (A, B, C, D, E or X).** ***Do not write answers in the 'Mark' column.***

TARGET TIME
:10
**10 minutes**

**!** Note: the questions in this test are challenging, and are intended to find out which skills you may need to develop to achieve success in the 11+ tests.

---

Pick out the section with **no** spelling errors. If they are all correct, choose X.

Mark

**1** Examples of microbes include bacterias and (A) | fungii like yeast. Some (B) | varitys are helpful to us (C) | and others are harmful and can cause illness. (D) | X ______

**2** Remember, these things are tiny, so (A) | we don't have to look at them, unlike bigger 'nastys' (B) | like heads louses or (C) | mosquitos, which make us run for our lifes! (D) | X ______

**3** Virusses are also microbes, spreading (A) | easily among people and causing things (B) | like the driping noses of colds and the (C) | spoty skin associated with chicken pox. (D) | X ______

**4** Most of us have suffered from (A) | an illness caused by microbes (B) | though on the whole we are lucky, (C) | getting better quite quickly. (D) | X ______

**5** Microbes can envade your (A) | body, if you are carless and don't (B) | wash your hands carefully, but your (C) | immune system usually neutralases them. (D) | X ______

**6** Illnesses can easely be caused by (A) | bacteria and moulds found in foods (B) | not properley cooked or (C) | stored in unsuitible conditions. (D) | X ______

**7** Many microbes cause deseases, (A) | some break down autum leaves into (B) | nutrients and there are others witch help (C) | to produce foods like yoghurt. (D) | X ______

**8** Choose the option in which all three words are spelled correctly to complete the sentence.

Our understanding of microbes has been … through the work of … which … how they live and grow.

**A** derveloped, laboratries, investegate
**B** developed, laboratories, investigate
**C** developed, labratories, investigate
**D** diveloped, laboratories, investigate
**E** developed, lavoratories, investergate ______

**TEST ENDS**

# Writing stories

## You must be able to...

 work within a given genre

 create the plot, setting and characters

 create a balanced text appropriate to the genre, mood and atmosphere through choice of language.

##  Working within a given genre

It is important to understand the characteristics of each genre as you will need to include these in your writing.

*Refer to the table below as a reminder.*

##  Creating the plot, setting and characters

### *Plot*

Planning the plot is one of the most important aspects of story writing.

Your story should include an introduction to the problem/mystery, a climax and a resolution.

*Create a pattern to plan out where the events occur. Use a spider diagram to list key events to follow as you write.*

*Experiment with a known story, moving the climax to different parts of the story. An early climax gives you the opportunity to introduce flashbacks.*

### *Setting*

The setting should be decided before you begin.

*Think about the senses when you are writing about setting. Try to include hearing, seeing, smelling and tasting (if appropriate).*

### *Characters*

As well as describing what your characters look like, it is important to say something about who they are.

##  Creating a balanced and descriptive text

### *Balance of text*

The balance of text styles can add to the maturity of your story writing and you can also plan this out before you begin writing.

*Plan the structure of your writing, splitting it between narrative, description and dialogue. Think of your story as a recipe! For example, two parts narrative, to two parts description, to one part dialogue.*

 **Watch out!** 

Dialogue should only be used to move the story on as it can be distracting.

### *Mood and atmosphere through language*

The mood and atmosphere in a text is created by the choice of words, figurative language (such as alliteration and metaphor) and sentence structure.

*If a passage has fast action, consider longer sentences; if there is drama, think about where short sentences and dialogue can be used for effect.*

Adverbial phrases used to explain 'where?', 'how?', 'why?' and 'when?' can help to bring a story to life:

*Jake ran into the room incredibly quickly.*

**Skills practice** 

1. Write the story of Little Red Riding Hood in your own style, starting with the climax at the beginning, where the woodsman has killed the wolf in Grandma's clothing.
2. Rewrite this sentence to convey the atmosphere of a) a sunny day, b) a windy day.

   *The fog drifted mysteriously over the ink-black river like smoke from the dying embers of a deserted fire.*

| | Plot | Setting | Characters |
|---|---|---|---|
| **Adventure** | a quest, action and danger | often historic | heroes and villains |
| **Mystery** | something to solve | any | somebody who has done something they shouldn't, detective (can be amateur) |
| **Historical fiction** | various | moment in history | various |
| **Science fiction** | man *vs* technology, man *vs* aliens | future, space, parallel world | usually a hero and alien creatures |
| **Fantasy** | magical adventure, mystery | fantasy world | various |
| **Contemporary fiction** | usually conflict | modern day | various |
| **Dilemma stories** | story with a moral purpose | generally contemporary | often young people and characters that can be identified with |
| **Myths** | beliefs to explain how things began | time before recorded history | gods and mythical creatures |
| **Legends** | adventures with fantasy elements | historical time | humans and often real characters, such as Robin Hood |

## You must be able to...

 understand how a script works

 create the plot, setting and characters

create a balanced text using script writing techniques and different language features.

##  Understanding how a script works

It is important to understand the characteristics of play scripts as you will need to include these in your writing.

*Use the table opposite as a checklist to make sure that you are clear about the features of play scripts.*

##  Creating the structure

### Plot

Planning the plot is one of the most important aspects of play-script writing. Planning enables you to create a storyline that your characters will need to convey to the audience. The plot must be explained by the characters in their dialogue.

*Your play should include a problem/mystery, a climax and a resolution.*

### Setting

The setting should be decided before you begin.

*Use your characters to add information about the setting by what they say. Add description about the setting into the stage directions.*

### Characters

The characters are introduced in the cast list. There is often a brief description of their personality and their relationship to other characters.

*Develop your characters by considering what they say and do and how the other characters react to them. Individual characters can speak directly to the audience (asides) to share their personal thoughts.*

##  Creating a balanced text

Unlike in story writing, script writing relies on dialogue to convey the plot, setting and characters' personalities.

*Use your stage directions to provide information to the actors on where to move, how to react and deliver lines and where to show emotion.*

*A good 'recipe mix' for a play would be… four parts dialogue, to two parts stage directions, to one part additional information.*

| Feature | Purpose |
|---|---|
| Acts | Acts in plays are like the chapters in a book. |
| Actor | Actors are the people who play the characters. |
| Cast list | The cast list comes at the start of a play script and lists the characters and outlines their character and relationships within the play. |
| Characters | People in the play script. The names are written on the left-hand side of the page followed by a colon. What they say follows the colon. |
| Costume | Costume is the clothing that the actors wear. Information on costume is often placed after the cast list. |
| Dialogue | Dialogue is the words the characters speak. |
| Narrator | The narrator is someone who tells or recounts the story to help move the story or action on. |
| Play script | The play script is the text that is written for the actors to learn and act. |
| Props | Props are the objects needed on stage. |
| Scene | Place of action. Each scene has either a new setting, point in time or both. |
| Scenery | The scenery gives the audience a sense of the setting. Often there is a painted background or painted back cloth. |
| Stage | This is the area where the play takes place. Sometimes this is in the middle of a hall or sometimes it is a raised platform at the end of a theatre or hall. |
| Stage directions | Stage directions describe the setting and tell the actor where to move, how to deliver the lines and the emotions to show. |

### Skills practice

1 Write a play script for 'Three blind mice', imagining the mice can speak.

2 Write ten exchanges of dialogue between two people talking about a setting familiar to you and your family. Ask your family to guess where the characters are situated.

# Writing poems

## You must be able to...

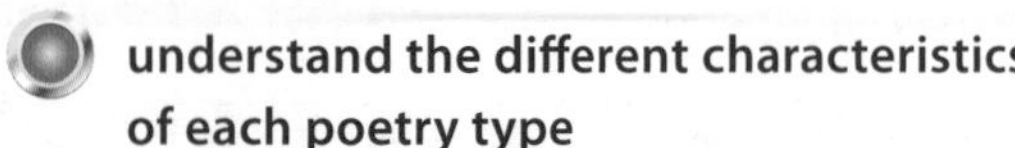
understand the different characteristics of each poetry type

plan the structure of a poem using these characteristics

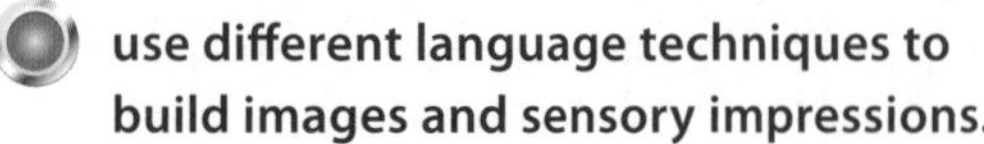
use different language techniques to build images and sensory impressions.

## 1 Understanding the characteristics of poetry types

In order to write a poem you need to know the characteristics of different poetry styles.

*Use the table below as a checklist for some different types of poem.*

## 2 Planning a poem using the correct characteristics

It is helpful to use a well-known poem written in the correct form as a starting point.

*If you are going to use a style that needs rhyme, it is useful to jot down words linked to the subject and then look for those with rhyming endings.*

ducks: drake – lake duck – muck wings – sings

*If you need to use a certain number of beats, then arrange your word choices according to the numbers of beats or syllables within each word.*

## 3 Using different language techniques

Poetry is all about creating images with carefully chosen words. They are meant to be read aloud.

*Your choices need to create sound patterns as well as visual patterns. The words and phrases need to convey the image in the most effective way.*

### *Parts of speech*

Think about the use of adjectives and adverbs to clarify ideas and images.

### *Figurative language*

Think about similes and metaphors to compare and contrast the images.

*Think about using alliteration or onomatopoeia to add to the sound effect of the poem and personification to bring the inanimate objects to life.*

### Skills practice

1 Sort these sporting words into a) groups of words that rhyme, b) groups of words with the same number of syllables (beats).

celebrate, choose, racing, dispute, lose, pacing, medal, pedal, shoes, shoot, placing

2 Make a table with the following headings to describe an alien…

Body part Adjectives Rhyming words

Now list five body parts in the first column and fill in the table.

| | Form | Rhyme | Rhythm |
|---|---|---|---|
| Acrostic | A poem where the initial letter of each line forms a word. | optional | optional |
| Ballad | A poem that tells a story, written in verse.<br>It often contains a repeated refrain, like a song. | Ballads typically have four-line verses, of which two or more rhyme.<br>Common rhyme schemes are… aabb / abab / abcb | Every line needs the same number of beats/syllables and the number of accented beats/syllables need to support the rhyme pattern. |
| Blank verse | These poems are all about building pictures from words. | no rhyme | Iambic verse<br>Five unstressed syllables followed by one stressed. |
| Concrete poems | The words are arranged in a shape that adds something to the meaning. For example, poems written about buildings may be arranged in the shape of that building. | optional | optional |
| Haiku | Haiku poems consist of three lines. | The lines rarely rhyme. | The first and last lines of a Haiku have five syllables and the middle line has seven syllables. |
| Limerick | An amusing poem of five lines. | First, second and fifth lines rhyme. The third and fourth lines rhyme with each other. | First, second and fifth lines have the same number of beats/syllables. The third and fourth lines have the same number of syllables (typically five or six). |
| Sonnet | A poem of 14 lines.<br>Three four-line stanzas and a closing couplet. | Rhyming scheme:<br>abab / cdcd / efef / gg | Each line of the stanza should have no more and no less than ten syllables. |

# Writing discussion and explanatory texts

## Discussion texts

**You must be able to...**

- look at a topic from different perspectives
- list the contrasting arguments and the links between them
- create a balanced text using appropriate language.

**Example:** School holidays should be reduced to four weeks a year so that homework can be abolished.

### 1 Looking at a topic from different perspectives

Well-written discussion texts provide a balanced text showing both sides of the argument.

*Although you will probably have your own views on the topic given, the skill is to contrast these thoughts with the opposing point of view.*

### 2 Listing and connecting contrasting arguments

To make sure that your text tackles both points of view, make a list of 'for' and 'against' points. These will be the subjects of your paragraphs.

*Link your contrasting ideas with arrows to help plan your paragraphs.*

### 3 Creating a balanced text

Discussion texts begin with an introduction and finish with a concluding paragraph that introduce and sum up the views expressed within the text. Don't be tempted to express a personal opinion, even at the end!

*Decide whether you are going to link your ideas within one paragraph or over two contrasting paragraphs.*

Connectives such as 'although' and 'however' can be useful to move between contrasting views.

**Skills practice** >>>

Write two points, both 'for' and 'against' the discussion topic about school holidays above, then write both the opening and concluding paragraphs.

## Explanatory texts

**You must be able to...**

- select the important points of the process to be explained
- organise your points clearly and logically
- create a balanced text using appropriate language.

**Example:** How rainbows are formed.

### 1 Selecting the important points

Explanatory texts explain a process or event. In order to write them effectively, you must understand the key points in the process you are explaining.

*Deciding on your audience before you begin will help you to choose the information you include and exclude.*

### 2 Organising points clearly and logically

Plan out the key facts you are going to put across and organise your information into a table.

*Numbering your points will help you to check that you have included everything.*

| How rainbows are formed | |
|---|---|
| *Topics* | *Important facts* |
| 1 Light | • Light travels in waves.<br>• Short – blue, long – red. |
| 2 Sunlight | • Made up from different wavelengths. |
| 3 Rain | • Light bends in water.<br>• Splits according to wavelength into colours. |

### 3 Creating a balanced text

One or two sentences are often enough to begin an explanatory text and a conclusion may not be needed, depending on the subject.

*Use the present tense (unless the subject is historical) and connections such as 'then', 'because' and 'afterwards' to join the content together.*

**Skills practice** >>>

Choose one section from the table above and write the paragraphs to explain this part of the process.

# Writing instructional texts and reports

## Instructional, procedural texts

### You must be able to...

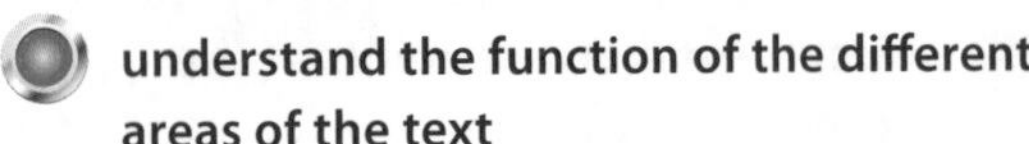

- understand the function of the different areas of the text

- list the important information and stages
- create an appropriate, balanced text for the intended purpose.

**Example:** A recipe for orange jelly faces.

### 1 Understanding the function of different areas of the text

Instructional and procedural texts have a number of essential elements that must be included for them to be effective.

*Before beginning these texts, create a plan of these essential elements. For example…*

Type of text: recipe

Areas of text: ingredients, utensils, method, illustration and captions

*Link each point to the subject area you are writing about.*

### 2 Listing important information and stages

The audience you are writing for should decide the information you include. This example relates to the orange jelly faces recipe for a children's audience over the age of nine.

Notes: include safety information when heating jelly and using knives.

*Include this specific information as you plan your writing.*

### 3 Creating a balanced text

Make sure that the essential information is included and listed in a clear order.

*For example, make sure that all the ingredients are included in an ingredients list rather than scattered through the instructions. If an oven should be pre-heated, don't mention this just before it is needed!*

The style of instruction text should be straightforward and clear.

#### Skills practice

Plan and make notes for an instructional text on how to organise your pencil case.

## Non-chronological reports

### You must be able to...

- structure a report for a specific purpose and given audience

- choose the important points to put across and plan your report

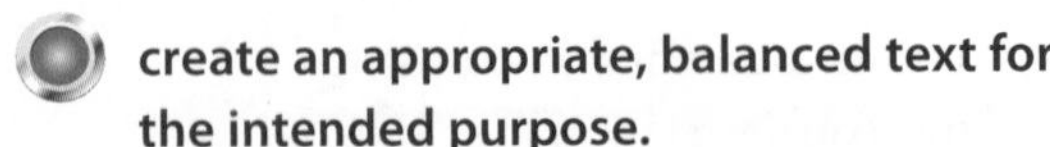

- create an appropriate, balanced text for the intended purpose.

**Example:** Preventing the spread of headlice in schools.

### 1 Structuring a report

Because non-chronological reports (reports that do not describe a sequence of events) are not structured in a particular order, the length, content and language style should be targeted at your audience before you begin.

*If you are writing for a younger audience you will need to have fewer categories and clearly separated points.*

### 2 Planning a report

Determining the essential information you want to put across will help you to decide the order of text and how much space you give to each topic.

*Draw a spider diagram to plan your thoughts.*

### 3 Creating a balanced text

Once you have created your spider diagram, briefly list the contents of each paragraph in the order you intend to write them:

- *Paragraph 1*: introduce the subject and the topics covered in your plan.
- *Central paragraphs*: work through your essential points in a logical order.
- *Final paragraph*: summarise each main point and add an interesting conclusion.

*Consider the language style and level of descriptive words suitable for your audience.*

#### Skills practice

Create a spider diagram for a non-chronological report for parents, based on the topic in the example above, about headlice.

# Persuasive writing and recounts

## Persuasive writing

### You must be able to...

- choose a perspective to write from

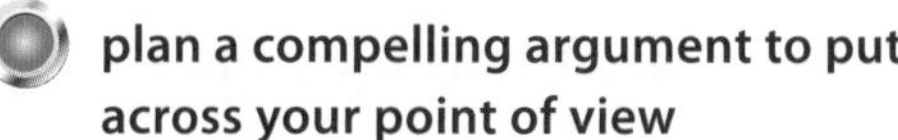

- plan a compelling argument to put across your point of view

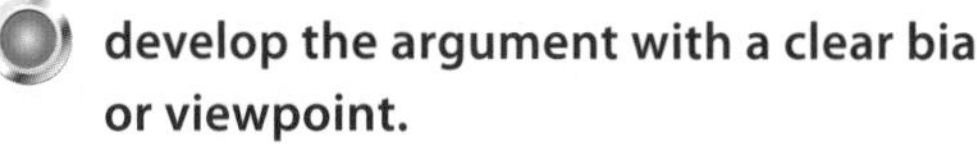

- develop the argument with a clear bias or viewpoint.

**Example:** Write a persuasive text to be presented at the School Council either for or against the following statement:
*Schools should be self-sufficient, growing their own vegetables and animals and generating their own energy.*

### 1 Choosing a perspective

To write a convincing persuasive text you will need a list of reasons for holding your point of view.

*Begin by creating a list so that you know you will have enough points to argue effectively. For example…*

Schools should be self-sufficient because:

- educational projects help children appreciate food
- it is healthier to grow vegetables without pesticides
- generating your own energy saves money to spend on learning.

### 2 Planning a compelling argument

Choose the most effective arguments that you can think of to include in your text.

Creating a flowchart can help you think of how to direct your text convincingly.

*Make notes of the language techniques you want to use and examples to include.*

### 3 Developing the argument

Work through your chart progressively, backing up your points with powerful adjectives, sentences of contrasting lengths and a strong conclusion.

**Skills practice >>>**

Produce a flowchart to plan a persuasive text *against* the argument in the example above.

## Recounts

### You must be able to...

- link the key information needed
- organise your narrative clearly and chronologically
- create a balanced text using appropriate language.

**Example:** My school's sports day.

### 1 Linking the key information

Recounts should cover the questions listed in the spider diagram below.

*Remember these key words and write notes for each to link the points to your chosen topic.*

### 2 Organising points clearly and chronologically

Recounts are chronological (they describe a sequence of events) accounts and so should be written in the order in which the events happen. Don't jump about between events when you are writing these texts!

*Put your points in date order before you begin writing.*

### 3 Creating a balanced text

Use an introduction to set the context of the recount. The concluding paragraph can be used to sum up your thoughts on the events.

*Use the past tense and time connectives (such as 'then', 'next', 'later', 'after that') to pull your text together.*

**Skills practice**

Create a spider diagram with notes for a recount about your school sports day.

You must be able to...

 choose the correct format for the type of letter you are writing

 plan the contents depending on the purpose

 use the correct language style.

## 1 Choosing the correct format for your letter

The first thing to decide on is the sort of letter you are writing. Is it a formal business letter or a friendly informal letter?

### *Business letters*

Business letters use both formal language and formal layout. As such letters are often word-processed, it is important to know how to lay out your letter heading before you begin.

*Business letters may be letters of complaint, interest, apology, appeal, application or resignation.*

### *Friendly letters*

Friendly letters are written in a less formal style. They may be thank-you letters, friendly family letters or letters inviting the recipient to an event or party. Postcards are also written in a less formal way. For very personal letters, there are no style rules!

### *Other written communication*

Letters are being replaced by email and fax messages. Both of these message types can be written formally or informally, depending on whether they are being used for business or personal communication.

## 2 Planning the contents

Decide the purpose of the letter and list the main points that you need to include.

### *Formal letters*

Refer to the table opposite to help you remember how to write a formal letter. The first paragraph should be short and state the purpose of the letter.

The middle paragraphs should include all the relevant information linked to the purpose of the letter.

The final paragraph should set out what you want to happen in response to the letter or your intended course of action.

## 3 Using the correct language style

The vocabulary you choose and the sentence structure will depend on whether the letter is formal or informal. For business letters there are writing conventions that need to be followed.

### *Abbreviations used in letter writing:*

**asap** as soon as possible

**cc** carbon copy (used when you have also sent the letter to somebody else; this is followed by the name of the person the letter is copied to)

**enc** documents enclosed with the letter

**pp** per procurationem (Latin; meaning that the letter has been signed on somebody else's behalf)

**ps** postscript (additional information added after the letter has been signed and finished)

**PTO** – please turn over (usually in informal letters)

**RSVP** répondez si vous plaît (French; meaning that a reply is required).

### *Friendly letters*

These letters are written in the style of everyday speech. There are no formal language conventions. The salutations and endings are personal and varied.

Dear... Love from... Bye for now...

Your affectionate niece... Your good friend...

Looking forward to seeing you...

| Formal letters | |
|---|---|
| *Purpose* | *Example* |
| Salutations | • Dear Ms Jones<br>• Dear Sir or Madam |
| Beginnings | • We are writing to inform/to request...<br>• I would be interested in receiving... |
| Making a request | • We are writing to request...<br>• Would it be possible for... |
| When replying to a letter | • With reference to your letter of 14th December... |
| Complaining | • It is with regret that I write to...<br>• I am very dissatisfied with... |
| Regret | • I am extremely sorry for any inconvenience...<br>• We regret the late delivery of... |
| Final comments | • If you require more information...<br>• For further details of this order... |
| Ending a formal letter | • Yours sincerely (use for correspondence that begins with a name, e.g. Ms Jones)<br>• Yours faithfully (use for letters that begin with Dear Sir, Dear Madam)<br>• Regards (used formally on a regular basis) |

### Skills practice

Write the opening paragraph of a letter complaining about a computer game that you have bought that will not open on your laptop.

# Writing tasks

**Choose your writing task from the following selection.**

## Fiction, plays and poetry

### *Fiction*

1 Write a plan for a humorous story about a family who adopt a rescue dog.

2 'And that is why the cliffs of Dover are white.' Write a plan for a story that ends with this sentence.

3 Write a plan for a story called 'My baby brother is a spy!'

4 Write the opening paragraph for a story about a ride in a hot-air balloon.

5 Write the opening paragraph for a story about a mysterious new pupil who joins your class.

6 'At first, nobody noticed the strange little man carrying the green umbrella…' Continue the first paragraph of this story.

7 Write the final paragraph for a story about a school trip that ends in disaster because the coach driver could not read a map.

### *Play script*

8 Write the first scene for a play set in a zoo where a tiger has escaped from its enclosure.

9 Write a scene of your choice for a play about an argument with a close friend.

### *Poetry*

10 Write a short poem about waking up to snow.

## Non-fiction

11 Write planning notes for a discussion text about whether animals should be used in circuses.

12 Write the plan for a report about endangered species.

13 Plan a short text about a luxury ski resort, designed to encourage people to visit.

14 Plan a talk about a school trip you particularly enjoyed.

15 Write the opening paragraph of a report about a sport or hobby you enjoy.

16 Write a short argument in favour of banning the sale of sweets and crisps to children.

17 Write a brief explanatory text about how to care for a pet of your choice.

18 Write instructions for making a snack of your choice.

19 Write the text for a magazine advertisement for a new breakfast cereal.

20 Write a letter to your local council complaining about the removal of play equipment from a local park.

# Comprehension

**Read this text carefully before answering the questions that follow.**

The morning after the storm dawned bright and fresh, though the sky, painted with vivid streaks of crimson cloud, hinted at further inclemency ahead. Kate hurriedly pulled on her boots and shrugged on her coarse wool coat before racing out of the door to join Polly, who was hopping from foot to foot in an agitated fashion on the doorstep. Born on Christmas day, Polly was six months older than Kate and the daughter of a local fisherman. The girls had always been inseparable and Kate silently thanked her friend for including her in this morning's adventure.

'Come on!' hissed Polly, clattering down the deserted lane towards the beach at a sprint, her long legs easily outpacing Kate's tiny frame.

'What cargo, Polly?' shouted Kate, pulling at the rough collar of her coat as she struggled to keep up in the wake of her companion.

'Don't… know,' panted Polly. 'The first… crate's just… washed up. Dad's gone ahead… with a crowbar. Nobody else knows yet though, so… keep your voice down!'

Skirting a row of fishermen's cottages, the girls came in sight of the sea. Impaled on the rocky headland, they saw the stricken wreck of a merchant ship reaching sadly into the sky, its mast broken and its sails in tatters. Its cargo bobbed on the now calm water, like the toy boats the youngest inhabitants of the village liked to sail on the pond. Further down the beach the girls saw Polly's father wrestling to breach a large crate that had come to rest in the shallow water among splintered planks from the ship's shattered hull and scraps of sail fabric. Levering off the lid, he reached into the crate and in triumph held up bolts of ruby and jade fabric which glinted in the sun.
Kate had never seen anything so colourful.

'It's silk,' he called. 'And it's *dry*. Fetch your mothers!'

**Write your answers on the lines provided, unless you are instructed otherwise. When you are given a choice of answers, write the option you think is correct (A, B, C, D, E or X) on the lines provided. *Do not write answers in the 'Mark' column.***

TARGET TIME :55 **55 minutes**

**!** Note: the questions in this test are challenging, and are intended to find out which skills you may need to develop to achieve success in the 11+ tests.

**Mark**

**1** What do the village children like to play with on the pond?

______________________________

**2** What was the village like when the story took place?

**A** bustling **B** stormy **C** quiet **D** crowded **E** dark ______

Mark

**3** How is Polly feeling at the start of the story?

**A** nervous **B** frightened **C** impatient **D** angry **E** surprised ______

**4** Find two things from this list, mentioned in the story, that were washed up on the beach.

1 the broken mast
2 scraps of sail fabric
3 toy boats
4 a crate
5 shells

**A** 1 and 4 only
**B** 2 and 5 only
**C** 3 and 4 only
**D** 2 and 4 only
**E** 1 and 2 only ______

**5** Why did Polly include Kate in what she was doing?

______

**6** Which of the two girls is the taller?

______

**7** In what month was Kate born?

**A** April **B** June **C** August **D** September **E** December ______

**8** Why do you think none of the other villagers knew about the wreck yet?

**A** Only the fishermen could see the sea from their homes.
**B** It was early morning and they were still sleeping.
**C** It was the middle of the night.
**D** They were already at work.
**E** The shipwreck had only just happened. ______

**9** Why did Polly want to keep the discovery secret from the other villagers?

______

**10** Why does the writer include ellipsis (…) for when Polly is explaining to Kate about the crate washing up (lines 12–13)?

**A** to break the sentence up and make it easier to read
**B** to give the impression that Polly keeps forgetting what she is saying
**C** to give the impression that Polly is out of breath
**D** it is a typing error
**E** to give the impression that Polly is speaking very quietly. ______

**11** What effect does the use of italics have for 'dry' (line 23)?

______

**12** Which of these phrases best describes what the fifth paragraph is about?

**A** the shipwreck
**B** what is in the crate
**C** the weather
**D** Polly's father
**E** what the girls see ______

**13** Why do you think the writer says that the ship was 'impaled' at the start of the sentence, rather than in the middle (line 14)?

______

**14** What do you think the word 'coarse' means in line 3?

**A** rough **B** straight **C** plain **D** cheap **E** warm ______

Mark

**15** Why did the writer choose the words 'ruby' and 'jade' to describe the colours of the fabrics (line 21)?

______________________________

**16** Why do you think Polly's father does not mind that Kate comes to the beach with Polly, even though the other villagers are not told about the crate on the beach?

______________________________

**17** Which three words best create the impression that the ship has been devastated by being wrecked?

**A** coarse, bobbed, wreck
**B** impaled, sadly, cargo
**C** broken, shattered, splintered
**D** tatters, scraps, crate
**E** deserted, crowbar, wrestling ______

**18** Which of these facts most strongly suggests that the story is set in the past?

**A** Kate wears boots.
**B** The fishermen live in cottages.
**C** Polly's father is a fisherman.
**D** The ship has sails.
**E** The village children play with toy boats. ______

**19** Why do you think Kate had never seen anything as colourful as the silk in the crate?

______________________________

# Grammar

**20** **The girls had always been inseparable and Kate silently thanked her friend for including her in this morning's adventure.**

What part of speech is the word 'inseparable' in the above sentence?

**A** noun **B** adjective **C** preposition **D** adverb **E** verb ______

**21** **Skirting a row of fishermen's cottages, the girls came in sight of the sea.**

What part of speech is the word 'skirting' in the above sentence?

**A** verb **B** preposition **C** pronoun **D** possessive pronoun
**E** adjective ______

**22** **Its cargo bobbed on the now calm water, like the toy boats the youngest inhabitants of the village liked to sail on the pond.**

What part of speech is the word 'Its' in the above sentence?

**A** adverb **B** definite article **C** verb
**D** noun **E** pronoun ______

**23** What sort of language technique has the author used when describing the 'crimson cloud' (line 2)?

**A** onomatopoeia **B** metaphor **C** alliteration
**D** simile **E** assonance ______

Mark

**24** What sort of language technique has the author used when describing how Polly 'hissed' at Kate (line 8)?

**A** metaphor **B** simile **C** personification

**D** onomatopoeia **E** alliteration ______

**25** What sort of language technique has the author used when describing how the wreck was 'reaching sadly' into the sky (line 15)?

**A** personification **B** alliteration **C** simile

**D** metaphor **E** onomatopoeia ______

Choose the word that will fit best at the beginning of these sentences. Write the letter for the answer you think is correct on the lines provided.

**26 … cargo from shipwrecks was an important source of income for the villagers.**

**A** Huge **B** Safe **C** Risking **D** Salvaging **E** Crate ______

**27 … crew members were given food and shelter by the families of the fishermen.**

**A** Hurrying **B** Rescued **C** Captain **D** Them **E** Wreck ______

**28** Circle a verb from each of the pairs so that the text makes sense and the verbs agree.

**Sometimes a ship would *run/ran* aground and *lose/loose* its cargo, *risked/risking* the lives of the crew who *were/was* often unable to swim.**

**29** Circle a verb from each of the pairs so that the text makes sense and the verbs agree.

**Historically, seaside communities would *make/made* use of everything they *find/found* on the beach to *provided/provide* extra luxuries their families would not have *had/has* otherwise.**

**30** Select the correct verb to complete the sentence.

None of the villagers

| knows | knowed | knew | knowing | known |
|---|---|---|---|---|
| A | B | C | D | E |

**what was inside the other crates.** ______

**31** Choose the correct word to complete this sentence so that it makes sense.

The rocky headlands

| does | do | did | didn't | done |
|---|---|---|---|---|
| A | B | C | D | E |

**still pose a risk to ships today.** ______

## Punctuation

**32** Pick out the section with the punctuation error. If they are all correct, choose X.

| Running back to fetch their mothers the | girls encountered groups of villagers |
|---|---|
| A | B |

| heading in the opposite direction, | towards the beach. | |
|---|---|---|
| C | D | X |

______

Mark

**33** Rewrite the text with the punctuation corrected.

**as each crate was opened the crowd held its breath. would this be the crate to make them all rich**

________________________________________

________________________________________

**34** Pick out the section with the punctuation error. If they are all correct, choose X.

| Sturdy crates, their lids | removed and their contents plundered, littered | | |
|---|---|---|---|
| **A** | **B** | | |
| **the shoreline as the villagers headed** | **for home with their bounty.** | | |
| **C** | **D** | **X** | ______ |

**35** Pick out the section with the punctuation error. If they are all correct, choose X.

| 'I shall have a dress out of | this!' giggled Polly, holding up a length | | |
|---|---|---|---|
| **A** | **B** | | |
| **of jade silk, and so shall** | **you, Katie!'** | | |
| **C** | **D** | **X** | ______ |

**36** Rewrite the sentence with the punctuation corrected.

**Its a good thing we got to the beach before the others remarked Dad as they sat around the fire that evening.**

________________________________________

________________________________________

**37** Pick out the section with the punctuation error. If they are all correct, choose X.

| When the villagers had finished with | the crates washed up on the | |
|---|---|---|
| **A** | **B** | |
| **beach, they turned their attention to the stricken** | | |
| **C** | | |
| **ship itself there would certainly be further treasures inside.** | | |
| **D** | **X** | ______ |

## Spelling

**38** Pick out the section with **no** spelling errors. If they are all correct, choose X.

| The storms had damaged many of | the roovs of the cottages and all over | |
|---|---|---|
| **A** | **B** | |
| **the villige mans were up ladders replacing loose tiles** | | |
| **C** | | |
| **and patching larger holees with oilcloths.** | | |
| **D** | **X** | ______ |

Mark

**39** Copy the sentence below, correcting any spelling errors.

**Polly's father brought donkies from his fields to pull the trollies that were filled with boltes of silk, carved wooden boxs and china vazes.**

______________________________

______________________________

**40** Pick out the section with **no** spelling errors. If they are all correct, choose X.

**If geting to the shipwreck was difficult, clambering** (A) **over the rocks themselves, nobly with** (B) **limpets and covered with slimmy seaweed,** (C) **was even more challenging.** (D) X ______

**41** Choose the option in which all three words are spelt correctly to complete the sentence.

**…, a large section of mast broke free and … into the … below.**

**A** suddenly, clatered, water **B** sudenly, clattered, watter **C** suddenly, clatered, water
**D** suddenly, clattered, water **E** sudenly, clattered, water ______

**42** Pick out the section with **no** spelling errors. If they are all correct, choose X.

**The unexpected arrivle of so** (A) **much valuable cloth was an** (B)
**amazing boost for the plainley dressed village** (C)
**women who longed to be fashionnable.** (D) X ______

**43** Copy the sentence below, correcting any spelling errors.

**Allthough there was a worked lighthouse on the dangeros headland, it was inpossible for disfortunate ships to avoid the perilous rocks in high winds.**

______________________________

______________________________

**44** Pick out the section with **no** spelling errors. If they are all correct, choose X.

**Like their neighbours, Kate's family** (A) **lived in poverty and were always greatful** (B)
**when her friend brougt** (C) **them serials from the farm.** (D) X ______

**45** Choose the option in which all three words are spelt correctly to complete the sentence.

**The village pub displayed a … , ancient … , recovered after a violent storm, which was studded with … jewels.**

**A** valuble, chalice, precious
**B** valuable, chalice, precious
**C** valuable, challice, precios
**D** valuble, chalace, presious
**E** valueble, challice, precous ______

**TEST ENDS**

 

# Placement test *answer grid*

*Follow the instructions on pages 4–5 to fill in and use this grid.*

| Test score | | Practice planner | | | | |
|---|---|---|---|---|---|---|
| *Question* | *Error* | *Skill* | *Page* | *To do* | *Achieved* | *Time (mins)* |
| **1 Understanding fiction and non-fiction** | | | | | | |
| | | Understanding fiction, plays and poetry | 6 | | | 75 |
| | | **Comprehension *test 1*** | 10 | | | 20 |
| | | Understanding non-fiction | 12 | | | 130 |
| | | **Comprehension *test 2*** | 19 | | | 20 |
| **2 Test skills** | | | | | **Total Section 1** | **145** |
| ***Comprehension*** | | | | | | |
| 1 | | Skimming and scanning text | 21 | 17 mins | 7 mins | |
| 2 | | | | | | |
| 3 | | Finding information | 22 | 17 mins | 7 mins | |
| 4 | | | | | | |
| 5 | | | | | | |
| 6 | | | | | | |
| 7 | | Deduction and inference | 23 | 17 mins | 7 mins | |
| 8 | | | | | | |
| 9 | | | | | | |
| 10 | | Organisation of text | 24 | 17 mins | 7 mins | |
| 11 | | | | | | |
| 12 | | | | | | |
| 13 | | | | | | |
| 14 | | How writers use language | 25 | 17 mins | 7 mins | |
| 15 | | | | | | |
| 16 | | Writer's viewpoint | 26 | 17 mins | 7 mins | |
| 17 | | | | | | |
| 18 | | Traditional and social context | 27 | 17 mins | 7 mins | |
| 19 | | | | | | |
| | | **Comprehension *test 3*** | 28 | | | 18 |
| ***Grammar*** | | | | | | |
| 20 | | Parts of speech | 30 | 17 mins | 7 mins | |
| 21 | | | | | | |
| 22 | | | | | | |
| 23 | | Figurative language | 31 | 17 mins | 7 mins | |
| 24 | | | | | | |
| 25 | | | | | | |
| 26 | | Starting sentences | 32 | 17 mins | 7 mins | |
| 27 | | | | | | |
| 28 | | Agreement in sentences | 33 | 17 mins | 7 mins | |
| 29 | | | | | | |
| 30 | | | | | | |
| 31 | | | | | | |
| | | **Grammar *test*** | 34 | | | 18 |
| ***Punctuation*** | | | | | | |
| 32 | | Basic punctuation | 36 | 17 mins | 7 mins | |
| 33 | | | | | | |
| 34 | | | | | | |
| 35 | | More about punctuation | 37 | 17 mins | 7 mins | |
| 36 | | | | | | |
| 37 | | | | | | |
| | | **Punctuation *test*** | 38 | | | 10 |
| ***Spelling*** | | | | | | |
| 38 | | Plurals and spelling rules | 39 | 17 mins | 7 mins | |
| 39 | | | | | | |
| 40 | | Doubling letters | 40 | 17 mins | 7 mins | |
| 41 | | | | | | |
| 42 | | Prefixes and suffixes | 41 | 17 mins | 7 mins | |
| 43 | | | | | | |
| 44 | | Tricky spellings | 42 | 17 mins | 7 mins | |
| 45 | | | | | | |
| | | **Spelling *test*** | 43 | | | 10 |
| | | | | | **Total Section 2** | |
| **Total** | | Count up the boxes that you **have not** put crosses in and write this total in the box. | **Total test score** / **45** × 100 = | | % | |
| **3 Writing skills** | | | | | | |
| | | Writing fiction, plays and poetry | 44 | | | 60 |
| | | Writing non-fiction | 47 | | | 125 |
| | | **Writing tasks** | 51 | | | 15 |
| | | | | | **Total Section 3** | **200** |
| | | | | | **Total practice time** | |

# Practice tests answer grids

*Follow the instructions on page 5 to fill in and use these grids.*

## Comprehension *test 1* (Fiction) — Page 10

| Question | Error | Skill | Page | Notes | Review × | Achieved ✓ |
|---|---|---|---|---|---|---|
| 1 | | Skimming and scanning text | 21 | | | |
| 2 | | | | | | |
| 3 | | Finding information | 22 | | | |
| 4 | | | | | | |
| 5 | | Deduction and inference | 23 | | | |
| 6 | | | | | | |
| 7 | | | | | | |
| 8 | | | | | | |
| 9 | | Organisation of text | 24 | | | |
| 10 | | How writers use language | 25 | | | |
| 11 | | | | | | |
| 12 | | Writer's viewpoint | 26 | | | |
| 13 | | | | | | |
| 14 | | Traditional and social context | 27 | | | |
| 15 | | | | | | |

**Total** [ ] Count up the boxes that you **have not** put crosses in and write this total in the box.

$\frac{\text{Test score}}{15} \times 100 =$ [ ] %

## Comprehension *test 2* (Non-fiction) — Page 19

| Question | Error | Skill | Page | Notes | Review × | Achieved ✓ |
|---|---|---|---|---|---|---|
| 1 | | Skimming and scanning text | 21 | | | |
| 2 | | | | | | |
| 3 | | Finding information | 22 | | | |
| 4 | | | | | | |
| 5 | | Deduction and inference | 23 | | | |
| 6 | | | | | | |
| 7 | | | | | | |
| 8 | | Organisation of text | 24 | | | |
| 9 | | | | | | |
| 10 | | How writers use language | 25 | | | |
| 11 | | | | | | |
| 12 | | Writer's viewpoint | 26 | | | |
| 13 | | | | | | |
| 14 | | Traditional and social context | 27 | | | |
| 15 | | | | | | |

**Total** [ ] Count up the boxes that you **have not** put crosses in and write this total in the box.

$\frac{\text{Test score}}{15} \times 100 =$ [ ] %

## Comprehension *test 3* — Page 28

| Question | Error | Skill | Page | Notes | | Review × | Achieved ✓ |
|---|---|---|---|---|---|---|---|
| **Fiction** | | | | | | | |
| 1 | | Skimming and scanning text | 21 | | | | |
| 2 | | Finding information | 22 | | | | |
| 3 | | Deduction and inference | 23 | | | | |
| 4 | | Organisation of text | 24 | | | | |
| 5 | | How writers use language | 25 | | | | |
| 6 | | Writer's viewpoint | 26 | | | | |
| 7 | | Traditional and social context | 27 | | | | |
| **Non-fiction** | | | | | | | |
| 8 | | Skimming and scanning text | 21 | | | | |
| 9 | | Finding information | 22 | | | | |
| 10 | | Deduction and inference | 23 | | | | |
| 11 | | Organisation of text | 24 | | | | |
| 12 | | How writers use language | 25 | | | | |
| 13 | | Writer's viewpoint | 26 | | | | |
| 14 | | Traditional and social context | 27 | | | | |

**Total** [ ] Count up the boxes that you **have not** put crosses in and write this total in the box.

$\frac{\text{Test score}}{14} \times 100 =$ [ ] %

# Practice tests *answer grids*

*Follow the instructions on page 5 to fill in and use these grids.*

## Grammar *test* — Page 34

| Question | Error | Skill | Page | Notes | Review × | Achieved ✓ |
|---|---|---|---|---|---|---|
| 1 | | Parts of speech | 30 | | | |
| 2 | | | | | | |
| 3 | | | | | | |
| 4 | | Figurative language | 31 | | | |
| 5 | | | | | | |
| 6 | | | | | | |
| 7 | | Starting sentences | 32 | | | |
| 8 | | | | | | |
| 9 | | | | | | |
| 10 | | Agreement in sentences | 33 | | | |
| 11 | | | | | | |
| 12 | | | | | | |
| 13 | | | | | | |
| 14 | | | | | | |
| 15 | | | | | | |

**Total** [ ] Count up the boxes that you **have not** put crosses in and write this total in the box.

$\frac{\text{Test score}}{15} \times 100 =$ [ ] %

## Punctuation *test* — Page 38

| Question | Error | Skill | Page | Notes | Review × | Achieved ✓ |
|---|---|---|---|---|---|---|
| 1 | | Basic punctuation | 36 | | | |
| 2 | | | | | | |
| 3 | | | | | | |
| 4 | | | | | | |
| 5 | | More about punctuation | 37 | | | |
| 6 | | | | | | |
| 7 | | | | | | |
| 8 | | | | | | |

**Total** [ ] Count up the boxes that you **have not** put crosses in and write this total in the box.

$\frac{\text{Test score}}{8} \times 100 =$ [ ] %

## Spelling *test* — Page 43

| Question | Error | Skill | Page | Notes | Review × | Achieved ✓ |
|---|---|---|---|---|---|---|
| 1 | | Plurals and spelling rules | 39 | | | |
| 2 | | | | | | |
| 3 | | Doubling letters | 40 | | | |
| 4 | | | | | | |
| 5 | | Prefixes and suffixes | 41 | | | |
| 6 | | | | | | |
| 7 | | Tricky spellings | 42 | | | |
| 8 | | | | | | |

**Total** [ ] Count up the boxes that you **have not** put crosses in and write this total in the box.

$\frac{\text{Test score}}{8} \times 100 =$ [ ] %

# Writing tasks *checklist*

*Go to the question number of the Writing task you have completed, as shown below. Tick the boxes for each skill you feel you have achieved successfully. Consider completing another Writing task if you have missed any skills.*

## Fiction, plays and poetry

### *Fiction*

| Question | Planning stories | |
|---|---|---|
| 1, 2, 3 | Spider diagram or similar plan | ☐ |
| | Outline of where story begins, problem/mystery, resolution | ☐ |
| | Outline of key events | ☐ |
| | Outline of setting and characters | ☐ |
| | Notes on balance of text (narrative, description and dialogue) | ☐ |
| | **Opening paragraphs** | |
| 4, 5, 6 | Opening sentence that captures the reader's interest (Qs 4, 5) | ☐ |
| | An introduction to what will happen | ☐ |
| | Use of description to create the mood and atmosphere | ☐ |
| | Reference to the setting and at least one of the characters | ☐ |
| | **Concluding paragraphs** | |
| 7 | Concluding sentence that creates impact | ☐ |
| | A clear resolution or climax | ☐ |
| | Use of description to create the mood and atmosphere | ☐ |
| | Reference to the setting and at least one of the characters | ☐ |

### *Play script*

| | | |
|---|---|---|
| 8, 9 | Cast list of actors (at least 2) who appear in the scene | ☐ |
| | Stage directions giving outline of setting and position of characters | ☐ |
| | Text laid out with actors' names followed by their dialogue | ☐ |
| | Clear development of the storyline through the scene | ☐ |
| | Use of description to create the mood and atmosphere | ☐ |

### *Poetry*

| | | |
|---|---|---|
| 10 | Structure matches the chosen form (see table on page 46) | ☐ |
| | Rhyming pattern (if used) carried through poem | ☐ |
| | Varied use of description, e.g. similes, metaphors, alliteration | ☐ |
| | Description that includes more than one sense, e.g. taste, sound | ☐ |

## Non-fiction

| Question | Planning non-fiction | |
|---|---|---|
| 11, 12, 13, 14 | Spider diagram or similar plan with notes on paragraph contents | ☐ |
| | Notes for content of introduction and conclusion | ☐ |
| | Notes on audience being addressed | ☐ |
| | Balanced points listed for discussion text (Q11); Biased points listed for persuasive text (Q13); what?, when?, who?, why?, where?, how? questions listed for recount (Q14) | ☐ |
| | **Opening paragraphs** | |
| 15 | Opening sentence that captures the reader's interest | ☐ |
| | An introduction to the points to be explained | ☐ |
| | Language level suitable for audience being addressed | ☐ |
| | Detail of content suitable for audience being addressed | ☐ |
| | **Complete texts** | |
| 16, 17, 18, 19, 20 | Features of text type link to chart on page 24 | ☐ |
| | Clear introduction/opening and conclusion (Qs 16, 17, 20) | ☐ |
| | Instructions/points in a clear and logical order including all steps (Qs 18, 20) | ☐ |
| | Language appropriate to the text type, e.g. powerful adjectives (Qs 16, 19, 20), clear explanations (Q17), imperative verbs (Q18) | ☐ |

# Placement test

## Comprehension

1 They like to sail toy boats.
2 C: quiet. The second paragraph mentions the lane was 'deserted'.
3 C: impatient. Polly was 'hopping from foot to foot in an agitated fashion', suggesting that she was eager to go.
4 D: 2 and 4 only
5 Polly included Kate because they had been close friends for a long time. The first paragraph mentions that the girls had 'always been inseparable'.
6 Polly. The text mentions Polly's 'long legs' and that she was 'outpacing Kate's tiny frame'.
7 B: June. The first paragraph mentions that Polly is six months older than Kate.
8 B: It was early morning and they were still sleeping.
9 An answer that explains that by keeping the wreck a secret, Polly's family and Kate would be able to see what had been washed up before anyone else and therefore might be able to keep the most valuable things for themselves.
10 C: to give the impression that Polly is out of breath
11 An answer that explains that italics can be used to highlight something unusual or important; that it is unusual and lucky for cargo from a wreck to remain dry and that the silk will be worth more because it is dry.
12 E: what the girls see
13 An answer that explains that 'impaled' is a dramatic word and placing it at the beginning of a sentence creates a powerful impression of the sight that greeted the girls as they arrived at the beach.
14 A: rough. We are told the collar is 'rough' in line 10.
15 An answer that recognises that as well as describing the colours of the silk, jade and ruby are precious stones and that this highlights the value as well as the beauty of the silk.
16 An answer that explains that Polly's father understands that Kate is a close friend of Polly.
17 C: broken, shattered, splintered
18 D: The ship has sails.
19 An answer that explains that Kate probably lives quite a plain life and would not be able to afford expensive and colourful clothes/travel to exotic places.

## Grammar

20 B: adjective
21 A: verb
22 E: pronoun
23 C: alliteration
24 D: onomatopoeia
25 A: personification
26 D: Salvaging
27 B: Rescued
28 run; lose; risking; were
29 make; found; provide; had
30 C: knew
31 B: do

## Punctuation

32 A: Running back to fetch their mothers, the
33 As each crate was opened, the crowd held its breath. Would this be the crate to make them all rich?
34 X – they are all correct.
35 C: of jade silk, 'and so shall
36 "It's a good thing we got to the beach before the others," remarked Dad, as they sat around the fire that evening.
37 D: ship itself; there would certainly be further treasures inside.

## Spelling

38 A: The storms had damaged many of…
39 Polly's father brought <u>donkeys</u> from his fields to pull the <u>trolleys</u> that were filled with <u>bolts</u> of silk, carved wooden <u>boxes</u> and china <u>vases</u>.
40 D: was even more challenging.
41 D: suddenly, clattered, water
42 B: …much valuable cloth was an…
43 <u>Although</u> there was a <u>working</u> lighthouse on the <u>dangerous</u> headland, it was <u>impossible</u> for <u>unfortunate</u> ships to avoid the perilous rocks in high winds.
44 A: Like their neighbours, Kate's family…
45 B: valuable, chalice, precious

# Skills practice

## 1 Understanding fiction and non-fiction

## Understanding fiction, plays and poetry

### Stories 7

1 Contemporary fiction (set in the present day, and cannot be put into any other genre sensibly)
2 The weather was wet (because the ground was muddy).
3 B: because the earth holds on to her wellies.

### Plays 8

1 To scare away the wolf.
2 It goes out. / An eclipse occurs.

### Poetry 9

1 structured poem – verse (because of the verses, this is clearly a structured poem, but the pattern of 'beats' does not fit into any of the standard forms described on page 46)
2 D: A, A, B, B
3 buzzes

## Understanding non-fiction

### Discussion texts 12

1 Should all children be provided with a laptop by their school?
2 The author doesn't think the government should fund computers for every child.
3 A: a government representative

### Explanatory texts 13

1 The tides are either higher or lower than usual.
2 The last paragraph

### Instructional and procedural texts 14

1 B: bulleted list
2 oven, baking paper, square tin, weighing scales, medium pan, brush, knife, stirring spoon, chopping board, grater for lemon zest
3 4 (remove, leave to cool, turn out, cut)

### Non-chronological reports 15

1 Paragraph 2 is an explanation of the design of bows and arrows.
Paragraph 4 is about hunting with bows and arrows/using bows and arrows as survival tools.
2 Any three of the following: not structured by time; unlikely to have headings; arranged in paragraphs; may include glossaries, additional references and illustrations; do not have bias; factual.
3 D: to provide general information about bows and arrows.

### Persuasive writing 16

1 C: 1 and 2 (because 'detritus' means 'waste' and 'jargonese' means 'difficult to understand')
2 Shorter meetings, more productivity and higher profits for British business.

### Recount texts 17

1 middle-aged or older (she has grey hair)
2 She thought the statue would be coming home as her Uncle always lets her have her own way/spoils her.
3 C: It had been bombed.

### Letter writing 18

1 B: I am at the end of my tether
2 To prevent Mary bringing her lamb to school.

## 2 Test skills

## Comprehension

### Skimming and scanning text 21

The answer is 'games', although it would be easy to answer 'celebrity programmes' if you did not read the text closely.

### Finding information 22

The answer should include that the text will be about the city of Athens and will give information about where to go and what to do.

### Deduction and inference 23

Text 1 is written in technical language that is obviously intended for a specialist audience. Text 2 is written in less technical language, which suggests it is for a more general audience.

### Organisation of text 24

Historical; play script

# Skills practice answers

## How writers use language 25

1 Metaphor

2 Personification

## Writer's viewpoint 26

"What do you mean?" I asked, knowing exactly what Ann had implied.

"There were six sweets left and now there are two" stated Ann. She always knew how to annoy me.

Answers will vary.

## Traditional and social context 27

The reef, as well as the names of the towns, give clues as to this Australian location. The activities make it clear the place described is on a warm coast.

# Grammar

## Parts of speech 30

1 Sylvie went shopping and bought some *green* gloves, some *blue* tights and a *bobble* hat. (nouns underlined, adjectives italic).

**He** *played* quietly on **his** games console on Saturday morning. (pronouns bold, verbs italic, adverbs underlined)

The mouse raced across the room, under the piano and into his hole, *which* infuriated the cat. (prepositions underlined, conjunction italic)

## Figurative language 31

1 The poisonous mushroom looked like a sinister umbrella dripping black blood on to the emerald grass it grew from.

2 a – A; b – E; c – D

3 D

## Starting sentences 32

1 a – A; b – E; c – B

2 a – A; b – E

## Agreement in sentences 33

1 drifted, covering

2 I drove to the shop and bought a carton of milk.

3 try

4 C; C

# Punctuation

## Basic punctuation 36

1 Stop! Where are you going? I want to know.

2 On Tuesday, Abeshek, Kylie and Yang were playing Monopoly in the kitchen.

## More about punctuation 37

1 1 and 2 are correct

2 3 This sentence needs brackets to show the stage direction.

Hannah: I don't want to come to your party. (starting to snivel)

# Spelling

## Plurals and spelling rules 39

1 The witches collected frogs, leaves, teeth, elves and deer ready for the mystery quizzes.

2 The oxen carried the children to the fields where the sheep were grazing.

3 The beautiful maiden happily skipped gracefully down the castle steps.

4 Hopping across the field the hare enjoyed the autumn weather.

## Doubling letters 40

1 I was hoping for a new bike for my birthday but I got swimming lessons instead.

2 I was feeling hungry so my mum brought me some broccoli quiche.

3 Generally I go shopping with Mum but this weekend I went with Grandma.

4 Occasionally I misspell words when I am not concentrating.

## Prefixes and suffixes 41

1 The hamburger restaurant was overpriced.

2 The bicyclist was thinking of purchasing a unicycle.

## Tricky spellings 42

1 The boy was not allowed to see his birthday present.

2 The profit from the business deal was less than the board was expecting.

3 The knitting pattern required a pair of size eight needles.

# 3 Writing skills

# Writing fiction, plays and poetry

## Writing stories 44

1 The order of text should follow the outline in the question. *Answers will vary.*

2 Adjectives and nouns should be relevant to a sunny day or windy day. *Answers will vary.*

## Writing plays 45

1 The conventions of play scripts, outlined in the text, should be followed. *Answers will vary.*

2 Ten exchanges should be included. *Answers will vary.*

## Writing poems 46

1 **a** Rhyming words: pedal, medal; shoot, dispute; racing, pacing, placing; lose, shoes, choose

**b** Syllables: 1: choose, lose, shoes, shoot; 2: dispute, pedal, medal, swimming, running, cycling; 3: celebrate

2 The table should be split into the categories stated. *Any relevant answers are acceptable.*

# Writing non-fiction

## Discussion texts 47

*Answers will vary.*

## Explanatory texts 47

*Answers will vary.*

## Instructional, procedural texts 48

*Answers will vary.*

## Non-chronological reports 48

*Answers will vary.*

## Persuasive writing 49

*Answers will vary.*

## Recounts 49

*Answers will vary.*

## Letter writing 50

*Answers will vary.*

# Practice tests

## Comprehension *test 1* (Fiction) 10

1 An answer that explains that Tom captured the creature by putting a glass mixing bowl over it.

This is stated in line 12.

2 B: plastic bags

This is stated in line 7.

3 E: tiles

The first sentence states it was a 'tiled hallway'.

4 Barney is the family dog.

This is stated in line 6.

5 D: brothers

The reference to 'their driveway' means that these are brothers living in the same house, rather than friends.

6 B: Mum's car

The conversation makes it clear that Mum will be home soon and won't be pleased. When the scrunch of gravel is heard, the boys make it clear they know Mum has arrived home.

7 An answer that acknowledges that Tom seems to know more about the origin of the creature and/or that Max notes that it is Tom who will be in trouble when Mum gets home.

8 An answer that recognises that the writer wants to maintain some mystery about exactly what the creature is, in order to interest the reader in finding out more.

9 B: to stress that Max believes it must be an alien

10 An answer that explains that 'skitter' creates the impression of rapid and chaotic movement and/or skitter is an onomatopoeia which describes the scratching noise the creature made while skidding on the tiled floor.

11 A: havoc

The description in the following sentence signals this is the correct answer.

12 B: menacing

13 An answer that explains that by not revealing what the creature is, the writer encourages the readers to make up their own minds about it.

14 An answer that argues that the story is set in the present, near past or near future, because the boys' mother drives a car and the existence of aliens is thought possible by some people.

15 B: very unlikely to think it was an alien rather than a goblin or a pixie

## Comprehension *test 2* (Non-fiction) 19

1 An answer that explains that the Romans built their communal toilets two thousand years ago.

2 D: clothes

This is explained in line 15.

3 B: open

Line 12 states that they were 'open drains in the street'.

4 An answer that explains that Roman communal toilets were built to have a social purpose and that people went there to meet their friends.

5 C: 19th century.

The text says that flushing toilets were invented in the 18th century and sewers were mainly built a century later.

6 C: because almost all houses in the UK have indoor toilets today.

This is implied in paragraph 1.

7 An answer that explains that covered drains are less smelly and more hygienic.

8 An answer that explains that the title reveals what the text is about and/or an answer that explains that the writer has used alliteration to make the heading stand out.

9 C: Paragraph 3 is about toilets in Roman times.

10 An answer that explains that 'stench' is a descriptive word meaning a bad odour, chosen to help the reader understand how terrible the smell would have been.

11 A: complex

The following sentence in paragraph 3 explains that the Romans had 'large communal toilets', suggesting that this is the correct answer.

12 B: medieval

The writer states 'Things took a turn for the worse' in paragraph 4 and also goes into detail, describing the stench.

13 An answer that explains that the writer starts the description of the medieval period with the words 'Things took a turn for the worse' and/or the writer says that the smell was 'overpowering'.

14 An answer that explains that today we usually go the toilet in private and have other places to meet our friends.

15 C: They would think that disposing of toilet waste in the streets was a bad idea.

## Comprehension *test 3* 28

1 In the sky. The poem describes a 'castle cloud world', suggesting a sky with variously shaped clouds.

2 Two. The 'twin owners' are mentioned.

3 E: kites

4 The first part of the poem is about the kites, the second about the children flying them.

5 D: answer C also contains words relating to birds but 'soar' isn't in the poem and 'swoop' appears only as 'swooping'.

6 The author approves because the poem talks about the children being excited and the joyful language used suggests the game is something enjoyable.

7 B: The salt pans, water buffalo and the Asian name Parvati together suggest the poem is set in Asia.

8 Three and above. The first paragraph states the toys are 'not suitable for children under three'.

9 Four, including the initial meeting.

10 A: to cancel a contract with NVX Marketing Inc.

11 B: dissatisfaction, consequence, action

12 Formal (or similar word)

13 E: Should NVX Marketing Inc. wish to dispute our position…

14 C: business

## Grammar *test* 34

1 E: noun

2 D: verb

3 B: noun

4 B: alliteration

5 A: metaphor

6 C: simile

7 D: Opportunities

8 B: Creative

9 D: If

10 enjoys, gives, capture, experience

11 gather, using, create, is

12 believe, have, understand, read

13 D: went

14 C: their

15 A: are

## Punctuation *test* 38

1 D: …children, in Victorian factories?

2 C: …were still running! As a result,

3 Others worked in match factories, dipping matchsticks in a chemical called phosphorus that can cause lung disease, tooth decay and other illnesses.

4 B: …orphanages, factory owners paid…

5 First-hand accounts from Victorian children have survived, with one nine-year-old girl explaining, "I work from five in the morning until after dark every day but Sunday."

6 C: …worked; they were also…

7 A: It's hard to imagine how much children…

8 X

## Spelling *test* 43

*Misspelt words in the answers are underlined and corrected.*

1 D: and others are harmful and can cause illness.

Examples of microbes include bacteria and fungi like yeast. Some varieties are helpful to us and others are harmful and can cause illness.

2 A: Remember, these things are tiny, so…

Remember, these things are tiny, so you don't have to look at them, unlike bigger 'nasties' like headlice or mosquitos, which make us run for our lives!

3 B: …easily among people and causing things …

Viruses are also microbes, spreading easily among people and causing things like the dripping noses of colds and the spotty skin associated with chicken pox.

4 X

5 C: …wash your hands carefully, but your…

Microbes can invade your body, if you are careless and don't wash your hands carefully, but your immune system usually neutralises them.

6 B: …bacteria and moulds found in foods…

Illnesses can easily be caused by bacteria and moulds found in foods not properly cooked or stored in unsuitable conditions.

7 D: …to produce foods like yoghurt.

Many microbes cause diseases, some break down autumn leaves into nutrients and there are others which help to produce foods like yoghurt.

8 B: developed, laboratories, investigate

# Reading

Dr Frank Spooncer

## Notes for Parents and Teachers

Most adults find it difficult to recall a time when they could not read, and often have only hazy ideas about how they learned to do so. The tests in this book highlight some of the many skills which come together in the smooth reading of the mature reader.

Each test focuses on a different aspect of reading, so that together they will not only give you an understanding of the processes involved, but also of how an individual child is progressing in them. You will be able to gauge the overall level of attainment, and get some indication of any areas which are particularly well, or perhaps less well, developed.

Although the tests are similar to those used in many schools, they are not designed to give a precise 'Reading Age'. Instead, by means of the table at the end of the book you will be able to form an impression of your child's performance in relation to that of average children of the same age.

Test material of this nature should always be presented as informally as possible, more as a game than as an examination. Please therefore adopt a relaxed approach, whilst of course keeping to the instructions which introduce each test.

We hope this small book will give you a greater understanding of reading, and thus help you to cooperate even more fully with your child's school in fostering it.

This Headway edition first published 1989
by Hodder and Stoughton Educational,
a division of Hodder and Stoughton Ltd,
Mill Road, Dunton Green, Sevenoaks, Kent

ISBN 0 340 50576 1



Printed and bound in Great Britain by CW Print Group, Loughton, Essex.

# The Early Skills

After the child has realised that the marks in books are not meaningless scribble, but have a systematic relation to spoken language, he is likely to progress to the stage of 'Word Recognition'. At this stage, there will be a 'Basic Sight Vocabulary' of words which he recognises, perhaps because of their shape, or some distinctive feature, such as tall letters like 'l' or 'k'. This stage is very helpful in giving the child confidence that he can read, but of course he cannot learn the thousands of words in print by this means alone. He will thus gradually learn some of the rules of written English – that the double *ee* of 'meet' represents a different sound from the single *e* of 'met', or, later, that the sound represented by *ea* in 'meat' is different from that represented by the same letters in 'feather'. Developing knowledge of these rules will help the child to 'attack' words he has not seen before, and thus extend the range of words he can read. Tests 1–3 assess the child's ability to read individual words.

## 1. Reading words aloud (6–7 yrs)

This test contains fifty words commonly used in material for young children. The child should be asked to read each word aloud, working across each line, and a note kept of the number of words read correctly. The test should not be continued after the child has made ten consecutive errors. The score is then the number of words read correctly.

| | | | | |
|---|---|---|---|---|
| is | man | car | are | with |
| into | has | went | sun | down |
| here | said | stop | make | sat |
| they | took | yet | were | must |
| work | train | away | brother | small |
| back | bring | along | around | right |
| because | afternoon | nice | water | poor |
| still | over | people | where | morning |
| when | father | three | uncle | grow |
| cold | watch | new | would | many |

(…/50)

## 2. Word-picture matching (6–7 yrs)

Tell the child to put a ring round the word that goes with each picture, and count the number of correct answers.

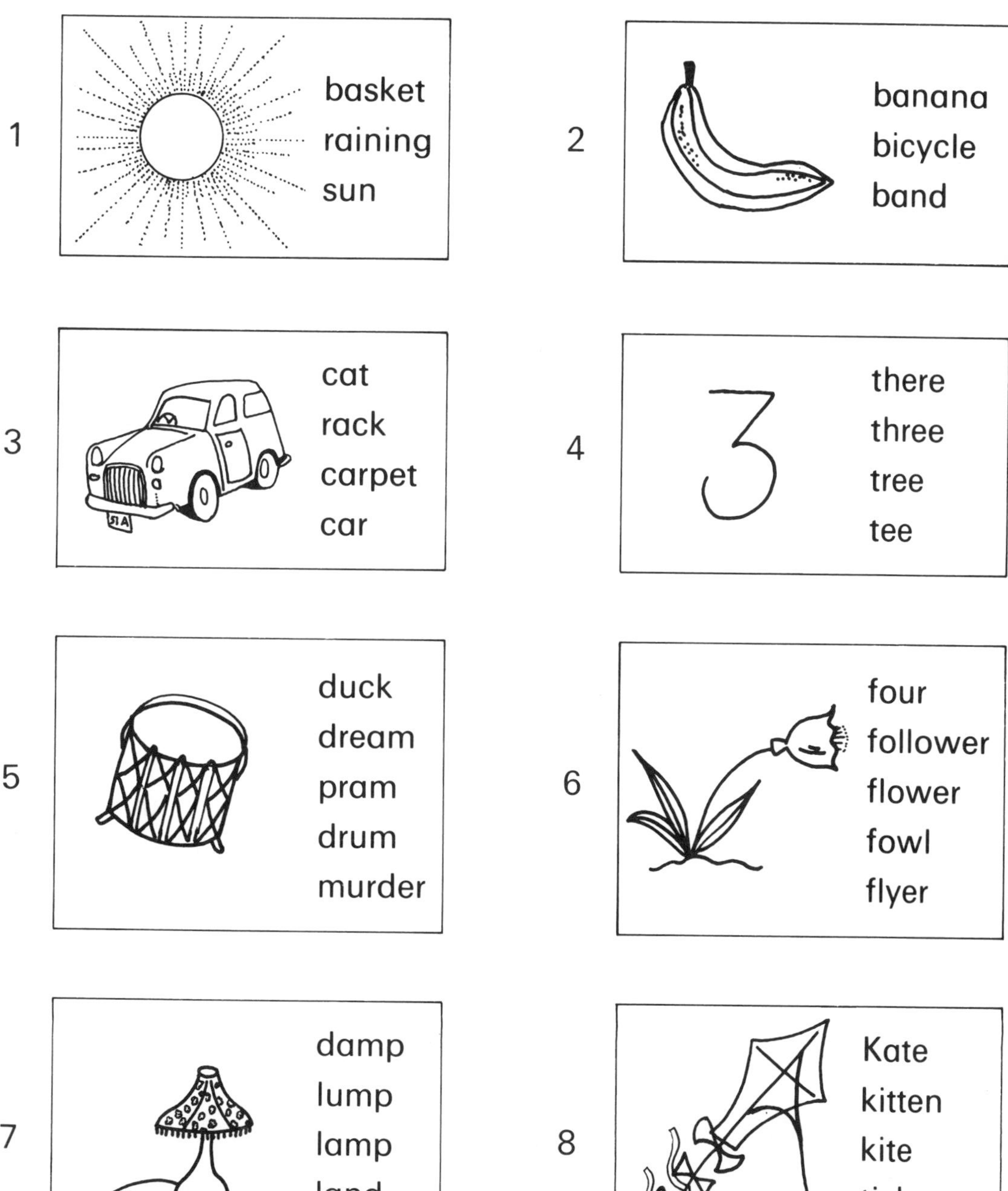

9

spat
spear
spare
pads
spade

10

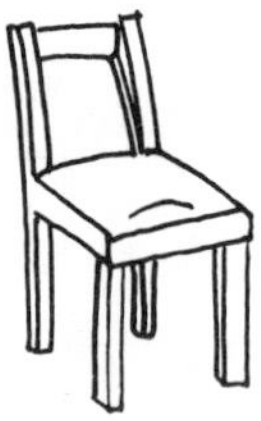

choir
chair
share
care
cheer

11

appeal
applaud
ankle
apple
addle

12

squire
scare
quakes
square
scarce

13

leader
ladder
larder
lender
loader

14

show
chew
shower
sew
shoe

15

house
happy
hours
horse
hers

16

sold
shoulder
solider
soldier
smoulder

(…/16)

### 3. Putting words together (7–11 yrs)

This assesses the ability to combine elements of words together to make sensible units. Use the example to show the child how to take each of the letters or groups of letters on the left, with each of those on the right. He should write down all the 'real' words he finds each time. There are just the right number of lines to put the answers on for each question. Let him work the test by himself and count the number of correct 'real' words.

Example

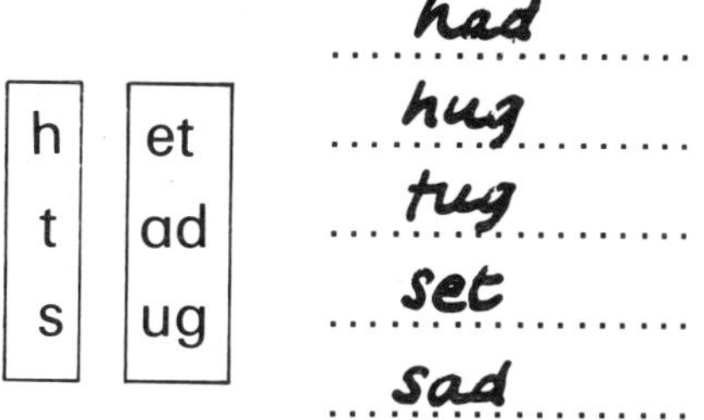


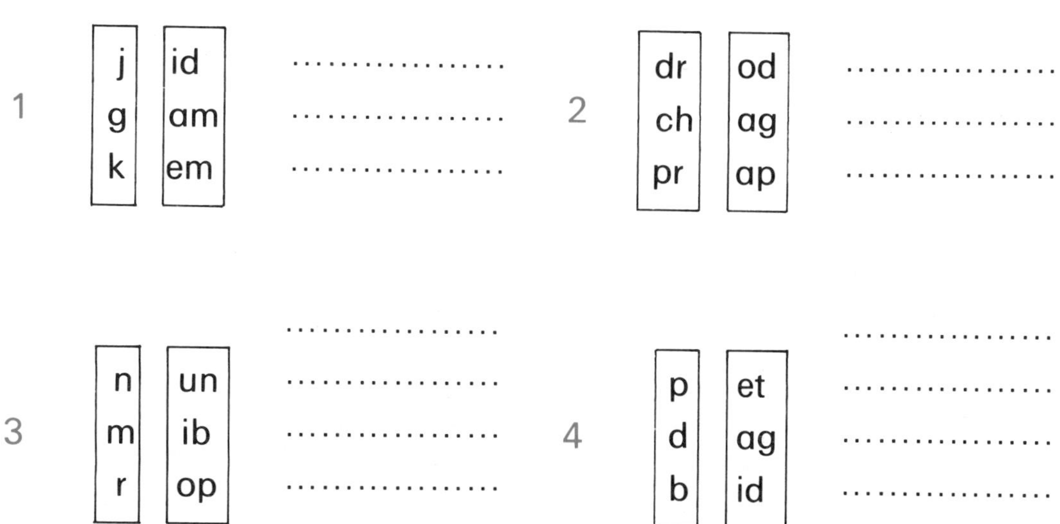

5

| | | |
|---|---|---|
| m | ome | .................. |
| h | ade | .................. |
| c | ube | .................. |
| | | .................. |

6

| | | |
|---|---|---|
| sh | ick | .................. |
| qu | en | .................. |
| th | ut | .................. |
| | | .................. |

7

| | | |
|---|---|---|
| sn | ute | .................. |
| fl | ade | .................. |
| gl | ake | .................. |
| | | .................. |

8

| | | |
|---|---|---|
| tr | ane | .................. |
| r | ein | .................. |
| cr | ead | .................. |
| | | .................. |

9

| | | |
|---|---|---|
| spr | eam | .................. |
| scr | eme | .................. |
| sch | ain | .................. |

10

| | | |
|---|---|---|
| gra | st | .................. |
| gna | ph | .................. |
| gho | w | .................. |

11

| | | |
|---|---|---|
| sta | tain | .................. |
| cer | ious | .................. |
| cur | tion | .................. |
| | | .................. |

12

| | | |
|---|---|---|
| sh | eel | .................. |
| wh | awl | .................. |
| squ | all | .................. |
| | | .................. |

| 15 | | | |
|---|---|---|---|
| mist | ache | .................. | |
| moust | ery | .................. | |
| myst | ake | .................. | |

| 16 | | | |
|---|---|---|---|
| ps | ism | .................. | |
| sp | alm | .................. | |
| pr | asm | .................. | |

(.../60)

From this section you may have gained some idea of the way your child tackles individual words. Ideally, he should be learning to combine the 'sight' and 'sound' approaches. Too much reliance on guessing from the 'look' of words may lead later to careless reading, and to difficulties with spelling. Overlong reliance on a slow building-up of words from their constituent sounds may later interfere with the smooth reading of complete passages, and thus cause a loss of understanding.

# From Words to Sentences

We don't normally read words in isolation, of course, but in sentences. In so doing, the fluent reader combines his knowledge of individual words with clues from the grammar and meaning of the sentence to guide his expectations of what will come next. Tests 4–6 assess the child's ability to combine a single-word approach with the use of such clues.

## 4. Reading sentences aloud (6–9 yrs)

This complements the testing of phonic development, assessed in Test 3 with individual words. This time, sentences containing most of the common 'sounds' of English are presented, to be read aloud by the child. Provided he is not completely struggling, he can be allowed to read all the sentences. The score is then the number of sentences read without a mistake.

1 A fox can run.

2 Fat men are big.

3 The pot had a red lid.

4 Ask Jack to sing next.

5 The act at the end was the best.

6 A frog will jump if you prod him.

7 You need five eggs to make a large cake.

8 Clap your hands as she skips.

9 The car went into a skid, and slid to a stop.

10 You can get cold if you camp in a tent.

11 Tell her that this church is shut.

12 Turn the chop over with a fork or it will burn.

13 The boy hoped he hadn't been too rude.

14 They enjoyed the boiled fish in its smooth white sauce.

15 The teacher counted the toys to see if his tale was true.

16 For the party, she wore a neat blue cloak over her dress.

17 Stir hard with a spoon, until the mix feels firm.

18 Throw these three darts at the board, one after the other.

19 At the level crossing, the train slowed down to a crawl.

20 A sprained knee or wrist can sometimes ache horribly.

21 The first problem was how to unwind the string from around his finger.

22 The mate told the seamen to haul in the lower sails.

23 The chemist can often assist in curing a cough.

24 Regular measurement of a child's weight can indicate his physical progress.

(.../24)

## 5. Reading sentences aloud (7–11 yrs)

Although children are encouraged to move towards 'silent reading' it is helpful, particularly at the early stages, to check on their reading aloud as well. Test 5 presents a set of sentences to be read aloud. As they are graded in order of difficulty, the test should be stopped at the end of the sentence in which the child makes his sixth error. His score is then the number of that sentence.

1 Play is fun.

2 Mother had some milk and an egg for tea.

3 Tom went to school by bus.

4 Mary loves to skip.

5 Most people do not like wet summers.

6 One night, John had a very strange dream.

7 The teacher told everyone that her kitten was full of mischief.

8 The fireman quickly carried the child downstairs to safety.

9 Juicy apples make a delicious dessert.

10 John's twisted ankle was quite a serious injury.

11 The crowd behaved extremely well in the sudden emergency.

12 The explorer's recent discoveries had made his rivals jealous.

13 The diver's behaviour in descending to the submerged wreck was quite heroic.

14 Roger's pathetic performance in the examination infuriated his parents.

15 His reputation as a philosopher rested on a single theory.

16 The police could not have anticipated the unique circumstances of the crime.

17 The magistrate sentenced the criminal to a brief period of imprisonment.

18 Microscopes enable scientists to study incredibly small organisms.

19 The journalist denied that his report was a grotesque misrepresentation of the facts.

20 The author was contemptuous of the trivial criticisms of his masterpiece.

(.../20)

## 6. Sentence completion (7–11 yrs)

A complementary test to Test 5, assessing silent reading by means of a multiple-choice presentation. The child should underline the word in brackets which best completes each sentence. The score is the number of correct answers made.

1 Tom is a (girl | boy | bad | bay).

2 A cat makes a good (pot | dog | animal | pet).

3 Ducks swim in a (bowl | water | pond | bath).

4 Bread can be cut with a (saw | board | knife | sandwich).

5 The birthday present was a great (surprise | occasion | pleasant | happy).

6 A trumpet is a musical (chair | choir | instrument | brass).

7 Treasure is usually very (worthless | valuable | pleasant | rich).

8 Good jewellery is (expensive | easy | expansive | cheap).

9 When Joan did not return immediately, her mother became (searching | ancient | anxious | hurried).

10 Mother and her friend enjoyed a long telephone (conversion | bell | comforting | conversation).

11 Remedies for headaches can be obtained from a (pain | chemist | church | sleep).

12 The boxer's opponent collapsed (happy | vertical | unconscious | fighting).

13 The soldiers were commanded by a (colonial | colonel | kernel | official).

14 They celebrated the occasion with great (wealth | ceremony | cemetery | castles).

15 The excavations on the site revealed remnants of an ancient (history | ruinous | civility | civilisation).

16 The professor encouraged his pupils to think (independently | problems | solutions | silently).

17 The achievement of second place was scarcely a (conversation | conversion | consolation | winner).

18 The victim swore vengeance on his (assailants | assistants | crimes | crooks).

19 Judicious examination of the artist's exhibition suggested an obsession with (cemetery | symmetry | money | frames).

20 The customer alleged that the purchase price had been (exorcised | absorbent | exorbitant | mislaid).

(.../20)

The importance of Tests 4–6 is that they may show up particular strengths or weaknesses in the child's ability to use a variety of approaches in his reading. Many children become remarkably expert in working out words they have never met before by using the 'context clues' of connected passages. Others will be surprisingly insensitive to the fact that they are reading nonsense!

# Understanding What we Read

It is very little use being able to make the right noises in response to marks on paper if we cannot understand the meaning of what we have read. 'Comprehension' is a term often used to indicate the child's ability to understand what he has read. This will depend on many things: his oral vocabulary, his ability to read the words, the level of language used in the passage, and its style and structure. Many different kinds of question can be used to test understanding, and the three test passages below give a range of types of question. In these, and all later tests, the instructions can be read by the child, with explanation by the adult if necessary, and the score is the total of correct answers.

A comparison of performance on Tests 4–6 with that on Tests 7–9 may be informative. Some children are quite accurate and fluent readers, but do not obtain the fullest meaning from their reading. Others may show good understanding, in spite of rather poor 'mechanical' reading. These children may be hindered in their reading, and indeed in school work generally, by slow development of the basic skills of reading. Again, the two processes of reading the words and understanding their message should ideally progress hand-in-hand.

## 7. 'A Trip to the Shops' (8–11 yrs)

Read the story and then look at the questions. Choose your answer and underline it.

Mother went to the shops, taking Peter with her. They went by bus, and Peter sat next to an old man with a green hat. When they reached the town, Mother and Peter got off the bus, leaving the man alone in the bus with the driver. They had come to the shops so that Mother could buy Peter either a coat or some trousers. After he had chosen a warm brown coat, Mother took Peter to the park, and bought him an ice-cream. 'And I don't want to go home before I've tried the swings,' he said.

1 Who went to the shops?
(Just Mother | Just Peter | An old man | Mother and Peter)

2 Who had a green hat?
(The man next to Peter | Peter | Mother | The bus-driver)

3 Who sat next to the old man when the bus left town?
(Peter | No one | The driver | Mother)

4 Who got the trousers? (Mother | Peter | No one | The man)

5 When did Mother buy the ice-cream?
(Before they went to the park |
After they got home |
Before they did the shopping |
Before they went home)

6 When did Peter want to try the swings?
(As soon as they got off the bus |
When they got home |
After they bought his coat |
Before they did the shopping)

(.../6)

## 8. 'A Battle between Friends' (8–11 yrs)

Read the story and then look at the questions. Choose your answer and underline it.

Jackie had prepared really well for the school sports. Together with her friend Claire, she had jogged for stamina, and sprinted for speed. 'Isn't it strange,' said Claire, 'We've been helping each other for weeks, but tomorrow we'll be trying to beat each other.'

Next afternoon, Jackie and Claire put on their differently coloured house bands, and took their places at opposite ends of the starting line, with four other girls between them. By the half-way mark, Jackie was already desperate. Only one girl was ahead of her: in the farthest lane, her friend's taller figure had forged two metres ahead! Their rival supporters screamed encouragement from each side, and Jackie responded by lengthening her stride. But it was no use. No one overtook her, but the younger girl was still fractionally ahead at the finish.

1 Jackie and Claire (went to different schools | disliked each other | were in the same house | were good friends).

2 Claire was (older and taller than Jackie | younger but taller than Jackie | older but shorter than Jackie | younger and shorter than Jackie).

3 The crowd (were all shouting for Jackie | were angry | were on opposite sides of the track | watched in silence).

4 How many girls were in the race?
(Four | Two | Six | You can't tell).

5 How long did Jackie spend preparing for the race?
(A week | More than a week | Less than a week | You can't tell).

6 Who was in the lead at half-way?
(You can't tell | Jackie | Claire | One of the other girls).

7 Who won the race?
(Claire | Jackie | You can't tell | Another girl).

(.../7)

**9. 'The Last Challenge' (8–11 yrs)**

Here is the last story. Read it right through, and then look at the questions. Choose the one answer you think is best for each, and underline it. Try to think *why* you chose it.

Zaradel knew exactly what was required. First, to escape Trowan, of the all-seeing eye, he must become invisible. Next, to soothe the venomous rage of Kelpan, he must sing like an enchanted bird. Finally, to reach the Golden Casket through the labyrinthine passages, he must borrow the brain of Mirosus.

He received the magic cloak of darkness from a smiling Nimador in return for a jest first heard from the lips of Roran, the Laughter-God. A pillow woven with the Silken Spider's aid took three months to make, but gained him the loan of Balan's song-giving harp. Whoever held that would chant ethereal music to its accompaniment. Lastly, the frail Mirosus, though now confined to his bed for ever, gave him, in return for promises of visits in the future, the secret password which would enable them to share their thoughts across the miles between.

1 Kelpan was (a great singer | a quiet man | a furious man | invisible).

2 Who helped Zaradel become invisible?
(Balan | Mirosus | Trowan | Nimador)

3 Zaradel needed the help of Mirosus, who was very (wise | lonely | ill | strong).

4 Nimador was (the Laughter-God | mean | fond of sleep | fond of jokes).

5 Who was.most likely to accompany Zaradel?
(No one | Mirosus | Nimador | Balan)

6 What was the last obstacle before the Golden Casket?
(A bird | A labyrinth | The anger of Kelpan | The eye of Trowan)

7 Whose help would eventually enable Zaradel to calm Kelpan?
(Nimador's | the Silken Spider's | Mirosus' | Trowan's)

8 The thing Zaradel desired most was the (song-giving harp | cloak of darkness | Golden Casket | secret password).

(.../8)

Total Score (Tests 7–9) .../21

# Filling the Gaps

A recent method of testing understanding, and the ability to use the 'context' clues referred to in the previous section, is the 'cloze' procedure. In this, words are removed from a passage, and the child has to 'fill the gaps'. Various methods for removal of words can be used, and the two passages below show a range of methods. Please accept as correct any word for which the child can make a convincing argument, since the value of the approach lies as much in the *way* the child finds an answer as in its correctness.

## 10. 'A Visit to the Zoo' (8–11 yrs)

Fill in the gaps in this story. Each dash stands for a missing letter, and sometimes letters have been put in to help you.

Tom and Mary went __ a small school. It was __ a village, far away ____ any town. At holiday time, ____ often visited their aunt, who lived n___ London. Sometimes, ___ took them to see the sights of the city, such as the Zoo.

The day they went __ the Zoo, there was g____ excitement, because a brand ___ panda was making his _____ appearance to the public. ____ had to queue for h____ to secure a place w___ a good view. At e_____y three o'clock, the panda ap______. The spectators called 'Aaah', be_____ he looked exactly like s___ great cuddly toy. No one t____ to feed him. His k_____ provided a special diet, w____ suited the panda's needs.

After the panda had dis________ to rest away from his ad______, Aunt Jane delighted Mary by taking her to the souvenir s___l, where she purchased a rep____ of the panda, in soft _____ and white. 'What will you call him?' a____ Tom, rather jealously. 'Peter will be p______ for him,' re_____ Mary. 'Peter the perfect _____.'

(.../29)

## 11. 'The Raid' (8–11 yrs)

In this next story, the words you need to fill the gaps are given in italics on the left.

---

*appearance*
*invented*
*anchor*
*invaders*
*inhabitants*

As night fell, the pirate schooner dropped .................. not far from the island. The .................. were dismayed by its sudden .................., but they quickly gathered together, and .................. a scheme to outwit the ..................

---

*possession*
*tormentors*
*crevices*
*population*
*particle*
*ceasing*
*barren*
*night*

The whole .................. laboured without .................. throughout the .................., transferring every .................. of food, and every personal .................. away from the clutches of their ................ Each family settled, unseen, in one of the caves or .............. in the .................. heights above the valley.

---

*destruction*
*pirates*
*precipitous*
*furnace*
*clambered*
*ascended*

Just before the sun .................. into the cloudless sky, the chief ran from hut to hut, starting a trail of .................. with his blazing torch. He .................. noiselessly up the .................. slopes in time to see the first of the .................. stagger back from the .............. that had once been a village.

---

*continue overleaf*

*thwarted*
*derision*
*abandoned*
*islanders*
*echoing*
*retreated*

The robbers, who had hoped to deprive the .................. of their homes, .................. their raid. As they .................., the islanders used their ............... heights to hurl shouts of .................. after their .................. enemy.

(.../25)

Total Score (Tests 10–11) .../54

If you have discussed the answers to the cloze passages, you will have gained some insight into the processes going on in the child's mind as he reads. You might find it interesting to try constructing your own cloze assessments on material of appropriate difficulty. Let the child discuss the possibilities with you, without trying to teach him the answers. Alternatively, let him try to construct some which might fool you!

# Reading and Vocabulary

The size of a child's reading vocabulary may be much less than his spoken, since sometimes he may be unable to read a word which he could well understand if he heard it. On the other hand, as pointed out previously, it is little use being able to read a word if you can't understand it. Tests 12 and 13 will indicate the child's ability to read and understand words in connected passages and on their own. The first is of course the easier task since the meaning of the passage enables the child to 'home in' on a word he might not understand out of context.

Let your child try the tests first on his own, and score his correct responses. Then let him ask you to pronounce (but not give the meaning of) any words he cannot read on his own. This may show you whether inability to read words is hindering his comprehension. If, on the other hand, he can read most of the words, but obtains a poor score, then his mechanical ability may be outstripping his vocabulary development.

## 12. Words in context (8–11 yrs)

One word in each of these sentences is underlined. Put a line under the answer in the brackets that means most nearly the same.

1 The real king came back to his own land. *(young | rich | true | first)*

2 The sea is very calm here. *(smooth | safe | pleasant | clear)*

3 Litter spoiled the look of the garden. *(insects | rubbish | pigs | letters)*

4 The new animal looked very peculiar. *(wonderful | terrible | strange | familiar)*

5 He cleared the bar with ease. *(no delay | some help | joy | no trouble)*

6 The rich aunt doted on her niece. *(gazed | spoilt | forgave | admired)*

7 The sheep had wandered far from the farm. *(hidden | strayed | walked | died)*

8 The life of a monk is a devout one. *(mature | considerate | religious | extraordinary)*

9 The actor shyly emerged from behind the curtain. *(crept | peered | retired | appeared)*

10 They were not certain when the game first originated. *(commenced | increased | decayed | changed)*

11 Please contribute some money for this worthy cause. *(withdraw | invest | provide | consider)*

12 The noise of the crowd subsided as the speaker began. *(renewed | increased | declined | continued)*

13 The chemist said that the remedy was very potent. *(powerful | efficient | expensive | important)*

14 The class's reaction to the story was instantaneous. *(unexpected | immediate | happy | excited)*

15 Plundering by soldiers was common in the Middle Ages. *(robbing | fighting | defence | burning)*

(.../15)

## 13. Words on their own (8–11 yrs)

One of the words on the right means the same, or nearly the same, as the word in capitals on the left. Underline the one you choose.

| | | |
|---|---|---|
| 1 | APPLE | *flower fruit tree eat* |
| 2 | WATCH | *hear listen wait see* |
| 3 | UNKIND | *unkempt polite cruel careful* |
| 4 | QUARREL | *argue bother ask fight* |
| 5 | SUPPLY | *annoy supple plenty provide* |
| 6 | EXACT | *increase precise guess estimate* |
| 7 | QUESTION | *answer search enquiry trouble* |
| 8 | DEBATE | *lower torment submit discuss* |
| 9 | PERILOUS | *tearful injured dangerous paralysed* |
| 10 | OBSTINATE | *obscure avoid stubborn instrument* |
| 11 | HAUGHTY | *puzzled pleasant serious proud* |
| 12 | SCHOLAR | *pupil schooner university leader* |
| 13 | TRIVIAL | *pointless racial unimportant trouble* |
| 14 | LEGACY | *inheritance decision reward will* |
| 15 | DEFECT | *remedy refuse failing correct* |
| 16 | ASCERTAIN | *foreign chemical discover accurate* |
| 17 | REMEDY | *receipt recipe prescription melody* |
| 18 | DIMINUTIVE | *hourly invisible tiny impertinent* |
| 19 | CONVENTIONAL | *courteous charming punctual orthodox* |
| 20 | ASSERT | *state accept threaten resource* |

(.../20)

Total Score (Tests 12–13) ....../35

Vocabulary development is essential to the transition from purely mechanical reading to reading with understanding. Improving the child's oral vocabulary is bound to help his understanding of what he reads, and can be fostered unobtrusively by games such as 'Call my Bluff', or by 'pairs' games in which one person has to find a word meaning the same as the one proposed by his opponent.

# Reading and Spelling

Although this book is primarily concerned with reading, some aspects of the child's spelling are worth investigating. Common problems in spelling occur when two words of the same sound but different meaning are spelt in different ways. Thus, the child who does not easily recognise the difference between, say, 'pray' and 'prey' may have the wrong expectations when reading a sentence beginning 'They preyed . . .'. Test 14 gives both a general indication of spelling ability, and, if scores on it are compared with scores on other sections, will show whether there is any great discrepancy between performance in spelling and in reading. Score as correct only when the spelling is perfect.

## 14. Spot the mistake (8–11 yrs)

One word in each of these sentences is not spelt correctly. The right word sounds just like it, but is spelt a different way. Put a line through the wrong word, and write the proper spelling in the space provided.

1 The son was shining. ............
2 Teacher asked to sea her book. ............
3 They maid a big castle on the beach. ............
4 The hole house fell down. ............
5 No one had ever herd of the place. ............
6 Her sister asked for sum toffee. ............
7 Mother asked Betty to meat her at the butcher's shop. ............
8 The boy told a long tail. ............
9 He tide the parcel with a knot. ............
10 Mind you don't brake the window. ............

*continue overleaf*

11 His grown was heard by the nurse. ............
12 The regal eagle is a bird of pray. ............
13 The crowd side as he fell. ............
14 The crown was throne into the ditch. ............
15 The assistant wade the groceries. ............
16 The dress fitted tightly around her waste. ............
17 The King had already been raining for ten years. ............
18 The travellers took the wrong root to the town. ............
19 Squirrels like to berry their acorns. ............
20 The bows of the tree creaked in the stormy weather. ............
21 At the hospital, the surgeon put some ointment on his brews. ............
22 The manager said he was an idol employee. ............
23 Exercise will gradually develop your mussels. ............
24 Always endeavour to practice what you preach. ............

( ....../24)

# Conclusion

Although the tests in this book have covered many of the aspects of reading, some skills have not been tested. There is, for instance, no 'speed' test. Testing of speed of reading has been omitted because speed of itself is not an indication of good reading. Too much emphasis on speed can lead to carelessness and misunderstanding. What is required is the ability to 'change speeds' – to read simple material quickly, but to give time and thought when more complex passages are encountered.

Another area not represented is that of 'information retrieval', to use a rather grand title. This includes such things as the use of a table of contents, or an index, or the paragraph headings of a non-fiction book, as well as the ability to choose material at an appropriate level for oneself, and to combine information from several sources. Whilst these are all obvious necessities for more advanced work, they are also capable of development in the earlier stages, and again parents can give gentle guidance on, for instance, projects chosen by the child.

Finally, of course, it is important that the child enjoys reading. Attitude to reading is not easy to test in any formal way, but once more the parent can watch to see how often the child turns to books, what sort he prefers, how ready he is to share pleasures in books, and so on.

We hope that the tests in this book have been of interest and have proved helpful, but bear in mind that they should not be taken as a model for teaching: this is the province of the teacher in the school.

# Rating Chart

The chart shows the normal range of scores likely to be achieved on each test by average children at the beginning of each year-group. Please note that, because the separate tests measure different skills of reading, a child should not be expected to perform at the same level throughout. Note also that the tests should not in general be given to children whose age lies outside the limits suggested.

| *Test* | *Age* 6+ | 7+ | 8+ | 9+ | 10+ | 11+ |
|---|---|---|---|---|---|---|
| 1 | 25–35 | 38–46 | — | — | — | — |
| 2 | 6–10 | 9–13 | — | — | — | — |
| 3 | — | — | 10–17 | 18–25 | 26–33 | 34–42 |
| 4 | 4–8 | 9–13 | 14–18 | 17–21 | — | — |
| 5 | — | 6–10 | 8–12 | 11–15 | 13–17 | 14–18 |
| 6 | — | 5–8 | 7–10 | 9–12 | 11–14 | 13–15 |
| 7–9 (total) | — | — | 5–8 | 6–9 | 8–11 | 9–12 |
| 10–11 (total) | — | — | 8–13 | 14–19 | 20–27 | 28–34 |
| 12–13 (total) | — | — | 8–11 | 11–15 | 15–18 | 18–22 |
| 14 | — | — | 4–7 | 7–10 | 10–13 | 12–15 |